Tony Corballis and Wayne Jennings

English for
MANAGEMENT
STUDIES

in Higher Education Studies

Teacher's Book

Series editor: Terry Phillips

English for Specific Academic Purposes

Published by
Garnet Publishing Ltd.
8 Southern Court
South Street
Reading RG1 4QS, UK

First published 2009
Reprinted 2009, 2012, 2018.

ISBN 978-1-85964-441-6

British Cataloguing-in-Publication Data
A catalogue record for this book is available
from the British Library.

Production
Series editor: Terry Phillips
Project management: Martin Moore, Bruce Nicholson,
Nicky Platt
Editorial team: Emily Clarke, Sarah Mellowes
Academic review: Evelyn Fenton, Henley Business School
at the University of Reading.
Design and layout: Neil Collier, Sarah Church
Photography: gettyimages.com, clipart.com, corbis.com

Audio recorded and produced by Tom, Dick & Debbie
Productions Ltd.

The authors and publisher would like to thank the following
for permission to reproduce copyright material:
easyGroup for their permission to reproduce the photograph
and logo on page 21.
Google for permission to reproduce the results listings on
page 74.

Printed and bound in Lebanon by International Press:
interpress@int-press.com

Contents

Book map

Unit	Topics
1 What is leadership? **Listening · Speaking**	• qualities of leaders • entrepreneurship
2 Culture and change **Reading · Writing**	• organizational culture • change management
3 Organizations and operations **Listening · Speaking**	• organizational structure and analysis • production methods
4 Production management **Reading · Writing**	• process engineering • MBO • project management • quality management
5 Strategy and the business environment **Listening · Speaking**	• crisis and contingency planning • international markets and situation analysis • competition
6 Finance for strategy **Reading · Writing**	• the time value of money • asset, bond and share valuation • project appraisal
7 Budgets, decisions and risk **Listening · Speaking**	• management accounting and budgetary control • quantitative decision-making • risk analysis
8 People as a resource **Reading · Writing**	• groups and teams • diversity • recruitment
9 Developing people **Listening · Speaking**	• motivation and rewards • learning and development • hard and soft HRM
10 Industrial relations **Reading · Writing**	• evolution of industrial relations • issues in industrial relations • typical procedures including industrial action
11 Marketing management **Listening · Speaking**	• marketing orientation and market share • marketing and brand strategy • the marketing process: from analysis to marketing mix formulation
12 Management information systems **Reading · Writing**	• management information systems

Vocabulary focus	Skills focus		Unit
• words from general English with a special meaning in management • prefixes and suffixes	Listening	• preparing for a lecture • predicting lecture content from the introduction • understanding lecture organization • choosing an appropriate form of notes • making lecture notes	**1**
	Speaking	• speaking from notes	
• English–English dictionaries: headwords · definitions · parts of speech · phonemes · stress markers · countable/uncountable · transitive/intransitive	Reading	• using research questions to focus on relevant information in a text • using topic sentences to get an overview of the text	**2**
	Writing	• writing topic sentences • summarizing a text	
• stress patterns in multi-syllable words • prefixes	Listening	• preparing for a lecture • predicting lecture content • making lecture notes • using different information sources	**3**
	Speaking	• reporting research findings • formulating questions	
• computer jargon • abbreviations and acronyms • discourse and stance markers • verb and noun suffixes	Reading	• identifying topic development within a paragraph • using the Internet effectively • evaluating Internet search results	**4**
	Writing	• reporting research findings	
• word sets: synonyms, antonyms, etc. • the language of trends • common lecture language	Listening	• understanding 'signpost language' in lectures • using symbols and abbreviations in note-taking	**5**
	Speaking	• making effective contributions to a seminar	
• synonyms, replacement subjects, etc., for sentence-level paraphrasing	Reading	• locating key information in complex sentences • writing complex sentences	**6**
	Writing	• reporting findings from other sources: paraphrasing	
• compound nouns • fixed phrases from management English • fixed phrases from academic English • common lecture language	Listening	• understanding speaker emphasis	**7**
	Speaking	• asking for clarification • responding to queries and requests for clarification	
• synonyms • nouns from verbs • definitions • common 'direction' verbs in essay titles (*discuss, analyze, evaluate*, etc.)	Reading	• understanding dependent clauses with passives	**8**
	Writing	• paraphrasing • expanding notes into complex sentences • recognizing different essay types/structures: descriptive · analytical · comparison/evaluation · argument • writing essay plans • writing essays	
• fixed phrases from management English • fixed phrases from academic English	Listening	• using the Cornell note-taking system • recognizing digressions in lectures	**9**
	Speaking	• making effective contributions to a seminar • referring to other people's ideas in a seminar	
• 'neutral' and 'marked' words • fixed phrases from industrial relations • fixed phrases from academic English	Reading	• recognizing the writer's stance and level of confidence or tentativeness • inferring implicit ideas	**10**
	Writing	• writing situation–problem–solution–evaluation essays • using direct quotations • compiling a bibliography/reference list	
• words/phrases used to link ideas (*moreover, as a result*, etc.) • stress patterns in noun phrases and compounds • fixed phrases from academic English	Listening	• recognizing the speaker's stance • writing up notes in full	**11**
	Speaking	• building an argument in a seminar • agreeing/disagreeing	
• verbs used to introduce ideas from other sources (*X contends/suggests/asserts that* …) • linking words/phrases conveying contrast (*whereas*), result (*consequently*), reasons (*due to*), etc. • words for quantities (*a significant minority*)	Reading	• understanding how ideas in a text are linked	**12**
	Writing	• deciding whether to use direct quotation or paraphrase • incorporating quotations • writing research reports • writing effective introductions/conclusions	

Introduction

The ESAP series

The aim of the titles in the ESAP series is to prepare students for academic study in a particular discipline. In this respect, the series is somewhat different from many ESP (English for Specific Purposes) series, which are aimed at people already working in the field, or about to enter the field. This focus on *study* in the discipline rather than *work* in the field has enabled the authors to focus much more specifically on the skills which a student of management studies needs.

It is assumed that prior to using titles in this series students will already have completed a general EAP (English for Academic Purposes) course such as *Skills in English* (Garnet Publishing, up to the end of at least Level 3), and will have achieved an IELTS level of at least 5.

English for Management Studies

English for Management Studies is designed for students who plan to take a management studies course entirely or partly in English. The principal aim of *English for Management Studies* is to teach students to cope with input texts, i.e., listening and reading, in the discipline. However, students will also be expected to produce output texts in speech and writing throughout the course.

The syllabus concentrates on key vocabulary for the discipline and on words and phrases commonly used in academic English. It covers key facts and concepts from the discipline, thereby giving students a flying start for when they meet the same points again in their faculty work. It also focuses on the skills that will enable students to get the most out of lectures and written texts. Finally, it presents the skills required to take part in seminars and tutorials and to produce essay assignments. For a summary of the course content, see the book map on pages 4–5.

Components of the course

The course comprises:

- the student Course Book
- this Teacher's Book, which provides detailed guidance on each lesson, full answer keys, audio transcripts and extra photocopiable resources
- audio CDs with lecture and seminar excerpts

Organization of the course

English for Management Studies has 12 units, each of which is based on a different aspect of management studies. Odd-numbered units are based on listening (lecture/seminar extracts). Even-numbered units are based on reading.

Each unit is divided into four lessons:

Lesson 1: vocabulary for the discipline; vocabulary skills such as word-building, use of affixes, use of synonyms for paraphrasing

Lesson 2: reading or listening text and skills development

Lesson 3: reading or listening skills extension. In addition, in later reading units, students are introduced to a writing assignment which is further developed in Lesson 4; in later listening units, students are introduced to a spoken language point (e.g., making an oral presentation at a seminar) which is further developed in Lesson 4

Lesson 4: a parallel listening or reading text to that presented in Lesson 2, which students have to use their new skills (Lesson 3) to decode; in addition, written or spoken work is further practised

The last two pages of each unit, *Vocabulary bank* and *Skills bank*, are a useful summary of the unit content.

Each unit provides between four and six hours of classroom activity with the possibility of a further two to four hours on the suggested extra activities. The course will be suitable, therefore, as the core component of a faculty-specific pre-sessional or foundation course of between 50 and 80 hours.

Vocabulary development

English for Management Studies attaches great importance to vocabulary. This is why one lesson out of four is devoted to vocabulary and why, in addition, the first exercise at least in many of the other three lessons is a vocabulary exercise. The vocabulary presented can be grouped into two main areas:

- key vocabulary for management studies
- key vocabulary for academic English

In addition to presenting specific items of vocabulary, the course concentrates on the vocabulary skills and strategies that will help students to make sense of lectures and texts. Examples include:

- understanding prefixes and suffixes and how these affect the meaning of the base word
- guessing words in context
- using an English–English dictionary effectively
- understanding how certain words/phrases link ideas
- understanding how certain words/phrases show the writer/speaker's point of view

Skills development

Listening and reading in the real world involve extracting communicative value in real time – i.e., as the spoken text is being produced or as you are reading written text. Good listeners and readers do not need to go back to listen or read again most of the time. Indeed, with listening to formal speech such as a lecture, there is no possibility of going back. In many ELT materials, second, third, even fourth listenings are common. The approach taken in the ESAP series is very different. We set out to teach and practise 'text-attack' skills – i.e., listening and reading strategies that will enable students to extract communicative value at a single listening or reading.

Students also need to become familiar with the way academic 'outputs' such as reports, essays and oral presentations are structured in English. Conventions may be different in their own language – for example, paragraphing conventions, or introduction–main body– conclusion structure. All students, whatever their background, will benefit from an awareness of the skills and strategies that will help them produce written work of a high standard.

Examples of specific skills practised in the course include:

Listening

- predicting lecture content and organization from the introduction
- following signposts to lecture organization
- choosing an appropriate form of lecture notes
- recognizing the lecturer's stance and level of confidence/tentativeness

Reading

- using research questions to focus on relevant information
- using topic sentences to get an overview of the text
- recognizing the writer's stance and level of confidence/tentativeness
- using the Internet effectively

Speaking

- making effective contributions to a seminar
- asking for clarification – formulating questions
- speaking from notes
- summarizing

Writing

- writing notes
- paraphrasing
- reporting findings from other sources – avoiding plagiarism
- recognizing different essay types and structures
- writing essay plans and essays
- compiling a bibliography/reference list

Specific activities

Certain types of activity are repeated on several occasions throughout the course. This is because these activities are particularly valuable in language learning.

Tasks to activate schemata

It has been known for many years, since the research of Bartlett in the 1930s, that we can only understand incoming information, written or spoken, if we can fit it into a schemata. It is essential that we build these schemata in students before exposing them to new information, so all lessons with listening and reading texts begin with one or more relevant activities.

Prediction activities

Before students are allowed to listen to a section of a lecture or read a text, they are encouraged to make predictions about the contents, in general or even specific terms, based on the context, the introduction to the text or, in the case of reading, the topic sentences in the text. This is based on the theory that active listening and reading involve the receiver in being ahead of the producer.

Working with illustrations, diagrams, figures

Some tasks require students to explain or interpret visual material. Students can be taken back to these visuals later on in the course to ensure that they have not forgotten how to describe and interpret them.

Vocabulary tasks

Many tasks ask students to group key management terms, to categorize them in some way or to find synonyms or antonyms. These tasks help students to build relationships between words which, research has shown, is a key element in remembering words. In these exercises, the target words are separated into blue boxes so you can quickly return to one of these activities for revision work later.

Gap-fill

Filling in missing words or phrases in a sentence or a text, or labelling a diagram, indicates comprehension both of the missing items and of the context in which they correctly fit. You can vary the activity by, for example, going through the gap-fill text with the whole class first orally, pens down, then setting the same task for individual completion. Gap-fill activities can be photocopied and set as revision at the end of the unit or later, with or without the missing items.

Breaking long sentences into key components

One feature of academic English is the average length of sentences. Traditionally, EFL classes teach students to cope with the complexity of the verb phrase, equating level with more and more arcane verb structures, such as the present perfect modal passive. However, research into academic language, including the corpus research which underlies the *Longman Grammar of Spoken and Written English*, suggests that complexity in academic language does not lie with the verb phrase but rather with the noun phrase and clause joining and embedding. For this reason, students are shown in many exercises later in the course how to break down long sentences into kernel elements, and find the subject, verb and object of each element. This receptive skill is then turned into a productive skill, by encouraging students to think in terms of kernel elements first before building them into complex sentences.

Activities with stance marking

Another key element of academic text is the attitude (or stance) of the writer or speaker to the information which is being imparted. This could be dogmatic, tentative, incredulous, sceptical, and so on. Students must learn the key skill of recognizing words and phrases marked for stance.

Crosswords and other word puzzles

One of the keys to vocabulary learning is repetition. However, the repetition must be active. It is no good if students are simply going through the motions. The course uses crosswords and other kinds of puzzles to bring words back into the students' consciousness through an engaging activity. However, it is understood by the writers that such playful activities are not always seen as serious and academic. The crosswords and other activities are therefore made available as photocopiable resources at the back of the Teacher's Book and can be used at the teacher's discretion, after explaining to the students why they are valuable.

Methodology points

Setting up tasks

The teaching notes for many of the exercises begin with the word *Set …* . This single word covers a number of vital functions for the teacher, as follows:

- Refer students to the rubric (instructions).
- Check that they understand **what** to do – get one or two students to explain the task in their own words.
- Tell students **how** they are to do the task, if this is not clear in the Course Book instructions – as individual work, pairwork or in groups.
- Go through the example, if there is one. If not, make it clear what the target output is – full sentences, short answers, notes, etc.
- Go through one or two of the items, working with a good student to elicit the required output.

Use of visuals

There is a considerable amount of visual material in the book. This should be exploited in a number of ways:

- before an exercise, to orientate students, to get them thinking about the situation or the task, and to provide an opportunity for a small amount of pre-teaching of vocabulary (be careful not to pre-empt any exercises, though)
- during the exercise, to remind students of important language
- after the activity, to help with related work or to revise the target language

Comparing answers in pairs

This is frequently suggested when students have completed a task individually. It provides all students with a chance to give and explain their answers, which is not possible if the teacher immediately goes through the answers with the whole class.

Self-checking

Learning only takes place after a person has noticed that there is something to learn. This noticing of an individual learning point does not happen at the same time for all students. In many cases, it does not even happen in a useful sense when a teacher has focused on it. So learning occurs to the individual timetable of each student in a group. For this reason, it is important to give students time to notice mistakes in their own work and try to correct them individually. Take every opportunity to get students to self-check to try to force the noticing stage.

Confirmation and correction

Many activities benefit from a learning tension, i.e., a period of time when students are not sure whether something is right or wrong. The advantages of this tension are:

- a chance for all students to become involved in an activity before the correct answers are given
- a higher level of concentration from the students (tension is quite enjoyable!)
- a greater focus on the item as students wait for the correct answer
- a greater involvement in the process – students become committed to their answers and want to know if they are right and, if not, why not

In cases where learning tension of this type is desirable, the teacher's notes say, *Do not confirm or correct (at this point)*.

Feedback

At the end of each task, there should be a feedback stage. During this stage, the correct answers (or a model answer in the case of freer exercises) are given, alternative answers (if any) are accepted, and wrong answers are discussed. Unless students' own answers are required (in the case of very free exercises), answers or model answers are provided in the teacher's notes.

Highlighting grammar

This course is not organized on a grammatical syllabus and does not focus on grammar specifically. It is assumed that students will have covered English grammar to at least upper intermediate level in their general English course. However, at times it will be necessary to focus on the grammar, and indeed occasionally the grammar is a main focus (for example, changing active to passive or vice versa when paraphrasing).

To highlight the grammar:

- focus students' attention on the grammar point, e.g., *Look at the word order in the first sentence.*
- write an example of the grammar point on the board
- ask a student to read out the sentence/phrase
- demonstrate the grammar point in an appropriate way (e.g., numbering to indicate word order; paradigms for verbs; time lines for tenses)
- refer to the board throughout the activity if students are making mistakes

Pronunciation

By itself, the mispronunciation of a single phoneme or a wrong word stress is unlikely to cause a breakdown in communication. However, most L2 users make multiple errors in a single utterance, including errors of word order, tense choice and vocabulary choice. We must therefore try to remove as many sources of error as possible. When you are working with a group of words, make sure that students can pronounce each word with reasonable accuracy in phonemic terms, and with the correct stress for multiple syllable words. Many researchers have found that getting the stress of a word wrong is a bigger cause of miscommunication than getting individual phonemes wrong.

Pair and group activities

Pairwork and group activities are, of course, an opportunity for students to produce spoken language. As mentioned above, this is not the main focus of this course. But the second benefit of these interactional patterns is that they provide an opportunity for the teacher to check three points:

- Are students performing the correct task, in the correct way?
- Do students understand the language of the task they are performing?
- Which elements need to be covered again for the benefit of the class, and which points need to be dealt with on an individual basis with particular students?

Vocabulary and Skills banks

Each unit has clear targets in terms of vocabulary extension and skills development. These are detailed in the checks at the end of the unit (*Vocabulary bank* and *Skills bank*). However, you may wish to refer students to one or both of these pages at the start of work on the unit, so they have a clear idea of the targets. You may also wish to refer to them from time to time during lessons.

1 WHAT IS LEADERSHIP?

This introductory unit explores what we understand by the term *leadership*. Students listen to an extract from a lecture which describes different styles of leadership and thinking in the study of leadership. They also listen to a series of mini-lectures which further explore certain aspects of leadership and introduce the idea of entrepreneurship.

Skills focus

🎧 Listening

- preparing for a lecture
- predicting lecture content from the introduction
- understanding lecture organization
- choosing an appropriate form of notes
- making lecture notes

Speaking

- speaking from notes

Vocabulary focus

- words from general English with a special meaning in management
- prefixes and suffixes

Key vocabulary

action	effective	paternal
atmosphere	empowerment	persuasive
autocratic	entrepreneur	productivity
capability	evaluate	project
capital	expert	quality
central	field	relationship
characteristic	flatter companies	role
charismatic	flexibility	see the bigger picture
committed	get caught up in detail	self-image
communication	goal	status
skills	hierarchy	style
concept	innovation	take ownership of
confident	innovative	task
consultative	inspire	team-based
controversy	laissez-faire	trained
creativity	manage	trend
debate	military	vision
decision	mix	welfare
delegating	model	workplace
democratic	obey	
dependent	participate	

1.1 Vocabulary

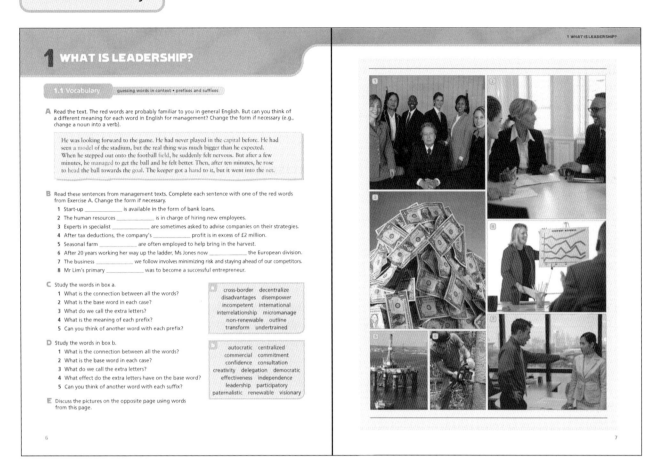

1 WHAT IS LEADERSHIP?

1.1 Vocabulary   guessing words in context • prefixes and suffixes

A Read the text. The red words are probably familiar to you in general English. But can you think of a different meaning for each word in English for management? Change the form if necessary (e.g., change a noun into a verb).

He was looking forward to the game. He had never played in the capital before. He had seen a model of the stadium, but the real thing was much bigger than he expected. When he stepped out onto the football field, he suddenly felt nervous. But after a few minutes, he managed to get the ball and he felt better. Then, after ten minutes, he rose to head the ball towards the goal. The keeper got a hand to it, but it went into the net.

B Read these sentences from management texts. Complete each sentence with one of the red words from Exercise A. Change the form if necessary.
1 Start-up _____ is available in the form of bank loans.
2 The human resources _____ is in charge of hiring new employees.
3 Experts in specialist _____ are sometimes asked to advise companies on their strategies.
4 After tax deductions, the company's _____ profit is in excess of £2 million.
5 Seasonal farm _____ are often employed to help bring in the harvest.
6 After 20 years working her way up the ladder, Ms Jones now _____ the European division.
7 The business _____ we follow involves minimizing risk and staying ahead of our competitors.
8 Mr Lim's primary _____ was to become a successful entrepreneur.

C Study the words in box a.
1 What is the connection between all the words?
2 What is the base word in each case?
3 What do we call the extra letters?
4 What is the meaning of each prefix?
5 Can you think of another word with each prefix?

> cross-border decentralize
> disadvantages disempower
> incompetent international
> interrelationship micromanage
> non-renewable outline
> transform undertrained

D Study the words in box b.
1 What is the connection between all the words?
2 What is the base word in each case?
3 What do we call the extra letters?
4 What effect do the extra letters have on the base word?
5 Can you think of another word with each suffix?

> autocratic centralized
> commercial commitment
> confidence consultation
> creativity delegation democratic
> effectiveness independence
> leadership participatory
> paternalistic renewable visionary

E Discuss the pictures on the opposite page using words from this page.

6

7

General note

Read the *Vocabulary bank* at the end of the Course Book unit. Decide when, if at all, to refer students to it. The best time is probably at the very end of the lesson or the beginning of the next lesson, as a summary/revision.

Lesson aims

- identify words for the discipline in context, including words which contain affixes
- gain fluency in the target vocabulary

Introduction

Write the words *management style* on the board. Ask students about the origin of the word *management*. Elicit *manage or manager* and from there get to *management*. Tell students that *manage* was first used in English to mean *to handle horses*.

Ask students where the word *style* comes from. Tell them it is from the Latin, *stilus*, which means *an instrument or way of writing*.

Language note

Ask students if they know where the word for *manager* in their language comes from.

Exercise A

Set for individual work and pairwork checking. Point out that the text introduces some important basic vocabulary related to management – although it may not seem like that at first glance. Do the first one as an example, e.g., in general English, *capital* means *the city where a country has its government*. In English for management, *capital* can mean *money used to set up a company*.

Point out that there is often a relationship between the general English meaning and a specific meaning, and if you know the general English meaning it can help to guess the management meaning (as in the case of *hand* and *goal*). Remind students to change the form if necessary, e.g., from verb to noun. Check students understand grammar or other changes.

Feed back, putting the management English meanings on the board. Tell students to use these structures where possible:

- *a(n) X is (a(n)) …* to define a noun
- *to X is to Y* to define a verb

Make sure students can say the words correctly, e.g.,

- /dʒ/ in *managed*
- /ə/ in *capital*
- /əʊ/ in *goal*

Answers

Model answers:

Word	Meaning	Comments
capital	money, especially for starting or expanding a business	change to uncountable
model	a statement of how something works or should work	
field	an area of study or type of work	
manage	to run a business or organize a group of people	
head	to be in control of a group or organization	
goal	an aim, something to be achieved	
hand	someone who does physical work	
net	the amount of money remaining after tax or costs have been deducted	part of speech has changed from noun to adjective

Exercise B

Set for individual work and pairwork checking. Make sure students understand that they should change the form if necessary, e.g., verb to noun.

Feed back with the whole class. Ask students for any other words they know which have a special meaning in management.

Answers

Model answers:

1 Start-up <u>capital</u> is available in the form of bank loans.

2 The human resources <u>manager</u> is in charge of hiring new employees.

3 Experts in specialist <u>fields</u> are sometimes asked to advise companies on their strategies.

4 After tax deductions, the company's <u>net</u> profit is in excess of £2 million.

5 Seasonal farm <u>hands</u> are often employed to help bring in the harvest.

6 After 20 years working her way up the ladder, Ms Jones now <u>heads</u> the European division.

7 The business <u>model</u> we follow involves minimizing risk and staying ahead of our competitors.

8 Mr Lim's primary <u>goal</u> was to become a successful entrepreneur.

Examples of other possible words from general English found in management:

campaign (n) – posters/advertisements that try to encourage people to buy a product

found (v) – to establish, to set up

go under – to fail, to go bust

labour – as well as work, it can refer to the people who work: the *labour force*

value (n) – something you believe in/what something is worth

Exercise C

Set the first question for pairwork. See which pair can work out the answer first.

Set the remainder for pairwork. Feed back, building up the table in the Answers section on the board.

Answers

Model answers:

1 They all have a base word + extra letters at the beginning/prefixes.

2 See table (below).

3 Prefix.

4 See table.

5 See table.

Prefix	Base word	Meaning of prefix	Another word
cross-	border	across	cross-company
de	centralize	revert/undo	deregulate
dis	advantage	not	discourage
dis	empower	not	disinherit
in	competent	not/no	inaccurate
inter	national	between	intergovernmental
inter	relationship	between	interlocking
micro	manage	very small	microprocessor
non-	renewable	not	non-aligned
out	line	used to form nouns	outlay
trans	form	change	translate
under	trained	not fully	underdeveloped

Language note

English is a lexemic language. In other words, the whole meaning of a word is usually contained within the word itself, rather than coming from a root meaning plus prefixes or suffixes (affixes). In most texts, written or spoken, there will only be a tiny number of words with affixes. However, these often add to a base meaning in a predictable way, and it is important that students learn to detach affixes from a new word and see if they can find a recognizable base word.

Some words beginning with letters from prefixes are NOT, in fact, base + prefix, e.g., *refuse*. In other cases, the base word does not exist anymore in English and therefore will not help students, e.g., *transfer*, *transit*, although even in these cases the root meaning of the prefix may be a guide to the meaning of the whole word.

Exercise D

Repeat the procedure from Exercise C.

Answers

Model answers:

1 They all have a base word + extra letters at the end/suffixes.
2 See table.
3 Suffix.
4 See table.
5 See table.

Base word	Suffix	Effect/meaning of suffix	Another word
autocrat	ic	noun ➜ adjective	democratic
centralize	ed	verb ➜ adjective (in fact, the two parts of speech, verb and adjective, have the same form, but the inflection shows that the change has occurred)	institutionalized
commerce	ial	noun ➜ adjective	controversial
commit	ment	verb ➜ noun	recruitment
confide	(e)nce	verb ➜ noun	competence
consult	(a)tion	verb ➜ noun	participation
creative	ity	adj ➜ noun	possibility
delegate	ion	verb ➜ noun	relation
democracy	tic	noun ➜ adjective	bureaucratic
effective	ness	adj ➜ noun	competitiveness
independent	ce	adj ➜ noun	competence
leader	ship	noun ➜ noun denoting ability	entrepreneurship
participate	ory	verb ➜ adjective	introductory
paternal	istic	adj ➜ adj denoting having some qualities of	modernistic
renew	able	verb ➜ adjective	transferable
vision	ary	noun ➜ adjective	voluntary

Language note

Note that with prefixes we rarely change the form of the base word. However, with suffixes, there are often changes to the base word, so students must:
- take off the suffix
- try to reconstruct the base word

Exercise E

Set for pairwork. Try to elicit more than just the words from this lesson. Students should describe the pictures as fully as they can at this stage.

Students may use the following words in their discussion of each picture:

1 heads, cross-border, international, interrelationship
2 paternalistic, manager, consultation, delegation, democratic, leadership, participatory
3 capital, net
4 decentralized, transform, confidence, effectiveness, participatory, visionary
5 non-renewable, disadvantages, commercial
6 renewable, effectiveness
7 autocratic, manage, incompetent, leadership

Closure

If you have not done so already, refer students to the *Vocabulary bank* at the end of Unit 1. Tell students to explain how this lesson can help them deal with new words in context. If you wish, make three groups. Group A looks at the first section, *Using related words*. Group B looks at the second section, *Removing prefixes*. Group C looks at the third section, *Removing suffixes*. Then make new groups of three with an ABC in each to explain to each other.

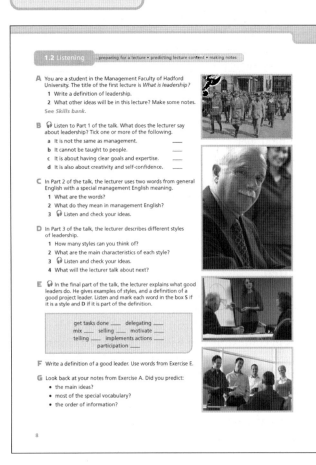

Introduction

1 Show students flashcards of some or all of the words from Lesson 1.1. Tell them to say the words correctly and quickly as you flash them. Give out each word to one of the students. Say the words again. The student with the word must hold it up. Repeat the process, saying the words in context.

2 Refer students to the photos. Briefly elicit ideas of what they depict. (They will look at the different styles of management in more detail in Exercise D.)

Exercise A

1 Set for pair or group work. Feed back, but do not confirm or correct at this time.

2 Set for pairwork. Elicit some ideas, but do not confirm or correct.

Methodology note

You may want to refer students to the *Skills bank – Making the most of lectures* at this point.
Set the following for individual work and pairwork checking. Tell students to cover the points and try to remember what was under each of the Ps – Plan, Prepare, Predict, Produce. Then tell students to work through the points to make sure they are prepared for the lecture they are about to hear.

🎧 Exercise B

Give students time to read the choices. Point out that they are only going to hear the introduction once, as in an authentic lecture situation. Then play Part 1. Feed back. If students' answers differ, discuss which is the best answer and why.

Answers

a It is not the same as management.

c It is about having clear goals and expertise.

d It is also about creativity and self-confidence.

General note

The recording should only be played once, since this reflects what happens in a real lecture. Students should be encouraged to listen for the important points, since this is what a native speaker would take from the text. However, students can be referred to the transcript at the end of the lesson to check their detailed understanding and word recognition, or to try to discover reasons for failing to comprehend.

Read the *Skills bank* at the end of the Course Book unit. Decide when, if at all, to refer students to it. The best time is probably at the very end of the lesson or the beginning of the next lesson, as a summary/revision.

Lesson aims

- prepare for a lecture
- predict lecture content
- make notes

Transcript 🎧 1.1

Part 1

Welcome to the Management School. A key issue, central to all management thinking, is the concept of leadership. And today I want to start you off by exploring this idea of what a leader is.

Does anyone here believe that leadership and management are the same thing? I'm afraid this isn't true: a manager is not always necessarily a leader … and being a good leader may not necessarily be part of a manager's role.

Another thing that is often discussed is the long-running debate over whether leaders are naturally charismatic people or whether people can be trained to become good leaders. Unfortunately, there is no easy answer to this 'nature versus nurture' controversy, though it might be that both arguments are true.

So what makes a good leader? Good leaders are able to keep their eye on overall goals at all times. Rather than get caught up in the detail, they can see the bigger picture. They are also usually experts in a field and generally quite knowledgeable. Look at Bill Gates, the founder of Microsoft. He began with incredible skills in software and computing. Good leaders can also see change and respond to it. They have natural creativity and a passion for ideas and solutions. Leaders also have good self-image. Their confidence helps give them charisma.

So, before we look more deeply at leadership, I am firstly going to outline for you a range of qualities or characteristics that leaders commonly have, and I shall talk for a while about leadership styles. OK, let's begin.

Methodology note

In many course books with listening activities, students are allowed to listen to material again and again. This does not mirror real-life exposure to spoken text. In this course, students are taught to expect only one hearing during the lesson, and are encouraged to develop coping strategies to enable them to extract the key points during this one hearing. Listening texts may be repeated for further analysis but not for initial comprehension.

🎧 Exercise C

Set the two questions for pairwork. Play Part 2. Feed back.

Answer

Model answers:

Word	General English meaning	Management meaning
goal	a point scored when a ball goes into a net in many sports	objective
hand	the part of the body at the end of the arm	a manual worker

Transcript 🎧 1.2

Part 2

Many words have an intrinsic or basic meaning. We use the words in different situations and they have different surface meanings, but the basic meaning remains the same. Let me give you an example. We use the word *goal* in everyday English. It is something a footballer scores when he kicks a ball into the back of a net. But we also use the word *goal* in management. It is a noun to mean something we want to achieve. Is there any connection between these two words? Yes, there is. For a footballer, putting balls into the net is what he wants to achieve. In management speak, it is something exact that we need to achieve.

Somehow, when we are learning our first language, we get a feeling for the basic meaning of words, which helps us to understand the same word in a new context. When we are learning another language, it is very important to find the basic meaning of a word because the direct translation in one context may not be the correct translation in another. For example, can you use the word in your language for *hand* in the context of *a factory hand*, meaning someone who works with his or her hands in a factory? Possibly not.

Language note

In English, we sometimes name a whole thing from one significant part, e.g., *hand* = a person who works with his/her hands.

🎧 Exercise D

1/2 Set for pairwork discussion before listening. Tell students to make notes.

3 Play Part 3. Feed back, building up a diagram on the board. Elicit detail. Explain that this is a *classification* diagram.

4 Set for general discussion.

Answers

Model answers:

1/2

Leadership styles				
1 autocratic	2 paternalistic	3 democratic		4 laissez-faire
• leader sets goals • leader tells staff what to do • staff obey	• leader makes all decisions • staff obey • leader cares about staff's welfare	consultative	persuasive	• employees work freely without much control
		• leader consults staff before making decisions	• leader makes decisions and persuades staff to follow	

4 The lecturer will now answer the question: What is the basic or intrinsic meaning of leadership?

Transcript 🎧 1.3

Part 3

So let me talk a little bit about leadership styles. There are a number of well-known styles.

The first is autocratic leadership. Have you ever come across a manager who sets his ... or her ... own goals, tells people what to do to achieve them, and demands that people obey? In this case, those he ... or she ... leads may become either dissatisfied or perhaps too dependent on him or her. In some cases, like the military, this kind of leadership is useful, but generally in business it is not.

Similar to autocratic leadership is paternalistic leadership. Paternalistic leaders still make all the decisions and expect workers to obey them. But while autocratic leaders don't care much about what their workers think and feel, paternalistic leaders are more interested in their welfare.

The third is democratic leadership, which can either be consultative – where, for example, a communications campaign leader may consult with her staff on ways forward before making strategy decisions – or it may be persuasive, where the leader decides first and then persuades her staff to follow the decision. While democratic leadership requires communication skills and takes more time than autocratic leadership, most people think it is more effective. It lets more people participate, letting everyone feel they belong and can take ownership of what they do, thereby motivating them and making them more committed. Besides, when staff have high levels of education, it is a good idea to respect people's ideas and draw on their knowledge and experience.

The fourth style of leadership is called laissez-faire. It's spelt l-a-i-s-s-e-z and f-a-i-r-e ... It's French and it means, roughly, *leave to do or happen*. Laissez-faire leaders let their employees work freely and without much control at all. Do you think this is an effective style? I can see some of you think not. Well, there are certain industries, like new media and other creative industries, which are quite informal and enjoy the freedom and relaxed atmosphere of this style. The danger is low productivity, but it can make for a very innovative workplace.

Next, I'm going to answer the question: What is the basic or intrinsic meaning of leadership?

Methodology note

Up to this point, you have not mentioned how students should record information. Have a look around to see what students are doing. If some are using good methods, make a note and mention it later in the unit.

🎧 Exercise E

Point out that we often define things before or after classifying them. Set for individual work and pairwork checking. Give students plenty of time to look at the words in the box. Play Part 4. Feed back, building up model definitions on the board.

Answers

get tasks done	D
delegating	S
mix	D
selling	S
motivate	D
telling	S
implements actions	D
participation	S

Transcript 🎧 **1.4**

Part 4

There are many great thinkers who have attempted to describe what leadership intrinsically is. Hersey and Blanchard, for example, have an excellent model that illustrates the difference between *task behaviour* and *relationship behaviour*. Task behaviour is about organizing what people need to do. Relationship behaviour is about the personal support they need. With the right balance, they say, a good leader can choose between some of the styles I mentioned earlier in the lecture, as well as some others like delegating (or giving power to others), for example ... or participation, as we talked about before ... or what they call 'selling' leadership (where they persuade others about a concept) ... or what they call 'telling' leadership (where workers are less mature and need to be clearly instructed).

As you know, the first decade of the 21st century has seen great changes. And so leadership styles need to adapt. One clear trend is a move away from the old hierarchy and ideas of status in a company. Companies are flatter, with fewer layers of management. Most companies now embrace a more team-based or project approach. A good team-based project leader these days can bring together the right mix of individuals to get things done. They can motivate staff and inspire them to see the same corporate objectives as they do and get their tasks done. Such a leader is good at standing back and evaluating the team and the actions it implements.

With this new level of flexibility and empowerment of people, leaders can tackle the challenges of the future: new technologies, international recruitment in a globalized world and cross-border mergers and acquisitions and the effects of these.

Exercise F

Set for individual work and pairwork checking. Feed back, building up a model definition on the board.

Answer

Possible answer:

Management means the planning, organization and supervision of people and processes to achieve an organization's goals. So leadership in management means ensuring that people plan, organize and supervise effectively to achieve the organization's goals.

Exercise G

Refer students back to their notes from Exercise A.

Closure

1 Ask students to give you examples of ways in which management in businesses has changed things for the better in recent times – particularly in students' own countries (e.g., less hierarchical organization, more openness and consultation between managers and the managed, etc.).

2 Refer students to the *Skills bank* if you have not done so already and work through the section *Making the most of lectures*.

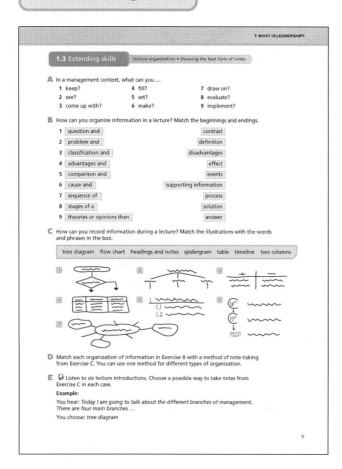

Lesson aims

- identify different types of lecture organization
- use the introduction to a lecture to decide the best form of notes to use

Introduction

Tell students to build up the four Ps of preparing for and attending a lecture: Plan, Prepare, Predict, Produce. You could put students into four groups, each group working on one of the stages, then feeding back to the rest of the class.

Exercise A

Set for pairwork. Feed back orally. The more students can say about these words, the better. Accept anything correct, but let students explain their choice if they choose a combination not given in the table.

Answers

Possible answers:

1	keep	a clear vision; an eye on goals
2	see	the bigger picture; an objective; something through
3	come up with	a plan; a proposal; an idea; a strategy
4	fill	a gap in the market
5	set	a goal; a target; an objective; a deadline
6	make	a decision; a profit
7	draw on	knowledge; resources; experience
8	evaluate	a team; a team's actions; a plan; individual performance; achievements
9	implement	a policy; a decision; an action plan; a model

Exercise B

Point out that you can understand a lecture better if you can predict the order of information. Point out also that there are many pairs and patterns in presenting information, e.g., *question and answer*, or a sequence of events in chronological order.

Set for pairwork. Feed back orally. Check pronunciation. Point out that lecturers may not actually use these words, but if you recognize that what a lecturer is saying is the first of a pair, or the beginning of a sequence, you are ready for the second or next stage later in the lecture.

Answers

1	question and	answer
2	problem and	solution
3	classification and	definition
4	advantages and	disadvantages
5	comparison and	contrast
6	cause and	effect
7	sequence of	events
8	stages of a	process
9	theories or opinions then	supporting information

Exercise C

Identify the first form of notes – a tree diagram. Set the rest for individual work and pairwork checking. Feed back, using an OHT or other visual medium if possible.

Answers

1 flow chart
2 tree diagram
3 two columns
4 table
5 headings and notes
6 timeline
7 spidergram

Methodology note

You might like to make larger versions of the illustrations of different note types and pin them up in the classroom for future reference.

Exercise D

Work through the first one as an example. Set for pairwork.

Feed back orally and encourage discussion. Demonstrate how each method of note-taking in Exercise C can be matched with an organizational structure. Point out that:

● a tree diagram is useful for hierarchically arranged information, such as when the information moves from general to specific/examples

● a spidergram is more fluid and flexible, and can be used to show connections between things, such as interactions, or causes and effects

Answers

Possible answers:

1 question and answer = headings and notes/two columns/spidergram
2 problem and solution = headings and notes/two columns
3 classification and definition = tree diagram/headings and notes/spidergram
4 advantages and disadvantages = two columns
5 comparison and contrast = table/two columns
6 cause and effect = spidergram/two columns
7 sequence of events = timeline/flow chart
8 stages of a process = flow chart (or circle if it is a cycle)
9 theories or opinions then supporting information = headings and notes/two columns/spidergram

🎧 Exercise E

Explain that students are going to hear the introductions to several different lectures. They do not have to take notes, only think about the organization of information and decide what type of notes would be appropriate. Work through the example.

Play each introduction. Pause after each one and allow students to discuss then feed back. After the first three, explain that sometimes lecturers move from one information organization to another, e.g., cause and effect then sequence of events. Play the final three. Feed back. Students may suggest different answers in some cases. Discuss.

Answers

Possible answers:

1 flow chart/timeline (stages of a process)
2 tree diagram/headings and notes (classification and definition)
3 two columns (advantages and disadvantages)
4 spidergram (cause and effect)
5 table (compare and contrast)
6 spidergram (question and answer)

Transcript 🎧 1.5

Introduction 1

In today's session, we're going to look at how enterprise evolves – how entrepreneurs take their ideas and business resources and bring the two together to try to become a success in the business world. Now, an entrepreneur is a person with a great talent in coming up with ideas and seeing how they can be turned into business opportunities and finally business activity.

So, what is this process, you might ask, that begins with an idea and ends with a business? Well, today's session will explain the stages in this process. I hope by the end of it you will have a clear picture of how these things progress. I shall use an example of a famous Greek entrepreneur, to make things easy to understand.

Introduction 2

Hi, everyone. At the most simple level of understanding managing business, we have to understand basic business resources commonly known as *factors of production*. In today's lecture, we shall classify these and explain what each one is. The factors of production are: land, labour, capital and enterprise. The last of these is where management acts as an *entrepreneur*. Well, let's get started, shall we?

OK. Land is not simply the location where a business sets itself up. What is meant by the word *land* here is more than land itself or physical premises. It might also include natural resources. Such resources are also classified – usually into two categories that you have probably already guessed. Yes, that's right: renewable and non-renewable.

Introduction 3

OK. Are we all ready? Right, I'll begin. This afternoon's topic is entrepreneurship, and I'm going to focus on the advantages and disadvantages of being an entrepreneur. Coming up with ideas is a fairly easy thing to do, and many people do it every day. Turning such ideas into a business is much harder. This is what entrepreneurs do. Today we are going to look at the pluses and the minuses of being an entrepreneur.

Introduction 4

OK. Settle down everyone. Thank you. I want to start by asking you to think about leadership and management. Are they the same? Do all leaders necessarily have authority? What do you think? In fact, no, they don't. Some leaders are not good managers, some managers are very poor leaders!

Today, we're going to look at one kind of leader – the charismatic leader. We'll see what happens when a leader is charismatic. We shall also look at a trend from what is called transactional management to transformational management and see what the effects are. I'll tell you what these mean shortly. But first … there has been a great deal of academic thinking on leadership in the last hundred years. And these areas have brought about a huge change to what we understand as good management. In today's lecture, I shall explore the consequences of these changes. What has all this brought about?

Introduction 5

Good morning, ladies and gentlemen. Today, we are going to examine leadership more closely. There are two typical concerns that leaders may have, and we are going to look for differences between these concerns. They are called concern for people and concern for production, or to some people: people orientation versus task orientation. The idea of viewing the leader's orientation in this way comes from two writers from the 1960s – Blake and Mouton. It has become a fundamental way of seeing management and leadership ever since. Basically, you need to construct a grid, with *production* across the top and *people* up the left side. You've got *high* in the top-left corner and *low* in the bottom-left corner. You've got another *high* in the top-right corner. OK. So, for example, *leadership* in the top-right of the grid has a high concern for people AND a high concern for production.

Introduction 6

Thanks for coming to my presentation. The faculty asked me here today as a guest lecturer to give you my thoughts on a simple question. Well, it's perhaps a simple question, but the answer is not quite so simple. The question is: *What qualities does an entrepreneur have?* or *What makes an entrepreneur tick?*, and they asked me because of my success in founding and developing my online travel agency, which now provides – in 25 countries – not just flights and hotels, but insurance and a whole suite of other travel-related services as well. Well, what makes people like me tick? OK, let's take a look and find out.

Closure

1 Test students on the pairs from Exercise B. Correct pronunciation again if necessary.
2 Refer students to the *Skills bank – Making perfect lecture notes*.

1.4 Extending skills

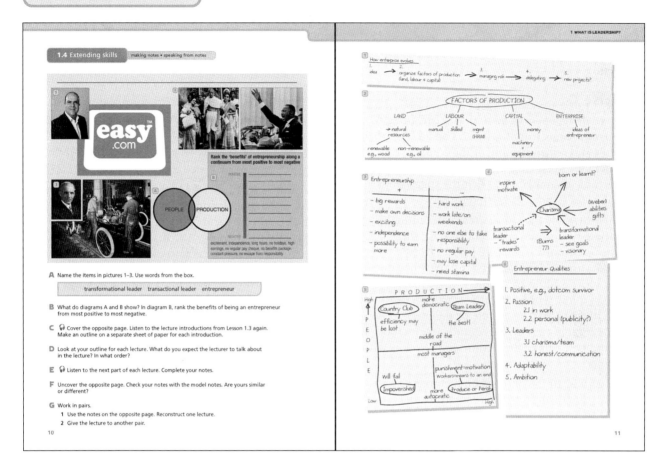

Lesson aims

- make outline notes from lecture introductions
- make notes from a variety of lecture types
- speak from notes

Further practice in:

- predicting lecture content

Introduction

Elicit as much information from the lecture in Lesson 1.2 as possible. If necessary, prompt students by reading parts of the transcript and pausing for students to complete in their own words.

Exercise A

Set for individual work and pairwork checking. Feed back orally, but do not confirm or correct. Point out that they are going to hear about all these things in today's lesson. You will return to these pictures at the end.

For reference, the pictures show:

1 composite photo of Stelios and the easy.com logo
2 composite of Martin Luther King with crowds and Mahatma Gandhi with crowds

3 composite of Henry Ford and an automobile production line

Answers

1 entrepreneur
2 transformational leader
3 transactional leader

Exercise B

Repeat the procedure from Exercise A – no confirmation or correction.

For reference, the diagrams show:

A   a Venn diagram showing people and production

B   Model answer:

a continuum from positive to negative:
excitement
independence
long hours
no holidays
high earnings
no regular pay cheque
no benefits package
constant pressure
no escape from responsibility

🎧 Exercise C

Make sure students understand that they are going to hear the introductions from Lesson 1.3 again. Ask them briefly if they can remember any of the content from the introductions. Spend a few moments on this if students are able to contribute. Elicit the suggestions for types of notes (Lesson 1.3, Exercise E).

Explain that this time they must create an outline using an appropriate type of notes. (You can refer them again to the *Skills bank – Making perfect lecture notes*.) Make sure students understand that they do not need to write a lot at this stage – outlines may consist of just a few words, e.g., the start of a spidergram, the first part of a table or diagram. Play each introduction in turn and give students time to choose a note-type, make the outline and check it with other students.

Feed back, getting all the outlines on the board – you may wish to copy them from the first part of the model notes on the right-hand page, or you may prefer to follow your students' suggestions. Clarify the meaning of new words and check pronunciation.

Transcript 🎧 1.5

Introduction 1

In today's session we're going to look at how enterprise evolves – how entrepreneurs take their ideas and business resources and bring the two together to try to become a success in the business world. Now, an entrepreneur is a person with a great talent in coming up with ideas and seeing how they can be turned into business opportunities and finally business activity.

So, what is this process, you might ask, that begins with an idea and ends with a business? Well, today's session will explain the stages in this process. I hope by the end of it you will have a clear picture of how these things progress. I shall use an example of a famous Greek entrepreneur, to make things easy to understand.

Introduction 2

Hi, everyone. At the most simple level of understanding managing business, we have to understand basic business resources commonly known as *factors of production*. In today's lecture, we shall classify these and explain what each one is. The factors of production are: land, labour, capital and enterprise. The last of these is where management acts as an *entrepreneur*. Well, let's get started, shall we?

Okay. Land is not simply the location where a business sets itself up. What is meant by the word *land* here is more than land itself or physical premises. It might also include natural resources. Such resources are also classified – usually into two categories that you have probably already guessed. Yes, that's right: renewable and non-renewable.

Introduction 3

OK. Are we all ready? Right, I'll begin. This afternoon's topic is entrepreneurship and I'm going to focus on the advantages and disadvantages of being an entrepreneur. Coming up with ideas is a fairly easy thing to do, and many people do it every day. Turning such ideas into a business is much harder. This is what entrepreneurs do. Today we are going to look at the pluses and the minuses of being an entrepreneur.

Introduction 4

OK. Settle down everyone. Thank you. I want to start by asking you to think about leadership and management. Are they the same? Do all leaders necessarily have authority? What do you think? In fact, no, they don't. Some leaders are not good managers, some managers are very poor leaders!

Today we're going to look at one kind of leader – the charismatic leader. We'll see what happens when a leader is charismatic. We shall also look at a trend from what is called transactional management to transformational management and see what the effects are. I'll tell you what these mean shortly. But first … There has been a great deal of academic thinking on leadership in the last hundred years. And these areas have brought about a huge change to what we understand as good management. In today's lecture, I shall explore the consequences of these changes. What has all this brought about?

Introduction 5

Good morning, ladies and gentlemen. Today, we are going to examine leadership more closely. There are two typical concerns that leaders may have and we are going to look for differences between these concerns. They are called concern for people and concern for production, or to some people: people orientation versus task orientation. The idea of viewing the leader's orientation in this way comes from two writers from the 1960s – Blake and Mouton. It has become a fundamental way of seeing management and leadership ever since. Basically you need to construct a grid, with *production* across the top and *people* up the left side. You've got *high* in the top-left corner and *low* in the bottom-left corner.

You've got another *high* in the top-right corner. OK. So, for example, *leadership* in the top-right of the grid has a high concern for people AND a high concern for production.

Introduction 6

Thanks for coming to my presentation. The faculty asked me here today as a guest lecturer to give you my thoughts on a simple question. Well, it's perhaps a simple question but the answer is not quite so simple. The question is *What qualities does an entrepreneur have?* or *What makes an entrepreneur tick?*, and they asked me because of my success in founding and developing my online travel agency which now provides – in 25 countries – not just flights and hotels, but insurance and a whole suite of other travel-related services as well. Well, what makes people like me tick? Okay, let's take a look and find out.

Methodology note

Spiral-bound or stitched/stapled notebooks are not the best way to keep lecture notes. It is impossible to reorganize or add extra information at a later date, or make a clean copy of notes after a lecture. Encourage students, therefore, to use a loose-leaf file, but make sure that they organize it in a sensible way, with file dividers, and keep it tidy. Tell students to use a separate piece of paper for each outline in this lecture.

Exercise D

Set for pair or group work. Feed back, but do not confirm or correct. Students should be able to predict reasonably well the kind of information which will fit into their outline.

🎧 Exercise E

Before you play the next part of each lecture, refer students to their outline notes again. Tell them to orally reconstruct the introduction from their notes. They do not have to be able to say the exact words, but they should be able to give the gist.

Remind students that they are only going to hear the next part of each lecture once. Play each extract in turn, pausing if necessary to allow students to make notes, but not replaying any section. Tell students to choose an appropriate type of notes for this part of the lecture – it could be a continuation of the type they chose for the introduction, or it could be a different type.

Transcript 🎧 1.6

Lecture 1

Most businesses begin with the ideas of an entrepreneur. Stelios Haji-Ioannou, for example, was a brilliantly innovative young entrepreneur born in a small village in Cyprus. He now heads a multi-billion-dollar empire called easyGroup, which includes the well-known airline, easyJet. This airline became a successful budget airline in the European market. The young Cypriot is known for simple, practical and innovative ideas.

So a new business usually begins with an idea. The next step is to organize the factors of production. An entrepreneur such as Stelios will bring together land, labour and capital to develop his goods and services and make them available to customers. He needs to make decisions about where the business will be located, how things will be produced and what the product design will be. He needs to think about the wages to pay people and the prices to charge consumers.

The next stage follows as the company grows. It is managing risk. The biggest risk is usually money. Money is always needed to develop the business, buy capital items and pay salaries. Some entrepreneurs use their own money to do this in the early stages. Stelios Haji-Ioannou, for example, received over $30 million when his family shipping firm was sold in 2005, so he had a good head start. So, like some business entrepreneurs, Stelios had a lot of money to support his young businesses, but he still carried the risk of losing it. Other people borrow from banks to start businesses, turning their hobbies or interests into commercial operations. Others still use redundancy money or inherited funds to get started. All these people risk losing their money, the business capital, if things go wrong. There is no guarantee that any business will sell its products and services.

Stelios began a range of companies with the word *easy* in the name. His idea was to make life easy for consumers. EasyJet was a company that started when he bought two aeroplanes and offered flights from just outside London to Edinburgh for £29, which was very cheap compared with other airlines at the time. Seven years later, the company was worth over a billion pounds. A few more years and it was huge, spanning the whole of Europe. Although the entrepreneur usually carries the risk of failing, in this case it was a success. The company had to borrow money in order to grow so fast. And whenever capital is involved, there is risk. Most people think entrepreneurs are small business owners who face a lot of risk. Many such small businesses become larger companies over time.

The final stage is to pass on responsibilities, or to delegate. Gradually, management jobs within the growing enterprise are given to others in the company. Stelios, in the early days, for example, would have quickly delegated decisions about prices and salaries and such things to other people.

Then, similarly, an entrepreneur may actually pass on the role as head of the company altogether, so he or she can begin new projects. In fact, Stelios handed over the running of easyJet to a new company chairman in 2002. This freed him up from the business to continue being an entrepreneur. The characteristics of running a huge company are very different from getting a small idea up and running as a company. Stelios, it seems, is good at the latter. True entrepreneurs tend to love continuing to be entrepreneurs.

🎧 **1.7**

Lecture 2

Renewable resources are things like water and the wood from pine forests … or other things that nature gradually replaces. Fish taken from the sea for food products is a renewable resource, although some would argue that we are using this resource too quickly and, in fact, faster than it can replace itself.

Non-renewable resources, on the other hand, are things that only exist in certain quantities and will not be replaced once they are used up. Oil, while some reserves still remain undiscovered, will definitely run out some day. The same could be said for coal and uranium.

The second factor of production is labour. Labour is another word for the people that are directly involved in business activity. Under labour there are three categories of worker. Can you guess what they might be? Well, one would be manual workers (that's those people who do mostly physical work). Then we have skilled workers (that's those people who do more mental work or work that you need education or training to do). And finally there are the management workers, who head up teams and delegate tasks to others. Human Resources is the name of the department that finds, employs and then trains and motivates these people to contribute to the organization.

The third factor is capital. This covers all the machinery and equipment and other assets that are used in the business activity. It also includes the money that the owners of the company raised to start the business.

The fourth and final of the factors of production is enterprise, and this is where we, as managers, come into the picture. This is a rather special factor, as it involves human thinking and ideas. Enterprise needs businesspeople who are *entrepreneurs* (that's spelt e-n-t-r-e-p-r-e-n-e-u-r … it comes from a French word, which is why the spelling looks a bit unusual). The word entrepreneur refers to the type of people who come up with and develop business ideas. They buy or hire the other factors of production that I already mentioned and organize them in such a way as to make their business work. If they invest capital themselves, then often they take quite a lot of risk and they may lose some or perhaps all of the money. But if successful, some money, called profit, will remain for the entrepreneur to enjoy. So I think you can see what drives the entrepreneur!

🎧 **1.8**

Lecture 3

Many people think that being an entrepreneur is creative and glamorous. In fact, being an entrepreneur is very hard work.

There is a common belief that entrepreneurs are great risk-takers. This is not quite true. It has been shown that most entrepreneurs are risk-averse – that is to say that they are very aware of risk, they manage risk carefully and avoid being exposed to too much risk.

And the rewards of the entrepreneur can be great. They include not only profits, but also the opportunity to make your own decisions and see those decisions turn into a successful enterprise.

So let's look a bit closer at these pros and cons. Entrepreneurship is certainly exciting and stimulating. As it involves risk, there is a sense of adventure, which many people love. It usually requires original thinking and ideas about services or products that have not been marketed before. It appeals to people's creativity.

Another great feature of being an entrepreneur is the independence. Many workers are tired of the stress of having those in authority telling them what to do. They find that the administration, rules and structure of a large company can be time-wasting and inefficient. This gets them down. Making their own decisions is very exciting for them. They want the flexibility that being an entrepreneur can provide them. For example, they can work according to their own schedule, freeing up time for family or other activities. I'm sure everyone here has dreamt of this before!

However, every coin has two sides. There are many aspects of an entrepreneur's working life that are not quite so positive.

For example, the working life of an entrepreneur is often full of surprises. An urgent matter may mean he … or she … will need to work late at night and at weekends for several weeks in a row. Entrepreneurs who dreamt of working flexibly may find themselves simply working all the time, with long hours and no holidays. And independence is a great thing, but if you make all your own decisions there is no one to blame but yourself. There is no one higher than you to take responsibility.

OK. Back to the positives. Employees in a corporation sometimes believe they can offer their employer's product or service to the customer at a lower cost, therefore sell it at a lower price. So, with such certain business potential (or business that seems certain), they think they will earn a lot of money. They may also feel that being an entrepreneur cuts out the management and company structure, letting them get paid in full for what they achieve.

While discussing money, let's turn back to the negatives. Starting your own company means giving up the safety of regular monthly pay. Not just that, but you will not receive anything like health insurance or other benefits until the company grows. And as mentioned earlier, you are taking full responsibility for the risk of the business venture, so as a worst case, you may earn no profits, and you may even lose some or all of your capital as well.

The most common complaint from entrepreneurs is keeping up the effort when the going gets tough. Has anyone heard of this before? Entrepreneurs really need to have stamina. With most start-up businesses going out of business in the first five years, there will certainly be times when all new businesses find it difficult. The entrepreneur is likely to have problems with incompetent new staff who don't understand what to do, as they don't have the experience of the entrepreneur, or market conditions that they didn't count on, like overwhelming pressure from larger competitors. It's never easy.

🎧 **1.9**

Lecture 4

Right. Let's start. The ideas I'm going to describe were written about by an academic called Burns in 1977. Burns said that a *transactional* leader is one who trades rewards for the efforts people make. This person leads by making promises. He or she understands what motivates employees, and then sets things up so that they get what they want if their performance is good. On the other hand, a *transformational* leader does things a bit differently.

He or she will raise a worker's awareness to see the whole picture, or the team's or company's goals. He or she will not aim to satisfy our needs with rewards, but will expand our needs to include greater goals. Some people say these leaders are visionary, as they get people to see beyond their own interests for the sake of a larger group. Transformational leaders are well known for bringing about change when change is needed. It is also said that these leaders are more charismatic.

So what is charisma? Another great thinker in management studies, Max Weber, believed that charisma is the influence people have over others. Charismatic people seem to have the ability to solve the problems of the people who follow them. Charismatic people are admired.

Academics have long argued over whether good leadership is a trait you are born with or something you can learn. Well, with more awareness of transformational leadership and charisma, leadership is now something that can be developed in people. Yes, some people are born leaders. However, it is true that leadership awareness can be developed in students on MBA courses and other programmes.

Another thing to consider is that a leader who understands and is aware of leadership styles can have a big effect on the organizations and teams he or she leads. People can be better motivated to get things done. Charismatic and transformational leaders will inspire people to act. People will see their vision and take it on. The consequence is getting things done through people … and doing it well.

The best leaders are not know-it-alls. They are not dominant or manipulative. Great transformational leaders like Martin Luther King and Mahatma Gandhi led by inspiring people through their vision.

🎧 **1.10**

Lecture 5

Right, as you can see here on this slide, Blake and Mouton have divided leadership styles into four parts. On this axis here on the left side is concern for people. And on this one up here is concern for production. Now, neither way is right or wrong and in fact, as you can see from this grid, most styles are a mix of both. But what exactly is the difference?

Leaders with concern for people want people to be satisfied and happy. Leaders with concern for production are those who prefer to set and enforce tight schedules, to get things done at any cost. The former, when they plan a project or task, like to think about the needs of team members, their interests, their training and how to develop them. The latter, when they plan a project or task, like to focus on clear and firm objectives and efficient productivity. The former is people-orientated whereas the latter is task-orientated.

The leadership style that has high concern for people and low concern for production was labelled *country club leadership* by Blake and Mouton. This is because it is probably the kind of leadership that might be found in this traditional kind of leisure club, where relationships and atmosphere are the most important things, and efficiency may have been lost.

The leadership style that has high concern for production and low concern for people, in contrast, they called *produce or perish*. This is really a warning. If you don't work efficiently and well, the enterprise dies and you die with it. These leaders see their workers as a means to an end. They tend to be autocratic and apply strict rules, policies and procedures. They see punishment as the best way to motivate people to work.

Here are the other two extremes you can see on the grid. This one, *impoverished leadership*, is where the leader has neither concern for people nor for task. This kind of leadership will fail. The other extreme is the most promising type. High concern for production and high concern for people. Blake and Mouton called this type *the team leader*. Managers with this combination are said to be the best leaders with the optimum management style. People led by this kind of leader will be involved in and understand the organization's purpose. They may have some share in the company success. Their own needs, therefore, come together with the company needs. Help one and you help the other. There is trust and job satisfaction.

People-orientation contrasts with task-orientation in other ways, too. In last week's lecture we talked about a number of leadership styles. These apply here, too.

Unlike task-orientated leaders, people-orientated leaders tend to be more democratic and use more consultative and participative styles. On the other hand, task-orientated leaders will tend to be more paternalistic or even, as I said before, a bit autocratic.

It is easy to draw a distinction between the two styles, but we must remember that neither is better than the other. They both have advantages, and a leader should not avoid one in preference for its counterpart. In fact, what Blake and Mouton also noted was that many businesses have management and leadership styles that they called *middle of the road*. These are a blend of both sides, and as you can see here, they are located in the middle of the grid.

🎧 **1.11**

Lecture 6

I suppose the main thing is that I have a great belief in market opportunity and I am ready to organize my resources to change what exists and turn it into something new. Some people think of us as gamblers. But I'd say that's simply not true. Entrepreneurs are people who accept personal and financial risk but manage it as experts, not as gamblers. We are people who are driven by what is called the *entrepreneurial spirit*. It's something that makes us the best we can be. And there are a few things that make this happen.

The first is that we tend to be very positive people. I believe in positive thinking. For me, every difficulty or challenge is an opportunity. When the dotcom crash happened at the end of the 1990s, I didn't give up. The newspapers criticized me and my online business and they predicted I would go under. But I came back with optimism. I confidently told them what we can do better than normal travel agents. And now our shares are back to where they were and higher.

Another great feature of entrepreneurs is passion. All the entrepreneurs I've met, from Joe Bloggs running a new corner shop in my street to Richard Branson, the founder of the 200 or more Virgin Group companies, all of them are brimming with excitement. Not just for business – most of us have a great passion for life as well. You might have seen on television my trips to tropical rainforests and coral reefs. Some say it was just to get publicity. But I can tell you now, it was more for the love of being there and trying to save these unique ecosystems.

I suppose it's also fairly obvious that entrepreneurs have to be good leaders. There has to be some charisma, and you have to be honest and show that you have good values. This inspires people to believe you and follow you. Liars and dishonest entrepreneurs never build long-term and large businesses. They generally pass from idea to idea, and while some are successful, most are not, and many fail.

Being a good leader makes you a team-orientated person and a good teacher. Entrepreneurs have to be clear communicators and should always be ready to communicate, as I have done by coming here to talk to you today. Not just talk – you also have to have the enthusiasm to motivate people to move and to act.

The next characteristic I think we tend to share is an ability to adapt to new situations. You have to be ready to customize a service to what the buyer wants. You must be ready to improve your product quickly. It's about being creative enough to come up with solutions ... and fast.

And finally, I reckon, one of the most important attributes of entrepreneurs is ambition. One thing I kept through the most difficult times was my headstrong determination and a clear vision of where I was going to be in the future. I never ever lose this focus. I know exactly what I want, and therefore I can work out how to get there. So never lose sight of your goals.

Exercise F

Allow students to uncover the opposite page or open their books. Give them plenty of time to compare their answers with the model notes. Feed back on the final question.

Exercise G

1 Ask students to work in pairs. Assign one set of notes to each pair. They must try to reconstruct the lecture orally – including the introduction – from the notes. It does not have to be exact, nor include all the detail.

2 Put the pairs together in groups of four, with different topics. Each pair should give their lecture to another pair.

Closure

1 Work on any problems you notice during the pairwork (Exercise G).

2 Refer back to the pictures at the top of the Course Book page. Students should now be able to name them with confidence.

Extra activities

1   Work through the *Vocabulary bank* and *Skills bank* if you have not already done so, or as a revision of previous study.

2   Use the *Activity bank* (Teacher's Book additional resources section, Resource 1A).

   A   Set the crossword for individual work (including homework) or pairwork.

   Answers

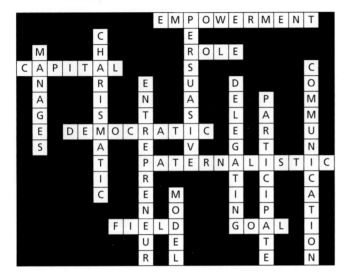

   B   Use the *Activity bank* (Teacher's Book additional resources section, Resource 1B).

   Tell students to play noughts and crosses in pairs, using the two boards. The first contains words with affixes, the second contains names, places and ideas mentioned in the lectures for this unit.

   Teach students how to play noughts and crosses if they do not know – they take it in turns to choose a word/phrase/name and try to use it in context or explain what it means. If they succeed, they can put their symbol – a nought 0 or a cross **X** – in that box. If a person gets three of their own symbols in a line, they win.

   First board: Tell students to remove the affixes to find the basic word in each case. Make sure they can tell you the meaning of the basic word (e.g., *flexible* for *flexibility*), but don't elicit the meaning of the affixed word at this stage. Put students in pairs to play the game. Monitor and adjudicate.

   Second board: Put students in different pairs to play the second game. This time they have to remember facts from the lectures. Don't let them look back at notes.

3   Each of the mini-lectures from Lesson 1.4 can lead on to a great deal more work. Tell students to research one of the following. Explain that they must come back and report to the rest of the class in the next lesson/next week.

Lecture	Research
1	The career of Richard Branson, Alan Sugar or another entrepreneur.
2	The problems associated with human resources in a company.
3	Compare what three successful entrepreneurs attribute their success to.
4	Research the leadership styles of Ricardo Semler and his father.
5	Find an example of a successful entrepreneur who has pioneered the use of renewable energy sources in his/her company.

4   Brainstorm note-taking techniques. For example:

   ● use spacing between points
   ● use abbreviations
   ● use symbols
   ● underline headings
   ● use capital letters
   ● use indenting
   ● make ordered points
   ● use different colours
   ● use key words only

2 CULTURE AND CHANGE

This unit explores what we understand by the term *culture*, especially extending its most common use – national or ethnic culture – into the context of an organization such as a company. It looks at how understanding culture can help managers involved in implementing change. Students read two academic texts covering these concepts. The second text elaborates on change management, exploring how managers can overcome resistance to change.

Skills focus

Reading

- using research questions to focus on relevant information in a text
- using topic sentences to get an overview of the text

Writing

- writing topic sentences
- summarizing a text

Vocabulary focus

- English–English dictionaries:
  headwords
  definitions
  parts of speech
  phonemes
  stress markers
  countable/uncountable
  transitive/intransitive

Key vocabulary

alliance	embrace	restructuring
artefact	entrepreneurialism	rumour
assumption	ethnic	strategic
attitude	evidence	take for granted
belief	guru	values
carbon-neutral	inevitable	visible
competition	innovation	
corporate	legislation	
courtesy	organizational	
cultural	piecemeal	
culture	pre-existing	
cutting-edge	redundant	
disseminate	resistance	

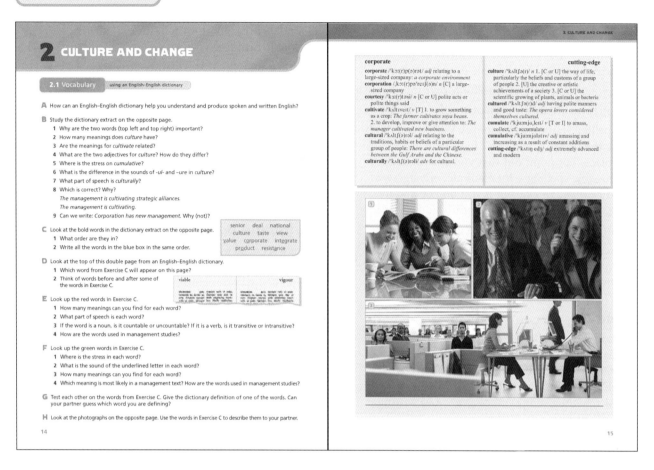

General note

Take in a set of English–English dictionaries.

Read the *Vocabulary bank* at the end of the Course Book unit. Decide when, if at all, to refer students to it. The best time is probably at the beginning of a later lesson, as a summary/revision.

Lesson aims

- learn how to make full use of an English–English dictionary
- gain fluency in the target vocabulary

Introduction

1 Revise the vocabulary from the last unit. Check:
- meaning
- pronunciation
- spelling

2 Ask students whether they use a translation (bilingual) dictionary or an English–English (monolingual) dictionary. Elicit the advantages and disadvantages of a translation dictionary.

Answers

Possible answers:

+	–
good when you know the word in your own language and need a translation into English	not good when there is more than one possible translation of a word – which is the correct one?
when you look up an English word, the translation into your language is easy to understand	English–English dictionaries often have more examples and precise definitions of each word

Methodology note

Recent research has shown that, despite the insistence of generations of language teachers on the use of English–English dictionaries in class, nearly 90 per cent of students use a translation dictionary when studying on their own.

Exercise A

Keep the question as a general discussion. Confirm but do not explain anything. Point out that the next exercise will make the value of this kind of dictionary clear.

Answers

Model answers:

The following information is useful for spoken English:

- stress
- pronunciation of individual phonemes – particularly when a phoneme has multiple pronunciations

The following information is useful for written English:

- information about the type of word – C/U; T/I
- the spelling – students might say that if you don't know the spelling, you can't find the word in the first place, but point out that you can often guess the possible spelling – for example, *management* could be *managment*, but if you do not find it there, you can try with an *e* in the middle
- examples of the word in use to memorize
- some synonyms for lexical cohesion – this is a very important point, although you may not want to elaborate on this now

Exercise B

Set for individual work and pairwork checking. Feed back, ideally using an OHT or other visual display of the dictionary extract to highlight points. You might suggest that students annotate the dictionary extract in their books, highlighting symbols, etc., and writing notes on the meaning and value.

Answers

Model answers:

1 They tell you the first and last words on the pages to help you locate the word you want.

2 *Culture* – three meanings as outlined in the dictionary excerpt; note that the second meaning is uncountable only.

3 Yes, the second meaning comes from idiomatic (metaphorical) use of the first.

4 *Cultured* and *cultural* are the adjectives for the two distinct meanings of the word *culture*. *Cultured* relates to someone who is well educated and knows a lot about the arts; *cultural* relates to a group, society or country, or to the arts.

5 'Cumulative* – on the first syllable.

6 *-ul-* is pronounced /ʌl/ and *–ure* is pronounced /ə(r)/.

7 An adverb.

8 The first sentence is correct because the verb is transitive and thus must have an object, in this case *strategic alliances*. The second is incorrect as there is no object.

9 No – because the noun *corporation* is countable and therefore needs *a* or *the*.

Exercise C

Note: If students are from a Roman alphabet background, you may want to omit this exercise.

1 Students should quickly be able to identify alphabetical order.

2 Set for individual work and pairwork checking. Feed back, getting the words on the board in the correct order. Don't worry about stress and individual phonemes at this point – students will check this later with their dictionaries.

Answers

corporate culture deal integrate national product resistance senior taste value view

> ### Language note
>
> It may seem self-evident that words in a dictionary are in alphabetical order. But students from certain languages may not automatically recognize this. In the famous Hans Wehr dictionary of written Arabic, for example, you must first convert a given word to its root and look that up, then find the derived form. So *aflaaj* (the plural of *falaj* = irrigation channel) will not be found under A but under F since the root is *f-l-j*.

Exercise D

1 Set for pairwork. Feed back orally, explaining the principle if necessary.

2 Set for pairwork. Feed back orally.

Answers

1 *View* will appear on the double-page spread.

2 Answers depend on which words students choose.

Exercise E

Give out dictionaries, if you have not already done so.

Remind students that dictionaries number multiple meanings of the same part of speech and multiple parts of speech. Remind them also of the countable/uncountable and transitive/intransitive markers. (Note that different dictionaries may use different methods for indicating these things. The *Oxford Advanced Learner's Dictionary*, for example, uses [V] for intransitive verbs and [Vn] for transitive verbs.)

Write the headings of the table in the Answers section on the board, and work through the first word as an example.

Set for pairwork. Feed back, building up the table in the Answers section on the board. (Students' answers will vary – accept any appropriate meanings and definitions.)

Answers

Model answers:

Word	Part of speech	Type	Main meaning in management	Main meaning(s) in general English
senior	adj		top-level	old/older
deal	n	C	a business agreement	the way you are treated by others
deal	v	T/I	to trade	to give out cards in a game/to cope
national	adj		owned by a government/relating to a country	relating to a country
culture	n	C/U	the way of life and beliefs of a group of people	the way of life, beliefs and customs of a group of people
culture	n	U		the creative or artistic achievements of a civilized society
taste	v	T		to try the flavour of food
taste	n	C/U	a preference (usually customers' purchasing patterns)	a preference/flavour
view	v	T	to consider something in a certain way	to look at something
view	n	C	an opinion	an area that can be seen, such as a landscape

Exercise F

Remind students how stress and the pronunciation of individual phonemes are shown in a dictionary. Refer them to the key to symbols in the dictionary if necessary. Write the headings of the table in the Answers section on the board, and work through the first word as an example.

Set for pairwork. Feed back, building up the table in the Answers section on the board.

Answers

Model answers:

Stress	Sound	Part of speech	Type	Main meaning in management	Main meaning (s) in general English
'value	/v/	v	T	to state how much something is worth	to consider something important
		n	C/U	the amount something is worth	1 the amount something is worth 2 the degree to which something is useful 3 a particular interesting quality that something has
'corporate	/ɔː/	adj		relating to companies	relating to companies
'integrate	/ɪ/	v	T	to blend things	to blend things
		v	I	to mix interpersonally	to mix socially
'product	/ɒ/	n	C/U	an item manufactured for sale	an item to buy/a consequence
re'sistance	/ə/	n		unwillingness	1 unwillingness 2 opposition to something 3 the ability to stop electricity

Exercise G

Demonstrate how to do the exercise by giving a few definitions and getting students to tell you the word (without reading from the board or their books, if possible). Stick to management usage rather than general English and encourage students to do the same.

Exercise H

Let the students discuss the pictures. If necessary, try to steer them towards the concepts listed below.

- Photo 1: Elicit words like *culture, national, taste*.
- Photo 2: Elicit words and phrases like *senior, view, value, corporate*.
- Photo 3: Elicit words like *culture, taste, corporate, integrate*.

Closure

1 Remind students that you can identify the part of speech of an unknown word by looking at the words before or after the word, i.e.,

- nouns often come before and after verbs, so if you know that X is a verb, the next content word before or after is probably a noun
- nouns often come immediately after articles
- verbs often come after names and pronouns
- adjectives come before nouns or after the verb *be*

Come back to this point when you are giving feedback on the reading texts in this unit.

2 Point out that dictionaries often use a small set of words that help to define, e.g., *method, process, role, way, kind, theory, object*. Give definitions using these words and tell students to identify what you are defining, e.g., *It's a role where you get things done through other people* (manager); *It's an object for sale* (product); *It's a way of finding new employees* (recruitment).

2.2 Reading

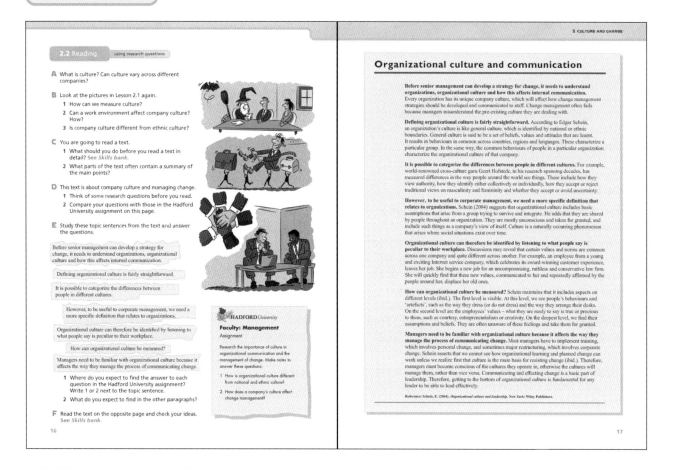

General note

Take in an English–English dictionary.

Read the *Skills bank* section on doing reading research at the end of the Course Book unit. Decide when, if at all, to refer students to it. The best time is probably at the very end of the lesson or the beginning of the next lesson, as a summary/revision.

Lesson aims

- prepare for reading research
- use research questions to structure reading research

Introduction

1 Hold up an English–English dictionary and say a word from Lesson 2.1. Ask students where approximately they will find it in the dictionary – i.e., beginning, middle, two-thirds of the way through, etc. Follow their advice and read the word at the top left. Ask students if the target word will be before or after. Continue until you get to the right page. Repeat with several more words from Lesson 2.1.

2 Give definitions of some words from Lesson 2.1 for students to identify.

Exercise A

Set the question for general discussion.

Answers

Culture refers to distinctive behaviours, values and beliefs that people in a group have in common. It can be ethnic (Kurdish, Berber, Palestinian, Maori), it may be provincial (Californian, Cornish, Northern English, Andalusian), it may be national (French, Polish, Japanese) or it may be regional (Chinese, Arabic, Latino). On the other hand, it may also be organizational (IBM, Google). IBM and Google make a good contrast: IBM, known as 'Big Blue' due to its alleged convention of wearing formal navy blue suits, has a more serious culture. Google, based in West-Coast America, prides itself on its creativity and its growth out of modest origins, and is more colourful, relaxed and daring in its organizational culture.

Language note

The word *behaviour* is used in general English as uncountable, e.g., *His behaviour is unacceptable.* But in many disciplines, it can be used as a countable noun, indicating that behaviour is not a single item but can vary, e.g., *People's attitudes and beliefs give rise to behaviours …* (different types of behaviour).

However, advise students to be very careful about trying to use the word as a countable noun. In most cases, uncountable usage is correct.

Exercise B

Tell students to discuss the questions in groups for a few minutes, then feed back as a whole class. If physical aspects of culture are not forthcoming, try to elicit them: *dress codes, hair, office arrangements, titles, name conventions.* Then try to elicit the non-physical: *what people believe is important to do and say in a workplace, who in the company they feel is a hero, whether they greet each other warmly or not,* etc. Find out which office environment they would prefer, and why. Stimulate their ideas with counter-offers if possible. The aim of the discussion is to raise interest and to elicit and share any previously learnt and relevant vocabulary.

Answers

Answers depend on the students.

Exercise C

Students may or may not be able to articulate preparation for reading. Elicit ideas. One thing they must identify – reading for a purpose. Point out that they should always be clear about the purpose of their reading. A series of questions to answer, or *research questions*, is one of the best purposes. Refer students to the *Skills bank* at this stage, if you wish.

Exercise D

1 Set for pairwork. Elicit some ideas, but do not confirm or correct.
2 Refer students to the Hadford University research questions at the bottom of the page. Check comprehension. If students have come up with better research questions, write them on the board for consideration during the actual reading.

Exercise E

Remind students about topic sentences if they haven't mentioned them already in Exercise C. Give them time to read the topic sentences in this exercise. Point out that the topic sentences are in order, so they give a rough overview of the whole text. Some topic sentences clearly announce what the paragraph will be about. Others may only give a hint of how it will develop. Let them discuss the questions in pairs.

1 The first research question is addressed in paragraphs 2, 3 and 4. The second research question is addressed in the last two paragraphs.
2 Answers depend on the students. Discuss and allow plenty of ideas but keep it brief.

Exercise F

Tell students to compare the contents of each paragraph with their predictions. A randomly chosen comparison in the class may provide a good prompt to the remainder of the class.

Encourage them to take notes as they read. If necessary, the reading can be set for homework.

Closure

1 After the reading, you might wish to apply the content of the reading text to a real-life example, to bring the text to life for the students.

   Discuss the ethnic, provincial, national or regional cultures represented in the room and (while being sensitive) elicit one or two related (positive) stereotypes.

   Then elicit any organizations that anyone in the room has had any contact with: the companies students' parents work at, companies students may have worked for, the school, college or university itself you are working in, etc. Brainstorm the behaviours, values or beliefs peculiar to the examples mentioned: fierce competitiveness, informality, bureaucratic inefficiency.

   Finally, elicit how managers would be able to change the culture in these organizations. Discuss how they might motivate people or disseminate information. It does not matter what ideas come up: it is the questioning that matters. This also relates to later activities in the unit.

2 As a further activity after reading, remind students of the note-taking skills practised in Unit 1. Discuss appropriate note-taking forms for this text. They can then write notes on the text. Tell them to keep their notes, as they will be useful for the summary exercise in Lesson 2.3.

3 Unless you have set the reading for homework, do some extra work on oral summarizing as a comprehension check after reading (see *Skills bank – Using topic sentences to summarize*). Students work in pairs. One student says a topic sentence and the other student summarizes the paragraph from memory in his/her own words, or if necessary reads the paragraph again and then summarizes it without looking.

4 You may also want to redo the text as a jigsaw – the text is reproduced in the additional resources section at the back of this Teacher's Book (Resource 2B) to facilitate this.

2.3 Extending skills

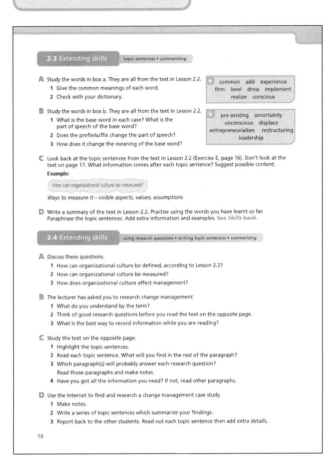

2.3 Extending skills — topic sentences • summarizing

A Study the words in box a. They are all from the text in Lesson 2.2.
1 Give the common meanings of each word.
2 Check with your dictionary.

common add experience
firm level dress implement
realize conscious

B Study the words in box b. They are all from the text in Lesson 2.2.
1 What is the base word in each case? What is the part of speech of the base word?
2 Does the prefix/suffix change the part of speech?
3 How does it change the meaning of the base word?

pre-existing uncertainty
unconscious displace
entrepreneurialism restructuring
leadership

C Look back at the topic sentences from the text in Lesson 2.2 (Exercise E, page 16). Don't look at the text on page 17. What information comes after each topic sentence? Suggest possible content.

Example:

How can organizational culture be measured?

Ways to measure it – visible aspects, values, assumptions

D Write a summary of the text in Lesson 2.2. Practise using the words you have learnt so far. Paraphrase the topic sentences. Add extra information and examples. See *Skills bank*.

2.4 Extending skills — using research questions • writing topic sentences • summarizing

A Discuss these questions.
1 How can organizational culture be defined, according to Lesson 2.2?
2 How can organizational culture be measured?
3 How does organizational culture affect management?

B The lecturer has asked you to research *change management*.
1 What do you understand by the term?
2 Think of good research questions before you read the text on the opposite page.
3 What is the best way to record information while you are reading?

C Study the text on the opposite page.
1 Highlight the topic sentences.
2 Read each topic sentence. What will you find in the rest of the paragraph?
3 Which paragraph(s) will probably answer each research question? Read those paragraphs and make notes.
4 Have you got all the information you need? If not, read other paragraphs.

D Use the Internet to find and research a change management case study.
1 Make notes.
2 Write a series of topic sentences which summarize your findings.
3 Report back to the other students. Read out each topic sentence then add extra details.

18

General note

Take in a set of English–English dictionaries.

Lesson aims

- produce good topic sentences and a summary text

Further practice in:

- vocabulary from Lesson 2.2

Introduction

Test students on the information from the previous lesson, e.g., *What's the difference between a leader and a manager? What's the difference between an entrepreneur and a manager?*

Exercise A

1 Set for pairwork. Refer students back to the text if necessary. Feed back.

2 Tell students to look up any cases where they could not think of two meanings. Feed back orally. (Students' answers will vary – accept any appropriate meanings and definitions.)

Methodology note

Don't help students to find words in a text. It's a key reading skill to be able to pattern match, i.e., get a word in your mind's eye and then find it on the page.

Answers

Possible answers:

		Meaning 1		Meaning 2
common	adj	usual or normal	adj	shared
add	v	to put things together	v	to say something more
experience	n	involvement recalled	v	to witness or be part of
firm	n	a company	adj	fixed or unchanging
level	adj	equal, balanced or flat	n	one stage or state in a process
dress	n	an item of clothing	v	putting clothes on/to adorn
implement	n	a tool	v	to put into action/ to use
realize	v	to become aware of	v	to sell an asset for cash
conscious	adj	awake	adj	aware and intentional

Exercise B

Set for individual work and pairwork checking. Students can check these points in a dictionary. Feed back, taking apart the words and showing how the affixes can change the meaning.

Answers

Model answers:

Word and part of speech	Base word	Affix and meaning
pre-existing (adj)	exist (v)	*pre* = before *ing* = participle for adjective form
uncertainty (n)	certain (adj)	*un* = not *ty* = adjective → noun
unconscious (adj)	conscious (adj)	*un* = not
displace (v)	place (n)	*dis* = opposite
entrepreneurialism (n)	entrepreneur (n)	*ial* = to form an adjective *ism* = to form an abstract noun
restructuring (gerund)	structure (n & v)	*re* = repeated again *ing* = participle for gerund form
leadership (n)	leader (n)	*ship* = to form an abstract noun Note: not related to a ship (boat)

Exercise C

Ideally, display the topic sentences (or give them on a handout) so that students do not have to turn back to pages 16 and 17. The topic sentences are reproduced in the additional resources section to facilitate this (Resource 2B). Work through the example, showing that you can deduce (or in this case, to some extent, remember) the contents of a paragraph from the topic sentence. Do another example orally. Set for pairwork.

Feed back, eliciting possible paragraph contents and sample information. Only correct ideas which are not based on the topic sentence. Allow students to check back with the text and self-mark.

Answers

See table below.

Discourse note

In academic writing, topic sentences often consist of a general point. The sentences that follow then support the general statement in various ways, such as:

- paraphrasing the topic sentence to expand or help clarify
- giving a definition and/or a description to explain
- extending by giving more information or detail
- illustrating though examples; explaining through practical application
- giving arguments or refuting counter-arguments
- giving reasons, causes, origins
- giving consequences, implications or effects
- concluding, recommending, or linking to a subsequent paragraph

Often – but not always – the type of sentence is shown by a 'discourse marker' – e.g., *for example, first of all*. This helps to signal to the reader how the writer sees the link between the sentences and is therefore a good clue as to the purpose of the sentences following the topic sentence.

Exercise D

Refer students to the *Skills bank*. Set for individual work. If students took notes in Lesson 2.2, Exercise F, they should use these notes as the basis for this exercise. Encourage students to add extra information or examples to fill out the summary. Tell students to start in class while you monitor and assist, and to finish for homework.

Methodology note

There are two reasons for students to use their own words in written work (except when quoting and acknowledging sources):

1 The work involved in rewording information and ideas helps us to mentally process them and to retain them in memory.

2 Copying whole sentences from the work of other writers is plagiarism (unless the quotation is acknowledged). Universities disapprove of plagiarism and will mark down students who plagiarize. In the commercial world, an accusation of plagiarism can cause legal problems, and in the academic world it can severely damage a teacher's reputation and career.

Topic sentence	Possible paragraph content	Supporting information/example(s)
Before senior management can develop a strategy for change, it needs to understand organizations, organizational culture and how this affects internal communication.	uniqueness of company culture	managers must understand it to change anything
Defining organizational culture is fairly straightforward.	definition of organizational culture	quoting Schein, comparison with general culture, behaviours in common
It is possible to categorize the differences between people in different cultures.	how to measure differences	example is Hofstede's work: how individually people identify, their views on male/female roles, etc.
However, to be useful to corporate management, we need a more specific definition that relates to organizations.	group assumptions	Schein: shared and unconscious, develop for people to 'survive/integrate'
Organizational culture can therefore be identified by listening to what people say is peculiar to their workplace.	find out values and norms	example: comparing those in an exciting Internet company and a ruthless law firm
How can organizational culture be measured?	ways to measure it	Schein: visible (e.g., clothes), values (e.g., creativity), assumptions
Managers need to be familiar with organizational culture because it affects the way they manage the process of communicating change.	how managers use culture to change	e.g., training including personal change, restructuring. Schein: leaders must understand culture to make change

Closure

Tell students to define some of the words from the reading text. Alternatively, give definitions of a few random words and ask students to identify them.

2.4 Extending skills

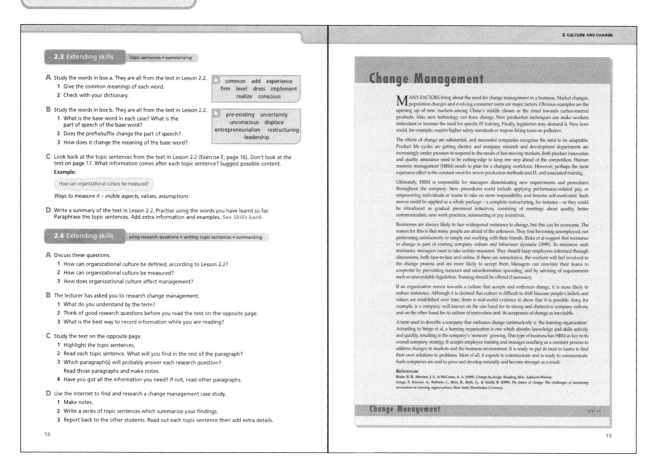

Lesson aims

- use research questions to structure reading research
- write topic sentences for a short summary of research done

Introduction

Give a word from the text in Lesson 2.2 which is part of a common phrase. Hint at the second word by providing the first one or two letters. Ask students to try to complete the phrase. It's probably better if you give the first word in the phrase, but you might also try giving the second word at times.

Possible two-word phrases:

consumer	tastes
middle	class
safety	standards
life	cycle
human	resources
information	technology
prevent	rumours
real	world
business	environment

Exercise A

Group discussion. Check students can remember and have understood the main content points from Lesson 2.2.

Answers

1 'According to Edgar Schein, an organization's culture is like general culture, which is identified by national or ethnic boundaries. General culture is said to be a set of beliefs, values and attitudes that are learnt. It results in behaviours in common, across countries, regions and languages. These characterize a particular group. In the same way, the common behaviours of people in a particular organization characterize the organizational culture of that company.'

2 'Schein maintains that it includes aspects on different levels (ibid.). The first level is visible. At this level, we see people's behaviours and 'artefacts', such as the way they dress (or do not dress) and the way they arrange their desks. On the second level are the employees' values – what they are ready to say is true or precious to them, such as courtesy, entrepreneurialism or creativity. On the deepest level, we find their assumptions and beliefs. They are often unaware of these feelings and take them for granted.'

3 Organizational culture affects the way managers manage the process of communicating change.

Exercise B

1 Refer students to the title of the text – *Change management*. Set for pairwork. Feed back orally.

2 Remind students of the importance of research questions – reading for a purpose. Set for pairwork. Feed back, writing up suitable questions on the board.

3 Elicit the different kinds of notes you can use – see Unit 1 *Skills bank*. Remind students to think about the best kind of notes before and while they are reading.

Methodology note

It is good for students to get into the habit of thinking about the form of their notes before they read a text in detail. If they don't do this, they will tend to be drawn into narrative notes rather than notes which are specifically designed to help them answer their research questions.

Answers

Possible answers:

1 Simply elicit what students have. No attempt to correct them is needed yet.

2 Examples: *How can managers make change happen? Do people resist? What's so important about change, anyway?*

3 See Unit 1 *Skills bank*.

Exercise C

1 Remind students of the importance of topic sentences. Set for individual work and pairwork checking.

2 Encourage students not to read ahead. Perhaps you should ask students to cover the text and only reveal each topic sentence in turn, then discuss possible contents of the paragraph. Remind them that this is a technique for previewing a text and at this point they do not need to read every part of the text. This will come later. If you have an OHP or other visual medium, you can tell students to close their books and just display the topic sentences (additional resources section, Resource 2C), or you can give them out as a handout.

3 Set the choice of paragraphs for pairwork. Students then read individually, make notes and compare them. Monitor and assist.

4 Give students time to read other paragraphs if they need to.

Discourse note

It is as well to be aware (though you may not feel it is appropriate to discuss with students at this point) that in real academic texts, the topic sentence may not be as obvious as in the texts in this unit. Sometimes there is not an explicit topic sentence, so that the overall topic of the paragraph must be inferred. Or the actual topic sentence for the paragraph can be near rather than at the beginning of the paragraph. Sometimes, also, the first sentence of a paragraph acts as a topic statement for a succession of paragraphs.

Answers

Possible answers:

Topic sentence	Possible paragraph content
Many factors bring about the need for change management in a business.	paragraph may list these causes
The effects of change are substantial, and successful companies recognize the need to be adaptable.	paragraph may outline what effects there are on companies and examples of what they may have to do
Ultimately, HRM is responsible for managers disseminating new requirements and procedures throughout the company.	paragraph may suggest ways that they do it
Businesses are always likely to face widespread resistance to change, but this can be overcome.	paragraph may outline reasons for resistance and how companies can overcome or minimize it
If an organization moves towards a culture that accepts and embraces change, it is more likely to reduce resistance.	paragraph may show an example of a company that did so effectively
A term used to describe a company that embraces change constructively is 'the learning organization'.	paragraph may define 'learning organization'

Exercise D

1 If it is possible to research on the Internet during the lesson, send students to the computers to work in pairs or groups. If not, set the task for homework and feed back next lesson.

2 Set for individual work and group checking.

3 The idea is that students, on the basis of the topic sentences, present their information to fellow students. Make sure students realize that they only have to write the topic sentences. They can add the details in orally. Encourage them to stick to information that is relevant to their research questions.

Closure

1 Project, display or write on the board some of the phrases and multi-word items from the text, including the ones below. Play a game where each student calls out a rough definition of an item without saying the item. The remainder of the class may guess the item by calling out suggestions. Note, that while they are all taken from the reading, some of the items here may have arisen already for discussion and other items may not. For those not yet taught, this serves to encourage guessing and to foreshadow their use in later units. Avoid long definitions and dictionary use at this stage, as it is a game.

carbon-neutral

quality assurance

made redundant

product life cycles

cutting-edge

competitive advantage

rumours and misinformation

real-world evidence

a learning organization

2 You may also want to redo the text as a jigsaw, as before – the text is reproduced in the additional resources section (Resource 2C) to facilitate this.

Extra activities

1 Work through the *Vocabulary bank* and *Skills bank* if you have not already done so, or as a revision of previous study.

2 Use the *Activity bank* (Teacher's Book additional resources section, Resource 2A).

A Set the wordsearch for individual work (including homework) or pairwork.

Answers

B Do the quiz as a whole class, or in teams, or set for homework – students can reread the texts to get the answers if necessary.

Answers

1 Firstly, ethnic, provincial, national or regional culture; and secondly, organizational culture

2 Beliefs, values and attitudes

3 A well-known guru in the study of cross-cultural communication

4 A well-known expert in organizational communication theory

5 Visible behaviours and artefacts; values; assumptions and beliefs

6 Extremely important

7 Factors which bring about a need for change management

8 The human resources department

9 Holding discussions and consultations to keep employees involved; informing on legislative requirements; providing training

10 A 'learning organization'

3 Ask students to work in small groups to research further their change management case study from Lesson 2.4, Exercise D. Remind students that they can't possibly read everything they find, so they must use the titles, introductions, conclusions and topic sentences to decide if a text is worth reading.

Have them agree their findings within their group first, and then report these individually to other groups. This can be done after regrouping, so that each new group has members of each former group.

4 Have a competition to practise finding words in a monolingual dictionary. Requirements:

● English–English dictionary for each student (or pair of students if necessary)

● Unit 2 key vocabulary list

Put students in teams with their dictionaries closed. Select a word from the vocabulary list and instruct students to open their dictionaries and find the word. The first student to find the word is awarded a point for their team. Additional points can be awarded if the student can give the correct pronunciation and meaning.

5 Set Resource 2D for individual work and pairwork checking.

Answers

1 if

2 because

3 because of

4 since

5 where

6 to

7 who

8 which

9 when

10 so

3 ORGANIZATIONS AND OPERATIONS

Unit 3 looks at the formal organization of company structure and the different organizational cultures that arise as a result. The first lecture examines these structures and the organization types they relate to. The second lecture looks at three ways of organizing production: job, batch and flow; and discusses two key concepts underlying this – *lean production* and *economies of scale*.

Skills focus

🎧 Listening

- preparing for a lecture
- predicting lecture content
- making lecture notes
- using different information sources

Speaking

- reporting research findings
- formulating questions

Vocabulary focus

- stress patterns in multi-syllable words
- prefixes

Key vocabulary

added value	flexible	project (n)
authority	flow production	representative
batch production	formal	reschedule
bureaucracy	hierarchy	responsibility
capital-intensive	horizontal	roles
centralized	independence	satisfaction
command	informal	span
decentralized	job production	specialized
decision-making	labour-intensive	status
delegate (v)	matrix	structure
division	network	traditional
efficiency	one-off	unscheduled
entrepreneurial	organizational	vertical
expert	procedure	

3.1 Vocabulary

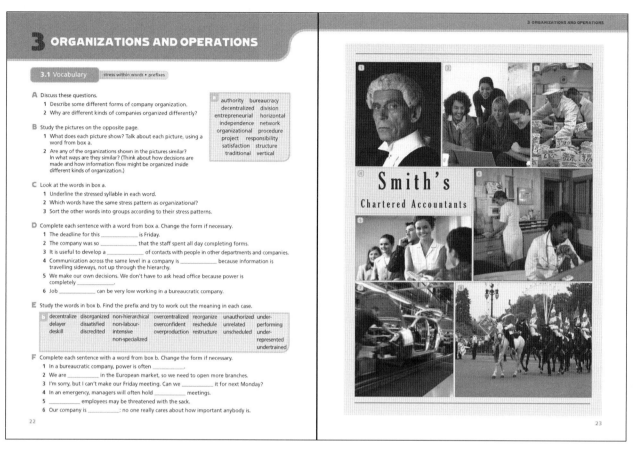

General note

Read the *Vocabulary bank* at the end of the Course Book unit. Decide when, if at all, to refer students to it. The best time is probably at the very end of the lesson or the beginning of the next lesson, as a summary/revision.

Dictionaries will be useful in this lesson.

Lesson aims

- gain a greater understanding of the importance of stress within words and some of the common patterns
- extend knowledge of words which contain prefixes
- gain fluency in the target vocabulary

Introduction

1 Revise the vocabulary from the first two units. Check:
- meaning
- pronunciation
- spelling

2 Ask students to think of different types of businesses they have seen in the high street, e.g., a multi-national bank, a supermarket, a newsagent's, a greengrocer's, etc. Encourage them to include businesses which sell services, such as solicitors and architects, as well as those that sell products. Ask them to think about who makes decisions in each company and how much independence staff may have. Write the different businesses on the board. Get students to work in pairs and decide where the centre of decision-making lies in each. Accept any reasonable answers, but push students to consider the questions seriously, e.g., *Who makes the decisions in a butcher's shop? How much freedom do his staff have to change prices, for instance? Why? The owner, because he is an entrepreneur and is responsible for the success of the business. He does not expect his staff to contradict his pricing. Compare this with a clerk working in a bank.*

Exercise A

1 Refer students to the first question. Point to the list of businesses on the board from the introductory exercise and ask: *Which of these business types are likely to organize their decision-making in similar ways?* You should be able to elicit at least the following:

- Most supermarkets' decisions are made at a centralized headquarters because their distribution networks are organized centrally. The shops are simply outlets for this organization. The military, banks and large international companies like Ford are organized in a similar way, with a centralized structure, decisions made at the centre and little autonomy for local-level managers.

- In small businesses, e.g., a newsagent's or a butcher's, decisions are made in the shop itself. The owner buys in the produce, makes all key decisions and decides how much autonomy to give the assistants.

- Solicitors, doctors and accountants work more as a community because each person is independent and has equal status or authority.

Check pronunciation of key words, e.g., *inde'pendent, 'structure, 'centralized, inter'national*, etc. Pay attention to the stress in the multi-syllable words.

2 Put students in pairs to discuss the second question. Feed back orally. If students use key vocabulary from the unit list, e.g., *decentralized*, accept but do not try to explain each word to the whole class. Point out that you are going to deal with this later.

Answers

Students may tell you about the organization of particular businesses, especially if they have direct experience of working within them. Accept this, but the key point here is that different kinds of businesses – by virtue of their unique natures – will develop their own organizational structures in response to their decision-making and decision-transmitting mechanisms.

Exercise B

Refer students to the pictures on the opposite page. Set questions 1 and 2 for pairwork. Tell students to select relevant words from the box – there are some extra words.

Feed back. As students describe different kinds of organization, check/correct pronunciation, especially the stress in multi-syllable words.

Answers

Possible answers:

1 1 authority/procedure
   2 project/decentralized
   3 independence/satisfaction
   4 procedure
   5 bureaucracy/traditional
   6 responsibility
   7 division (of labour)
   8 authority/vertical

2 Accept all reasonable suggestions.

Exercise C

Write *organizational* on the board. Ask students to say how many syllables there are in the word (there are six). Draw vertical lines to divide the syllables. Then ask students to say where the main stress is and draw a line under the syllable:

o r | g a | n i | <u>z a</u> | t i o n | a l

Point out the importance of stressed syllables in words – see *Language note* below. Although you can mark stress with a straight stress marker (') or diacritic, it may be easier for students to use an underline. Another possibility is to use capital letters for the stressed syllable: *organiZAtional*. Students will, however, find the straight marker in many dictionaries, so it is worth them getting into the habit of using it.

1 Set for pairwork. Tell students to identify the syllables first, then to underline the strongest stress. Feed back.

2 Ask students to find the words which have the same stress pattern as *organizational*. Write them on the board like this:

o r	g a	n i	<u>z a</u>	t i o n	a l
e n	t r e	p r e	<u>n e u r</u>	i	a l
r e	s p o n	s i	<u>b i</u>	l i	t y

3 Set for pairwork. Students should match words with the same number of syllables and with main stresses in the same place.

Stress sometimes moves to fit common patterns when you add a suffix, e.g., *e'lastic, elas'ticity*.

Sometimes it is difficult to be sure how exactly a word should be divided into syllables. Use vowel sounds as a guide to the number of syllables. If in doubt, consult a dictionary.

Answers

1. authority
   bureaucracy
   decentralized
   division
   entrepreneurial
   horizontal
   independence
   network
   organizational
   procedure
   project
   responsibility
   satisfaction
   structure
   traditional
   vertical
3. authority, bureaucracy, decentralized, traditional
   horizontal, independence, satisfaction
   division, procedure
   network, project, structure
   vertical

Exercise D

Set for individual work and pairwork checking. Not all words are needed. Feed back orally.

Answers

Model answers:

1. The deadline for this project is Friday.
2. The company was so bureaucratic that the staff spent all day completing forms.
3. It is useful to develop a network of contacts with people in other departments and companies.
4. Communication across the same level in a company is horizontal because information is travelling sideways, not up through the hierarchy.
5. We make our own decisions. We don't have to ask head office because power is completely decentralized.
6. Job satisfaction can be very low working in a bureaucratic company.

Exercise E

Set for pairwork. Students should look at all three words in each column to find and then deduce the meaning of the prefix. Encourage them to use a phrase as a definition rather than a single-word translation. They need to develop a sense of the broader meaning of the prefix. Feed back, getting the meanings on the board.

Answers

Model answers:

de = without, not
dis = without, not being something, not having something
non = not
over = more than is necessary
re = doing again, repeating
un = not having, not being, the opposite
under = less than it should be

Exercise F

This is further practice in using words with prefixes. Remind students that they must make sure the form of the word fits into the sentence. Feed back, checking pronunciation and stress patterns.

Answers

Model answers:

1. In a bureaucratic company, power is often over-centralized.
2. We are underrepresented in the European market, so we need to open more branches.
3. I'm sorry, but I can't make our Friday meeting. Can we reschedule it for next Monday?
4. In an emergency, managers will often hold unscheduled meetings.
5. Underperforming employees may be threatened with the sack.
6. Our company is non-hierarchical: no one really cares about how important anybody is.

Closure

1. Check meanings of words learnt in this lesson using the pictures on page 23. Ideally, copy the pictures onto an OHT or other visual medium and work through again how the words relate to organization types.
2. If you have not already done so, refer students to the *Vocabulary bank* at the end of Unit 3. Work through some or all of the stress patterns.

Language note

The patterns shown in the *Vocabulary bank* in Unit 3 are productive, i.e., they enable you to make more words or apply the rules accurately to other words. The words with unusual patterns tend to be the more common ones, so if students come across a new multi-syllable word at this level, it is likely to conform to the patterns shown. Native speakers recognize the patterns and will naturally apply them to unusual words, e.g., proper nouns. How, for example, would you pronounce these nonsense words?

felacom

bornessity

shimafy

emtonology

scolosphere

nemponium

cagoral

andimakinize

ortepanimation

3.2 Listening

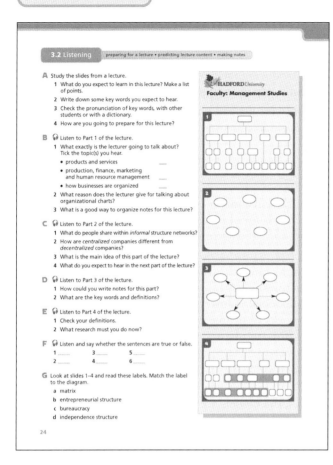

4 Elicit some points – the four Ps (Plan, Prepare, Predict, Produce). If necessary, refer students to Unit 1 *Skills bank* to review the preparation for a lecture. One way to help the students to make provisional notes is to:

- brainstorm what they would include
- organize their topics into a logical sequence

Answers

Answers depend on the students. Accept any reasonable and relevant answers.

🎧 Exercise B

1 Tell students they are only going to hear the introduction to the lecture. Ask what information they expect to get from the introduction (i.e., the outline of the lecture). Give students time to read the choices of topics. Check that they understand the meaning and relevance. Remind them they will only hear the introduction once, as in a lecture. Play Part 1. Allow them to compare answers.

Feed back. Ask them to justify their choice by saying what they heard that related to it. Confirm the correct answer.

2 Elicit ideas. Confirm or correct.

3 Elicit ideas.

Answers

Possible answers:

1 how businesses are organized

2 Organizational charts show lines of command, or where responsibility lies, and a manager's span of control, i.e., how far his/her influence stretches.

3 Perhaps into a table with organization types and their characteristics, or a mixture of headings and bullet points followed by a tree diagram.

Example:

Headings and bullet points:

Organizational charts

- …
- …
- …

Tree Diagram:

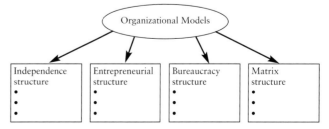

Lesson aims

Further practice in:

- planning and preparing for a lecture
- predicting lecture content
- choosing the best form of notes
- making notes

Introduction

Review key vocabulary by:

- using flashcards
- linking material to organization structures
- playing the alphabet game in the extra activities section at the end of this unit

Exercise A

Refer students to the handout and the slides. Write the title: *Ways businesses are organized* on the board.

1 Set for individual work and pairwork checking. Feed back, eliciting some ideas.

2 Brainstorm to elicit key words. Allow the class to decide whether a word should be included.

3 Set for pairwork.

Transcript 🎧 1.12

Part 1

OK. Is everyone here? Right, let's get started. Today, I'm going to talk about something that's quite basic to management … it's the way businesses are formally organized. We'll look at how they are put together and some popular models that work for different types of company. Of course, in broad terms, organizations may be divided into production, finance, marketing and human resource management. Or they could be organized according to products or services (for example, you might have a food products division that is quite separate from a soap products division). Organizations can also be organized geographically … you may manage the South-East Asian operation or the Middle Eastern one. Or there may be a mixture of these kinds of organization.

We can illustrate the formal organization of a company using an organizational chart, which shows diagrammatically exactly how the employees relate to one another. It is useful for communication and for seeing where responsibility lies, because it shows lines of command – in other words, who reports to whom – and each manager's span of control. By that I mean the number of people below the manager in the chart. In this lecture, we shall examine four possible models of business that we find in many organizations: they are the *independence structure*, the *entrepreneurial structure*, the *bureaucracy* and the *matrix*.

🎧 Exercise C

Before playing Part 2, refer students to the slides and make sure they recognize what they depict. Ask students what they expect to hear, based on the introduction. Give them time to read questions 1–4. Tell them to write only brief notes. The main task is to absorb the meaning.

Play Part 2. Give them time to answer questions 1–4. Allow them to compare their answers. Feed back.

When they thoroughly understand *ways of organizing companies*, ask them what they expect to hear in the next part of the lecture (question 4). Elicit ideas, but do not confirm or correct.

Answers

Model answers:

1 People in informal networks share trust, information and advice.

2 In centralized companies, people have less authority because authority lies in one central headquarters – less complicated, managers have more control, can be fair and processes can be standardized. In

decentralized companies, authority is delegated. Workers are motivated because they can make decisions, businesses are more flexible and local branch managers are permitted to use their local knowledge.

3 Defining formal and informal structures, and introducing the key idea of (de)centralized authority in companies.

4 Answers depend on the students. Accept any reasonable answer.

Transcript 🎧 1.13

Part 2

Now, I will explain each of these four models in a bit, but before I do so, I need to tell you why I call them formal structures.

In fact, Krackhardt and Hanson in 1993 demonstrated that there are also *informal* structures in organizations. They showed that in the financial industry, for instance, there are strong networks of people who trust each other enough to look for and share information and advice amongst themselves. These networks were not related to the lines of command in the organizational charts. They were informal.

Still, the models are important, and the different models suit different business activities. Some of the models are more centralized. This means individuals have less authority because all the authority lies in one central headquarters. Other businesses may suit more decentralized authority, where authority is delegated to individuals, or to different business units, rather than being in a single place.

There are advantages and disadvantages of both these models. Centralized authority can be less complicated if management is strong and decisions are clear. It lets managers keep more control and be fair. In addition, procedures can be standardized. On the other hand, decentralized authority has great advantages as well. It motivates and empowers workers by giving them decision-making power. And it allows businesses to be more flexible. It also recognizes the fact that local managers may have better local knowledge. It can prepare such individuals for greater management roles in the future.

🎧 Exercise D

1 Play the first sentence of Part 3. Ask the first question and elicit ideas.

2 Set the second question for individual work and pairwork checking. Play the rest of the recording. Tell students to take notes. Allow students to compare their definitions. Do not, at this stage, confirm the answers.

Answers

Model answers:

1 A table is good for definitions.

2 See Exercise E.

Transcript 🎧 1.14

Part 3

OK, now I'll look at each of these model structures and explain what they are.

First of all, the *independence structure* is rather a special case. It is where the job requires highly qualified professionals to work alone with their clients, and the organization only exists to support them to do so. Examples are law firms, accounting and consultancy firms, and private medical clinics. Power is essentially decentralized into each and every practising professional.

A complete contrast is the second model – the *entrepreneurial structure*. Here, the decision-making is completely centralized, and decisions are usually made quickly and easily. Businesses using this model are usually small because, as a business grows, it becomes too much for the central entrepreneur to make every decision. Good illustrations of this structure are a small corner shop, a family-run plumbing business or creative agencies in online media, advertising or media production. They are usually run by one expert who set up and developed the firm.

The third one is the *bureaucracy*. It's the traditional hierarchy that larger businesses tend to have, and decision-making is shared out according to the roles of people in the hierarchy. People's jobs are more specialized. A large number of procedures are set, and these decide how people work: what roles they have. Such larger businesses are sometimes criticized for not being able to change quickly enough to meet demand. For example, it takes a long time in a big bureaucratic corporation for a message or idea to reach every employee, because everything has to pass through lines of management. Opportunities may be lost.

However, all large companies need not be like this. The fourth and final model is the *matrix*, possibly the most common in large modern companies now. It accepts the hierarchy from top to bottom (vertical), but it adds another dimension (horizontal). It creates teams that cut across different departments. The members report not only to their line managers in the chain of command, but also to someone on their own level. Horizontal teams are often put together to work on special projects, such as those involving IT, or creating new ideas for quality. The benefit is that the team receives input from representatives from all areas of the company. This structure can solve the problems of a large bureaucracy, and it also gives people greater responsibility and therefore satisfaction. But there may be additional difficulties, like the confusion of workers having two bosses, or the need for extra admin support.

🎧 Exercise E

Part 4 summarizes the definitions of the four key words. Tell students that this is the last part of the lecture. What do they expect to hear? Confirm that it is a summary. Play Part 4.

1 Students should check their definitions as they listen. After the summary has finished, they should correct their definitions and complete their notes. Guide them to the correct answer: that is, the correct meaning, not necessarily the words given here.

2 Elicit ideas. Then set the research for students to work on in pairs or individually. They will need to report back in Lesson 3.3.

Answers

Model answers:

1

Key word	Definition
Independence structure	A structure where power is completely decentralized among individual professionals.
Entrepreneurial structure	A smaller structure where decision-making is completely centralized, quick in adapting to change, and effective.
Bureaucracy	A centralized structure where decision-making lies with individuals with status in the clear organization hierarchy.
Matrix	A structure that has a vertical hierarchy and also has teams that are organized across departmental boundaries.

2 Students should research production planning and how companies organize themselves for this.

Transcript 🎧 1.15

Part 4

So, to summarize what we've covered so far, the *independence structure* is the type of organization where independent professionals like accountants or architects work alone but under the same roof. The *entrepreneurial structure* is where one expert has strong central control in a smaller company. The *bureaucracy* is a larger and traditional structure based on hierarchies with set roles and procedures. And the *matrix* is a larger but more modern organization, where top-to-bottom hierarchies are criss-crossed with special teams with particular responsibilities.

Well, that's it for today. Next time, we'll look a bit more specifically into production planning and how companies organize themselves to meet their production objectives. Don't forget to do a bit of reading on that before you come. Thanks. See you soon.

🎧 Exercise F

These are sentences about the ideas in the lecture. Set for pairwork. Say or play the sentences. Give time for students to discuss and then respond. Students must justify their answers. Advise them to beware of statements containing absolutes such as *always, never, all*. These are rarely true.

Answers

1	false	It shows how information and decisions are transmitted through an organization.
2	true	
3	true	
4	true	
5	true	
6	false	A matrix structure gives workers more responsibility and satisfaction.

Transcript 🎧 1.16

1 An organizational chart shows how money moves through a company.

2 Within informal structures, staff share ideas and help one another.

3 Centralized authority can make management simpler if managers can make strong and clear decisions.

4 A large company is very likely to have a bureaucratic structure.

5 A matrix structure helps by making information flow both vertically and horizontally through a company.

6 A matrix structure makes the problems of a large hierarchical company worse.

Exercise G

Set for pairwork. Ask students to write the correct label on the line by the correct diagram. They should justify their choices.

Answers

1: a hierarchical tree = **bureaucratic structure (c).**

2: isolated circles in an oval = **independent structure (d).**

3: a spider's web with central hub = **entrepreneurial structure (b).**

4: a hierarchical tree with horizontal teams = **matrix structure (a).**

Closure

Ask students to explain in their own words:

● what links the four slides

● the different organizational characteristics of each

Note: Students will need their lecture notes from Lesson 3.2 in the next lesson.

3.3 Extending skills

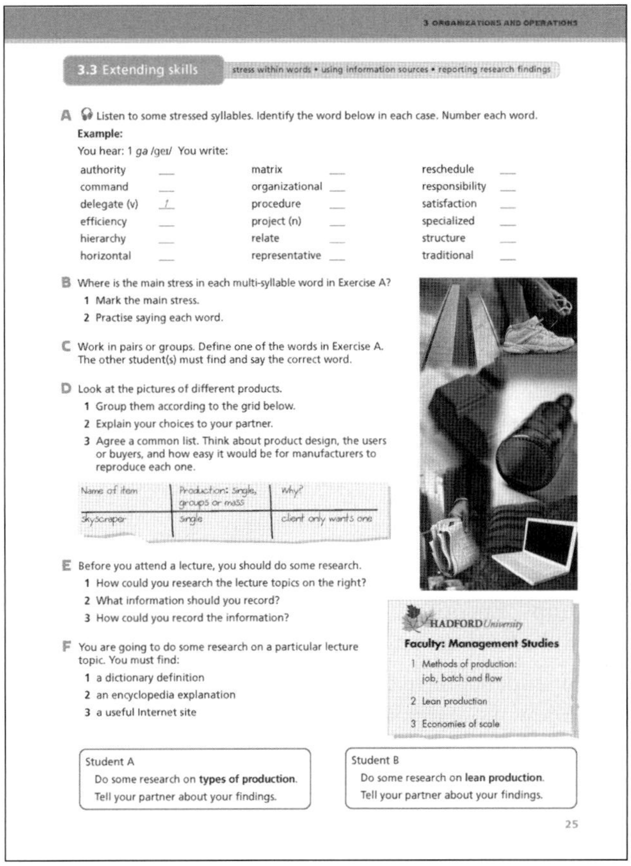

3 ORGANIZATIONS AND OPERATIONS

3.3 Extending skills — stress within words • using information sources • reporting research findings

A Listen to some stressed syllables. Identify the word below in each case. Number each word.

Example:

You hear: 1 *ga* /geɪ/ You write:

authority	___	matrix	___	reschedule	___
command	___	organizational	___	responsibility	___
delegate (v)	1	procedure	___	satisfaction	___
efficiency	___	project (n)	___	specialized	___
hierarchy	___	relate	___	structure	___
horizontal	___	representative	___	traditional	___

B Where is the main stress in each multi-syllable word in Exercise A?

1 Mark the main stress.

2 Practise saying each word.

C Work in pairs or groups. Define one of the words in Exercise A. The other student(s) must find and say the correct word.

D Look at the pictures of different products.

1 Group them according to the grid below.

2 Explain your choices to your partner.

3 Agree a common list. Think about product design, the users or buyers, and how easy it would be for manufacturers to reproduce each one.

Name of item	Production: single, groups or mass	Why?
skyscraper	single	client only wants one

E Before you attend a lecture, you should do some research.

1 How could you research the lecture topics on the right?

2 What information should you record?

3 How could you record the information?

F You are going to do some research on a particular lecture topic. You must find:

1 a dictionary definition

2 an encyclopedia explanation

3 a useful Internet site

HADFORD University

Faculty: Management Studies

1 Methods of production: job, batch and flow

2 Lean production

3 Economies of scale

Student A
Do some research on **types of production**.
Tell your partner about your findings.

Student B
Do some research on **lean production**.
Tell your partner about your findings.

25

General note

Read the *Skills bank* at the end of the Course Book unit. Decide when, if at all, to refer students to it. The best time is probably at the beginning of this lesson or the end of the next lesson, as a summary/revision.

Lesson aims

This lesson is the first in a series about writing an assignment or giving a presentation based on research. The principal objective of this lesson is to introduce students to sources of information.

Introduction

1 Tell students to ask you questions about the information in the lecture in Lesson 3.2 as if you were the lecturer. Refer them to the *Skills bank* for typical language if you wish.

2 Put students in pairs. Student A must ask Student B about the information in the lecture in Lesson 3.2 to help him/her complete the notes from the lecture. Then they reverse roles. Go round, helping students to identify gaps in their notes and to think of good questions to get the missing information. Refer them to the *Skills bank*, if you wish, for language to use in the pairwork.

Pairs then compare notes and decide what other information would be useful and where they could get it from. For example, definitions of the key terms might be useful, from a specialist dictionary or an encyclopedia. In the feedback, write a list of research sources on the board, at least including dictionaries, encyclopedias, specialist reference books and the Internet.

Point out that dictionaries are good for definitions, although you may need to go to a specialist dictionary for a technical word. Otherwise, try an encyclopedia, because technical words are often defined in articles when they are first used. You could also try Google's 'define' feature, i.e., type *define: economies of scale*. But remember you will get definitions from all disciplines, not just your own, so you need to scan to see which is relevant.

Exercise A

In this exercise, students will hear each word with the stressed syllable emphasized, and the rest of the syllables underspoken.

Play the recording, pausing after the first few to check that students understand the task. Feed back, perhaps playing the recording again for each word before checking. Ideally, mark up an OHT or other visual display of the words.

Answers

Model answers:

authority	7
command	3
delegate (v)	1
efficiency	15
hierarchy	12
horizontal	18
matrix	13
organizational	9
procedure	4
project (n)	10
relate (v)	14
representative	17
reschedule	6
responsibility	8
satisfaction	2
specialized	16
structure	5
traditional	11

Transcript 🎧 1.17

1 'delegate
2 satis'faction
3 co'mmand
4 pro'cedure
5 'structure
6 re'schedule
7 au'thority
8 responsi'bility
9 organi'zational
10 'project
11 tra'ditional
12 'hierarchy
13 'matrix
14 re'late
15 e'fficiency
16 'specialized
17 repre'sentative
18 hori'zontal

Exercise B

Erase the words or turn off the OHT. Ask students to guess or remember where the stressed syllable is on each word. Tell them to mark their idea with a light vertical stroke in pencil. Elicit and drill. Refer students to the *Vocabulary bank* at this stage if you wish.

Answers

See transcript for Exercise A.

Exercise C

Set for pair or group work. Go round and assist/correct.

Exercise D

Refer students to the picture and the table. Put students in groups. Encourage them to use the language from the *Skills bank* to get information from others.

When students have covered the items in the pictures, give a few more items – see the Answers section below.

Feed back, building up the table in the Answers section on the board. The more components students can name, the better.

Answers

Possible answers:

Name of item	Production: single, groups or mass	Why?
skyscraper	single	Client only wants one, design is specific to this one project.
trainers	group	Product changes according to fashion.
bottles	mass	Large quantities of bottles are produced for products that are continuously needed.
newspapers	group	Papers change each day, but the basic technology remains the same.
chocolate bars	mass	Company produces huge numbers of same product with no end in sight.
laptops	group	Consumers will stop buying it when it's out of date, so a limited number are made.
the Millennium Dome	single	Only one is needed, in time for a certain event.
microchip	mass	Will be used in all types of computer for many years.
an airport terminal	single	The government only wants one terminal – production processes cannot be changed to produce another easily.
high-street fashion item	group	Product changes according to fashion.

Exercise E

Remind students again about the four Ps. Refer students to the lecture topics and the questions. Make sure they understand what all three questions relate to before, rather than during, the lecture. Work through as a whole class if you wish.

Answers

Model answers:

1   Look up key words in a dictionary/encyclopedia/ on the Internet. Check pronunciation so you will recognize the words in the lecture.

2   Lecture 1: meanings of these key words; examples of job, batch and flow production.

Lecture 2: definition of *lean production*

Lecture 3: definition of *economies of scale*

3   Perhaps do a spidergram so that it is easier to brainstorm with fellow students and cover all the possible areas that the lecturer might focus on.

Exercise F

Set for pairwork, giving each member of the pair a different research task. If students have access in class to reference material, allow them to at least start the activity in class. Otherwise, set the task for homework. Before the feedback to partner stage, refer students to the *Skills bank – Reporting information to other people*.

Closure

Dictate sentences with words from Exercise A in context for students to identify the words again.

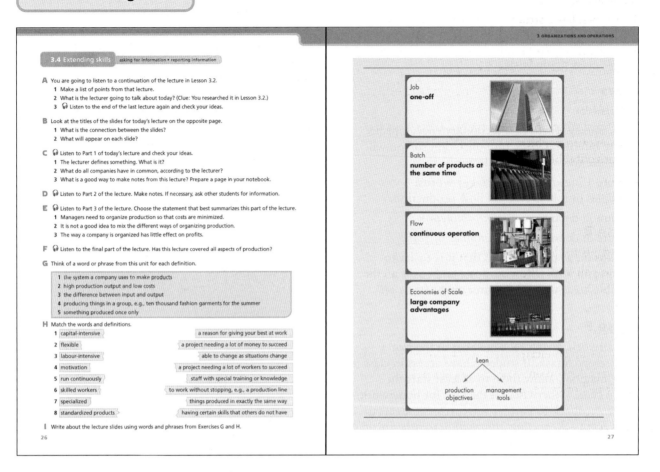

Lesson aims

- ask for information to complete notes

Further practice in:

- choosing the best form of notes
- making notes
- reporting information

Introduction

Elicit some information from the lecture in Lesson 3.2. If necessary, prompt students by reading parts of the transcript and pausing for students to complete in their own words. Don't spend too long on this, however.

🎧 Exercise A

Remind students of the language involved in asking for information about a lecture from other people – see *Skills bank*. Drill some of the sentences if you wish.

1/2 Set for pairwork. Encourage students to ask each other for information.

3 Play Part 4 of the lecture from Lesson 3.2 to enable students to check their answers. Feed back. Elicit information from the students' research. Do not

confirm or correct at this stage, except for pronunciation mistakes on key words.

Transcript 🎧 1.18

Part 4

So, to summarize what we've covered so far, the *independence structure* is the type of organization where independent professionals like accountants or architects work alone but under the same roof. The *entrepreneurial structure* is where one expert has strong central control in a smaller company. The *bureaucracy* is a larger and traditional structure based on hierarchies with set roles and procedures. And the *matrix* is a larger but more modern organization, where top-to-bottom hierarchies are criss-crossed with special teams with particular responsibilities.

Well, that's it for today. Next time, we'll look a bit more specifically into production planning and how companies organize themselves to meet their production objectives. Don't forget to do a bit of reading on that before you come. Thanks. See you soon.

Answers

Model answers:

1 1 Independence structure involves professionals working independently but under one roof.

  2 Entrepreneurial structure involves one expert who has strong control of a smaller company.

  3 Bureaucracy structure is a larger, traditional structure based on hierarchies.

  4 Matrix structure is a larger, modern structure where vertical hierarchies criss-cross with horizontal hierarchies.

2/3 production planning (economies of scale, lean production)

Exercise B

Refer students to the lecture slides.

1 Set for pairwork. Feed back orally.

2 Set for pairwork. Elicit some ideas, but do not confirm or correct.

Answers

1 They are all connected with production.

2 Answers depend on students and are not confirmed or corrected here.

🎧 Exercise C

Set the questions. Play Part 1. Allow students to discuss answers. Feed back orally.

Answers

1 *Added value* = the difference between input and output.

2 They all make something through input-process-output.

3 The notes could be written as headings with bullet points: the three ways of organizing production would be the headings, with room to make notes underneath each one. Economies of scale would be a separate heading with bullet points.

Language note

The word *job* has an obvious meaning, even in Management English, i.e., employment in a particular post. However, in *job production*, the word has a very specialist meaning, i.e., a particular task to be completed. Whereas in general English, this usage would tend to imply something quite small, in management it could be as big as constructing a skyscraper.

Subject note

Note that although this process is classically applied to the manufacture of products, it may also be applied to the provision of services as well, which can be easily understood with some illustration. The *input* may include human resources, education and training and its subsequent knowledge and skills, system design or intellectual property such as software, and many other resources. The *process* may include an online e-commerce procedure, a course in a university, a journey such as a flight, or a great range of other possible processes. The *output* may include the supply of intellectual property such as multimedia products or software, education qualifications, delivery to a destination, or a range of other outcomes that the customer experiences. In a nutshell, the model applies equally well to the production of services as for products.

Transcript 🎧 1.19

Part 1

In the last lecture, we looked at four models of formal organization. Now, looking a little deeper, the *input-process-output* of any organization is fundamental to its structure, so it's central to managers' concerns. A business takes input, applies processes that add value, and then provides output. Input-process-output is essentially how businesses make products. The difference between the input and the output is known as *added value*. This is production. Today, I'll outline three types of production (*job*, *batch* and *flow* production) that managers can choose from for commercial efficiency. And I'll also mention two important aspects of production: the idea of *being lean*, and the idea of *economies of scale*.

🎧 Exercise D

Play Part 2 of the lecture. Students should recognize the rhetorical structure – see Answers section below – and complete a table, in effect. When students have done their best individually, put them in pairs or small groups to complete their notes by asking for information from the other student(s).

Sum up this part by asking some specific questions, e.g.,

What are the advantages of job production? – motivating, easy to manage

What is the definition of flow production? – runs continuously

How can small companies try to achieve economies of scale? – e.g., mergers and acquisitions

Answers

Model answers:

Type of organization	Characteristics	Example
job production	– one product made – motivating for workers, uses skilled workers – easy to manage – easy to meet customers' needs – labour- and capital-intensive – no revenue until job is finished	repairing a tooth, building a skyscraper
batch production	– products made in groups or batches – each batch may be slightly different – flexible – labour less skilled than with job production – standardized labour focuses on one part of the operation	fashion items – shirts, bags
flow production	– operations run continuously – produces large numbers of standardized products – more capital-intensive than labour-intensive – technological automation expensive – workers may get bored – less need to store goods: can speed up/slow down production to meet demand	popular car production
lean production	– raise productivity, cut costs	– continuous improvement (get better each year) – just-in-time manufacturing (only produce what customers order)
economies of scale	– bigger production run = lower per-unit costs	smaller companies aim for this through organic growth/borrowing money/mergers and acquisitions

Transcript 🎧 1.20

Part 2

When production is one-off, we use the term *job production*. The company makes one product at a time. It could be as small as a dentist's repair job on a tooth, or as large as the building of a skyscraper. This approach is motivating to its skilled workers, easy to manage, and makes it easy to meet customers' needs. However, it is labour-intensive and capital-intensive. Workers and equipment are often specialized and may be expensive, and there usually is no revenue from a job until it is completed.

Batch production, on the other hand, is where a number of products are made at once. It could be ten or it could be thousands. When the next batch is made, the product may have to be slightly different than before. A good example is a company producing 10,000 fashion items like shirts or bags. Next year, they may make 12,000 but in a different colour. So batch production can be a bit flexible. And with the products being standardized, labour can be less skilled, as workers only focus on one part of the operation.

The third type is called *flow production*, where operations run continuously. When cars are manufactured, for instance, each one moves along the production line to have parts fitted. None of the operations ever stop, and at the end of the line, completed products – for example, new cars, appear. This type of production is used for producing large numbers of standardized products from large quantities of raw materials. It is more capital-intensive than labour-intensive. Usually, the technological automation is expensive. And it employs workers that may specialize in one part of the operation only, which they may find boring. This is called *division of labour*. But there is less need to store goods, because you can speed up or slow down production as demand changes.

Two ideas linked to production that we should consider when talking about production are *lean production* and *economies of scale*. *Lean production* means raising productivity and decreasing costs. The key idea is efficiency. Japanese and US businesses in the last century showed the world new ideas, like continuous improvement (where every aspect in a business aims to get better each year), or just-in-time manufacturing (where you only produce products as they are ordered, to save storage costs), and various other management tools that either save time or make workers more effective. Henry Ford and W. Edwards Deming were key thinkers in all of this. And key companies that developed these systems were Toyota and Motorola, while a key industry was Japanese shipping.

And then, finally, there's the idea of *economies of scale*. The bigger a production run is, the less each unit costs to make. So the cost per unit of making a million cars is much less than the cost per unit of making ten cars. This is called economies of scale. Smaller companies tend to want to grow and achieve these benefits that bigger ones enjoy. They can aim for organic growth – that is, sustainable and naturally developing growth – by simply reinvesting their profits. Or they can grow faster by borrowing money and by mergers and acquisitions (joining or taking over other companies).

🎧 Exercise E

Play Part 3 of the lecture. As before, give students time to do their own work, then set for pair or group work.

Answer

1 Managers need to organize production so that costs are minimized.

Transcript 🎧 1.21

Part 3

Of course, many operations can be a mix of all three: *job, batch* and *flow*. But thinking about the different systems of production individually does help us to understand how it is possible to arrange production. Management can choose from these systems, and plan and structure production to be as lean as possible, for commercial success. And the idea of economies of scale relates to job, batch and flow methods, too. While job production has the benefit of specialization, it may not enjoy economies of scale. Flow production, on the other hand, will usually be larger and will enjoy economies of scale. You can see how these all interrelate.

🎧 Exercise F

Set for individual work and pairwork checking. Play Part 4 of the lecture. Feed back orally. Point out that if students do miss information on the way through a lecture, they should wait for the recap, which often comes at the end. This recap may enable them to fill in some of the missing information.

Answer

Model answer:

No, it has only covered the most fundamental aspects.

Transcript 🎧 1.22

Part 4

So, to recap, we have taken a brief look at what production is and how it can be done. Of course, there are many aspects of production that are very complex that we haven't had time to look at, but I hope you can see the fundamentals of operations, which are important for all managers to understand.

Methodology note

End all listening lessons by referring students to the transcript at the back of the Course Book, so they can read the text while the aural memory is still clear. You could set this as standard homework after a listening lesson. You can also get students to highlight key sections and underline key sentences, as in Exercise F.

Exercise G

Set for individual work and pairwork checking. Feed back, getting the words and definitions on the board.

Answers

the system a company uses to make products	input-process-output
high production output and low costs	lean production
the difference between input and output	added value
producing things in a group, e.g., ten thousand fashion garments for the summer	batch production
something produced once only	job production

Exercise H

Set for pairwork. Monitor and assist. Feed back, writing the words on the board as students correctly identify them. Check pronunciation and stress patterns.

Answers

1	capital-intensive	a project needing a lot of money to succeed
2	flexible	able to change as situations change
3	labour-intensive	a project needing a lot of workers to succeed
4	motivation	a reason for giving your best at work
5	run continuously	to work without stopping, e.g., a production line
6	skilled workers	staff with special training or knowledge
7	specialized	having certain skills that others do not have
8	standardized products	things produced in exactly the same way

Exercise I

Set for individual work and pairwork checking.

Closure

Ask students to think of other products and how they are produced. Decide if the company producing each one used a job, batch or flow production model. Have them explain their choices to their partners and say why they think they are produced in this way.

Extra activities

1 Work through the *Vocabulary bank* and *Skills bank* if you have not already done so, or as a revision of previous study.

2 Use the *Activity bank* (Teacher's Book additional resources section, Resource 3A).

A Set the crossword for individual work (including homework). They can also copy the words into their notebooks and check the definitions of any words they cannot remember.

Answers

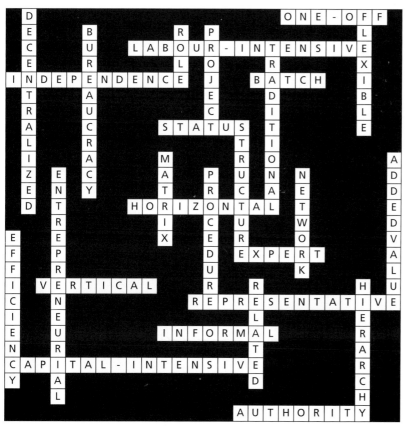

B This game practises pronunciation and meaning recognition. It can only be played in groups in class.

Students must think of one word for each of the categories on the bingo card. Allow them to use any of the vocabulary from this unit. They should write their words on card 1, or copy the bingo grid into their notebooks.

Each student says one of their own words at random once only, concentrating on the pronunciation. The others must identify the category and cross it out on card 2.

The winner is the first student to identify the correct category for all the words. If the teacher keeps a record of which words have been said, he/she can say when a successful card could have been completed.

3 Students can play this alphabet game by themselves or as a group/class. The aim is to think of a word related to management for each letter of the alphabet. For example:

Student A: authority

Student B: authority, bureaucracy

Student C: authority, bureaucracy, command

Each student adds something from the next letter of the alphabet. They should try to use words from the unit if possible. A student misses a turn if he/she can't remember the items, or can't add another letter.

4 Get students to research organization types which fit the models described in this unit.

Note that a lot of the details will be in complex English, and students should be warned of this, but they should be able to record the basic details to report back in the next lesson.

4 PRODUCTION MANAGEMENT

Unit 4 provides a glimpse into aspects of production and operations that relate closely to management. Students read a jargon-rich extract touching on four such ideas: process engineering, management by objectives, cellular manufacturing and project management, and quality management.

Skills focus

Reading
- identifying topic development within a paragraph

Writing
- reporting research findings

Vocabulary focus

- production management jargon
- abbreviations and acronyms
- discourse and stance markers
- verb and noun suffixes

Key vocabulary

accountable
agile manufacturing
benchmarking
cellular manufacturing
coordination
defects
delayering
downsizing

empower
management by
  objectives
measurable
  performance
mission statement
objectives
outcome

perspective
process engineering
project management
quality assurance
quality management

Abbreviations and acronyms

The Jargon Buster on page 31 of the Course Book lists the meanings of these.

ANOVA	COQ	SMART
ANSI	ISO	TQM
BM	JIT	USP
BPR	MBO	
CM	QA	

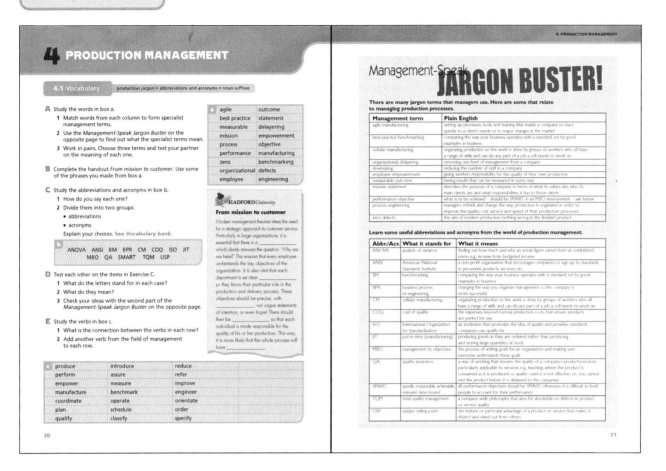

General note

Read the *Vocabulary bank* at the end of the Course Book unit. Decide when, if at all, to refer your students to it. The best point is probably Exercise C, or at the very end of the lesson or the beginning of the next lesson, as a summary/revision.

Lesson aims

- gain fluency in the meaning, pronunciation and spelling of key production management terms, abbreviations and acronyms
- understand how nouns can be formed from verbs through the addition of suffixes

Introduction

Show a visual of a production line. Write the words *production management* on the board. Ask students to define production management. Explain that businesses have particular types of management issues when they are producers.

Explain also that there is a lot of language shared by managers, and that this language often develops into jargon. Build up a typical jargon phrase on the board:

management

quality management

total quality management

Point out that after some time a phrase like this will become abbreviated into, e.g., TQM. Nobody in business will use the expanded phrase anymore.

Exercise A

1 Do one or two as examples, then set for individual work.

2 Refer students to the opposite page to self-check the phrases and the meanings.

3 Set for pairwork. Each student chooses three phrases and consults the Jargon Buster to find the meanings. A describes a term to B, and B tries to guess which term it is.

Answers

1 and 2

agile	manufacturing
best practice	benchmarking
measurable	outcome
mission	statement
process	engineering
performance	objective
zero	defects
organizational	delayering
employee	empowerment

Exercise B

Set for individual work and pairwork checking. Ensure that students read *all* the text and have a general understanding of it before they insert the missing phrases.

Feed back by reading the paragraph or by using an OHT or other visual display of the text. Verify whether errors are due to using new phrases or to misunderstanding the text.

Answers

Modern management theories stress the need for a strategic approach to customer service. Particularly in large organizations, it is essential that there is a <u>mission statement</u> which clearly answers the question: 'Why are we here?' This ensures that every employee understands the key objectives of the organization. It is also vital that each department is set clear <u>performance objectives</u> so they know their particular role in the production and delivery process. These objectives should be precise, with <u>measurable outcomes</u>, not vague statements of intention, or even hope! There should then be <u>employee empowerment</u> so that each individual is made responsible for the quality of his or her production. This way, it is more likely that the whole process will have <u>zero defects</u>.

Exercise C

Set for pairwork. Feed back, eliciting ideas on pronunciation and confirming or correcting. Build up the two lists on the board. Establish that one group are acronyms, i.e., they can be pronounced as words: ANOVA = /ænəʊvə/. The other group are abbreviations, i.e., they are pronounced as letters: BPR = B-P-R. Drill all the abbreviations and acronyms. Make sure students can say letter names and vowel sounds correctly.

Elicit that words with normal consonant/vowel patterns are *normally* pronounced as a word and those with unusual patterns are *normally* pronounced with single letters. However, there are exceptions, e.g., JIT. Refer to the *Vocabulary bank* at this stage if you wish.

Methodology note

Don't discuss the meanings at this point. This is covered in the next activity.

Answers

Acronyms	ANOVA /ænəʊvə/, ANSI /ænsiː/, SMART /smɑːt/
Abbreviations	BPR, BM, CM, COQ, ISO, JIT, MBO, QA, TQM, USP

Exercise D

1 Introduce the verb *stand for*. Elicit examples of common abbreviations and ask what they stand for. Set for pairwork. Tell students to pick out the ones they already know first. Next, they pick out the ones they are familiar with but do not know exactly what they stand for – and guess.

2 Elicit the meanings without reference to the *Jargon Buster* if possible.

3 Refer students to the *Jargon Buster* to verify their answers. As a follow-up, elicit other common abbreviations from management.

Language note

If students do not use acronyms or initial abbreviations in their language, a discussion about the reasons for using them is useful. They will then know how to find the meaning of new ones when they meet them. You might point out that abbreviations can sometimes be longer than the thing they abbreviate! For example, *World Wide Web* is three syllables, whereas *WWW* is six. It evolved because it is quicker to write, but it is longer, and harder, to say. Point out that the field of ICT in particular is developing at an incredible speed, and new acronyms and abbreviations are constantly being created.

Exercise E

Set for pairwork. If students are struggling, point out that the grouping has nothing to do with meaning. If they are still struggling, say:

produce – production
introduce – introduction
prevent – prevention

Feed back, highlighting the changes from verb to noun.

Answers

Each row forms its noun in a similar way, as shown. A suggested additional verb, which forms the noun in the same way, is in the final column.

produce	+ *tion*	*deduce*
perform	+ *ance/ence*	*insure*
empower	+ *ment*	*require*
manufacture	+ *ing*	*delayer*
coordinate	+ *ation*	*motivate*
plan	*same word*	*design*
qualify	+ *fication*	*identify*

Language and culture note

Movement from verb to noun does not have many productive rules. In other words, students cannot look at a verb and say – now I know what the noun will be. However, there are some common patterns, e.g.,

1. ~*uce* = uction
2. ~*ate* = ation
3. ~*fy* = fication

However, in terms of reading or listening, there is some value in recognizing noun endings. If you see a word ending in any of the following ways, it is probably a noun;

+ *tion* or + *fication*
+ *ance/ence*
+ *ment*
+ *fication*

In addition, if it has one of the above endings, it can probably be converted to a verb in a relatively systematic way, e.g.,

regulation – noun; verb = *regulate*
clarification – noun; verb = *clarify*
intention – noun; verb = *inten* (cannot be sure of final consonant)

Of course, as always in English, there are 'false friends', e.g.,

importance – noun; verb = *import*? No! At least, not in its modern meaning.

Closure

Ask students if they know the mission statements of any organizations.

If they do, get them on the board then discuss whether they help us understand why the organization exists.

If they don't, put a mission statement on the board, e.g.,

New York Police Department: To protect and serve

Ask students if they think this sums up the purpose of the organization.

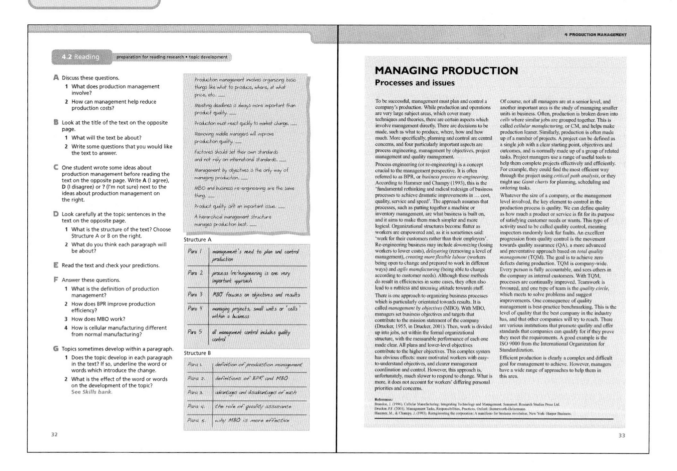

General note

Read the *Skills bank – Developing ideas in a paragraph* at the end of the Course Book unit. Decide when, if at all, to refer students to it. The best time is probably at the very end of the lesson or the beginning of the next lesson, as a summary/revision.

Lesson aims

- prepare to read a text by looking at title, figures, topic sentences
- understand the purpose of discourse markers and stance markers in the development of a topic

Introduction

Ask the students what the most important aspect of any business is. Some students may say finance, others may say marketing or human resource management. There is no correct answer, yet the strongest case exists for operations or production of a business being the most important aspect, as it essentially *is* the business. Elicit and prompt a brief discussion on how production sits centrally to other company functions.

Exercise A

1 Divide students into small groups. Show students a visual of a production line, e.g., a car assembly line or a newspaper press running. Ask students to brainstorm the possible management issues that might arise. Do not comment. Get students to prioritize their list. Allow students to debate differences of opinion. Encourage them to give examples if they can. Elicit from students the overall objectives of a production management team. Possible answers might be ideas related to the following, in some form:

- lowest possible price per unit
- lowest possible price per unit for a given product quality
- lowest possible staffing to output ratio
- benchmarked product quality
- flexibility of operations to market changes

Do not press them if nothing is forthcoming. From the well-read, you might get *management by objectives* or *total quality management*. Encourage these students to explain if they can. Keep it brief.

2 Set for pairwork.

Answers

Possible answers:

1 Production management is applying management functions to the principal operations that account for a business's production.

Other related ideas might include:

- resource management
- sourcing raw materials
- installation and management of equipment
- labour management
- supply-to-customer management
- effect of using robots in industrial production

2 By keeping resource costs and labour costs to a minimum, and by keeping layers of management to a minimum.

Exercise B

Write the title of the reading text on the board.
Set for pairwork. Tell students to think of four or five questions with different *Wh~* question words:

What ...?

Where ...?

When ...?

Why ...?

How ...?

Answers

Accept any suggestions from students.

Possible questions:

What exactly is business process engineering?
Where can I find examples of companies that use cellular management systems?
When do companies need to think about putting these theories into practice?
Who benefits most from BPR: shareholders or company staff?
Why is it necessary to change traditional ways of doing things?
How can old-fashioned companies integrate new management theories into the way they are organized?

Exercise C

1 Set for individual work and pairwork checking. Feed back, trying to get consensus on each point, but do not actually confirm or correct. Preface your remarks with phrases like: *So most of you think ... You all believe ...*

Elicit some more ideas, but once again, do not confirm or correct. Draw students' attention to words like *only* and *always*. Point out that these words make statements very strong. The truth may actually be better expressed with a limiting word, e.g., *most/some/many*, or with words which express

possibility such as *may* or *seem*, or adverbs such as *sometimes, usually, often*.

Remind students to look back at these predictions while they are reading the text (Exercise E).

Exercise D

Review paragraph structure – i.e., paragraphs usually begin with a topic sentence which makes a statement that is then expanded in the following sentences. Thus, topic sentences give an indication of the contents of the paragraph. You may wish to refer students to the *Skills bank* at this point.

1 Write the topic sentences from the text on an OHT or other visual display, or use Resource 4B from the additional resources section. Students should use only the topic sentences for this exercise. Set for individual work and pairwork checking.

2 Set for pairwork. Tell students that close analysis of the topic sentences will help them. Feed back with the whole class. Point out any language features which led them to draw their conclusions.

Answers

1 Structure A

2 Possible answers:

	Possible predicted content
Para 1	*management's need to plan and control production: information that introduces the content of the text on production*
Para 2	*process (re-)engineering is one very important approach: an explanation of what process engineering means*
Para 3	*MBO focuses on objectives and results: an outline of what MBO involves*
Para 4	*managing projects, small units or 'cells' within a business: introducing the concept of cells and projects and how they are best managed and scheduled*
Para 5	*all management control includes quality control: how quality control evolved, what total quality control is and what international standards are*

Exercise E

Set the reading. Students should make notes on the differences between their predictions and the text.

Exercise F

1/2 Ask students to write answers to these questions.

3/4 Set for general discussion and feedback.

Answers

Model answers:

1 Production management is the business of controlling operations and production through planning and the use of tools such as BPR and MBO, with quality control being a central concern.

2 BPR improves production efficiency by redesigning production systems so they are simpler and more logical, with fewer managers and a more flexible workforce. In addition, there is less hierarchy, and workers are empowered and so are more flexible.

3 Management by objectives is a system-wide approach that achieves goals through setting clear objectives and negotiating how they will be achieved with an empowered workforce.

4 Cellular manufacturing is leaner than normal manufacturing. It is a way of organizing tasks so that similar jobs are given to one cell of workers who are responsible for completing all of them. It differs from traditional manufacturing, where workers complete only one piece of a process and thus are not aware of the completed product at the end.

Exercise G

1/2 The purpose of this exercise is for students to try to identify the information structure of each paragraph and to see how a new step in the progression of ideas may be signalled by a rhetorical marker or phrase.

Refer also to the *Skills bank* at the end of this unit. Elicit more examples of discourse markers and stance markers.

Set for pairwork. Feed back. A good idea is to make an OHT or other visual display of the text and use a highlighter to indicate which are the relevant parts of the text. Students should notice that there is not a discernible topic development in every paragraph.

Answers

Possible answers:

	Discourse marker	Stance marker	Effect
Para 1	more specifically		to narrow the focus and signal coming examples
Para 2		crucial	to indicate something being of key importance
	although		to introduce a contradiction
		ruthless/uncaring	to indicate a negative opinion
Para 3	then		to signal the next stage of a process
		made clear	to show a positive improvement in management
	however		to signal a contrasting and negative consequence of MBO, i.e., that it can be slower to change
		unfortunately	to show that the negative consequence undermines the positive aspects of MBO
	what is more		to add another negative consequence
Para 4	of course		to introduce an obvious fact
	similarly		to introduce a parallel kind of situation – in this case, another example of breaking the total project into smaller ones
		useful	to show a positive attitude
	for example		to show a move from ideas to illustrations of the ideas
Para 5		more advanced	to show a better development
	one consequence of		to signal a result – in this case, quality control has led to the use of ISOs
	a good example		to introduce a single example
	however		placing the summary and the conclusion in contrast

Methodology note

It could be argued that words like *but, however*, and phrases like *on the other hand* do not fundamentally change the topic of a paragraph. Point this out if you wish. However, they do bring in a concessive element where the reader of a topic sentence might assume that the whole paragraph would be (for example) positive.

Imagine a school report with the topic sentence: *John is an extremely able student* which then proceeded with a great deal of praise, but ended with the following: *Despite his many good qualities, however, John will have some difficulty in gaining high marks in his exams unless he concentrates more in class.* We could justifiably claim either that:

1 the whole paragraph is about John and his school work

or

2 the paragraph has two topics – John's positive aspects and his negative aspects.

Closure

1 Divide the class into groups. Write the topic sentences on strips, or photocopy them from the additional resources section (Resource 4B). Make a copy for each group. Students must put them into the correct order.

Alternatively, divide the class into two teams. One team chooses a topic sentence and reads it aloud. The other team must call out information triggered by that topic sentence. Accept a prediction or the actual paragraph content. However, ask students which it is – prediction or actual.

Language note

There is no universal logic to the structuring of information in a text. The order of information is language-specific. For example, oriental languages tend to have a topic sentence or paragraph summary at the end, not the beginning, of the paragraph. Or students whose first language is Arabic might structure a particular type of discourse in a different way from native English speakers. So it is important for students to see what a native English writer would consider to be 'logical' ordering.

2 Refer students back to the sentences in Exercise C. Students should find it easier to comment on these now that they have read the text.

3 Focus on some of the vocabulary from the text, including:
accountable
agile manufacturing
benchmarking
cellular manufacturing
coordination
defects
delayering
downsizing
empower
management by objectives
measurable performance
mission statement
objectives
outcome
perspective
process engineering
project management
quality assurance
quality management

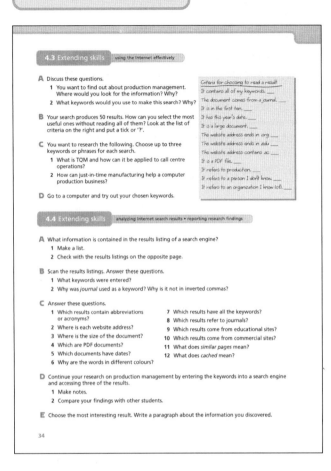

General note

Students will need access to a computer with an Internet connection. If computers are not available during the lesson, part of the lesson can be set for private study.

Lesson aims

- learn or practise how to use the Internet effectively for research

Introduction

Brainstorm the uses of the Internet. Then brainstorm what the important factors are when using the Internet. These should include:

- the search engines students use and why. Note that there is now a large number of search engines to suit different purposes. It is not necessarily a good idea to use Google exclusively.
- how to choose *and write* keywords in their preferred search engine
- how they extract the information they want from the results

Put students in groups and ask them to compare how they normally use a computer to find information. Ask each group to produce a set of advice for using the Internet. Then, as a class, produce an accepted set of advice.

Key words to elicit: *search engine, keyword, website, web page, website address, search result, subject directory*

Note: Where the subject is a new one or a fairly general topic, it is a good idea to start first with a subject directory which evaluates sites related to the topic and collects them in one place. Some examples are: Academic Info; BUBL LINK; INFOMINE; The WWW Virtual Library.

Exercise A

Write *production management* on the board.

1 Set for class discussion. Make sure students give reasons for their answers. Accept their answers at this stage.

2 Remind students that words in English often have more than one meaning, so care must be taken to get the desired result.

Answers

Possible answers:

1 In a management journal – very useful, as recent articles give the latest information.
On the Internet – good if the correct keywords are used and a careful selection of results is made. Since it is a general topic, it would benefit from a search with a subject directory such as The WWW Virtual Library on http://vlib.org/
In a textbook – useful if there is an up-to-date one, but books take time to publish, so even the latest book may be out of date in these technologically fast-moving times.

2 In this list of possible keywords, the first three are obvious starting points; others are also possible.

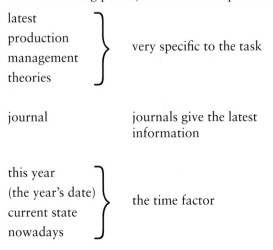

latest	
production	
management	very specific to the task
theories	

| journal | journals give the latest information |

this year	
(the year's date)	
current state	the time factor
nowadays	

BPR
MBO
agile manufacturing
cellular manufacturing
TQM
ISO
} specific to the field

Exercise B

Set for pairwork. Remind students of the research topic.

Feed back, encouraging students to give reasons for their decisions. Emphasize that we only know what *might* be useful at this stage. Establish that company sites often end in 'com'.

Answers

Possible answers:

- ✓ It contains all of my keywords. (*but check that the meaning is the same*)
- ✓ The document comes from a journal. (*current information*)
- ? It is in the first ten. (*a web page can have codes attached to put it high in the list*)
- ✓ It has this year's date. (*current information*)
- ? It is a large document. (*size is no indication of quality*)
- ✓ The website address ends in .org (*because it is a non-profit organization*)
- ✓ The website address ends in .edu (*because it is an educational establishment*)
- ✓ The website address contains .ac (*because it is an educational establishment*)
- ? It is a PDF file. (*file type is no indication of quality*)
- ? It refers to production. (*may not be relevant*)
- ? It refers to a person I don't know. (*may not be reliable*)
- ✓ It refers to an organization I know (of). (*reliable*)

Language note

PDF stands for *portable document format*. PDF documents look exactly like the original documents, and can be viewed and printed on most computers without the need for each computer to have the same software, fonts, etc. They are created with Adobe Acrobat software.

Exercise C

Set for individual work and pairwork checking. Ask students to compare their choice of keywords with their partner and justify their choice.

Answers

See Exercise D.

Exercise D

Students should try out different combinations to discover for themselves which gives the best results.

Answers

1 TQM, call centre, operations
2 Manufacturing, JIT, just-in-time, computer, production

Closure

Tell students to think of their own question for research, as in Exercise C, and find the best web page for the data by entering appropriate keywords.
Ask students to write their question on a piece of paper and sign it. Put all the questions in a box. Students pick out one of the questions at random and go online to find the best page of search results. From those results they can find the most useful web page. They should ask the questioner for verification.

4.4 Extending skills

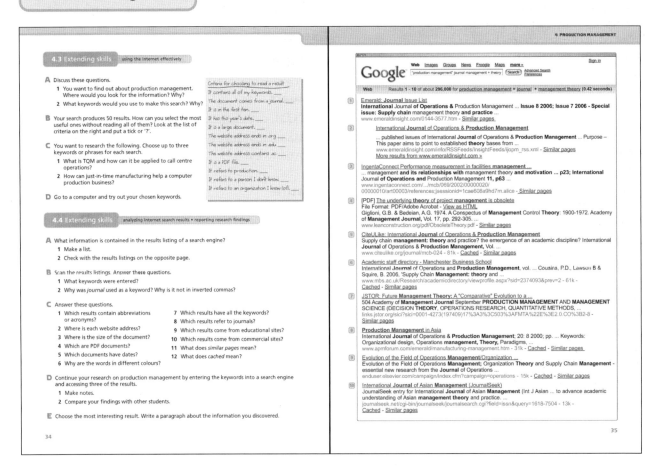

General note

Students will need access to a computer with an Internet connection. If computers are not available during the lesson, part of the lesson can be set for private study.

Lesson aims

- examine a page of Internet search results critically
- report Internet search findings in a short written summary

Introduction

Ask students what problems they had, what lessons they have learnt and what advice they can give from their Internet search experience in Lesson 4.3. Brainstorm the important factors when searching for information on the Internet and put them in order of importance.

Exercise A

Set for pairwork. Students should first make a list of information they expect to find in search engine results. (They should do this before they look at the search engine results on the right-hand page.) They should

then look at the page of results and identify any other information that is there.

Answers

Possible answers:

number of results
keywords used
time taken
title of document
type of document
quotations from the text with keywords highlighted
date
web address/URL

Exercise B

This is further reinforcement on keywords. Set for pairwork or whole-class discussion.

Answers

Model answers:

1 "production management" + journal management + theory

2 Because journals give the most current information. Inverted commas are put round a phrase to indicate that it is a single meaningful lexical item. In Google, *journal* does not need them, as it is one word.

74

Exercise C

This detailed examination of the results page should make students aware of the content, so that they can make an educated selection of a web page with useful information. Set for pairwork.

Make sure in feedback that students are aware of what the following abbreviations stand for: FTP (File Transfer Protocol), PDF (Portable Document Format), PPT (PowerPoint), RTF (Rich Text Format).

Answers

Possible answers:

1 Acronyms/abbreviations:
   Result 1: htm
   Result 2: (in website address) www, xml
   Result 3: (in website address) www, p
   Result 4: PDF, HTML, vol, pp
   Result 5: (in website address) www, vol, k
   Result 6: (in website address) www, k
   Result 7:
   Result 8: (in website address) www, htm, k
   Result 9: k
   Result 10: k
   Note: Students may identify further abbreviations in the website addresses.
2 At the end
3 At the end (if it is given), e.g., 81k
4 Result 4
5 Results 1, 4, 6, 8
6 For ease of reference: blue = titles and viewing information; green = website address; black = keywords.
7 Results 1, 2, 3, 5, 6, 7, 8
8 All results
9 Result 6
10 Results 1, 2, 3, 8, 9 and 10
11 There were other very similar results, so the search engine ignored them. They are available if you click on the words.
12 It is a more efficient way of storing information. (It means that you can go to a copy of the page stored by Google, in case the actual website happens to be down at the time of the search; of course, it could be a little out of date.)

Exercise D

1 Set the search for individual work. Students should input the keywords again. They will not get exactly the same results page as here, but the results should be comparable. Tell them to take notes.

2 Set for pairwork. Feed back, getting students to tell the rest of the class about their most interesting findings. Encourage other students to ask questions.

Exercise E

Set for individual work. Students can complete it in class or for homework.

Closure

1 Focus on some of the vocabulary connected with using the Internet, including:
   website
   web(site) address/URL
   search engine
   search results
   input
   keyword
   key in
   log in/log on
   username
   password
   access

2 The importance of the care needed when selecting keywords can be demonstrated by a simple classroom activity. Tell the class you are thinking of a particular student who you want to stand up. Say (for example):
   It's a man. (all the men stand up and remain standing)
   He has dark hair. (only those with dark hair remain standing)
   He has a beard.
   He has glasses.
   He's tall.
   His name begins with A.
   And so on.
   When only one student remains, ask the class to list the minimum number of keywords necessary to identify only that student. Make sure they discard unnecessary ones. For example, if all students have dark hair, that is unnecessary.

3 Finding the keywords for familiar topics is another activity, done in groups. For example, they could:
   ● find their own college record (name, ID number or date of entry)
   ● find their last exam results (name, class, subject, date)
   ● find a book in the library about robotics used in production lines (robotics, production line, manufacturing, factory, etc.)

1 Work through the *Vocabulary bank* and *Skills bank* if you have not already done so, or as a revision of previous study.

2 Use the *Activity bank* (Teacher's Book additional resources section, Resource 4A).

A Set the wordsearch for individual work (including homework) or pairwork.

Answers

Verb	Noun
centralize	centralization
communicate	communication
conceptualize	conceptualization
coordinate	coordination
debate	debate
delayer	delayering
delegate	delegation
downsize	downsizing
embrace	embracing
empower	empowerment
evaluate	evaluation
improve	improvement
inspire	inspiration
manage	management
motivate	motivation
organize	organization
participate	participation
qualify	qualification
reschedule	rescheduling
specialize	specialization

B Set for pairwork. Teach students how to play noughts and crosses if they don't know – they take it in turns to say the abbreviation or acronym, and what it stands for. If they succeed, they can put their symbol – a nought 0 or a cross X – in that box. If a person gets three of their own symbols in a line, they win.

3 Write the acronyms and abbreviations from the unit on cards, or photocopy them from the additional resources section (Resource 4C). Divide the class into two teams. A student selects a card and reads it correctly. (Speed is of the essence.) Alternatively, one team picks a card with an acronym or abbreviation; the other team gives the actual words.

4 Elicit other acronyms and abbreviations from the students – in particular, common/useful ones from the field of management.

5 Have a class debate: 'MBO does not work. It is better for managers just to tell people what to do.' Ask two students to prepare an opening argument for and against.

Some points:

For

● people need clear direction
● managers know better than workers how to do a job
● some people are not clever enough to understand objectives
● it has been suggested that the world works by the 90:10 rule – 90% of people are happy to be told what to do by the other 10%
● some jobs do not need 'objectives' because the objective is obvious – clean the road, empty the bins, etc.
● managers are hopeless at setting SMART objectives

Against

● managers do not necessarily know the best way to do every task in their organizations
● always give a person a map not a route – that way they can find the best way through a task
● everyone needs to know exactly how they will be judged
● even mundane jobs have different ways of doing them; the operative should be able to make operational decisions which will achieve the objectives
● workers can help to set SMART objectives if the manager had a feedback/consultation loop

6 Write *What makes a good lesson?* on the board. Put students in small groups to make a list of things that they think make a good lesson – tell them to consider three things before, during and after the actual lesson.

Remind students about TQM and the idea of quality assurance – that you need to provide good inputs to achieve good outcomes.

Ask students to design a quality assurance checklist for a lesson, e.g.,

Does the teacher have a clear objective for the lesson?

Does the teacher have the correct course materials in the appropriate quantity, etc.

5 STRATEGY AND THE BUSINESS ENVIRONMENT

Much of the study of management is the study of strategy. Unit 5 takes a look at sample factors that influence strategy building. Students listen to extracts from a lecture which introduces the idea of the business environment, especially in a globalized world. It goes on to explore the fundamental concept of competition. Finally, it explains how contingency planning is an indispensable part of any strategy.

Skills focus

🎧 Listening

- understanding 'signpost language' in lectures
- using symbols and abbreviations in note-taking

Speaking

- making effective contributions to a seminar

Vocabulary focus

- word sets: synonyms, antonyms, etc.
- the language of trends
- common lecture language

Key vocabulary

alternative	environment	outsource
challenge	expansion	PESTEL analysis
competition	feasible	rival
competitor analysis	incentive	situation analysis
contingency planning	inflation	stakeholders
crisis	infrastructure	strategy
currency	mission	substitute
demographic	monopoly	supplier
deregulate	multinational	
diversify	new entrant	

5.1 Vocabulary

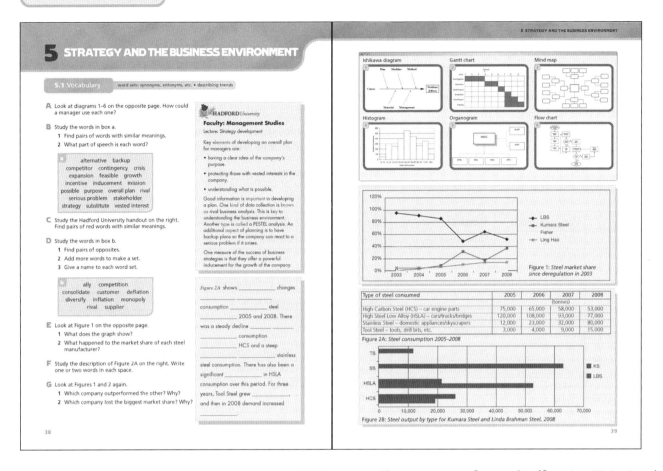

General note

Read the *Vocabulary bank – Vocabulary sets* and *Describing trends* at the end of the Course Book unit. Decide when, if at all, to refer your students to it. The best time is probably at the very end of the lesson or the beginning of the next lesson, as a summary/revision.

Lesson aims

- gain an understanding of lexical cohesion in texts through building word sets, synonyms and opposites/converses
- use appropriate language for describing trends

Introduction

Do some vocabulary revision from the previous units. For example:

1 Choose some words with different meanings in general and management English (see Units 1 and 2). Ask students to say or write two sentences using each word with a different meaning. Some examples are: *cell, capital, goal, hand, net*, etc. If necessary, students can work with their dictionaries.

2 Choose some prefixes and suffixes (see Units 1 and 4). Write them on the board. Ask students to give the meaning of the affix and an example of a word.

3 Dictate some of the key vocabulary from Unit 3. Ask students to check their spellings (with a dictionary) and group the words according to their stress patterns.

Exercise A

Set the question for pairwork discussion and whole-class feedback. Do not comment or correct at this point.

Elicit the general word *diagram* and write it on the board. Ask for some other examples of diagrams and write these on the board under *diagram* (e.g., *Venn diagram, line graph*, etc).

Language note

General words like *diagram* are called hypernyms or superordinate terms. Words like *spidergram* and *bar graph* are called hyponyms or class members.

Answers

1 Accept all reasonable answers.

    1 An Ishikawa diagram shows a manager how a problem is the effect of a number of contributing causes.

2 Gantt charts are used to help managers plan and complete project stages to meet deadlines.

3 A mind map is most often used as a brainstorming tool.

4 A histogram gives a manager accurate information about, for instance, production figures over a period of time.

5 Managers use an organogram to show the structure of an organization.

6 Flow charts are used to describe processes.

Exercise B

The purpose of this exercise is to build sets of synonyms. This not only helps in understanding textual cohesion, but is useful for paraphrasing.

Set both questions for pairwork. Students should look for pairs of words/items. Tell them to use their dictionaries if necessary to check the grammatical information, and to note if they find other words with similar meanings.

Feed back with the whole class, building up a table on the board and eliciting other words which can be used with the same meaning.

Answers

See table.

Word 1	Part of speech	Word 2	Part of speech	Words with similar meanings/notes
alternative	n (C)	substitute	n (C)	choice
backup	n (C)	contingency	n (C)	*backup* would normally mean support, but in a business context it is often used as an alternative for *contingency*
competitor	n (U)	rival	n (U)	opponent
crisis	n (C)	serious problem	n (C)	crunch point
expansion	n (U)	growth	n (U)	enlargement
feasible	adj	possible	adj	doable, achievable
incentive	n (C)	inducement	n (C)	motivation
mission	n (C)	purpose	n (C)	goal
overall plan	n phr.	strategy	n (C/U)	scheme
stakeholder	n (C)	vested interest	n phr. (C)	concerned party, involved person

Exercise C

Set for individual work and pairwork checking. Feed back with the whole class. The incomplete handout is reproduced in the additional resources section (Resource 5B) to use as an OHT or handout. Discuss alternative ideas and decide whether they are acceptable. Check the meaning of any unknown words in the text.

Answers

Model answers:

element	aspect
important	key
kind	type
known as	called

Exercise D

1 Set for pairwork. Feed back. Start with the first column of the table as shown in the Answers section.

2 Do the first pair of words with the whole class as an example. Set the remainder for pairwork. Feed back, completing the second column of the table on the board.

3 Because the word set names will be difficult for students to articulate, it will help the students if you put the names on an OHT or other visual

display and ask them to choose the most appropriate. Discuss with the whole class. Elicit a word or phrase which describes the whole set of words and add this to the table.

Answers

Model answers:

Opposites	Other words	Name for set
ally/rival	competitor, partner	business relationship
competition/monopoly	free market, closed market	market type
consolidate/diversify	downsize, spread	business development
customer/supplier	client source	business relationship
deflation/inflation	growth, recession	economic situation

Exercise E

Introduce *market share*. Elicit or give a definition, e.g., *Market share is a company's sales of a product as a percentage of the total sales in the market*. With the whole class, discuss what Figure 1 shows. Elicit some of the verbs and adverbs which students may need in order to discuss question 1. For example:

Go up	No change	Go down	Adverbs
boom	doesn't change	decrease	dramatically
grow	is unchanged	decline	gradually
improve	remain at …	drop	sharply
increase	stay the same	fall	significantly
rise		worsen	slightly
soar			steadily

Verbs	Nouns	Adverbs	Adjectives
rise	a rise	gradually	gradual
increase	an increase	sharply	sharp
grow	growth*	slightly	slight
improve	improvement	markedly	marked
fall	a fall	significantly	significant
decrease	a decrease	rapidly	rapid
drop	a drop	steeply	steep
decline	a decline	steadily	steady

* usually (but not always) uncountable in this sense

Note: These verbs are generally used intransitively when describing trends.

1 Discuss with the whole class. The answer to this question should be one sentence giving the topic of the graph.

2 Set for pairwork. Students should write or say two sentences about LBS and KS, and one sentence about the other companies. Feed back, eliciting sentences from the students. Write correct sentences on the board, or display the model answers on an OHT or other visual display. Make sure that students notice the prepositions used with the numbers and dates.

Answers

Model answers:

1 The graph shows changes in the steel market share for four steel manufacturers between 2003 and 2008.

2 LBS's market share fell steadily from 96 per cent in 2003 to 85 per cent in 2005. In 2005, LBS's market share dropped very sharply to 49 per cent of the market, and climbed above 60 per cent in 2007 before falling again to about 50 per cent in 2008.

KS's market share increased steadily between 2003 and 2005, it then rose sharply to 33 per cent in 2006. After that, KS's market share fell significantly from about 33 per cent in 2006 to 18 per cent in 2007. It then rose steadily to 36 per cent in 2008.

Ling Hao's market share has increased gradually between 2003 and 2008.

Fisher's market share has remained stationary at 1 per cent for the full five-year period.

Underline the verbs and adverbs. Ask students to make nouns from the verbs and adjectives from the adverbs. Alternatively, you could reproduce the table (minus the noun and adjective forms) on the board, on an OHT or on a handout. The incomplete table is reproduced in the additional resources section (Resource 5C) to facilitate this.

Return to the original answer sentences and ask students to make sentences with the same meaning, using the nouns and adjectives in place of the verbs and adverbs. Note that when using the noun + adjective, sentences can be made using *There was …* or *showed*. Do one or two examples orally, then ask students to write the remaining sentences. Feed back.

Answers

Model answers:

LBS's market share fell steadily from 96 per cent in 2003 to 85 per cent in 2005.	There was a steady fall in LBS's market share from 96 per cent in 2003 to 85 per cent in 2005.
In 2005 LBS's market share dropped very sharply to 49 per cent of the market.	There was a very sharp drop in LBS's market share from 85 per cent to 49 per cent in 2005.
KS's market share increased steadily between 2003 and 2005, it then rose sharply to 33 per cent in 2006.	There was a steady increase in KS's market share until 2005, and then a sharp rise to 33 per cent in 2006.
After that, Kumara Steel's market share fell significantly from about 33 per cent in 2006 to 18 per cent in 2007. Since then it has risen steadily to its current figure of 36 per cent.	After that, there was a significant fall in Kumara Steel's market share, from about 33 per cent in 2006 to 18 per cent in 2007. Since then there has been a steady rise to its current figure of 36 per cent.
Ling Hao's market share has increased gradually to 11 per cent between 2003 and 2008.	Ling Hao's market share has shown a gradual increase to 11 per cent between 2003 and 2008.
Fisher's market share has remained stationary at 1 per cent for the full five-year period.	Fisher's market share has shown no change at 1 per cent for the full five-year period.

Exercise F

First ask students to look at Figure 2A and discuss in pairs the information it shows. Feed back. Elicit two types of sentence using a verb and a noun to express the changes. For example:

There was a fall of 10,000 tonnes in HCS consumption between 2005 and 2006.

HCS consumption fell by 10,000 tonnes between 2005 and 2006.

Again, make sure that students notice the prepositions, especially the use of *by* to show the size of the fall.

Set the text completion for individual work and pairwork checking.

Answers

Model answer:

Figure 2A shows the changes in the consumption of steel between 2005 and 2008. There was a steady decline in the consumption of HCS and a steep increase in stainless steel consumption. There has also been a significant decrease/decline in HSLA consumption over this period. For three years, Tool Steel grew steadily/slowly, and then in 2008 demand increased sharply/markedly/significantly.

Exercise G

Check the meaning of *outperformed*. Tell students to look at all the information on the right-hand page, i.e., the table and the two graphs. Set for pairwork. Feed back with the whole class. You could take the discussion further by asking why students think these increases and decreases took place.

Answers

Model answers:

1 KS outperformed LBS because it had products that fitted the patterns of consumption.

2 LBS lost the biggest market share because it did not diversify, so when demand for HSLA and HCS shrank, it could not respond to the market, i.e., greater demand for stainless steel and tool steel.

Closure

Role play. Tell students to work in groups. They should imagine they are members of the board of LBS. They should brainstorm strategies for recovering market share and countering the increasing threat from KS and Ling Hao.

Possible factors to consider:

- Current inflation running at 20 per cent.
- Measures to make the company economically viable:
  - Downsizing the present staff requirements
  - Alternative production structures
- Cost of new product development
- Need to diversify the product range
- Sourcing capital investment for new plant and facilities
- Alternative markets in nearby countries that could be developed for their current product range

5.2 Listening

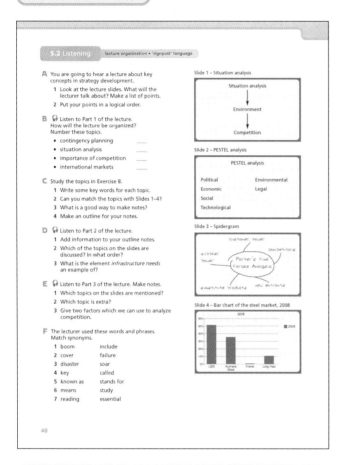

General note

Read the *Skills bank – Signpost language in a lecture* at the end of the Course Book unit. Decide when, if at all, to refer students to it. The best time is probably at the very end of the lesson or the beginning of the next lesson, as a summary/revision.

Lesson aims

- improve comprehension through understanding of signposts and lexical cohesion
- deal with disorganization in lectures/fractured text

Further practice in:

- predicting content from own background knowledge and from the lecture introduction
- using the introduction to decide the best form of notes to use

Introduction

Review key vocabulary by writing a selection of words from Lesson 5.1 on the board and asking students to put the words in groups, giving reasons for their decisions.

Exercise A

Remind students that when lecturers begin their talks, they usually provide their listeners with an outline. Remind/tell students about the *signpost language* which speakers use at the beginning to list the areas they will cover. On the board, build the table below, eliciting suggestions from the students. Alternatively (or in addition), you could refer to the *Skills bank* at this point.

Sequencing words		Verbs
To start with, Firstly,		begin/start by …ing discuss
Secondly, Then … After that,	I'll	examine consider mention
Finally,		talk about look at define give a(n) outline/overview/ definition/summary of … end/finish/conclude by …ing

Language note

Speakers will usually avoid repeating words. So they would be unlikely to say *To start with, I'll start by … .*

Refer students to the lecture slides. Set the exercise for pairwork.

Ask students to feed back their possible lecture ideas to the whole class, using the signpost language on the board to order their points. Accept any reasonable ideas. One possibility is given below.

Answer

Possible answer:

To start with, he/she will talk about situation analysis. After that, he/she will talk about PESTEL analysis and then about Porter's Five Forces Analysis. He/she will finish by discussing the steel market.

Methodology note

If students are new to the subject of strategy, they may only be able to make simple points about the slides, as in the model answer above. If they already know something about the subject, they may realize that the slides illustrate the concepts which the lecturer will discuss, e.g., Slide 1: situation analysis: the business environment and competition; Slide 2: PESTEL analysis: political, economic, social, technological, environmental and legal aspects of a market; Slide 3: Porter's Five Forces Analysis: competition from new entrants, substitute products, other competitors in the market and the possible threats/opportunities from both suppliers and customers; Slide 4: presents a bar chart showing market share of the steel market in 2008.

🎧 Exercise B

Tell students they are only going to hear the introduction to the lecture. Give students time to read the topics. Check that they understand the meaning. Remind them they will only hear the introduction once, as in a lecture. Tell them to listen out for the signpost language on the board. While they listen, they should number the topics from 1–4 in the order in which the lecturer will talk about them.

Play Part 1. Allow students to compare answers. Feed back. Ask students to say what signpost language they heard related to each topic. Confirm the correct answers.

Answers

contingency planning – 4 (*Finally, I'll finish up by …*)
situation analysis – 2 (*Secondly, …*)
importance of competition – 3 (*Next, I'll explain …*)
international markets – 1 (*to start with, we need to consider …*)

Transcript 🎧 1.23

Part 1

Good morning, everyone. This morning, we're going to continue looking at the topic of strategy. You'll recall that strategy is how actions and decisions are arranged to achieve the mission of a business. In this talk, I'm going to give you an overview of *four* more key concepts, and then more on strategic planning will be dealt with next week. So … er … let's see – yes – to start with, we need to consider firstly an idea many international managers are faced with. It's the idea of international markets. Secondly, I want to talk to you about situation analysis. In other words, how do managers understand the environment of other countries, especially the markets they wish to enter? Next, I'll explain a little bit about why competition is so important in strategy. Yes, understanding your rivals is, very definitely, key. Finally, I'll finish up by briefly mentioning crisis and contingency planning because, among a number of considerations, planning for possible disaster or failure is something every manager should know about and every strategy should include.

Exercise C

1 Set for pairwork. Divide the topics up among the pairs so that each pair concentrates on one topic. Feed back. Accept any reasonable suggestions.

2 Refer students to the lecture slides. Students should try to guess which of the topics each slide could refer to. Set for individual work and pairwork checking. Feed back, but do not confirm or correct yet.

3 Elicit suggestions from the whole class. If you wish, refer to students to Unit 1 *Skills bank*.

4 Set for individual work. Students should prepare an outline on a sheet of paper, preferably using either numbered points (with enough space between the points to allow for notes to be added) or a mind map/spidergram (see example below).

Answer

Possible answers:

1 Some key words are:

contingency planning – *alternative, backup, crisis, emergency, failure, plan*

situation analysis – *business environment, competition, inflation, market conditions*

importance of competition – *competition, competitor, challenge, danger, rival, threat*

international markets – *expansion, gain entry to, globalization, MNE, multinational*

2 Accept any reasonable answers with good justifications.

3/4 Example of spidergram:

Methodology note

There is no need to teach all the words given in the model answers for question 1. However, if students suggest words that others do not know, it would, of course, be reasonable to check/clarify meanings of such words at this point.

🎧 Exercise D

Tell students to use their outline from Exercise C to take notes. Which topics do they expect to hear in this section?

Play Part 2. Put students in pairs to compare their notes and discuss the questions.

Feed back. When it becomes clear that the lecturer did not develop her first point very well and therefore did not quite stick to the plan, say that this happens very often in lectures. Lecturers are human! Although it is a good idea to prepare outline notes, students need to be ready to alter and amend these. Discuss how best to do this. One obvious way is to use a non-linear approach,

such as a mind map or spidergram, where new topics can be easily added.

After checking answers to questions 2 and 3, build a complete set of notes on the board as a spidergram, as in the example in the Answers section.

Answer

Possible answers:

1 Example notes: see diagram below.

2 Discussed first: importance of environment; second: definition of situation analysis; third: PESTEL analysis

3 *infrastructure needs* is an example of a technological research

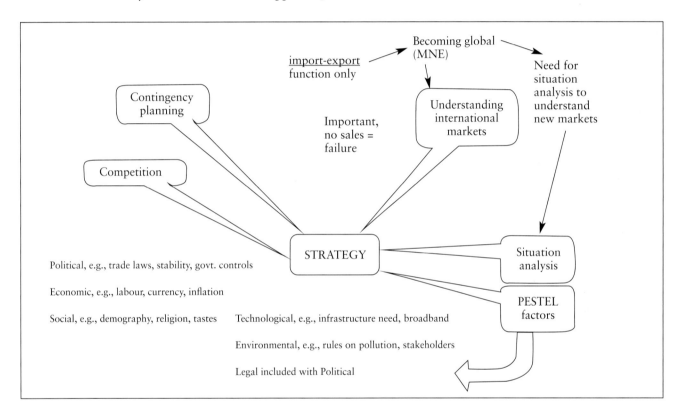

Transcript 🎧 1.24

Part 2

Actually, understanding the environment is arguably *the* most important aspect of strategy nowadays, especially for a company that wants to become an MNE (that's a multinational enterprise). That's the result of globalization. So, it follows that an international manager has to perform situation analysis if expansion is going to succeed.

One common tool that is used for situation analysis is known as PESTEL. This stands for political, economic, social, technological, environmental and legal. So what happens is, you analyze all these aspects within the country you want to enter to see if it's feasible to enter. What I

mean is that you do a lot of research. Political and legal questions you might ask could cover stability, government controls and trade laws. Economic questions might cover local labour or currency and inflation issues. Social research might include studying demographic and cultural aspects like religion and consumer tastes, while technological research might examine whether the country in question has the infrastructure necessary for business. A good example of this is the local broadband uptake. And, of course, environmental research means examining rules on pollution and what steps may need to be taken to protect local stakeholders affected by your business. Altogether, the analysis will give you the information you need to understand the market.

🎧 Exercise E

Ask students what they expect to hear about in the next part. Refer students to their outline again. Give them time to read the questions. Note that the final part of the lecture will be heard in Lesson 5.3, but there is no need to tell them this at this point. Play Part 3. Set the questions for pairwork. Students should use their notes to help them answer the questions.

Feed back. Note that there is no need to build a set of notes on the board at this point – this will be done in Lesson 5.3. Ask students if they can remember exactly what the lecturer said to indicate that she had lost her place (Fisher's market share. (*Er ... Where was I? Oh, yes.*)

Answers

Model answers:

1 PESTEL, Porter's Five Forces Analysis, steel market
2 extra situation analysis
3 Who is the competition? What are they doing?

Transcript 🎧 1.25

Part 3

Anyway, er ... to return to the main point – fundamentally, building a successful strategy depends on understanding the business environment. So what else is there apart from PESTEL analysis? Well, first and foremost is analyzing and understanding your competition. For example, if you are Nokia, your competition includes Sony Ericsson and Motorola.

If there are more competitors, your prices (and so your revenues) normally decrease. So it's essential to perform competitor analysis. That's to say, you need to find out who your rivals are and what they are doing. For example, does one of your competitors have a virtual monopoly? That is to say, does the rival have most of the market to itself?

Naturally, you'll have to do some reading on this, and Michael Porter is the one to read. His model, called the Five Forces Analysis, is essential for your study, and you will be using it for your assignment. It covers the threats of competitors, of new entrants in the market and of substitutes for your product. It also covers the power of your suppliers and customers. As management, this is helpful in informing your strategy.

OK. You'll be looking at a case study in the seminar. In the case study, we'll be using the same company in the same foreign market as we mentioned last week. As you can see, five years ago Linda Brahman Steelmakers (LBS) had a virtual monopoly, with a 96 per cent share of the steel market. But, following government deregulation of steelmaking, the competition has boomed. LBS's market share has declined to 53 per cent. The market share of new entrant Kumara Steel has soared and today stands at 36 per cent, while Ling Hao now makes up 11 per cent of the market. And what's more, Fisher has remained stationary at 1 per cent throughout the five years. ... er ... where was I? Oh, yes. In terms of the seminar, we'll be applying Porter's model to Linda Brahman Steelmakers, so be sure to read this competition case study carefully.

Exercise F

This gives further practice in identifying words and phrases used synonymously in a particular context.

Set for individual work and pairwork checking.

Answers

1	boom	soar
2	cover	include
3	disaster	failure
4	key	essential
5	known as	called
6	means	stands for
7	reading	study

Closure

1 Put students in groups. Ask students to look at the information available in Figures 1, 2A and 2B in Lesson 5.1. Ask them to decide what extra information they will need if they are to conduct a full PESTEL analysis of LBS's situation in 2006. Ask them to brainstorm how they would find this information, i.e., what kind of sources they would use.

Answer

Possible answer:

- They would need to look at their customer base to find out why car sales are falling. This information could come from sales data or market research.
- They would need to look into issues like labour costs, inflation issues, currency stability – this information could come from government statistics, banks, economic journals and websites.
- They would need to investigate environmental regulation – so they would need to look at laws passed and how they affect LBS.
- They would need to look at technological issues, like how up-to-date their own production processes are, and whether their competitors are able to produce a cheaper product because they are using a

more cost-effective technology. This would entail research on the Internet, and research into Kumara Steel's production processes.

- They would need to try to find out what the government felt about the success of the deregulation process, and how this was going to affect future government policy. They would need to discuss these matters with politicians or informed journalists or academics who have a more neutral stance.

2 Check that students understand some of the concepts and vocabulary in the unit so far, including:

business environment

competition

competitor analysis

contingency planning

crisis

currency

demographic

deregulate

diversify

expansion

feasible

incentive

inflation

infrastructure

mission

monopoly

multinational

new entrant

outsource

PESTEL analysis

rival

situation analysis

stakeholders

strategy

substitute

supplier

5.3 Extending skills note-taking symbols • stress within words • lecture language

Lesson aims

- use symbols in note-taking
- understand and use lecture language such as stance adverbials (*obviously, arguably*), restatement (*in other words ...*) and other commentary-type phrases

Further practice in:

- stress within words
- asking for information
- formulating polite questions

Introduction

As in Unit 3, encourage students to ask you questions about the information in the lecture in Lesson 5.2 as if you were the lecturer. Remind them about asking for information politely. If they can't remember how to do this, you could tell them to revise the *Skills bank* for Unit 3.

Put students in pairs. Student A must ask Student B about the information in the lecture in Lesson 5.2 to help him/her complete the notes from the lecture. Then they reverse roles. Again, they can revise language for this in the *Skills bank* for Unit 3.

Exercise A

1 Revise/introduce the idea of using symbols and abbreviations when making notes. Ask students to look at the example notes and find the symbols and abbreviated forms. Do they know what these mean? If not, they should try to guess.

If you wish, expand the table in the Answers section below with more symbols and abbreviations that will be useful for the students. There is also a list at the back of the Course Book for students' reference.

2 Ask students to tell you what kind of notes these are (linear and numbered). Set the question for pairwork. Students will need to agree what the notes are saying and then make the corrections.

3 Set for individual work. Feed back with the whole class and build the spidergram in the Answers section on the board.

Answers

Model answers:

1

Symbol/abbreviation	Meaning
no.	number
=	equals, the same as, is
↓	decreases or falls
→	to, towards, leads to
i.e.	that is
e.g.	(for) example
US	United States
Mkt.	market
"	ditto = repeat the same information

2 Suggested corrections:

3) i. no. of competitors = price ↓
   → competitor analysis
   i.e., find out about rivals, e.g., monopoly?
   ii. Porter <u>5</u> Forces Analysis

4) case study <u>Kazdjikistan</u> steel <u>production</u> mkt.
   i. LBS 96 per cent market share →53 per cent (2003–2008)
   ii. KS ↑ to 36 per cent

3

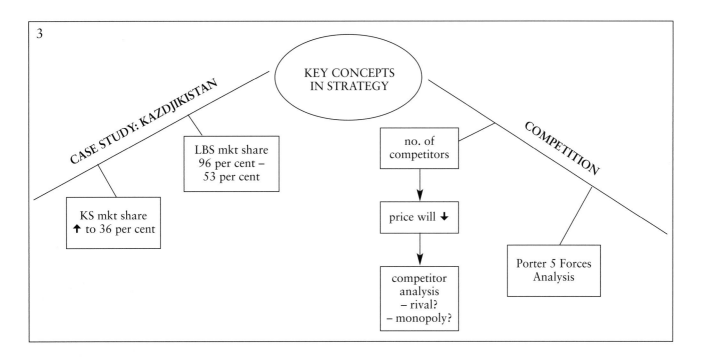

Language note

Some abbreviations are universal and some are personal. People often develop their own personal system of symbols and abbreviations. For example, *bn* for billion is used by many people, but *mkt* is an example of a longer word abbreviated by the individual who wrote these notes.

🎧 Exercise B

Tell students they will hear the final part of the lecture. Give them time to read the questions. They should complete the final leg of the spidergram.

Play Part 4. Put students in pairs to compare their notes and discuss the questions. Feed back. For question 2, ask students if they can remember the exact words used by the lecturer (*oh, dear ... sadly, I see that we've run out of time*).

Answers

Model answers:

1

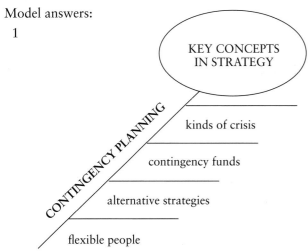

2 Because there is no more time.

3 The research task is to find out whether or what contingency plan LBS had prepared in preparation for government deregulation and the possibility of losing its monopoly.

Transcript 🎧 1.26

Part 4

Now, even the best strategy can't plan for everything. Organizations can face financial crises or industrial action. There can be sudden environmental issues which affect company image. Legal problems can occur from time to time. Contingency planning is being ready for these challenges. Every strategy should have backup, which is what we're talking about here. Often this means having contingency funds, or alternatives to fall back on, or good flexible people in your firm. However, ... oh dear ... sadly, I see that we've run out of time. This means that I'll have to ask *you* to do some research. I'd like you to find out whether LBS had any contingency plan in place for government deregulation and the possibility of losing its monopoly. We'll discuss what you've found out next time I see you.

🎧 Exercise C

Remind students of the importance of stressed syllables in words (see the teaching notes for Unit 3, Lesson 3, Exercise A). Play the recording, pausing after the first few to check that students understand the task.

Feed back, perhaps playing the recording again for each word before checking. Ideally, mark up an OHT or other visual display with the words.

Answers

analyze	8
anticipate	7
assignment	3
category	11
characteristics	5
identify	10
incredibly	9
overview	2
seminar	1
strategy	4
successful	6
variety	12

Transcript 🎧 1.27

1 'seminar
2 'overview
3 a'ssignment
4 'strategy
5 character'istics
6 suc'cessful
7 an'ticipate
8 'analyze
9 in'credibly
10 i'dentify
11 'category
12 va'riety

🎧 Exercise D

This exercise gives students a chance to focus on some typical lecture language.

1 Set for pairwork. Students should try to think of a word for each of the blank spaces. Note that they should *not* try to use the words from the box for this. Do not feed back at this point.

2 Tell students they will hear the sentences from the lecture and should fill in the missing words as they listen. There will be pauses at the end of each sentence, but you will play the recording straight through without stopping (as a kind of dictation). Feed back with the whole class, playing the sentences again if necessary. Check the meanings and functions of the words and phrases. Ask students to repeat the sentences for pronunciation practice, making sure that the stress and intonation are copied from the model.

3 Set for individual work and pairwork checking. Students should check in their dictionaries for meanings or pronunciations of words from the box that they don't know. Feed back, building the first two columns of the table in the Answers section on the board.

4 Elicit suggestions from the whole class for a third column: *Other similar words*.
If you wish, students can practise saying the sentences in question 2 but this time with words from questions 3 and 4.
After completing Exercise D, students can be referred to the *Vocabulary bank – Stance* and the *Skills bank – Signpost language in a lecture* for consolidation.

Answers

Model answers:

1/2

Actually, because of globalization, understanding the environment is arguably *the* most important aspect of strategy for companies thinking big. You can become an MNE, but if nobody out there buys your product, your business will fail. So, it follows that an international manager has to perform a situation analysis.

So what happens is you analyze all these aspects to see if it's feasible to enter. What I mean is that you do a lot of research. Anyway, er … to return to the main point – fundamentally, building a successful strategy depends on understanding the business environment. Well, first and foremost is analyzing and understanding your competition. Naturally, you'll have to do some reading on this, and Michael Porter is the one to read. His model, called the Five Forces Analysis, is essential for your study.

3/4

Word/phrase from the lecture	Words/phrases from the box	Other similar words/phrases
actually	in fact	in reality
arguably	probably, possibly, some people say	perhaps
it follows that	we can see that	logically
what I mean is that	that is to say, in other words	or, by that I mean, to put it another way
to return to the main point	as I was saying	going back to the main point
fundamentally	basically	in essence, really
naturally	of course, obviously, clearly	certainly
essential	crucial	important

Transcript 🎧 1.28

Actually, because of globalization, understanding the environment is arguably *the* most important aspect of strategy for companies thinking big.

You can become an MNE, but if nobody out there buys your product, your business will fail. So, it follows that an international manager has to perform a situation analysis.

So what happens is you analyze all these aspects to see if it's feasible to enter. What I mean is that you do a lot of research.

Anyway, er … to return to the main point – fundamentally, building a successful strategy depends on understanding the business environment. Well, first and foremost is analyzing and understanding your competition.

Naturally, you'll have to do some reading on this, and Michael Porter is the one to read. His model, called the Five Forces Analysis, is essential for your study.

Language note

There are three main categories of language here:

1 Stance markers. These are words or phrases that speakers use to show what they feel or think about what they are saying. Adverbs used like this are generally (though not always) positioned at the beginning of the sentence.

2 Phrases used to indicate a restatement. It is very important for students both to understand and to be able to use these, since speakers frequently need to repeat and explain their points.

3 Phrases used to show that the speaker has deviated from the main point and is now about to return to it. Again, this type of phrase is very common in lectures and discussions.

Exercise E

Remind students of the task set by the lecturer at the end of Part 4. Set the questions for pairwork discussion. Students should first list the sort of information they will need to find, then discuss and make notes on what they already know. Then they should compile a list of possible sources of information.

Feed back on all three tasks with the whole class. Do not discuss further at this point, as the topic will be taken up in the next lesson.

Answers

Possible answers:

1 Definition of a good contingency plan, i.e., what it is likely to include. Information from LBS regarding reaction and anything else that is relevant. Company history, market environment, competitors, demand/supply, deregulation.

2 Answers depend on the students – direct them to Figures 1 and 2B.

3 Internet, professional and academic journals, subject textbooks, etc.

Closure

Play a version of the game *Just a minute*. Put students in groups of four. Give them an envelope in which they will find topics written on slips of paper. Students take turns to take a slip of paper from the envelope and then talk for one minute on the topic. Encourage them to use as many of the words and phrases from Exercises C and D as they can. Each person should talk for up to a minute without stopping. If they can talk for one minute they get a point. If they deviate from their topic or cannot think of anything more to say, they have to stop. The person who has the most points is the winner.

Suggestions for topics follow. Or if you prefer, you can use other topics unrelated to business.

- PESTEL analysis (give students one element to discuss)

  political and legal

  economic

  social

  technological

  environmental

- Porter's Five Forces Analysis
- contingency planning
- situation analysis
- competition
- discussing a graph
- the steel market they have studied

5.4 Extending skills

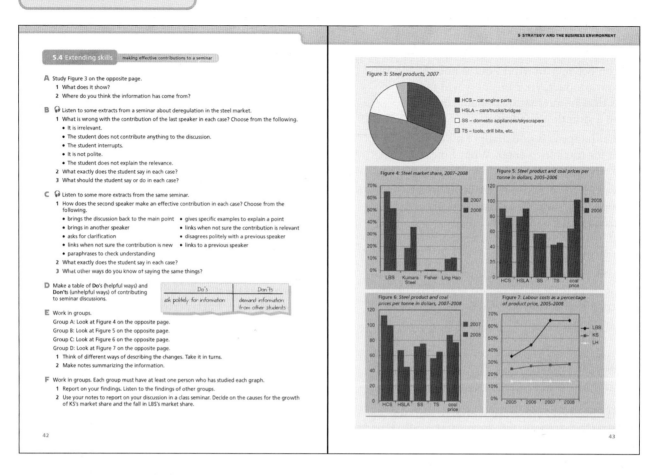

5.4 Extending skills making effective contributions to a seminar

A Study Figure 3 on the opposite page.
  1 What does it show?
  2 Where do you think the information has come from?

B 🎧 Listen to some extracts from a seminar about deregulation in the steel market.
  1 What is wrong with the contribution of the last speaker in each case? Choose from the following.
    • It is irrelevant.
    • The student does not contribute anything to the discussion.
    • The student interrupts.
    • It is not polite.
    • The student does not explain the relevance.
  2 What exactly does the student say in each case?
  3 What should the student say or do in each case?

C 🎧 Listen to some more extracts from the same seminar.
  1 How does the second speaker make an effective contribution in each case? Choose from the following.
    • brings the discussion back to the main point   • gives specific examples to explain a point
    • brings in another speaker   • links when not sure the contribution is relevant
    • asks for clarification   • disagrees politely with a previous speaker
    • links when not sure the contribution is new   • links to a previous speaker
    • paraphrases to check understanding
  2 What exactly does the student say in each case?
  3 What other ways do you know of saying the same things?

D Make a table of **Do's** (helpful ways) and **Don'ts** (unhelpful ways) of contributing to seminar discussions.

Do's	Don'ts
ask politely for information	demand information from other students

E Work in groups.
  Group A: Look at Figure 4 on the opposite page.
  Group B: Look at Figure 5 on the opposite page.
  Group C: Look at Figure 6 on the opposite page.
  Group D: Look at Figure 7 on the opposite page.
  1 Think of different ways of describing the changes. Take it in turns.
  2 Make notes summarizing the information.

F Work in groups. Each group must have at least one person who has studied each graph.
  1 Report on your findings. Listen to the findings of other groups.
  2 Use your notes to report on your discussion in a class seminar. Decide on the causes for the growth of KS's market share and the fall in LBS's market share.

42

43

Lesson aims

• make effective and appropriate contributions to a seminar

Further practice in:

• speaking from notes
• reporting information

Introduction

Revise stance words and restatement/deviation phrases from the previous lesson. Give a word or phrase and ask students to give one with a similar meaning. Alternatively, give a sentence or phrase from the lecture in Lessons 5.2 and 5.3 and ask students to tell you the accompanying stance word or restatement/deviation phrase.

Exercise A

1 Tell students to look at the pie chart. Set for pairwork discussion.

2 Ask students to use what they know about the case study in Lesson 5.3 to speculate on the answer. Feed back, accepting any reasonable suggestions.

Answers

Possible answers:

1 Steel product market share per product in 2007.

2 The information has probably come from some form of market analysis – from a journal/source that has analyzed figures published by the companies involved.

🎧 Exercise B

In this exercise, students will hear examples of how *not* to contribute to a group discussion.

1/2 Allow students time to read the questions. Tell them they will hear five extracts. They should choose a different answer for each one. Set for individual work and pairwork checking. Play all the extracts through once.

Play the extracts a second time, pausing after each one. Students should write down the actual words, as in a dictation, then check in pairs. When students have completed questions 1 and 2, feed back with the whole class, maybe building up columns 1 and 2 of the table in the Answers section on the board.

3 Set for pairwork discussion. Feed back, adding a third column to the table on the board.

Answers

Model answers:

	Contribution is poor because	Exact words	How to improve
Extract 1	it is irrelevant	Dina: I love Chinese food.	say something relevant: for example, something about Chinese entrants into other markets
Extract 2	it is not polite	Dina: That's rubbish. They obviously didn't do that.	use polite (tentative) language when disagreeing, e.g., *Actually, I don't think that's quite right. Logic suggests they did something different.*
Extract 3	the student does not contribute anything to the discussion	Ramon: Well, erm … I'm not sure really.	be ready to contribute something when brought into the discussion by the lecturer or other students
Extract 4	the student interrupts	Bruce: … too slow. So the company got in financial trouble when it happened.	he should wait until the speaker has finished
Extract 5	the student does not explain the relevance	Elena: Outsource.	the comment is relevant to the topic, but Elena doesn't explain why. She should say, for example, what she said later after the lecturer asked her to explain (i.e., *they could have outsourced their production*).

Transcript 🎧 1.29

Extract 1

LECTURER: Right, Elena and Dina, what did you find out about the new entrants in this steel market?

ELENA: Well, first of all, there were two new competitors for LBS. Then a third, a Chinese firm, entered the market, too.

DINA: I love Chinese food.

Extract 2

LECTURER: And what else did you find out?

ELENA: The Chinese firm undercut prices, so LBS was forced to lower its prices, too.

DINA: That's rubbish. They obviously didn't do that.

Extract 3

LECTURER: Elena, can you give us an explanation of your chart?

ELENA: Well, yes, it has a vertical axis for market share and a horizontal axis for time. Five years. And as you can see, this is how the competition changed.

LECTURER: What do the rest of you think? Ramon, what about you? What do you make of this?

RAMON: Well, erm … I'm not sure really.

Extract 4

LECTURER: Dina, can you explain what

contingency plan the company had for the possibility of deregulation?

DINA: Well, yes, it knew it might happen and had tried to diversify into other industries. But it was too …

BRUCE: … (interrupting) too slow. So the company got in financial trouble when it happened.

Extract 5

LECTURER: When you gave an example of a contingency plan, what did you mean by *alternative sources of production*, Bruce?

BRUCE: I meant it's a backup. If something went wrong, the company could move its production to Brazil but keep control of it.

ELENA: Outsource.

🎧 Exercise C

1/2 This time, students will hear good ways of contributing to a discussion. Follow the same procedure as for 1 and 2 in Exercise B above. Again, when students have completed 1 and 2, feed back with the whole class, maybe building up a table on the board. If you wish, students can look at the transcript in the Course Book.

3 Ask the whole class for other words or phrases that can be used for the strategy and add a third column to the table on the board.

Answers

Model answers:

	Helpful strategy	Exact words	Other ways to say it
Extract 6	brings in another speaker	Dina: *Didn't they, Elena?*	Isn't that right, Elena? What do you think, Elena? What do you make of this, Elena?
Extract 7	asks for clarification	Bruce: *Sorry, I don't follow. Could you possibly explain …?*	I don't quite understand. Could you say a bit more about …?
Extract 8	gives specific examples to explain a point	Elena: *Like Venezuela owning its own oil industry … For example, here, there used to be …*	For instance …
Extract 9	paraphrases to check understanding	Bruce: *If I understand you correctly, you're saying that …*	So what you're saying is …
Extract 10	brings the discussion back to the main point	Ramon: *Yes, but if we just go back to the topic …*	Thinking about …/If we can go back to … for a moment, …
Extract 11	disagrees politely with a previous speaker	Dina: *I'm not sure that's true.*	I don't think I agree with that. In my opinion, …
Extract 12	links to a previous speaker	Ramon: *As Elena said earlier …*	Going back to what Leila said a while ago …
Extract 13	links when not sure the contribution is new	Bruce: *I'm sorry. Has anybody made the point that …*	I don't know if this has been said already, but …
Extract 14	linking when not sure the contribution is relevant	Elena: *I don't know if this is relevant.*	This might be a little off the point, but …

Transcript 🎧 1.30

Extract 6

LECTURER: Let's go back to this steel market and talk about the power of suppliers and customers. What can you tell us?

DINA: Well, LBS had a fixed number of customers – all local manufacturers – and the country is small, so there weren't many. Didn't they, Elena?

ELENA: Yes, absolutely. And after deregulation, globalization increased, too, so suddenly there were more opportunities to export, that is, more potential customers overseas.

Extract 7

DINA: With sudden deregulation and Russian immigrants investing heavily, and also new opportunities to export to overseas manufacturers, there was a real incentive for new businesses to emerge.

BRUCE: Sorry, I don't follow. Could you possibly explain how that works?

DINA: Well, basically, new companies suddenly had good reasons to enter the steel business.

Extract 8

RAMON: I don't understand how deregulation works.

ELENA: Well, governments with strong central control often own key industries in their countries. Like Venezuela owning its oil industry. Deregulation is when they open up and sell to private enterprise to increase competition and make it more efficient. For example, here, there used to be one government-owned phone company – now there are dozens.

Extract 9

DINA: Yes, and deregulation is a way for governments to make money by selling the state-owned organizations. It's also a way to make these organizations more efficient.

BRUCE: If I understand you correctly, you're saying that governments are selling to private companies things that the country owns.

DINA: Yes, that's right.

Extract 10

LECTURER: This is all quite interesting, isn't it?

RAMON: Yes, but if we just go back to the topic: the power of suppliers and customers, we forgot to talk about the power of suppliers.

DINA: Correct! So who are the steelmakers' suppliers, then?

Extract 11

BRUCE: Deregulation is just robbery. I mean, a government can't just sell off and gain from assets that already belong to the people of a country.

DINA: I'm not sure that's true. I think they are just making industry more efficient. And their gains from sales are then spent on the public good anyway.

Extract 12

LECTURER: So what do you think is the most important point about these diagrams?

RAMON: As Elena said earlier, they help to show how much competition has changed in the industry.

Extract 13

LECTURER: Any other ideas?

BRUCE: I'm sorry. Has anybody made the point that deregulation happened about the same time as intense economic globalization? Surely, because it opened up the world, everything became more competitive.

LECTURER: Yes, actually. Elena did say that earlier, but it's an important point.

Extract 14

LECTURER: So what is the difference between the 'threat of new entrants' and the 'threat of substitutes'?

ELENA: I don't know if this is relevant, but maybe other types of metal are substitutes; I don't know, perhaps some alloys or something. Not steel, but one that can be used the same way in building. Only new steelmakers are new entrants.

LECTURER: Yes, that's right, and a good example of a substitute is … *[fades]*

Exercise D

Set for group work. Tell students to brainstorm suggestions for more good and bad seminar strategies. They should think about what helps a seminar discussion to be successful. It may help to think about having seminar discussions in their own language, but they should also think about what is involved in having a seminar discussion in English. Aspects to consider include language, how to contribute to discussions and how to behave.

Feed back, making a list on the board.

Answers

Possible answers:

Do's	Don'ts
ask politely for information	demand information from other students
try to use correct language	use inappropriate language (register)
speak clearly	mumble, whisper or shout
say when you agree with someone	get angry if someone disagrees with you
contribute to the discussion	sit quietly and say nothing
link correctly with previous speakers	ignore what other speakers say
build on points made by other speakers	undermine points made by other speakers
be constructive	be negative
explain your point clearly	wander off the point or be long-winded
listen carefully to what others say	start a side conversation
allow others to speak	dominate the discussion
make a contribution, even if you are not sure if it is new or relevant	stay silent, waiting for 'the perfect moment'

Exercise E

Set students to work in groups of five or six. Give the groups a letter. Group A looks at Figure 4, group B at Figure 5, group C at Figure 6 and group D at Figure 7.

In each group there should be one or two observers and three or four discussing. Groups should also appoint one person to take notes on the discussion, since they will have to present their findings to another group. During the discussion, they will need to identify key variables. They will also need to identify the key trends or facts that the graphs indicate and produce a summary of this information. While students are talking, you can listen in and note where students may need help with language, and where particularly good examples of language are used.

The students acting as observers for the discussion should use a checklist of things to watch for. One observer can concentrate on poor contributions and the other on good contributions. Sample checklists are provided in the additional resources section (Resource 5D) – students simply mark in each cell whenever the behaviour occurs.

Exercise F

Mix up the students and tell them to work in groups containing one student from group A, B, C and D. You will also need to distribute the observers into the new groups. Make sure each of the new groups has a 'secretary', who records group decisions. Groups need to decide on the answer to question 2 – the causes of growth in KS's market increase and the fall in LBS's market share.

Before the groups report on their discussion, remind them about speaking from notes (see Unit 1 *Skills bank*).

First, the observers should give an overview of how the seminar discussion went and should highlight especially good practice. They can also report on poor contributions, but this needs to be done carefully and constructively (possibly without mentioning names), so that individuals are not embarrassed or upset.

Then the person who took notes should present the decisions of their group to the other groups.

Finally, feed back to the whole class on what you heard as you listened in on the groups. Suggest improvements for words and phrases, and highlight good practice.

Closure

1 If you wish, refer students to the *Skills bank – Seminar language* for consolidation.

2 Focus on some of the vocabulary connected with research from Lessons 5.2 and 5.4. For example:

> *analyze (v)*
>
> *analysis*
>
> *axis*
>
> *category*
>
> *concept*
>
> *data*
>
> *define*
>
> *definition*
>
> *examine*
>
> *horizontal*
>
> *identify*
>
> *overview*
>
> *sources*
>
> *trend*
>
> *vertical*

Extra activities

1 Work through the *Vocabulary bank* and *Skills bank* if you have not already done so, or as a revision of previous study.

2 Use the *Activity bank* (Teacher's Book additional resources section, Resource 5A).

   A Set the crossword for individual work (including homework) or pairwork.

   Answers

Students' words	Teacher's words
competition	partnership
decrease	increase
diversify	consolidate
expansion	contraction
feasible	impossible
inflation	deflation
monopoly	competition
rigid	flexible
rise	fall
rival	ally
sharply	gradually
slightly	significantly
slow	rapid

B Students should select any six words from the box (listed in *Students' words* column). Call out words at random from the *Teacher's words* column, not forgetting to note which words you have called. Students cross out the antonym if they have it on their card. When someone has managed to cross out all the words on his/her bingo card, he/she should call out *Bingo!* Check to see if all the words are correctly crossed out. The first person to correctly cross out all the words on his/her bingo card is the winner.

An alternative is to put students in groups to play the game, with one student acting as the teacher. In this case, you will need to prepare a list of teacher's words for each group.

6 FINANCE FOR STRATEGY

Unit 6 introduces the theme of finance, focusing on areas most relevant to senior management and centred around a reading text. After the context is set with preliminary exercises, the reading then firstly explains the time value of money, a difficult concept that is fundamental to finance, and follows with a description of cost and depreciation. It then explores what valuation is in the context of investment and project appraisal, and introduces the idea of financial ratios, along with a few popular methods used in valuing. Finally, it explains some methodological problems with valuation, including the manipulation of accounts by managers. The unit finishes with a case study of the valuation of a young company, Kumara Steel.

Skills focus

Reading
- locating key information in complex sentences

Writing
- reporting findings from other sources: paraphrasing
- writing complex sentences

Vocabulary focus
- synonyms, replacement subjects, etc., for sentence-level paraphrasing

---

Key vocabulary

account	intangible	shareholding
appraisal	issue (v)	share market
asset	manipulate	share price
capital	market capitalization	takeover
depreciation	merger/de-merger	technique
discounted cash flow	minus	time value of money
earnings	net book value	to place value on
earnings per share	net present value	valuation
expenditure	price-to-earnings ratio	value (v)
fixed sum	ratio	viability
goodwill	return on investment	
historical cost	scandal	

6.1 Vocabulary

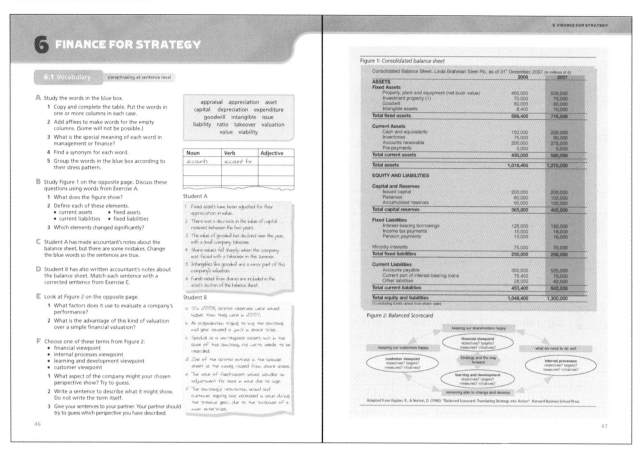

General note

Read the *Vocabulary bank* at the end of the Course Book unit. Decide when, if at all, to refer students to it. The best time is probably at the very end of the lesson or the beginning of the next lesson, as a summary/revision.

Lesson aims

- paraphrase at sentence level using passives, synonyms, negatives, replacement subjects

Further practice in:

- affixes
- words with different meanings in general English
- stress within words
- word sets – synonyms, antonyms

Introduction

1 Revise affixes, e.g., *re~, un~, in~, out~, ~ize, ~al, ~ty, ~ly, ~ion, ~ive*. Do this by dividing the class into small groups. Give each group one affix. Allow three or four minutes only. The group which can list the most words is the winner.

2 Revise words describing graphs (from Unit 5). Draw a line graph on the board. The line should rise and fall, sharply and gradually, and have a peak and a point where it levels off. Point to each part of the line and ask students to give you the appropriate verb and adverb. Alternatively, draw your own line graph and describe it. Students should try to draw an identical line graph from your description while you are talking.

Exercise A

1 Tell students to make a table with three columns and 18 rows in their notebooks. Go through the example in the Course Book. Set the exercise for individual work and pairwork checking. Tell students to use their dictionaries if they need to check meanings, grammatical category, etc. Feed back with the whole class, building the first three columns of the table in the Answers section on the board. Ask students to say what general meanings they can give for the words.

2 Refer to the example (*accounts*) in the Course Book. Ask students to suggest a form of *account* which is an adjective (*accountable*). Set for pairwork. Students should try to fill as many empty columns as possible with words with appropriate

99

affixes. They should continue to use their dictionaries to check meanings and spellings. Note that it is possible to use the participle of a verb as an adjective if there is no other possibility. Feed back with the whole class, checking meanings of the words added to the table.

3 Add a fourth column on the board and give it the heading *Management/finance meaning*. Underline or highlight the words as shown in the table below,

and with the whole class, ask students to suggest (or find in their dictionaries) meanings specific to management for these words.

4 Work in a similar way with the fifth column, *Management/finance synonym*. Limit the synonyms to those for the underlined words.

5 Set for pairwork. Feed back with the whole class, checking pronunciation.

Answers

Model answers:
1–4

Noun	Verb	Adjective	Mgmt/finance meaning	Mgmt/finance synonym
appraisal	appraise		an assessment of the value of a company	assessment, valuation
appreciation	appreciate	appreciable	increase in value	capital growth
asset			something a company owns that has real value	land, plant, equipment, premises, capital
capital	capitalize	capitalized	money available for or spent on investment	finance, funding
depreciation	depreciate	depreciating	loss in value of assets or currency	decline in value
expenditure	spend	expenditure-related	the amount of money spent on something	spending cost(s)
goodwill			the amount added to a company's value because it has a semi-guaranteed customer base and income	
	intangibility	intangible	something that has value but is not concrete, e.g., goodwill	abstract, non-concrete
issue	issue	issued	releasing shares for sale on the share market	release
liability		liable	the amount a company owes	debt, expense
ratio			a fixed proportional relationship	a set proportion
takeover	takeover		the act of buying and running another company	buy out/merger (depending on the financial context)
valuation	value	valued	(n) a description of a company's worth, often prior to its sale (v) the process of deciding what a company is worth	appraisal appraise
viability		viable	how well a company or project can survive under current conditions	life expectancy

5

Oo	asset, issue, ratio, value
oO	account, goodwill
Ooo	capital, takeover
oOo	appraisal
oOoo	intangible, expenditure
ooOo	valuation
ooOoo	liability, viability
oooOo	appreciation, depreciation

Language note

Some grammatical forms of the words may have particular meanings that are unlikely (though probably not impossible) in a business context, e.g., *goodwill = a nice feeling towards someone; capital = most important city in a country, issue (n) = important area/topic*. Point this out if necessary, but don't spend much time on these words.

Exercise B

1 Set for pairwork discussion. Students should refer to the words they have looked at in Exercise A to help describe the balance sheet. Monitor but do not assist. Feed back with the whole class, checking that students can identify the different parts of the balance sheet. Elicit words which can be used from Exercise A (underlined below, including synonyms).

2 Set for pairwork discussion. Feed back with the whole class, using information in the Answers if necessary to check that they are defining items correctly.

3 Set for group work. Hopefully, someone in each group will recognize that *significance* relates to the size of the original item and the difference between the two years. So a huge change in a tiny item may not be significant, but the reverse might be. Groups should also recognize that they need to calculate percentage to reveal significance.

Answers

Model answers:

1 The diagram shows a consolidated balance sheet. It is a tool for evaluating the current financial situation of a company by comparing it with the financial performance of the company in the previous year. It is one important tool for use in company valuation or appraisal.

2 **Current assets:** are sums of money owing to the business or money earned for things it has done in the past. For LBS, they have increased by 30 per cent.

Fixed assets: include land, equipment, goodwill, etc., i.e., things the company owns. They are often

subject to depreciation. For LBS, their value has risen over the year by 25 per cent.

Current liabilities: are monies owed by a company in the current year. They are payments to suppliers, for instance, that would normally be completed within a 12-month period. They have risen considerably over the period by about 40 per cent.

Fixed liabilities: are debts that last longer than one year, for example mortgages, debentures or long-term loans from the bank. For LBS, there has been an increase in the value of fixed liabilities by about 11 per cent.

3 There are significant changes in:
- fixed assets as a result of changes in property and goodwill
- current assets as a result of changes in cash and accounts receivable
- current liabilities as a result of changes in accounts payable and other

The change in fixed liabilities may not be significant, certainly compared with the other large changes.

Exercise C

As well as requiring the use of antonyms, this exercise checks that students have understood the balance sheet in Exercise B. Set for individual work and pairwork checking. Feed back with the whole class. A good way to do this is to use an OHT (or projected page) with blanks for the blue words (see additional resources section, Resource 6B).

Answers

Model answers:

1 Fixed assets have been adjusted for their *depreciation* in value.

2 There was *an increase* in the value of capital reserves between the two years.

3 The value of goodwill has *risen* over the year, with a small company takeover.

4 Share values *rose* sharply when the company was faced with a takeover in the summer.

5 Intangibles like goodwill are an *essential/important* part of this company's valuation.

6 Funds raised from shares are included in the *capital side* of the balance sheet.

Exercise D

Introduce the idea of paraphrasing – or restating. Elicit from the students the main ways to do this at sentence level, namely:
- using different grammar
- using different words
- reordering the information

Write these points on the board. Also make the point very strongly that a paraphrase is not a paraphrase unless 90 per cent of the language is different. There are some words which must remain the same, but these are very few, and are likely to be words specific to the subject, such as *cash flow*, *fixed assets*, *liabilities*, etc. It is best to try to use all three of the above strategies, if possible.

Students should look carefully at the corrected sentences from Exercise C and then compare them with the paraphrases. The first step is to identify which sentences match. Set for individual work and pairwork checking. It may be helpful for the students if you reproduce the corrected sentences from Exercise C and the sentences in Exercise D on strips of paper so that they can move them around. Both sets of sentences are reproduced in the additional resources section (Resource 6C) to facilitate this.

Feed back with the whole class. A good way to do this is to reproduce the sentences on OHTs, with each sentence cut into a separate strip. Lay the sentences on the OHP one at a time, as you agree what is the correct match.

Once the sentences are correctly paired, ask students to locate the parts of each sentence which seem to match. They will need to look at the overall meaning of each phrase, using what they know about the subject, to make sure that the phrases are similar. Set for pairwork. Feed back with the whole group, using the OHT strips and highlighting the matching parts with coloured pens.

Answers

Model answers:

1 Fixed assets have been adjusted for their depreciation in value.	e The value of fixed-asset values includes an adjustment for loss in value due to age.
2 There was an increase in the value of capital reserves between the two years.	a In 2008, capital reserves were valued higher than they were in 2007.
3 The value of goodwill has risen over the year, with a small company takeover.	f The company's reputation, brand and customer loyalty has increased in value during the previous year, due to the purchase of a minor enterprise.
4 Share values rose sharply when the company was faced with a takeover in the summer.	b An organization trying to buy the company mid year caused a jump in share price.
5 Intangibles like goodwill are an essential/important part of this company's valuation.	c Goodwill is a non-physical asset, but in the case of this company, its worth needs to be recorded.
6 Funds raised from shares are included in the capital section of the balance sheet.	d One of the capital entries in the balance sheet is the money raised from share sales.

A final step is to discuss the changes that have been made in detail. Students should refer to the list of types of changes you have written on the board. Look at each paraphrase with the class and ask students what changes have been made. Be specific about the types of vocabulary or grammar changes. For example, in the first answer above, the paraphrase reorders the information and changes all the key vocabulary except for the technical term *fixed assets*.

Exercise E

Put students in pairs to discuss the balanced scorecard. Ask them to describe what they think it shows. Note that it is not essential for students to grasp the full meaning of the balanced scorecard, but this mention of it foreshadows another mention in the next unit.

Answer

Model answers:

1 The balanced scorecard uses four perspectives/ viewpoints to examine the performance of a company.

- The *financial viewpoint* gives a purely economic view of the company and is backward looking in that it focuses on past performance.

- The other three aspects: *internal processes*, *learning and development* and *customer viewpoint*, all look at present performance and measure it against how well company objectives are being achieved.

2 The value of this kind of appraisal is that it is targeted on objectives, including financial objectives, and tries to show how well the company is meeting these objectives. It gives managers a much more precise picture of company performance and gives them an effective basis for planning future changes.

Exercise F

1/2 Set as individual work. Although the balanced
scorecard is an extension to the financial topic of
this unit, it is somewhat relevant, and it
foreshadows its mention in a later unit. Students
use the term, their prior knowledge and perhaps
their dictionaries to guess at what their chosen
point of view within a company is (these are
viewpoints from which performance can be
measured, setting financial performance into
context amid others). They then compose a
sentence to explain it.

3 Set as pairwork.

Answers

Possible answers:

- The *financial viewpoint* is looking at a company in
  terms of the money it has or is owed and owes, and
  the movements of money in, out and within it. This
  is easily quantified.

- The *internal processes viewpoint* looks at a
  company in terms of the operations that are central
  to it and the process and tasks that make them up.
  This can be quantified and measured.

- The *learning and development viewpoint* regards a
  company in terms of the knowledge and skills that
  are contained within its human resources and looks
  to exploit this, addressing shortfalls. This can be
  quantified and measured.

- The *customer viewpoint* looks at a company in
  terms of the consumer's or customer's experience:
  their experience of the product or service, of
  customer service, their perception of the brand, and
  so on. This can, in fact, be quantified and measured.

Teaching note

If short on time, Exercise F could easily be omitted
without jeopardizing the unit's aims.

Closure

Discussion:

1 What are the advantages and disadvantages
  of using purely financial indicators to assess
  a company?

2 What is the benefit to managers of using a balanced
  scorecard as a tool for appraisal of a company's
  performance?

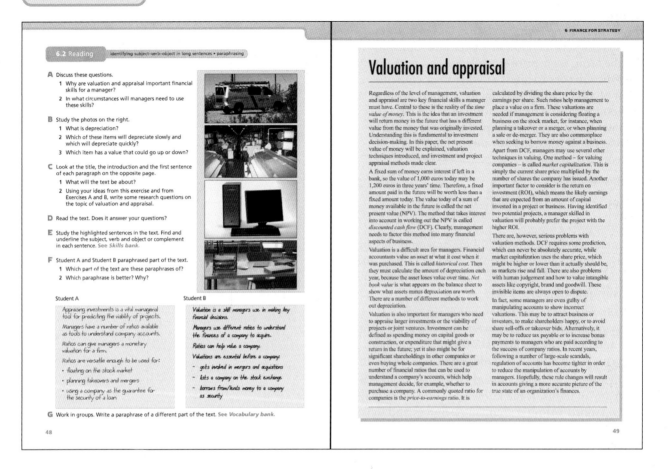

General note

Read the *Skills bank* at the end of the Course Book unit. Decide when, if at all, to refer students to it. The best time is probably at the very end of the lesson or the beginning of the next lesson, as a summary/revision.

Lesson aims

- identify the kernel SVC/O of a long sentence

Further practice in:

- research questions
- topic sentences
- paraphrasing

Introduction

Remind the class about techniques when using written texts for research. Ask:

What is it a good idea to do:

- *before reading?* (think of research questions)
- *while you are reading?* (look for topic sentences)
- *after reading?* (check answers to the research questions)

What words in a text signal the development of a topic in a new direction? (markers showing contrast such as *but, however, at the same time, on the other hand*, etc.)

If you wish, refer students to Unit 4 *Skills bank*.

Exercise A

Set for general discussion. Allow students to debate differences of opinion. Encourage them to give examples if they can. Do not correct or give information at this point, as these topics will be dealt with in the text.

Subject note

Valuation and *appraisal* are important skills because they enable a manager to assess the financial capabilities of an enterprise. Valuation and appraisal are used when managers need to assess the viability of projects, joint ventures or buying other companies.

Exercise B

Refer students to the photos.

1 Students work in pairs to articulate a definition. As a class, compare definitions. Accept any reasonable suggestions.

2/3 Allow students a few minutes to speculate on these, in pairs.

Answers

1 It is the loss of value of an asset due to time and wear.

Suggested answers:

2 Items that will depreciate slowly: office furniture; items that will depreciate quickly: commercial vehicle, computer.

3 Item which has a value that could go up or down: commercial premises.

Exercise C

1 Set for pairwork discussion. Feed back with the whole class. Accept any reasonable answers. If students do not know, do not tell them, but say they may find out in the text.

2 Discuss with the whole class. Elicit ideas, but do not confirm or correct. Accept any sensible suggestions.

Answers

1/2 Students' own answers.

Exercise D

Set for individual work and pairwork checking.

Exercise E

Draw a table with the headings from the Answers section on the board. If you wish, students can also draw a similar table in their notebooks. Explain that in academic writing, sentences can seem very complex. This is often not so much because the sentence structure is highly complex in itself, but that the subjects and objects/complements may consist of clauses or complex noun phrases. Often the verb is quite simple. But in order to fully understand a text, the grammar of a sentence must be understood. Subject + verb + object or complement is the basic sentence structure of English. Students need to be able to locate the subjects, main verbs and their objects or complements.

Elicit from students the subject, main verb and object for the first sentence. Ask students for the *headword* of each subject, main verb and object (underlined in the table in the Answers section). Write them in the table on the board. Using high-speed questioning, get students to build the whole phrase that constitutes the subject/main verb/object/complement.

Example 1:

This example shows how to deal with *is* + complement.

<u>Valuation and appraisal</u> are two key financial skills a manager must have.

What is this sentence about in general? = valuation and appraisal
What's the main verb in this sentence? = is
So what is important? = two key financial skills
Because? = a manager must have them

The idea is that students should be able to extract something which contains the kernel, even if it does not make complete sense without the full phrase.

Set the remainder of the exercise for individual work followed by pairwork checking. Finally, feed back with the whole class.

You may wish to refer students to the *Skills bank – Finding the main information*.

Example 2:

Net book value is what appears on the balance sheet to show what assets minus depreciation are worth.

What is this sentence about? = net book value (subject)
What does net book value do? = is (verb)
What 'is' it? = what appears on the balance sheet (object)
Why? = to show what assets minus depreciation are worth (extension – here an infinitive clause containing a relative clause).

The headword in the subject is *value*.

The object is a clause. The headword in the object is *what*.

Answers

Model answers:

Subject	Verb	Object/complement
<u>valuation and appraisal</u>	<u>are</u>	two key financial <u>skills</u> a manager must have
a fixed <u>amount</u> paid in the future	<u>will be</u>	<u>worth less than a fixed amount today.</u>
Net book value	<u>is</u>	<u>what appears on the balance sheet to show what assets minus depreciation are worth.</u>
A commonly quoted <u>ratio</u> for companies	<u>is</u>	<u>the *price-to-earnings* ratio.</u>
a <u>manager</u> skilled in valuation	<u>will</u> probably <u>prefer</u>	<u>the project</u> with the higher ROI.
<u>regulation</u> of accounts	has become	<u>tighter</u>, in order to reduce the manipulation of accounts by managers.

Exercise F

Set for individual work and pairwork checking. Make sure that students identify the original phrases in the text first (paragraph 4, though the definition of investment is omitted) before looking at the paraphrases.

Feed back with the whole class. A good way to demonstrate how Student A's text contains too many words from the original is to use an OHT or other visual display and highlight the common words in colour. (A table giving the sentences plus commentary is included in the additional resources section – Resources 6D and 6E.) Check that students are able to say which parts of the paraphrase match with the original, and which structures have been used.

Answers

1 Paragraph 4
2 Student B's paraphrase is better, because it uses fewer words from the original text.

> ### Language note
>
> It is important that students understand that when paraphrasing, it is not sufficient to change a word here and there and leave most of the words and the basic sentence structure unchanged. This approach is known as 'patch-writing' and is considered to be plagiarism. It is also important when paraphrasing not to change the meaning of the original – also quite hard to do.

Exercise G

Refer students to the *Vocabulary bank* at this stage. Review paraphrasing skills with the whole class before starting this exercise.

Divide the text into parts. For example, each paragraph can be divided into two so that there are eight different sections (though, of course, you should not use the first part of paragraph 4). Give each section to different students to work on. Alternatively, you could choose one part of the text for all students to work on, for example the second part of paragraph 4. This can be done in class or, if you prefer, as individual work/homework.

If students are doing the work in class in groups or pairs, a good way to provide feedback is to get them to write their paraphrase on an OHT. Show each paraphrase (or a selection) to the class and ask for comments. Say what is good about the work. Point out where there are errors and ask for suggestions on how to improve it. Make any corrections on the OHT with a different coloured pen.

Closure

1 Divide the class into two teams. Write the six topic sentences from the reading text on strips, or photocopy them from the additional resources section (Resource 6F). One team chooses a topic sentence and reads it aloud. The other team must give the information triggered by that topic sentence. Accept only the actual paragraph content.

2 Dictate the following to the class:

Some important terms we use in valuation are:

… the value of an asset when it is bought.

… a ratio that is calculated by dividing share price by the amount each share earns.

… a way of valuing a company by multiplying the number of shares by the share price.

… money your company owes, short-term loans.

Students work in pairs and scan the article to find the information. The first pair to find the correct term for each description wins. Feed back with the whole class.

6.3 Extending skills

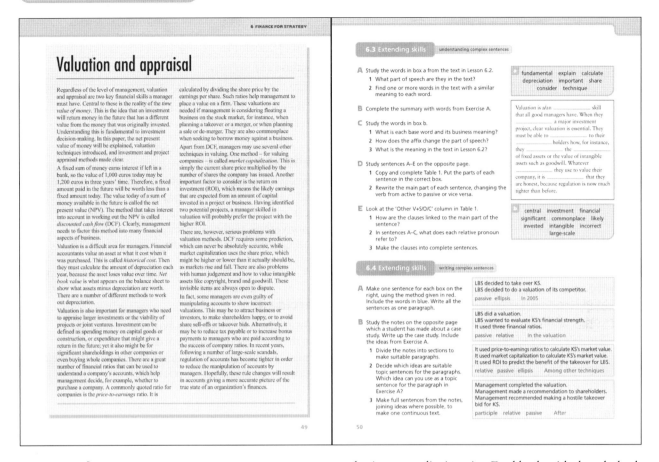

Lesson aims

- study sentence structure in more detail
- identify the main information in:

  an active sentence

  a passive sentence

  a complex sentence with participles

  a complex sentence with embedded clauses

Further practice in:

- vocabulary from Lesson 6.2

Introduction

Ask students to see how many phrases or compound nouns they can make with the word *share*. Tell students to brainstorm a list in pairs. Feed back with the whole class.

Possible answers: *share price, share market, shareholdings, share value, shareholder, share broker, share dividends.*

Exercise A

Ask students to study the words in the box and to find the words in the text. Set for individual work and pairwork checking. Tell students not to use their dictionaries to begin with but to use what they know to guess meanings and parts of speech. If necessary, they should use dictionaries when checking in pairs. Deal with any common problems with the whole class.

Answers

Model answers (paragraph numbers in brackets):

Word	Part of speech	Similar meaning
fundamental (1)	adj	key (1), important (4)
explain (1)	v (T/I)	make clear (1)
calculate (3)	v (T)	work out (3)
depreciation (3)	n (U)	lose value (3)
important (4)	adj	significant (4), key (1)

Word	Part of speech	Similar meaning
share (4)	usually n (C); here part of compounds *shareholdings* and *share price*, so in adjectival position	stock, a unit of a company that is sold on the stock market. When it is sold, the purchaser owns a part of the company.
consider (4)	v (T/I)	plan (4), seek (4)
technique (5)	n (C/U)	method (5)

Exercise B

Set for individual work and pairwork checking. Students should make use of all the words they have discussed in Exercise A (i.e., the synonyms as well as the words in the box). Feed back with the whole class.

Answers

Model answers:

Valuation is a/an <u>fundamental/important</u> skill that all good managers have. When they <u>consider/plan/seek</u> a major investment project, clear valuation is essential. They must be able to <u>explain/make clear</u> to their <u>share/stock</u>holders how, for instance, they <u>calculate/work out</u> the <u>depreciation/loss in value</u> of fixed assets or the value of intangible assets such as goodwill. Whatever <u>technique/method</u> they use to value their company, it is <u>important/significant/key</u>

that they are honest, because regulation is now much tighter than before.

Language note

The use of words as synonyms often depends on the context. For example, although the base meanings of *important* and *significant* are synonymous as they are used in paragraph 4 of the reading text, in the last sentence of the gap-fill text they are not.

Exercise C

Set for pairwork. Feed back with the whole class. Note that not all the base words have specifically business meanings. Tell students to explain the meaning in business terms as far as possible.

Answers

Model answers:

Word	Base and meaning	Effect of affix	Meaning in text
central	centre (n, C) – the middle	~al = adjective ending	most important
investment	invest (v, T/I) – to spend money on something with a hope of future profit or benefit	~ment = a noun or adjective ending	what to spend money on
financial	finance 1 (n, U) – money and matters concerning money 2 (v, T) – to provide money for something	~ial = adjective ending	related to the use of money/investment
significant	signify (v, T/I) – mean, indicate	~icant = adjective ending	having sufficient shares to influence decision-making
commonplace	common (adj) – normal or ordinary	~place = adjective ending	fairly frequently used
likely	like (adj) – similar to	~ly = adverbial ending, but here used as an adjective ending	possible, potential
invested	invest (v, T/I) – to put money into a product or organization with a view to getting a financial return	~ed = past simple verb ending. Here it is used as a verb despite looking like an adjective.	describing the use of money to help a project succeed
intangible	tangible (adj) – something that has a physical reality, i.e., you can touch it	in~ = not	difficult to quantify elements of business like goodwill, brand value, etc.
incorrect	correct (adj) – something is factually true	in~ = not	inaccurate, untrue

large-scale	large (adj) – used to describe the relative size of an organization	~scale = size	involving big organizations or a lot of people, and attended by a lot of publicity

Exercise D

1 Copy the table headings from the Answers section onto the board and complete the example with the students. Tell them that when they look at the 'other verbs' column they may well find several, and should number each verb and subject/object/complement section separately. Point out that the order of each part of the sentence is not reflected in the table: the table is just a way to analyze the sentences.

Set the rest of the sentences for individual work and pairwork checking. Feed back with the whole class. Draw their attention to the 'main' parts of the sentence: it is very important in reading that they should be able to identify these. Notice also that the main parts can stand on their own and make complete sentences.

2 Set for individual work. If the clause is active, it should be changed to passive, and vice versa.

Answers

1 Model answers (see table):

	Main subject	Main verb	Main object/complement	Other verbs + their subjects + objects/complements	Adverbial phrases
A	the name (of the steel company)	has changed	to HSH (Haka Steel Holdings)	which* was known as LBS	in the UK, previously
B	three of the many ways	will be described		in which financial ratios can be calculated	here
C	managers	can also use	the DCF	which is useful, which requires some prediction, which is uncertain	obviously
D	a manager	must understand	the new, tighter financial accounts regulations	as well as not manipulating accounts	fully deliberately
E	some managers	have caused	a number of serious scandals	having manipulated accounts in the process of valuation	

*underlined text = means by which dependent clause is joined to main clause

2 Possible answers:
- A The board of directors/The company changed its name to HSH.
- B I/the author will describe three (of the many) ways (to calculate financial ratios).
- C The DCF can also be used (by managers).
- D Tighter financial accounts regulations must be understood (by a manager).
- E Serious scandals have been caused by managers.

Exercise E

This exercise involves looking carefully at the dependent clauses in sentences A–E.

1 Say that these clauses have special ways to link them to the main part of the sentence. Do this exercise with the whole class, using an OHT or other visual display of the table in Exercise D, and a highlighter pen to mark the relevant words. (A version of the table without underlining is included in the additional resources section – Resource 6G.) Go through the clauses, asking students what words or other ways are used to link the clauses to the main part of the sentence.

2 Set for individual work and pairwork checking. Students should look at each sentence and identify the antecedents of the relative pronouns. You could ask them to use a highlighter pen or to draw circles and arrows linking the words.

3 Students must be able to get the basic or kernel meaning of the clause. Take sentence A as an example and write it on the board. Point out that the relative pronouns and other ways of linking these clauses to the main clause will need to be changed or got rid of. Students should aim to write something that makes good sense as a complete sentence. They can break a sentence into shorter sentences if necessary.

Set the remaining clauses for individual work. Feed back with the whole class. Accept anything that makes good sense.

Answers

1 See table in Exercise D on the previous page. Sentences A–C use relative clauses. D and E use reduced or participle clauses.

2 A *which* = the old name of the company/LBS

  B *which* = ways

  C 1 *which* = the DCF

    2 *which* = the DCF

    3 *which* = prediction

3 Possible answers:

  A The steel company/HSH was previously known as LBS.

  B A financial ratio can be calculated in many ways.

  C 1 The DCF is useful.

    2 The DCF includes prediction.

    3 This element of prediction makes the reliability of DCF uncertain.

  D A manager must not deliberately manipulate accounts.

  E Some managers have manipulated their valuations.

Language note

A dependent clause contains a verb and a subject and is a secondary part of a sentence. It is dependent because it 'depends' on the main clause. A main clause can stand by itself as a complete sentence in its own right (usually). A dependent clause always goes with a main clause and cannot stand by itself as a sentence in its own right.

Dependent clauses are typically joined to main clauses with certain types of words: for example, relative pronouns (e.g., *who, which*), linking adverbials (e.g., *if, when, before, although, whereas*); words associated with reporting speech (e.g., *that,* a *Wh~* word such as *what* or *why*) and so on.

Some dependent clauses are non-finite; that is, they don't have a 'full verb' but a participle form (e.g., *having finished, opening*) and the subject may not be stated.

For more on this, see a good grammar reference book.

Closure

Write the following underlined beginnings and endings of words on the board or dictate them. Ask students to give the (or a) complete word. Accept alternatives and other parts of speech.

ob(ject)

bene(fit)

supp(ort)

fin(ance)

vers(ion)

(serv)ice

(strat)egy

(succ)ess

(portfo)lio

(analy)sis

(custo)mer

6.4 Extending skills

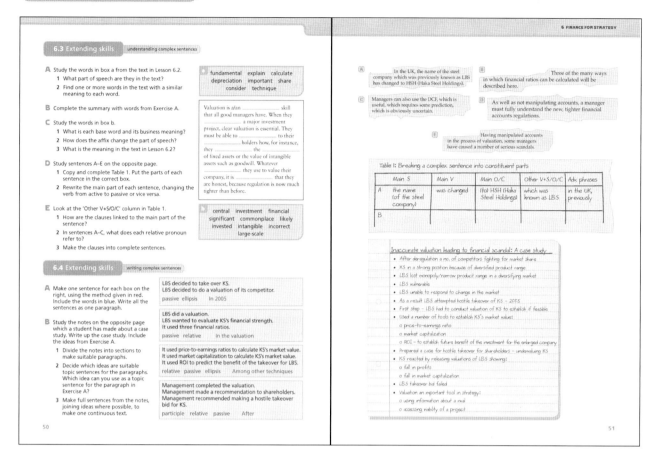

Lesson aims

- write complex sentences:

  with passives

  joining with participles

  embedding clauses

  adding prepositional phrases

Further practice in:

- writing topic sentences
- expanding a topic sentence into a paragraph

Introduction

Ask students to think about and discuss the following questions:

1 When might a company carry out a valuation of itself?

2 When might it carry out a valuation of another company?

Exercise A

Set for individual work and pairwork checking. If necessary, do the first box with the students. Make sure students understand that they should write the four sentences as a continuous paragraph.

Feed back with the whole class. Accept any answers that make good sense. Point out where the phrases in blue act as linkers between the sentences to make a continuous paragraph.

Answer

Possible answer:

In 2005, a decision was made by LBS to undertake a valuation of its competitor, Kumara Steel, and prepare for a takeover. In the valuation which was done to evaluate KS's financial strength in the market, financial ratios were used. Among other techniques, price-to-earnings ratio and market capitalization were used to calculate KS's market value, and then ROI was used to predict the benefit of the takeover to LBS. After completing the valuation, a recommendation was made to shareholders that LBS should mount a hostile takeover.

Exercise B

In this exercise, students are required to use all they have practised about sentence structure as well as revise what they know about topic sentences and paragraphing. Set for pairwork. Do not feed back after each question, but allow students to work through the questions, proceeding to write up the whole text.

They will need to decide where is the best place for the paragraph in Exercise A, and should also add this to their text. Students can change the wording and add extra phrases to help the flow of the text, as long as the sense remains the same.

If possible, pairs should write their text on an OHT or other visual display. Select two or three OHTs for display and comment by the whole class. Make any corrections on the text yourself with a coloured pen. Alternatively, circulate the transparencies to other pairs to correct and comment on. These pairs then display the corrected work and explain why they have made the corrections.

Answers

Possible answers:

1/2 Paragraph divisions are given below, with the possible topic sentences underlined. Note that other answers may be possible.

• _Inaccurate valuation leading to financial scandal_ • _After deregulation a no. of competitors fighting for market share_ • _KS in a strong position because of diversified product range_ • _LBS lost monopoly/narrow product range in diversifying market_ • _LBS vulnerable_ • _LBS unable to respond to change in the market_

• _As a result, LBS attempted hostile takeover of KS – 2005_
• First step – LBS had to conduct valuation of KS to establish if feasible
• Used a number of tools to establish KS's market value:
  – price-to-earnings ratio
  – market capitalization
  – ROI – to establish future benefit of the investment for the enlarged company
• Prepared a case for hostile takeover for shareholders – undervaluing KS

• _KS reacted by releasing valuations of LBS showing_
  – _fall in profits_
  – _fall in market capitalization_
• LBS takeover bid failed

• _Valuation is an important tool in strategy_
  – _using information about a rival_
  – _assessing viability of a project_

3 How can an inaccurate valuation lead to financial scandal? A good example is the case study of LBS in the steel market. After deregulation, a number of competitors were fighting for market share, one of which, KS, had a strong position because it had a diversified product range. LBS had lost its monopoly and had a narrow product range in a diversifying market. It was vulnerable and unable to react to market conditions.

In 2005, a decision was made by LBS to undertake a valuation of its competitor Kumara Steel and prepare for a takeover. In the valuation which was done to evaluate KS's financial strength in the market, financial ratios were used. Among other techniques, price-to-earnings ratio and market capitalization were used to calculate KS's market value, and then, ROI was used to predict the benefit of the takeover to LBS. After completing the valuation which had undervalued KS significantly, a recommendation was made to shareholders that LBS should mount a hostile takeover.

KS reacted to the takeover bid by releasing its own valuations of LBS. Its valuations showed that LBS was suffering from a fall in profits and market capitalization. The result of these revelations was that the takeover bid failed.

One conclusion we can draw from this case study is that valuation is an important tool for managers on two counts, first in assessing information and understanding rivals, and second, in assessing how viable an investment project, such as a takeover, may be.

Closure

Give students some very simple three- or four-word SVO/C sentences from the unit (or make some yourself) and ask them to add as many phrases and clauses as they can to make a long complex sentence. Who can make the longest sentence?

For example:

Valuation is effective.

➔ _As a tool for analyzing the financial position of a company, particularly if they use ratios such as price-to-earnings, market capitalization or return on investment, managers will find that valuation is effective, as long as they present information accurately, because inaccurate valuations can and often have in the past, led to financial scandals and the downfall of the managers concerned ..._
(62 words)

Extra activities

1 Work through the *Vocabulary bank* and *Skills bank* if you have not already done so, or as a revision of previous study.

2 Use the *Activity bank* (Teacher's Book additional resources section, Resource 6A).

  A Set the wordsearch for individual work (including homework) or pairwork.

    Answers

  B Students work in pairs or small groups and try to think of word pairs. They should be able to explain the meaning.

  Alternatively, photocopy (enlarged) the words from the additional resources section (Resource 6H) and cut up into cards. Put the A and B words into separate envelopes. Put students into groups of four. Make one set of A and one set of B words for each group. Give one pair in each group the A words and the other pair the B words. Each pair takes it in turns to pick a word from their envelope. The other pair must try to find a word from their own envelope which can go with it.

Accept all reasonable word pairs. Possible pairs are:

A	B
added	value
asset	management
cash	flow
competitor	analysis
current	asset
current	liabilities
customer	services
fixed	asset
fixed	liabilities
float	a company
historical	cost
human	judgement
investment	capital
labour	intensive
loan	money
market	capitalization
share	holding
share	portfolio
share	price
share	value
situation	analysis
unit	cost

7 BUDGETS, DECISIONS AND RISK

Unit 7 continues the theme of finance, homing in on two aspects of management accounting that are relevant to managers. The two ideas that are introduced by means of lecture excerpts are, firstly, management accounting and more specifically budgetary control, and, secondly, quantitative decision-making. The second listening extract is from a seminar discussion introducing the ideas behind risk analysis.

Skills focus

🎧 Listening
- understanding speaker emphasis

Speaking
- asking for clarification
- responding to queries and requests for clarification

Vocabulary focus
- compound nouns
- fixed phrases from management studies
- fixed phrases from academic English
- common lecture language

Key vocabulary
See also the list of fixed phrases from academic English in the *Vocabulary bank* (Course Book page 60).

accurate	forecasting (gerund)	profit/profitability
adverse	formula	qualitative
allocate	index	quantitative
alternative	indicator	resources
assumption	labour	revenue
break-even point	likelihood	risk
budget	liquidity	seasonal
budgetary control	long-term	short-term
contingency plan	management	statistical
course of action	accounting	target (n)
cyclical	mitigate (risk)	techniques
database	monitor	the former
deviation	multiplied by	the latter
eliminate	optimistic	threat
estimate	outcome	trends
favourable	overheads	uncertainty
financial accounting	performance	variable costs
fixed costs	pessimistic	variance
fluctuation	potential	
forecast (n and v)	predict	

7.1 Vocabulary

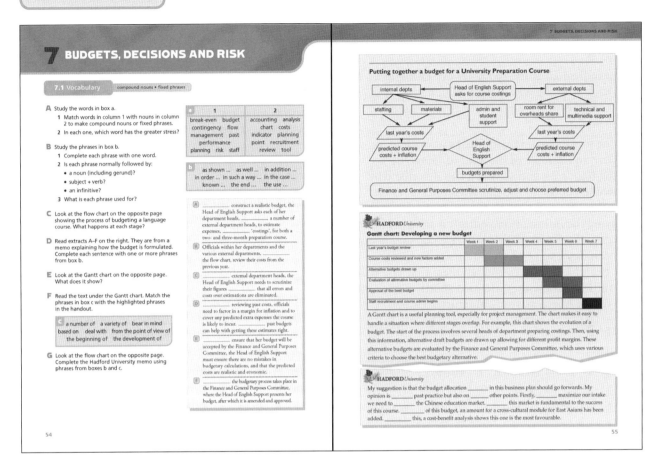

General note

Read the *Vocabulary bank* at the end of the Course Book unit. Decide when, if at all, to refer students to it. The best time is probably at the very end of the lesson or the beginning of the next lesson, as a summary/revision.

Lesson aims

- understand and use some general academic fixed phrases
- understand and use fixed phrases and compound nouns from the discipline

Introduction

1 Revise some noun phrases (noun + noun, adjective + noun) from previous units. Give students two or three minutes to make word stars with a base word, trying to find as many possible combinations as they can (preferably without having to look at dictionaries). For example:

Other base words which could be used are *job, company, goods, management, finance*. If they are stuck for ideas, tell them to look back at previous units.

2 Introduce the topic of the lesson by finding out what students know about what a budget is, what processes are involved in preparing a budget and what factors a manager would have to consider when preparing a budget.

Exercise A

Set for individual work and pairwork checking. Feed back with the whole class, making sure that the stress pattern is correct. Ask students to suggest other fixed phrases which could be made using the words in column 2.

Answers

Model answers:

break-'even	point
'management	accounting
per'formance	indicator
'past	costs
con'tingency	planning
'flow	chart
'staff	recruitment

115

'budget	review
'planning	tool
'risk	analysis

Exercise B

1/2 Set for individual work and pairwork checking. Feed back with the whole class, building the first three columns of the table in the Answers section on the board.

3 Add the fourth column with the heading 'Use to …'. Give an example of the kind of thing you are looking for, i.e., a phrase which can describe why you would choose to use this fixed phrase. Elicit suggestions from the students to complete the table, supplying the information yourself if students do not know the answer. If students are not sure about the meaning of some of the phrases, give them some example sentences and tell them that you will look further at how they are used shortly. Leave the table on the board as you will return to it.

Answers

Model answers:

Phrase		Followed by …	Use to …
as shown	in/by	noun/gerund	indicate a diagram or table or case law
as well	as	noun/gerund	add information
in addition	to	noun/gerund	add information
in order	to	infinitive	give the purpose for doing something
in such a way	that*	subject + verb	give the result of doing something
in the case	of	noun/gerund	mention something
known	as	noun	give the special name for something
the end	of	noun	refer to the end of something
the use	of	noun	refer to the use of something

*as to is also possible after *in such a way*, although in this exercise, one word is required

Exercise C

Set for pairwork. Students should try to identify what each stage of the flow chart represents. One pair can describe each stage to the whole class. On the board, build up as many key words to describe the process as students can come up with. If students do not know some important words, assure them they will come across them shortly.

Answers

Answers depend on the students.

Exercise D

Explain that the information from the leaflet goes with the flow chart they have just discussed. Each extract (A–F) goes with one stage. Students should first read the extracts, checking words they cannot guess in the dictionary. They should not pay attention to the spaces at this point.

Set for individual work. Refer back to the box in Exercise B, which will help students to choose the correct phrase. Feed back with the whole class.

Answers

Model answers:

A <u>In order to</u> construct a realistic budget, the Head of English Support asks each of her department heads, <u>as well as</u> a number of external department heads, to estimate expenses, known as 'costings', for both a two- and three-month preparation course.
B Officials within her departments and the various external departments, <u>as shown in</u> the flow chart, review their costs from the previous year.
C <u>In the case of</u> external department heads, the Head of English Support needs to scrutinize their figures <u>in such a way</u> that all errors and costs over estimations are eliminated.
D <u>In addition</u> to reviewing past costs, officials need to factor in a margin for inflation and to cover any predicted extra expenses the course is likely to incur. <u>The use of</u> past budgets can help with getting these estimates right.
E <u>In order to</u> ensure that her budget will be accepted by the Finance and General Purposes Committee, the Head of English Support must ensure there are no mistakes in budgetary calculations, and that the predicted costs are realistic and economic.
F <u>The end of</u> the budgetary process takes place in the Finance and General Purposes Committee, where the Head of English Support presents her budget, after which it is amended and approved.

If you wish, ask students to return to the table in Exercise B and write one sentence for each of the fixed phrases to show their meaning.

Exercise E

Introduce the Gantt chart – if students have not seen one before – by saying that it is a highly important tool in project management. It shows how different stages in a process follow each other and/or overlap.

Set for pairwork discussion. Feed back with the whole group, making sure that students understand the concept behind the chart. Do not correct or confirm students' views of the content at this point.

Subject note

The Gantt chart was the invention of Henry Laurence Gantt (1861–1919), who was a mechanical engineer. Gantt developed his charts in the early 20th century. His invention was hugely important in management then as well as now. It can be used for large-scale projects as well as for small pieces of work that an individual person may have to do.

Exercise F

Set for individual work and pairwork checking. Students should use their dictionaries if they are not sure of the meaning of the phrases. Note that some phrases can be used for the same thing, but it is a good idea to use a different word to avoid repetition. Ask students to say which sentence goes with which part of the chart. Which part of the diagram is not mentioned?

Answers

Model answers:

A Gantt chart is a useful planning tool, especially (*for*) from the point of view of project management. The chart makes it easy to (*handle*) deal with a situation where (*different*) a number of stages overlap. For example, this chart shows (*the evolution of*) the development of a budget. (*The start of*) The beginning of the process involves (*several*) a number of heads of department preparing costings. Then, (*using*) based on this information, alternative draft budgets are drawn up allowing for different profit margins. These alternative budgets are evaluated by the Finance and General Purposes Committee, which (*uses*) bears in mind (*various*) a number of/a variety of criteria to choose the best budgetary alternative.

Language note

The fixed phrases here are used in a situation which describes a series of chronological stages. However, the same words can be used when writing or talking in more general abstract academic terms, for example when introducing an essay, lecture or piece of research. This use of these words will be covered later in the unit.

Exercise G

Set for pairwork. Feed back with the whole class.

Answers

Model answers:

My suggestion is that the budget allocation (as) shown in this business plan should go forwards. My opinion is based on past practice but also on a number of other

points. Firstly, in order to maximize our intake we need to bear in mind the Chinese education market. The development of this market is fundamental to the success of this course. In the case of this budget, an amount for a cross-cultural module for East Asians has been added. In addition to/As well as this, a cost-benefit analysis shows this one is the most favourable.

Closure

Tell students to close their books and then describe:

- the typical main stages of a planning process, e.g., budget formulation
- what a typical Gantt chart looks like and what it includes

7.2 Listening

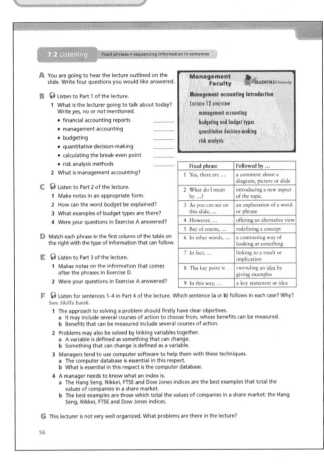

Lesson aims

- improve comprehension through recognition of fixed phrases and what follows them in terms of words/type of information
- understand how information can be sequenced in different ways within a sentence, e.g., for emphasis (see *Skills bank*).

Further practice in:
- understanding fractured text

General note

Read the *Skills bank – 'Given' and 'new' information in sentences* at the end of the Course Book unit. Decide when, if at all, to refer students to it. The best time, as before, is probably at the very end of the lesson or the beginning of the next lesson, as a summary/revision. Alternatively, use the *Skills bank* in conjunction with Exercise F.

Introduction

Review key vocabulary by writing a selection of words from Lesson 7.1 on the board and asking students to put them into phrases of two or more words.

Exercise A

Remind students about preparing for a lecture. If you wish, review Unit 1 *Skills bank – Making the most of lectures*. Remind students that, when they begin their talks, lecturers usually provide their listeners with an outline in order to aid comprehension. Elicit from the students the kinds of signpost words lecturers might use (e.g., *To start with, … , Firstly, … , I'll begin/start by ~ing*, etc.). If necessary, refer students to Unit 5.

Refer students to the lecture slide. Tell them to look at the title and bullet points and to list ideas/make questions for each bullet point. At this stage, do not explain any words from the slide or allow students to check in their dictionaries, as the meanings will be dealt with in the lecture. Set the exercise for pairwork.

Feed back with the whole class: ask several students to read out their questions. Write some of the questions on the board.

🎧 Exercise B

Tell students they are going to hear the introduction to the lecture – not the whole thing. Give students time to read questions 1 and 2. Remind them they will only hear the recording once. Play Part 1. Allow students to compare their answers.

Feed back. Confirm the correct answers.

Answers

Model answers:

1

financial accounting reports	no
management accounting	yes
budgeting	yes
quantitative decision-making	yes
calculating the break-even point	no
risk analysis methods	not mentioned

2 Management accounting is generally about the *future* and *possibility*. It includes costing items or projects to break even or make profit, and controlling budgeting based on forecasting turnover and expenditure.

Transcript 🎧 1.31

Part 1

Good morning, everyone. What I'm going to talk about today is the financial concerns of managers at all levels: that is, budgeting and quantitative decision-making. These come under the heading of management accounting … though bear in mind that management accounting is quite different from financial accounting. The former is about budgets and reports that help managers think about the *future* within a company in their day-to-day work, whereas the latter – financial accounting – is about producing reports about the present and *past* for people outside the company, such as the tax department or shareholders, plus of course, the general public, including students like you! So the likes of budgeting control *inside* a company, just for managers ... is known as 'management accounting'. It includes forecasting sales or revenues coming in, and allocating budgets for spending. It's all about controlling and reviewing these budgets to manage a business's working capital and liquidity.

Now, um ... in later lectures, we'll go into more detail on costing jobs and projects and calculating break-even point – what I mean by that is the lowest level of sales so that your profits just cover your costs. It's the minimum to survive and not make a loss. But today we will just deal with budgeting and quantitative decision-making. OK, let's begin ...

🎧 Exercise C

Refer students to the second point on the lecture slide ('budgeting and budget types'). Ask students to suggest an appropriate type of notes. The key word here is *types*, which should trigger the idea of a tree diagram (see Unit 1).

Give students time to read the questions. Play Part 2.

Put students in pairs to compare their diagrams and discuss the questions. Because the information in the lecture is compact, if the class is weak or notes are patchy, you may wish to replay Part 2.

With the whole class, ask students how many answers to their questions in Exercise A they heard. Build the tree diagram from the Answers, at the same time checking the answers to questions 2 and 3.

Answer

Model answers:

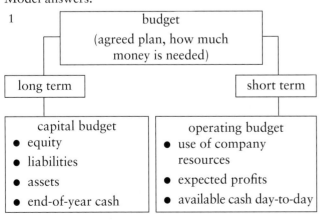

2 an agreed plan of money needed

3 capital budget, operating budget, short-term, long-term

4 Answers depend on students' questions.

Transcript 🎧 1.32
Part 2

As we have seen in the seminars this week, a budget is usually thought of as an 'agreed plan', usually made one year in advance, which details how much money is needed. As I said, a budget normally has to be prepared every year, but there can be short-term as well as long-term ones. Examples of the long-term are capital budgets. These look at equity, liabilities, assets and end-of-year cash over longer periods. On the other hand, shorter-term ones include operating budgets which plan the use of a company's resources over time, looking at the profits expected – perhaps daily, weekly or monthly – and the day-to-day cash available.

Exercise D

Explain that these are common phrases in an academic context such as a lecture. Knowing the meaning of the phrases will help a lot with comprehension. Make sure students understand that the items in the second column are not in the correct order.

Set for individual work and pairwork checking. Tell students to check the meaning of any words they do not know in a dictionary. They should be able to guess the meanings of the phrases, even if they do not actually know the phrases.

Feed back with the whole class, completing the first two columns of the chart in the Answers section for Exercise E on the board. (Alternatively, make an OHT from Resource 7B in the additional resources section.) Once this is completed, it will act as a predictive support for Part 3 of the lecture.

Methodology note

Two-column activities are good for pair checking and practice. Once students have got the correct answers, they can test each other in pairs. Student A covers the first column and tries to remember the phrases, then B covers the second column and tries to remember the purpose of each phrase.

You can then check memory by getting students to close their books and giving a phrase; students (as a group or individually) must give its purpose. Then change roles.

🎧 Exercise E

1 Tell students that in the next part of the lecture they will hear the phrases in Exercise D. They

know now what *type* of information is likely to follow. Now they must try to hear what *actual* information is given. If you wish, photocopy the table in the additional resources section (Resource 7B) for students to write their answers on.

Do the first one as an example. Play the first sentence and stop after *difficulties in budgeting*. Ask students: *What is the important concept?* (Answer: *difficulties in budgeting.*)

Play the rest of the recording, pausing briefly now and again to allow students to make notes. Put students in pairs to check their answers.

Feed back with the whole class, asking questions based on the words in the 'Followed by ...' column. For example:
After phrase number 2, what is the word or phrase that is explained?
After phrase number 3, what is the diagram that is commented on?

2 Refer back to students' questions in Exercise A. Discuss with the whole class whether they heard any answers to their questions. Note that this task builds on and reinforces task C4.

Answers

Model answers:

1

Fixed phrase	Followed by ...	Actual information (suggested answers)
1 Yes, there are ...	introducing a new aspect of the topic	difficulties of budgeting
2 What do I mean by ...?	an explanation of a word or phrase	explanation of historical data
3 As you can see on this slide, ...	a comment about a diagram, picture or slide	example on a slide
4 However, ...	a contrasting way of looking at something	qualitative approaches
5 But of course, ...	offering an alternative view	advantages of budgets (having looked at problems)
6 In other words, ...	redefining a concept	redefining favourable and adverse variance
7 In fact, ...	extending an idea by giving examples	different types of variances
8 The key point is ...	a key statement or idea	the idea of analyzing variance
9 In this way, ...	linking to a result or implication	the importance of accuracy of budgets

2 Answers depend on students' questions.

Transcript 🎧 1.33

Part 3

Yes, there are difficulties in budgeting: it is hard to rely on historical data for predicting what will come in the future. What do I mean by 'historical data'? Forecasting is usually based on 'back data' (data from the past), and managers will use it to try to look for trends or predictable changes, such as cyclical or seasonal fluctuations. This kind of predicting is usually *quantitative*, which means mathematical. (As you can see on this slide, an example of a tool to use for this is 'time series analysis').

However, looking at it another way, there are *qualitative* approaches. This is the opposite of quantitative, and it means asking experts for their opinions.

So it's not straightforward. There are challenges in predicting. And all of this is costly. Yes, quite expensive. It is also difficult to collect all the information for budgets and it takes time. Budgeting may also cause conflict over limited funds between departments or staff.

But, of course, budgeting has its advantages: budgets help control spending, and they let managers review and correct problems. They make managers more responsible and give them clearer targets and easier coordination and communication.

A budget can have a favourable variance or an adverse variance. In other words, if the revenues or savings are better than expected, it is 'favourable' variance, and if they are worse than expected, it is 'adverse' variance. In fact, managers may experience many different kinds: profit variances, materials or labour variances, or overheads variances. They might have sales margin variances or cash variances.

Why does this matter? Well, the point is that analyzing the variance from what was budgeted allows the manager to monitor performance and then find the causes. In this way, they can be more accurate in the future.

🎧 Exercise F

The purpose of this exercise is to look at how information tends to be structured in sentences. It also requires very close attention to the listening text.

Before listening, allow students time to read through the sentences. In pairs, set them to discuss which sentence (**a** or **b**) they think will follow the numbered sentences.

Play Part 4 all the way through. Students should choose sentence **a** or **b**. Put them in pairs to check and discuss why **a** or **b** was the sentence they heard.

Feed back with the whole class. Deal with sentences 1 and 2 first. Tell students that all the sentences are correct, but sentence a 'sounds better' when it comes after the first sentence. This is because of the way that sentences go together and the way in which information is organized in a sentence. Draw the table below on the board. Show how the underlined words in the second sentence have been mentioned in the first sentence. In the second sentence, the underlined words are 'old' or 'given' information. When sentences follow each other

in a conversation (or a piece of writing), usually the 'given' information comes in the first part of a sentence.

Now look at sentences 3 and 4. These are different. The normal choice would be the a sentences. However, here the speaker wanted to emphasize the idea of 'important' and 'different'. So a Wh~ cleft sentence structure was used, which changes the usual order of information. Show this on the table, as below. This 'fronting' of information has the effect of special focus for emphasis.

First sentence		Second sentence	
		Given information	New information
1 The approach to solving a problem should firstly have clear objectives.		It may include ...	... several courses of action to choose from, whose benefits can be measured.
2 Problems may also be solved by linking variables together.		A variable ...	... is defined as something that can change.
3 Managers tend to use computer software to help them with these techniques.	normal order	a The computer ...	... database is essential in this respect.
	special focus	b What is essential in this respect is the computer ...	... database.
4 A manager needs to know what an index is.	normal order	a The Hang Seng, Nikkei, FTSE and Dow Jones indices are the best examples ...	that total the values of companies in a share market.
	special focus	b The best examples are those which ...	total the values of companies in a share market: the Hang Seng, Nikkei, FTSE and Dow Jones indices.

Further examples of different ways to 'front' information and more practice will be given in Lesson 7.3.

Language note

In English, important information can be placed at the beginning or at the end of a sentence. There are two types of important information. The first part of the sentence contains the topic and the second part contains some kind of information or comment about the topic. Usually, the comment is the more syntactically complicated part of the sentence.

Once a piece of text or a piece of conversation (i.e., a piece of discourse) has gone beyond the first sentence, a 'given'/'new' principle operates. Information which is 'given', in other words that has already been mentioned, goes at the beginning of the sentence. Normally speaking, information which is new goes at the end of the sentence. So in the second sentence of a piece of discourse, an aspect of the comment from the previous sentence may become the topic. Thus, the topic of the second sentence, if it has already been mentioned in the previous sentence, is also 'given'. Of course, the given information may not be referred to with

exactly the same words in the second sentence. Other ways to refer to the given information include reference words (*it, he, she, this, that, these, those,* etc.) or vocabulary items with similar meanings.

Information structure is covered in the *Skills bank* in the Course Book unit.

Transcript 🎧 1.34

Part 4

Now ... er ... let's see ... oh dear, we're running short of time ... but perhaps I should just say something about *quantitative decision-making*, as it is a basic tool for all managers.

In a nutshell, quantitative analysis is an important skill for managers involved in the business decision-making process, and they use various methods for solving problems using statistical techniques, such as the normal distribution model, and others.

The approach to solving a problem should firstly have clear objectives. It may include several courses of action to choose from, whose benefits can be measured. That is to say, they should have measurable options to compare. Each option, being uncertain, has a probability attached to the outcome. The manager, therefore, applies probabilities to each alternative outcome. A probability is a likelihood – how likely it is that something will happen. It measures uncertainty. Each option has a percentage probability applied to it.

Problems may also be solved by linking variables together. A variable is defined as something that can change. For example, it may be useful to know if you can find a relationship between one variable – the summertime fall in sales of a product, for instance – and another – say, the summer demand for certain product types in a market. Maths and statistics can help us find such connections.

Managers tend to use computer software to help them with these techniques. What is essential in this respect is the computer database. Company and government databases, for instance, are good places to find financial information. Managers must learn how to get computers to help them manipulate data such as cost data, profit and revenue data or supply and demand data.

And I must mention indices, too. A manager needs to know what an index is – it's an average number based on several sources to illustrate a trend. The best examples are those which total the values of companies in a share market: the Hang Seng, Nikkei, FTSE and Dow Jones indices. And then, of course, there are ratios. Now ... ah, OK ... I see that time is moving on. So, I'm just going to ...

which features belong to its type of accounting. When they have finished, ask each group to compare its choices with those of the other group. Help students to formulate a correct list as a whole-class activity.

is for public consumption ➜ information is for departmental use

includes summary info on assets ➜ includes daily cash flow analysis

includes summary info on liabilities ➜ allocates future spending

is mostly concerned with reporting the past ➜ forecasts sales

reports on revenue – how it was spent ➜ asks why variances exist

Model answer:

management accounting	financial accounting
information is for departmental use	is for public consumption
can involve a range of different time scales	includes summary info on assets
includes daily cash flow analysis	includes summary info on liabilities
allocates future spending	is mostly concerned with reporting the past
forecasts sales	reports on revenue – how it was spent
asks why variances exist	

Exercise G

Set for pairwork discussion. Feed back with the whole class. Note that the lecture has not yet finished. The last part will be heard in Lesson 7.3.

Answer

Model answers:

The lecturer is running out of time. He has not had time to talk about ratios.

Closure

Write the terms *management accounting* and *financial accounting* on the board. Group students into two groups, A and B. Assign group A students to *management accounting* and group B students to *financial accounting*. Give each group the list below. Alternatively, for a stronger group, write the phrases on the board in a random order. Ask each group to decide

7.3 Extending skills

Lesson aims

- extend knowledge of fixed phrases commonly used in lectures
- give sentences a special focus (see *Skills bank*)

Further practice in:

- stress within words

Introduction

As in Units 3 and 5, tell students to ask you questions about the information in the lecture in Lesson 7.2 as if you were the lecturer. Remind them about asking for information politely. If they need to revise how to do this, tell them to look back at the *Skills bank* for Unit 3.

🎧 Exercise A

Remind students of the importance of stressed syllables in words (see the teaching notes for Unit 3, Lesson 3.3, Exercise A). Play the recording, pausing after the first few to check that students understand the task.

Feed back, perhaps playing the recording again for each word before checking. Ideally, mark up an OHT or other visual projection of the words. Finally, check students' pronunciation of the words.

Answers

Possible answers:

allocate	7
alternative	10
contingency	1
database	8
financial	11
fluctuation	2
index	9
liquidity	5
mitigate	12
quantitative	4
technique	6
variance	3

Transcript 🎧 1.35

1 con'tingency
2 fluctu'ation
3 'variance
4 'quantitative
5 li'quidity
6 tech'nique
7 'allocate
8 'database
9 'index
10 al'ternative
11 fi'nancial
12 'mitigate

🎧 Exercise B

Write these words on the board and ask students to say what symbols you can use for them when taking notes. Put the symbols on the board.

∵	because
e.g.	for example
=	is, means
→	invented, leads to*
←	from
cf.	compare(d) with
∴	therefore, so
& +	and
numbers or bullet points	a list
/	or
>	is greater than
<	is less than

*the arrow has a wide range of possible meanings, including *made, produced, did, causes, results in.*

Ask students what other symbols they use when taking notes. Add them to the list on the board.

Tell students they will hear the final part of the lecture. Ask them to read the notes through. Remind them also to listen for their research task. Play Part 5.

Put students in pairs to compare their symbols. Feed back with the whole class, if possible using an OHT of the notes. Discuss acceptable alternatives, e.g., *start & finish* instead of *start/finish*.

Answers

Model answers:

1 Budgetary control = highly complex task ...
  1 some factors = outside mgmnt control
    (controllable/uncontrollable costs)
      e.g., dept's ad budget = controllable
    co-wide ad budget = uncontrollable
  2 fixed/variable costs
      fixed costs = like admin salaries
      variable costs = costs depend'g on production
  3 managers' budgeting target ∴ variation from budget <10%
  4 Balanced Scorecard → Kaplan & Norton (1992)
      • Measures key performance indicators → see if strategies are successful
      e.g., Mobil adopts BSC, ∴ movement (last → first place profitab.)

2 They must research what business risks mean for a manager.

Transcript 🎧 1.36

Part 5

I'm going to finish off with some final comments on this area of management accounting – in other words, budgetary control.

Now, the fact of the matter is, for management, it's a highly complex task to plan a budget. The reason for this is that calculating future costs and sales using forecasting techniques is highly involved and assessing the results is equally so – not to mention the fact that some factors are totally outside the control of management.

Let's take costs: we talk about controllable and uncontrollable costs, and it is important for a manager to be able to identify which is which. Your department's advertising might be controllable as you can reduce the expense if you need to. Yet, company-wide advertising spending might be uncontrollable.

You've probably heard about fixed costs and variable costs. Fixed costs are your overheads that stay the same no matter how much you produce (like the receptionist's and CEO's salaries). Many fixed costs are uncontrollable but some are controllable. Variable costs depend on how much you produce, or use (so for an airline, fuel is a variable cost).

Plus there's the fact that forecasting never completely eliminates uncertainty. Optimistic forecasts mean cash is tied up in slow-moving stocks. Pessimistic forecasts mean poor revenues or unhappy customers. You can test assumptions of your budgeting, collect relevant facts to be informed, compare past forecasts with current performance, etcetera, etcetera, to try to make the deviation from your budget less than ten per cent.

Now to quickly mention the 'Balanced Scorecard'. It was Kaplan and Norton who came up with this very simple idea to help managers measure. It looks at key performance indicators for seeing if strategy is successful, and what we've covered today (internal financial performance) is one key indicator. The advantage of the Balanced Scorecard is that it works. It really makes companies perform. Exxon Mobil moved from last to first in its industry in terms of profitability after adopting the Balanced Scorecard. It was in 1992 that Kaplan and Norton came up with this tool, and it is very much in use today.

To sum up, then, budgets must be carefully planned. Let me put it another way ... planning is a sophisticated quantitative process involving forecasting and understanding costs.

Oh, I almost forgot to mention your research topic. We've mentioned quantitative decision-making. OK, well, what's very important for any manager to have is skills in decision-making involving the assessment of *risk*. So I'd like you to find out what business risk actually means for a manager. See you next week.

Exercise C

Set for pairwork. Feed back with the whole class. If necessary, play the relevant sections again. Ask for other phrases which have similar meanings, particularly from earlier in the unit, and also from Unit 5. Build the table in the Answers section on the board. Accept any suitable words or phrases for the third column.

Answers

Model answers:

Use	Fixed phrase	Other phrases
to introduce a new topic	You've probably heard about …	Now, an important concept is …
to emphasize a major point	The fact of the matter is, …	Actually, … In fact, … The point is that …
to add points	Not to mention the fact that … Plus there's the fact that …	also, and, too
to finish a list	etcetera	and so on, among others
to give an example	Let's take …	For example, … e.g., … Let's look at an example of this. For instance, …
to restate	In other words, … Let me put it another way.	What I mean is … That is to say, … By that I mean … To put it another way, …

Language note

The phrases above are appropriate in speaking. Some are less suitable for written language, for which different phrases should be used.

Exercise D

Students need to restructure each sentence in order to rewrite them. Depending on the class, they can work in pairs or individually first.

Feed back with the whole class. Take each sentence in turn. Ask for suggestions as to which aspect could receive special emphasis (actual words are underlined below). Accept any reasonable answers. If you wish, replay Part 5 of the lecture for students to check their answers. Note that:

- sentences 1, 2 and the first part of 4 use an *It* construction to give the special focus
- sentence 3 uses a *Wh~* cleft sentence already seen in Lesson 7.2
- sentences 4 and 5 introduce new, general words (often found in academic contexts) followed by *is* plus a *that* clause

Answers

Model answers:

1 Kaplan and Norton came up with an idea to help with measuring performance. (*It*)
It was Kaplan and Norton who came up with an idea to help with measuring performance.

2 Kaplan and Norton invented the Balanced Scorecard in 1992. (*It*)
It was in 1992 that Kaplan and Norton invented the Balanced Scorecard.

3 Management accounting is very important for managing working capital and liquidity. (*What*)
What is very important for managing working capital and liquidity is management accounting.

4 Budgeting is complex because planning decisions are based on highly involved calculations. (*Two sentences. First = 'It'; Second = 'The reason'*)
It is a complex task to plan a budget. The reason for this is that planning decisions are based on highly involved calculations.

5 The Balanced Scorecard uses key performance indicators to measure the success of a strategy. (*The advantage*)
The advantage of the Balanced Scorecard is that it uses key performance indicators to measure the success of a strategy.

After completing Exercises C and D, students can be referred to the *Vocabulary bank* and the *Skills bank* for consolidation and preparation for Exercise E.

Exercise E

Set the initial preparation for individual work. Students can refer to their notes in Lesson 7.2 (Exercises C and E) or the notes for completion in Lesson 7.3 (Exercise B). They should think about how they can use the phrases they have looked at, and ways of giving special focus/ emphasis. (Note: They should not write out exactly what they are going to say in complete sentences and then read!)

Put students in pairs to give their oral summaries to each other, preferably pairing students who have chosen different sections to summarize.

Go around the class monitoring closely and noting any problems or especially good examples of language use.

You may wish to choose one or two individuals to give their summary to the whole class.

With the whole class, feed back on any language or other difficulties which you noticed.

Closure

Dictate some words for which students have learnt note-taking symbols or abbreviations such as *and, minus, approximately, less than, results in, therefore, because, etc., as, since, for example, approximately*. Students should write the symbol or abbreviation.

Remind them of the list of symbols and abbreviations at the back of the Course Book.

7.4 Extending skills

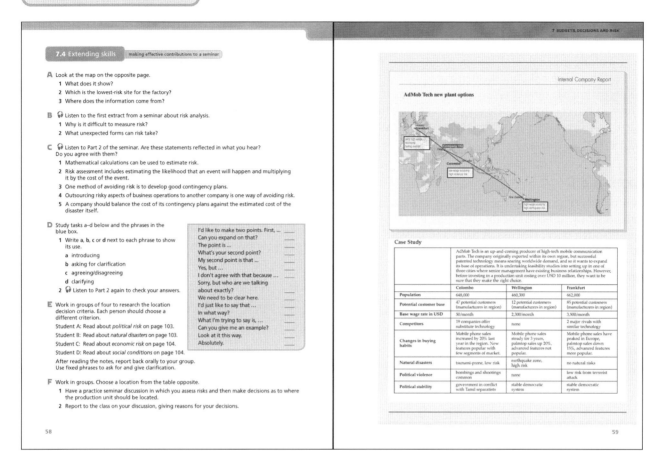

7 BUDGETS, DECISIONS AND RISK

7.4 Extending skills | making effective contributions to a seminar

A Look at the map on the opposite page.
1 What does it show?
2 Which is the lowest-risk site for the factory?
3 Where does the information come from?

B Listen to the first extract from a seminar about risk analysis.
1 Why is it difficult to measure risk?
2 What unexpected forms can risk take?

C Listen to Part 2 of the seminar. Are these statements reflected in what you hear? Do you agree with them?
1 Mathematical calculations can be used to estimate risk.
2 Risk assessment includes estimating the likelihood that an event will happen and multiplying it by the cost of the event.
3 One method of avoiding risk is to develop good contingency plans.
4 Outsourcing risky aspects of business operations to another company is one way of avoiding risk.
5 A company should balance the cost of its contingency plans against the estimated cost of the disaster itself.

D Study tasks a–d below and the phrases in the blue box.
1 Write a, b, c or d next to each phrase to show its use.
a introducing
b asking for clarification
c agreeing/disagreeing
d clarifying
2 Listen to Part 2 again to check your answers.

E Work in groups of four to research the location decision criteria. Each person should choose a different criterion.
Student A: Read about *political risk* on page 103.
Student B: Read about *natural disasters* on page 103.
Student C: Read about *economic risk* on page 104.
Student D: Read about *social conditions* on page 104.
After reading the notes, report back orally to your group. Use fixed phrases to ask for and give clarification.

F Work in groups. Choose a location from the table opposite.
1 Have a practice seminar discussion in which you assess risks and then make decisions as to where the production unit should be located.
2 Report to the class on your discussion, giving reasons for your decisions.

I'd like to make two points. First, …
Can you expand on that?
The point is …
What's your second point?
My second point is that …
Yes, but …
I don't agree with that because …
Sorry, but who are we talking about exactly?
We need to be clear here.
I'd just like to say that …
In what way?
What I'm trying to say is, …
Can you give me an example?
Look at it this way.
Absolutely.

Internal Company Report

AdMob Tech new plant options

Case Study

AdMob Tech is an up-and-coming producer of high-tech mobile communication parts. The company originally exported within its own region, but successful patented technology means soaring worldwide demand, and so it wants to expand its base of operations. It is undertaking feasibility studies into setting up in one of three cities where senior management have existing business relationships. However, before investing in a production unit costing over USD 10 million, they want to be sure that they make the right choice.

	Colombo	Wellington	Frankfurt
Population	648,000	460,300	662,000
Potential customer base	47 potential customers (manufacturers in region)	12 potential customers (manufacturers in region)	85 potential customers (manufacturers in region)
Base wage rate in USD	50/month	2,300/month	3,500/month
Competitors	39 companies offer substitute technology	none	2 major rivals with similar technology
Changes in buying habits	Mobile phone sales increased by 20% last year in the region. New features popular with few segments of market.	Mobile phone sales steady for 3 years, palmtop sales up 20%, advanced features not popular.	Mobile phone sales have peaked in Europe, palmtop sales down 15%, advanced features more popular.
Natural disasters	tsunami-prone, low risk	earthquake zone, high risk	no natural risks
Political violence	bombings and shootings common	none	low risk from terrorist attack
Political stability	government in conflict with Tamil separatists	stable democratic system	stable democratic system

58

59

Lesson aims

- make effective contributions to a seminar:
  using pre-organizers – *I'd like to make two points; I don't agree with that because …*
  responding to queries by clarifying – *What I'm trying to say is … ; What I meant was …*

Introduction

Revise phrases from the previous lessons. Give a word or phrase and ask students to give one with a similar meaning. Ask for phrases from the previous lesson which can be used to:

- introduce a new topic
- emphasize a major point
- add a point
- finish a list
- give an example

Exercise A

Set for pairwork discussion. Feed back.

Answers

Possible answers:

1 It shows four potential cities for a new plant for AdMob Tech.

2 Accept any reasonable answer as long as students can justify their choice.

3 The information comes from an internal company report.

🎧 Exercise B

Allow students time to read the two questions. Play Part 1 once only. Check answers in pairs. Feed back with the whole class.

Answers

Model answers:

1 We can try to measure risk, but it often takes unexpected forms.

2 Some of the unexpected forms risk can take include new competitors, changes in buyers' habits and disasters that are outside your control.

Transcript 🎧 1.37

Part 1

Now, as we know, *risk analysis* is a complex process that every manager must be familiar with before making investment decisions of any sort. We can try to measure risk, but it often takes unexpected forms: new competitors appearing, changes in buyers' habits, disasters outside of your control that delay a project. So, let's have some of your views.

🎧 Exercise C

Allow students time to read the questions and discuss them. Check any difficult vocabulary. Play Part 2 straight through once. Discuss in pairs and/or with the whole class.

Answers

All these statements are reflected in the seminar. Accept any reasonable additional comments from students.

Transcript 🎧 1.38

Note: The underlining relates to Exercise D.

Part 2

JACK: Well, <u>I'd like to make two points. First,</u> risk can be defined as the 'perceived extent of potential losses'.

LEILA: <u>Can you expand on that,</u> Jack?

JACK: Sure, Leila. Different people are affected differently by the outcomes of things. So a small risk for you or me may potentially destroy the life of someone else.

LEILA: So?

JACK: So <u>the point is</u> that there are different views about what business risk actually means in a given situation – different points of view.

LECTURER: OK. So, <u>what's your second point,</u> Jack?

JACK: I was coming to that! <u>My second point is that</u> there is a good formula for working out risk. Risk equals the likelihood of an event multiplied by the cost of the event. This way, you can compare risks objectively.

LEILA: <u>Yes, but</u> … that doesn't really work for all things. It kind of depends on the type of risk, doesn't it? I mean, there's human illness or death, there's loss of reputation through scandals, there's risk of natural disasters like floods or disease … all of them quite different from your usual risks like political change, share market crashes or projects taking too long.

MAJED: Well, <u>I don't agree with that,</u> Leila, <u>because</u> from what I've read, you just apply the formula to anything. You just have to understand the probability of it properly.

EVIE: <u>Sorry, but who are we talking about exactly?</u> Small businesses? Big businesses? Managers in charge of projects? What size?

MAJED: Yes, <u>we need to be clear here</u>. It must be all of them, but it's especially relevant for larger businesses, I think. <u>I'd just like to say that</u> according to what I've read, risk analysts have very clear jobs. They estimate what threats they face. Then they estimate the chance of it happening. Then they multiply them together. And thus they have a value to compare with other scenarios. They can use this when they are managing risk.

EVIE: <u>In what way?</u>

LEILA: Well, when you manage risk there is no point in spending more in avoiding the risk than the cost of the event if it happened.

EVIE: I don't get that. What do you mean?

LEILA: <u>What I'm trying to say is,</u> some risks you have to accept rather than using too much of your resources trying to avoid.

MAJED: I still don't understand. <u>Can you give me an example,</u> Leila?

LEILA: OK. <u>Look at it this way</u>. You could avoid risk by making your operations more efficient or making people more accountable for things. Or you could develop contingency plans for when things go wrong – like having an emergency fund. Or you could outsource the risky aspects to another company to do and pay them to make them carry the risk. They guarantee to deliver the goods to you, whatever happens. But all of these choices are expensive. None of them should cost more than what would happen if the threat actually happened.

MAJED: Like if a competitor came and took your market share, or if an earthquake destroyed your factory and left you with no stock to sell one year, your backup plan shouldn't cost you more than what you stand to lose in such events?

LECTURER: <u>Absolutely</u>. In making a decision to mitigate risk or develop a contingency fund, companies have to think about what they are protecting against, and weigh the costs of the decision against the costs of the danger.

MAJED: Yes, OK. That makes perfect sense.

🎧 Exercise D

Check the meaning of 'introducing' phrases. This means a phrase to use before your main statement to announce that you are going to say something. It may also signal how much you are going to say, or how important you think what you are going to say is.

1 Set for individual work and pairwork checking. Feed back.

2 Play Part 2 from Exercise C. Ask students to tell you to stop when they hear each phrase (underlined in the transcript above). Check what kind of phrase they think it is. Get students to repeat the phrase to copy the intonation.

If you wish, ask students to suggest other phrases that could be used in the same way.

Answers

Model answers:

I'd like to make two points. First, …	a
Can you expand on that?	b
The point is …	d
What's your second point?	b
My second point is that …	a
Yes, but …	c
I don't agree with that because …	c
Sorry, but who are we talking about exactly?	b
We need to be clear here.	d
I'd just like to say that …	a
In what way?	b
What I'm trying to say is, …	d
Can you give me an example?	b
Look at it this way.	d
Absolutely.	c

Exercise E

With the whole class, revise asking for information. Remind students of the questions used by the lecturer in Unit 5, Lesson 5.3 (see Unit 5 *Skills bank*). Remind students also about reporting information to people (see Unit 3 *Skills bank*).

Set students to work in groups of four. Each student should choose one aspect of location and turn to the relevant page to make notes on the information. When everyone is ready, they should feed back to their group, giving an oral report on the information. It is important that they do not simply read aloud the information, but use it to inform their speaking.

Alternatively, the research activity can be done as a 'wall dictation' as follows. Use Resource 7C in the additional resources section. Make large A3 (or A4) size copies of the location information (one type of research per page) and pin the sheets on the classroom walls. Each student should leave his/her seat and go to the wall to find the information he/she needs. Students should not write anything down: instead they should read and try to remember the information. Then they return to their group and tell them the information. If they forget something, they can go back to the wall to have another look.

Circulate, encouraging students to ask for clarification and to use the appropriate phrases when giving clarification. Note where students are having difficulty with language and where things are going well. When everyone has finished, feed back to the class on points you have noticed while listening in to the discussions.

Exercise F

Encourage students to make this as relevant as possible by choosing a site for a new production unit after having factored in different kinds of risk. Emphasize or remind students that most business risk is in the changing behaviour of consumers, so especially to think about risk involved in distribution and markets after the location has been chosen.

Alternatively, you could have a 'pyramid discussion'. Choose one product or service for the whole class to debate and put students in pairs to discuss a suitable location. After a short while, the pair should join together with another pair. This group of four should then come to an agreement on a suitable location. The group of four should then join another group of four. One or two people from each group of eight should then present the decision and the reasons for the decision to the class. It will help their presentation if they use visual aids such as maps or diagrams. Finally, the whole class should try to reach agreement on the site decision, taking a vote if necessary.

Remind students about agreeing and disagreeing, and about good and bad ways to contribute to seminar discussions (refer to Unit 5 if necessary).

While the representatives are presenting their group decisions, you should occasionally interrupt with a wrong interpretation so that students are forced to clarify their statements. Or you could ask for clarification.

Closure

Remind students that for a company to invest in new business, possibly the greatest risk is failing to understand ever-changing consumer behaviour as well as the competition does. Consider Vodafone's failed subsidiary J-Phone in Japan: the company simply did not understand the sophisticated expectations of the Japanese mobile consumer. The subsidiary was sold. Similarly, Uniqlo's less-than-successful understanding of the British market meant it took more than one attempt and an uphill struggle to become a successful high street brand. This Japanese company had misunderstood the British clothes shopper's buying habits.

Ask student groups to choose a different product or service than before. They brainstorm and report to the class:

- Changes in consumer behaviour that could put the company out of business.
- What probability they would attach to this risk.

Extra activities

1 Work through the *Vocabulary bank* and *Skills bank* if you have not already done so, or as a revision of previous study.

2 Use the *Activity bank* (Teacher's Book additional resources section, Resources 7A–C).

A Set the crossword (7A) for individual work (including homework) or pairwork.

Answers

3 Make some statements about what you're going to do after the class and ask students to transform them into *Wh~* cleft sentences. For example:

I'm going to have a coffee after the class.

→ *What you're going to do after the class is have a coffee.*

I might go to a film tonight.

→ *What you might do tonight is go to a film.*

Put students in pairs to practise.

8 PEOPLE AS A RESOURCE

This is the first of two units on aspects of human resource management that are relevant to all levels of management. This unit initially looks at the concepts of the individual, personality and roles in groups and teams, the need for diversity, and understanding how workforces operate well. Then, it explains the process of recruitment. The reading text discusses these concepts in building up a picture of how management sees people as a resource.

Skills focus

Reading

- understanding dependent clauses with passives

Writing

- paraphrasing
- expanding notes into complex sentences
- recognizing different essay types/structures:
  descriptive
  analytical
  comparison/evaluation
  argument
- writing essay plans
- writing essays

Vocabulary focus

- synonyms
- nouns from verbs
- definitions
- common 'direction' verbs in essay titles (*discuss, analyze, evaluate*, etc.)

Key vocabulary

adaptor	impress someone	personality
analytical	induction training	physically disabled
comprise/comprised of	innovator/innovative	popular
cooperation	intelligence	psychological
deadline-focused	interdependence	reliable
discrimination	interview	role
diversity	job analysis	rules and norms
emotional intelligence	job description	stable/unstable
enter a contract	job evaluation	sympathetic
equal opportunities	labour turnover	team
evaluate	minority	team building
extrovert/introvert	motivating	traits
forecasting	overcome hurdles	trust
human resources	person specification	workplace stress

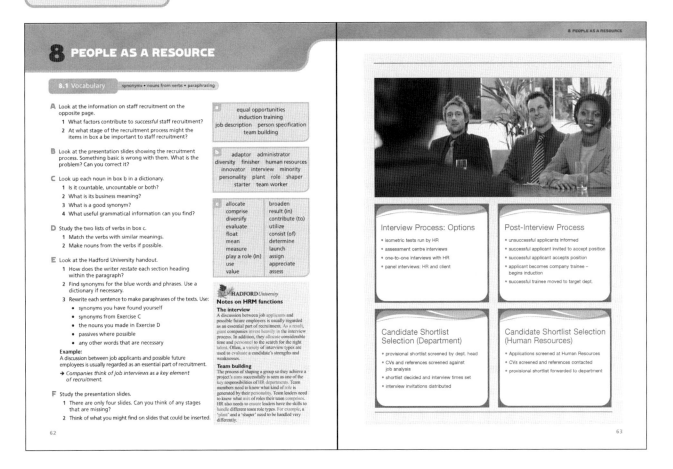

Lesson aims

- extend knowledge of synonyms and word sets (enables paraphrasing at word level)
- make nouns and noun phrases from verbs (enables paraphrasing at sentence level)

Further practice in paraphrasing at sentence level with:

- passives
- synonymous phrases
- negatives
- replacement subjects

Introduction

Revise ways of paraphrasing sentences. Write the following sentences on the board and ask students to say what changes have been made to the paraphrased sentences.

Original sentence: *Increasing external recruitment means that in-house vacancies are reduced.*

Paraphrase: *The company will solve its staff shortages once they start to recruit outside the firm.*
(answer: change in word order, passive to active, use of synonyms)

Original sentence: *In an interview, a candidate shouldn't be afraid to ask questions.*

Paraphrase: *Interviewees should feel able to ask their interviewer questions in an interview.*
(answer: change in word order, use of synonyms, replacement subject)

Exercise A

Set for pairwork or class discussion. Accept any reasonable answers.

Answers

Possible answers:

1 A good job description, careful screening and a careful interview process that uses a two- or three-step process to identify the right people to fit the job requirements.

2 **equal opportunities:** is borne in mind when the job is advertised. Modern companies tend to be equal opportunities employers, so the advertisement needs to make this clear. It should also be important during the shortlist selection and interview processes.

induction training: successful job applicants would normally be put through this process after having been interviewed, the job offered and accepted.

job description: is necessary for drafting the advertisement. But it is also important in deciding on the kind of candidate the interviewers will be looking for.

person specification: this may appear on the application form and may form part of the shortlist selection (screening) process.

team building: this could appear as a skill on a CV, or it could be a requirement in a manager's skill set and therefore be specified in the job description and advertisement.

Exercise B

Set for pairwork discussion. Check that students understand the technical vocabulary shown in the flow chart (*assessment centre, isometric test, panel interview*).

Assessment centre interviews = interviews where groups of applicants complete tasks in teams.

Isometric tests = tests to define the characteristic and trait set each applicant has.

Panel interview = an interview, usually at departmental level, in which three or more interviewers question one applicant at a time.

Tell students to bear in mind the points they have just

discussed. Feed back with the whole class. Avoid getting too bogged down in the items on the slides, as the exercise is merely introductory.

Answers

The slides are not in order. The correct order is: Interview Process: Options; Candidate Shortlist Selection (Human Resources); Candidate Shortlist Selection (Department); Post-Interview Process.

Exercise C

Set for pairwork. You may wish to divide the work up between different pairs. For question 4 (useful grammatical information), tell students to look out for words that can have the same form when used as a noun or verb, nouns that can be only singular or only plural, nouns that change their meaning when used as uncountable or countable, etc.

Feed back, building up the table in the Answers section on the board or in a projection.

Answers

Model answers:

Word	C/U	Meaning in business	Synonym	Useful grammatical information
adaptor	C	A team member who is flexible and able to take on challenges		Describes a type of team role. Usually used in the singular with a definite article, e.g., *the adaptor is ...*
administrator	C	1. a person whose main function is to administer 2. a reliable member of a team who can be relied on to carry out set tasks	executor, official	A label for a type of team member. Usually used in the singular and carries a definite article, e.g., *the administrator*. adj = administrative v = administer
diversity	U	a range of differences in people or organizations	differences	used with singular verbs, e.g., *Our aim is diversity.*
finisher	C	a team member who meets deadlines and encourages others to meet deadlines	completer	Countable, but usually used in the singular because it defines a type of team member.
human resources	C/U	a department in a company that is responsible for recruitment, training and other aspects of managing people	personnel	Can be seen as a single department or as the people in the department, so can be followed by either singular or plural verbs, e.g., *HR is upstairs. HR are offering us three new graduates.*
innovator	C	a team member who thinks of new ways of meeting challenges	ideas man/woman	Describes a team member type, so often used with the definite article, e.g., *The innovator is a ...*
interview	C	an event in a company involving questions and discussion to determine if an applicant is right for a job	job interview	C = an event V = the action of screening applicants and choosing a future employee. People involved in an interview: interviewer = company employee who asks the applicant questions interviewee = a job applicant being interviewed

minority	C	A group with a strong identity, such as ethnic or religious, living within a larger society. Usually it defines itself by its differences from the host society.		
personality	C	the mixture of characteristics that people have which make them unique	character	
plant	C	1. a heavy industrial factory 2. a team member who has expert knowledge but is introverted and socially uncooperative	1. factory, unit 2. specialist	1. used by production teams 2. is usually used to define or discuss a type of team member
role	C	type of person necessary to make a team operate successfully	function	
shaper	C	A team role, a person whose strength is working with other people's ideas and making them work in a practical way. He/she is often a good motivator and keeps the team moving forwards.	coordinator	In HR and management, used to define a particular kind of team member. Often used with the definite article.
starter	C	a person who initiates actions	initiator	In HR and management, used to define a particular kind of team member. Often used with the definite article.
team worker	C	A team role, a person who works to complete decisions made by the team.	co-worker	In HR and management, used to define a particular kind of team member. Often used with the definite article.

Exercise D

Set for individual work and pairwork checking. Make sure students understand that they should find a verb in the second column with a similar meaning to one of the verbs in the first column.

Feed back with the whole class, discussing the extent to which the verbs are exact synonyms, and if not, identifying any differences in meaning.

Answers

Model answers:

Verb	Noun	Verb	Noun
allocate	allocation	assign	assignment
comprise	–	consist (of)	constituent
diversify	diversification	broaden	broadening (of)
evaluate	evaluation	assess	assessment
float	flotation	launch	launch
mean	no noun for this meaning	result (in)	result
measure	measurement	determine	determination
play a role (in)	–	contribute (to)	contribution
use	use, usage	utilize	utilization
value	no noun for this meaning	appreciate	appreciation

Exercise E

This is an exercise in paraphrasing based on word- and sentence-level techniques. As well as finding their own synonyms from memory and using the synonyms already discussed in Exercises C and D, students will use noun phrases in place of verb phrases as a technique in paraphrasing. Students should also make passive sentences wherever they can.

1 Set for individual work. Feed back with the whole class.

2 Set for individual work and pairwork checking.

3 Set for pairwork; pairs then check with other pairs. Alternatively, tell some students to write their answers on an OHT, or create a file for projection, for discussion by the whole class.

Answers

Model answers:

1 The interview = discussion between job applicants and possible future employees

Team building = the process of shaping a group so they achieve a project's aims successfully

2 Possible synonyms (including synonyms from Exercises C and D):

The Interview

A discussion between job (*applicants*) candidates and possible future employers is usually regarded as an essential part of recruitment. (*As a result*) therefore/so/consequently/, (*giant*) large/big/huge/multinational companies (*invest heavily in*) spend a lot of money on/give a lot of resources to the interview process. In addition, they (*allocate*) set aside/assign considerable time and (*personnel*) staff/people in the search for the right (*talent*) people/skill set/knowledge and experience/people with the right skills. Often, a (*variety*) range of/number of different interview types are used to (*evaluate*) assess/measure/gauge a candidate's strengths and weaknesses.

Team building

The process of shaping a group so they achieve a project's (*aims*) objectives/targets successfully is seen as one of the (*key*) chief/main/principal/primary responsibilities of (*HR departments*) personnel departments. Team members need to know what kind of (*role*) performance is generated by their (*personality*) character. Team leaders need to know what (*mix*) mixture/blend of roles their team (*comprises*) includes/is made up of. HR also needs to (*ensure*) make sure/make certain leaders have the skills to (*handle*) deal with/cope with/manage different team role types. (*For example*) For instance, a ('*plant*') ideas man and a 'shaper' need to be handled very differently.

3 Possible paraphrases:

The interview

Companies think of job interviews as a key element of recruitment.
Consequently, huge firms spend a lot of money organizing interviews.
Employers also assign time and staff to finding appropriately skilled applicants.
Frequently, a job applicant's personality is assessed using different kinds of interview.

Team building

Personnel Departments view team building as a primary function.
People in a team should be aware that their character affects the type of team member they are.
It is essential for a person leading a team to be aware of which team roles he has in his team.
An important responsibility of a personnel department is to make certain team leaders are skilful enough to manage different team types.
For instance, a 'shaper' needs to be managed very differently from an 'ideas man'.

Exercise F

Ask students if they think the slides shown have any important stages missing. Set for pairwork. When complete, pairs compare with other pairs. Accept any reasonable answers.

Answers

Possible answers:

1 An obvious stage that is missing is the pre-interview process. This may include an analysis of the job, the writing of a job description and advertising the job in suitable media.

2 Information that could be added to slides includes job analysis, job description, considering internal recruitment, collating applications received, collating interview data, assessing applications and interview information, selecting the best few candidates (in case the best refuses), evaluating the recruitment and selection process.

Closure

Ask students to work in pairs or small groups to draw a flow chart on an OHT, or create a file to project, showing the full recruitment process they think would work best for a large corporation. Feed back as a class, with students giving a mini presentation explaining their flow chart.

8.2 Reading

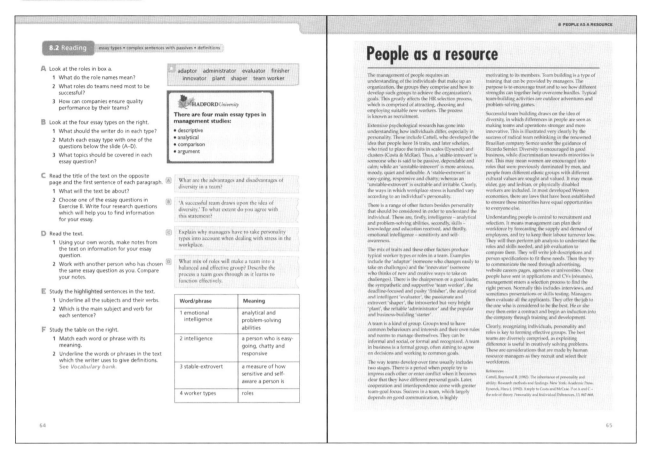

General note

Read the *Vocabulary bank* and *Skills bank* at the end of the Course Book unit. Decide when, if at all, to refer students to them. The *Vocabulary bank* section *Understanding new words: using definitions* is relevant to Lesson 8.2; the *Skills bank* will be more relevant to Lessons 8.3 and 8.4.

Lesson aims

- understand essay types
- interpret essay titles
- find the main information in a passive clause
- understand internal definitions (see *Vocabulary bank*)

Further practice in:
- reading research
- finding the kernel of a long sentence

Introduction

With the whole class, discuss how to use written texts as sources of information when writing an answer for an essay question. Ask students:

1 *How can you choose useful sources?* (To get an idea of whether a text might be useful, survey the text, i.e., look at the title, look at the beginning and the end and the first line of each paragraph; in other words, skim-read to get an approximate idea of the text contents.)

2 *If you decide that a text is going to be useful, what is it a good idea to do ...*

- *... before reading?* (think of questions related to the essay question to which you would like to find some answers)

- *... while reading?* (identify useful parts of the text; make notes **in your own words**)

- *... after reading?* (check answers to the questions)

Exercise A

Divide the class into pairs and ask students to brainstorm the advantages and disadvantages of working in a team. Elicit the words *team* and *role*, and ask for examples of team roles. Accept any roles students offer, but ask what the contribution of each role is to the functioning of the team as a whole.

Set the questions for pairwork discussion with whole-class feedback.

Answers

Possible answers:

1

role name	meaning
adaptor	a person who accepts change and thus solves problems efficiently
administrator	someone who handles detail and keeps teams running smoothly
evaluator	an analyst who weighs up and tests ideas
finisher	someone focused on deadlines and who encourages others to complete tasks
innovator	a person who finds new and creative ways of meeting challenges
plant	an ideas man or woman, sometimes rather shy or not very sociable
shaper	a leader who 'shapes' and influences the team to complete tasks
team worker	a reliable, hardworking 'doer'

2 A successful team is said to need a good leader, an adaptor, a team worker, a shaper, a plant and an innovator. What it does not need is too many of any one type, because they may cause conflict and the team might then fail to meet its goals.

3 A manager can ensure quality performance in his/her teams by choosing the right balance of roles in the first place. Secondly, by monitoring the teamwork the manager ensures that conflicts within the team are not destructive. The team will probably move from its first stage of coming together or forming, through its 'storming' or conflict stage to the stage where it is functioning efficiently. However, the manager needs to monitor this process and ensure that the team does not lose sight of its goals.

Exercise B

1 Refer students to the lecture slide. Discuss this question with the whole class. Build up the table in the Answers section on the board.

2 Set for pairwork. Feed back with the whole class. Ask the class to say which key words in each title tell you what type of writing it is.

3 Set for pairwork. Feed back, using the second table in the Answers section, discussing with the whole class what topics will need to be included in each essay. Add the notes in the third column.

Answers

Possible answers:

1

	What the writer should do
Descriptive writing	describe or summarize key ideas/events/points. Give the plain facts. Could involve writing about: a narrative description (a history of something); a process (how something happens); key ideas in a theory; main points of an article (answers the question *What is/are ...?*)
Analytical writing	try to analyze (= go behind the plain facts) or explain something or give reasons for a situation; may also question accepted ideas and assumptions (answers the question *Why/How ...?*)
Comparison	compare two or more aspects/ideas/things/people, etc., usually also evaluate, i.e., say which is better/bigger, etc.
Argument writing	give an opinion and support the opinion with evidence/reasons, etc., likely to also give opposing opinions (counter-arguments) and show how they are wrong

2/3 Key words are underlined. (See table below.)

Type of writing	Question	Topics
descriptive	D <u>What mix of roles</u> will make a team into a balanced and effective group? <u>Describe</u> the process a team goes through as it learns to function effectively.	<ul><li>importance of a balance of roles in a team</li><li>key team roles: what they are</li><li>the contribution each role makes</li><li>problems each role could create</li><li>the balance of types a team needs to function effectively</li><li>stages teams go through as they acquire team focus</li></ul>
analytical	C <u>Explain why</u> managers have to take personality types into account when dealing with stress in the workplace.	<ul><li>different personality types</li><li>how different personality types interact – the need for balance in a team</li><li>different team roles matched to personality types</li><li>matching the strengths of different roles to form an effective team</li></ul>

comparison	A What are the advantages and disadvantages of diversity in a team?	<ul><li>the ways in which diversity affects a team's effective functioning</li><li>examples of advantages of diversity of team roles in a company's project</li><li>examples of uniformity of team roles and the problems this creates for the team</li><li>diversity is an essential element of a successful team</li></ul>
argument	B 'A successful team draws upon the idea of diversity.' To what extent do you agree with this statement?	<ul><li>the factors that contribute to a team's success</li><li>the impact of diversity on a team's functioning – action roles and ideas roles</li><li>the impact of role uniformity on a team's functioning (refuting counter-argument)</li><li>examples from business which demonstrate the validity of the quotation</li></ul>

Exercise C

1 Set for individual work. Feed back with the whole class. Accept all reasonable answers.

2 If necessary, remind students of the purpose of research questions and do one or two examples as a class. Set for individual work and pairwork checking. Feed back, getting good research questions for each essay topic on the board.

Answer

Possible answers:

1 The title of the text suggests that the text will look at the value people can bring to a company and ways in which managers can harness the human resources available to them. The use of resources suggests two ideas: something that can be utilized and something that has value. The implication is that managers need to have the awareness to assess the value of their staff accurately and make effective decisions about staff deployment so that it works to the benefit of the company.

Paragraph 1 will explain the basic concept of the text: people management involves understanding how individuals impact on an organization and how groups work and can be developed, and how all of this affects staff recruitment.

Paragraph 2 will explore and give examples of different personality types identified by psychological research.

Paragraph 3 will provide factors beyond mere personality that affect an individual's effectiveness in the workplace.

Paragraph 4 will introduce and describe typical worker roles in companies.

Paragraph 5 will explain how a team behaves as a group.

Paragraph 6 will indicate the main stages in a team's development.

Paragraph 7 will explain how diversity benefits a team.

Paragraph 8 will show how individuals, personality and roles are interrelated, and how all these themes tie in together in the human resources management function.

2 Answers depend on the students.

Exercise D

Set for individual work and pairwork comparison/ checking. If you wish, students can make notes under the headings in the 'Topics' column of the table in Exercise B above. Encourage students to make notes in their own words.

Answer

Possible answers:

A *What are the advantages and disadvantages of diversity in a team?*

Advantages
<ul><li>different kinds of people have different strengths</li><li>may find women doing jobs that traditionally went to men</li><li>a range of cultures and values can be included</li></ul>

Disadvantages
<ul><li>the text doesn't mention any specific disadvantages.</li></ul>

B '*A successful team draws upon the idea of diversity.*' *To what extent do you agree* with this statement?
<ul><li>Successful team building draws on idea of diversity</li><li>Differences in people make teams stronger and more creative, e.g., Semler and Semco</li><li>Team success depends on good interaction, communication and motivation</li><li>Successful teams include a range of roles, e.g., chairperson who provides leadership, team worker who provides support, innovator who comes up with creative ideas, adaptor who responds effectively to new challenges</li></ul>

C _Explain why_ managers have to take personality types into account when dealing with stress in the workplace.

- different personality types – what are they, how can they be measured and how well do they interact, e.g., Cattell's 16 character traits; Eysenck's trait scales; Costa and McRae's clusters – different ways of measuring them.
- four different personality types definitions:
  - stable-introvert – passive, dependable, calm
  - unstable-introvert – anxious, moody, quiet, inflexible
  - stable-extrovert – easy-going, responsive, chatty
  - unstable-extrovert – excitable, irritable
- Workplace stress will create different reactions in different personality types.

D _What mix of roles_ will make a team into a balanced and effective group? _Describe_ the process a team goes through as it learns to function effectively.

- ten common team roles – what are they?, e.g., adaptor, administrator, finisher, etc.
- each role = a unique blend of strengths it brings to the team. adaptor = s.o. who adapts to situations well – finisher focuses on deadlines – administrator provides reliability, etc.
- a team needs a variety of roles – combination of strengths is necessary
- two stages of development – conflict because people try to impress each other – cooperation and interaction with goal focus

Exercise E

Set for individual work and pairwork checking. Students could copy out the sentences in their notebooks and then underline all the verbs and subjects. Feed back with the whole class, building up the table in the Answers section on the board. Point out that each sentence has two verbs, which means that each sentence has two _clauses_. This means that the sentences are complex. (A simple sentence has only one main verb and subject.) To enable students to identify which is the 'main' part of the sentence (in bold in the table below), ask how the two clauses are 'joined' and add the joining words (here: relative pronouns _which_, _in which_ [twice], and _that_). The main part of the sentence is linked to the dependent part with these words.

Check understanding of the passives in each case by asking how each clause and sentence could be rephrased with an active verb, e.g.,

1 This greatly affects the HR selection process, which is comprised of attracting, choosing and employing suitable new workers.

1 Attracting, choosing and employing suitable new workers comprises the HR selection process which this greatly affects.

2 Clearly, the ways in which workplace stress is handled vary according to an individual's personality.

2 Clearly, the ways in which one handles workplace stress vary according to an individual's personality.

3 There is a range of other factors besides personality that should be considered in order to understand the individual.

3 There is a range of other factors besides personality that we should consider in order to understand the individual.

4 Team building is a type of training that can be provided by managers.

4 Team building is a type of training that managers can provide.

Answers

Possible answers:

	Joining word	Subject	Verb	Object/complement
1		This	affects	**the human resource <u>process</u>***
	which		is comprised of	attracting, choosing and employing suitable workers.
2	(Clearly),	**the <u>ways</u>**	vary	**according to an individual's responsibility**
	in which	workplace <u>stress</u>	is handled	
3		**There**	is	**a <u>range</u> of other factors besides personality**
	that		should be considered	in order to understand the individual.
4		**Team building**	is	**a <u>type</u> of training**
	that		can be provided by	managers.
5		**Successful <u>team building</u>**	draws on	**the idea of diversity**
	in which	<u>differences</u> in people	are seen	as making teams and operations stronger and more innovative.

*the underlined noun is the head word of the noun phrase

5 Successful team building draws on the idea of diversity, in which differences in people are seen as making teams and operations stronger and more innovative.

5 Successful team building draws on the idea of diversity, in which we see differences in people as making teams and operations stronger and more innovative.

> ### Language note
>
> The choice of whether to use an active or a passive construction often depends on how the writer wants to structure the information. Refer to Unit 7 *Skills bank* for a note on information structure.

Exercise F

Set for individual work and pairwork checking. In question 2, tell students to look for the actual words used and the punctuation, grammatical devices and vocabulary devices which are used to indicate meanings.

Feed back with the whole class, pointing out the structures given in the third column of the table for question 2 in the Answers section. If you wish, refer students to the *Vocabulary bank – Understanding new words: using definitions*.

Answers

1

Word/phrase	Meaning
1 emotional intelligence	a measure of how sensitive and self-aware a person is
2 intelligence	analytical and problem-solving abilities
3 stable-extrovert	a person who is easy-going, chatty and responsive
4 worker types	roles

2 Model answers:

Word/phrase	Actual words giving the meaning	Punctuation/vocab/structure
emotional intelligence	– sensitive and self-aware	word/phrase followed by *dash + noun and noun*
intelligence	– analytical and problem-solving abilities	word followed by *dash + adj + and + compound adj + noun*
adaptor	(someone who changes easily to take on challenges)	word followed by *open brackets + someone who + v + adv + to-phrasal v + obj (noun) + close brackets*
innovator	(someone who thinks of new and creative ways to take on challenges)	word followed by *open brackets + someone who + v + objs + to-phrasal v + obj (noun) + close brackets*
stable-extrovert	..., on the other hand, is easy-going, responsive and chatty	word/phrase followed by comma + *is + adj, adj and adj*
worker types	or roles	*or + synonym (noun or noun phrase)*

Closure

Tell students to make a list of jobs they have done; this can include anything:

● intern work with companies
● holiday jobs
● working within a family business
● Saturday jobs
● part-time work to finance their course of study

Students should work in small groups and share experiences. Then they should discuss the following:

1 What stages were involved in the recruitment process?

  a Was there an advertisement of the job with a job description, etc.? If not, how did the person find out about the job?

  b What kind of interview occurred?

  c Did the process involve assessment of qualifications and experience? Give examples.

  d What discussion of duties and benefits was involved?

  e What kind of induction process or job training was offered, if any? If none, what kind of induction or job training would have made you more effective as a worker?

2 In your work, what involvement in teams was there?

  a How big was the team?

  b Was it created for a specific project or was it a 'general' team?

  c What role/s did you adopt, and what roles did other people adopt?

  d Describe how the group learnt to work together.

3 How could the team management have been improved?

8.3 Extending skills

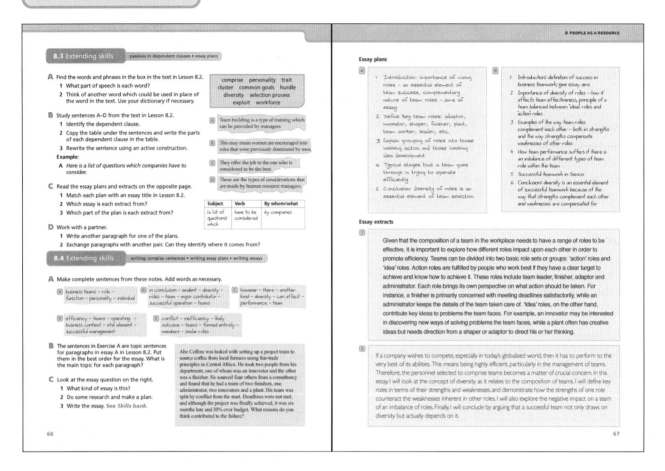

Lesson aims

- find the main information in a passive dependent clause
- recognize appropriate writing plans for essay types

Further practice in:

- vocabulary from Lesson 8.2

Introduction

Choose about 10–15 words from the previous unit which you think that students should revise. Write them in a random arrangement and at different angles (i.e., not in a vertical list) on an OHT, projection or on the board. Allow students two minutes to look at and remember the words, and then take them away. Students should write down all the words they can remember.

Exercise A

Set for individual work and pairwork checking. Feed back with the whole class.

Answers

Model answers:

Word	Part of speech	Another word/s
comprise	v	include
personality	n (U/C)	character
trait	n (C)	characteristic
cluster	n (C)	group
common goals	n (C)	shared objective
hurdle	n (C)	difficulty, problem, obstacle
diversity	n (U)	difference
selection process	n (C)	recruitment
exploit	v	use, utilize
workforce	n (U/C)	staff, labour

Exercise B

Set for individual work and pairwork checking. Make sure that students can correctly identify the main clause, the dependent clause and the linking word. Do the first transformation with the class to check that they know what to do. Note that they do not need to rewrite the main clauses. Also, if no agent is given they will need to supply one themselves.

Answers

Model answers:

1/2

Main clause	Linking word	Subject	Verb	By whom/what
A Team building is a type of training	which	(training type) which*	can be provided	by managers.
B This may mean women are encouraged into roles	that	(roles) that*	were previously dominated	by men.
C They offer the job to the one	who	(the one) who*	is considered	(to be the best).
D These are the types of considerations	that	(considerations) that*	are made	by human resource managers.

*note that the relative pronoun is the subject of the dependent clause.

3 Suggested answers:

A Team building is a type of training that managers can provide.

B These *[business trends]* may encourage women into roles that men previously dominated.

C They offer the job to the one they consider to be the best.

D Human resource managers consider these.

Exercise C

Tell students to look back at the essay questions in Lesson 8.2. You may also need to remind them of the topics which you all decided are suitable for the essay.

Set all three questions for individual work and pairwork checking. Feed back with the whole class. Ask students to say what aspects of the plans and the extracts enabled them to be identified. Check that students can match the parts of the extracts with the corresponding parts of the essay plan.

Answers

Model answers:

1 Plan B = essay title B: '*A successful team draws upon the idea of diversity.*' *To what extent do you agree with this statement?*

Plan A = essay title D: *What mix of roles will make a team into a balanced and effective group? Describe the process a team goes through as it learns to function effectively.*

2 Extract 1 = plan A

Extract 2 = plan B

3 Extract 1 = Plan A, point 3: **Importance of diversity of roles:** *action roles v idea roles, e.g., each set complements other roles in the department – weaknesses are compensated for*

Extract 2 = Plan B, intro: *Introduction:* **importance** *of diversity for efficiency of businesses today, esp. with regard to team operations and selection; aims of essay*

Exercise D

Remind students about writing topic sentences. Set for pairwork. Students who chose these two questions in Lesson 8.2 can refer to their notes. Students who did not make notes on these two questions in Lesson 8.2 can refer back to the reading text for information. In all cases, students should write using their own words, i.e., paraphrase the ideas in the text.

If you wish, you could ask some students – perhaps those who finish early – to write their paragraphs on an OHT or projected file for all the class to look at. As well as eliciting grammar/syntax correction from the class, comment on the extent to which students have managed to paraphrase, whether they have successfully covered the point in the plan, and whether their topic sentence is supported well by the sentences that follow.

Closure

Ask students to finish the following sentences as quickly as possible.

The basic objective of recruitment is …

An 'adaptor' is a … who …

'Emotional intelligence' means …

A 'stable-introvert' is someone who …

Job analysis involves …

'Equal opportunities' means …

A good example of team success is …

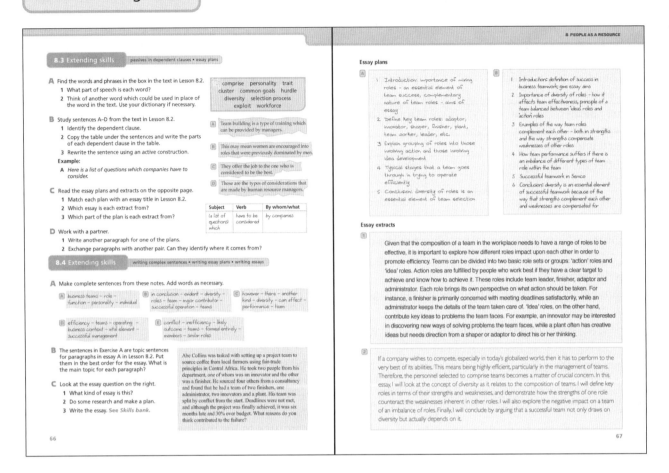

Lesson aims

- expand notes into complex sentences
- make an essay plan
- write an essay

Further practice in:

- writing topic sentences
- expanding a topic sentence into a paragraph
- writing complex sentences with passives
- identifying required essay type

Introduction

Remind students about complex and compound sentences – that is, sentences with more than one clause. Remind students that academic texts often consist of sentences with several clauses. Give the following simple sentences (or make your own) and ask students to add some more clauses to them:

Effective interviewing identifies talented applicants.
Successful businesses encourage diversity.
Companies must look at their fixed costs.
Efficiency requires excellent management.
Teams learn to work together over time.
Recruitment involves attracting the right talent.

Exercise A

Set for individual work and pairwork checking. Remind students that they should try to make sentences in a good 'academic' style. Also remind them to use passives where necessary, and to look out for ways of making dependent clauses, such as relative pronouns, linking words, etc. They will also need to pay attention to making correct verb tenses. Feed back with the whole class.

Answers

Possible answers:

A In business teams, roles can be seen as a function of the personality of the individual.

B In conclusion, it is evident that a diversity of roles in a team is a major contributor to the successful operation of teams.

C However, there is another kind of diversity that can affect the performance of a team.

D The efficiency of teams operating in a business context is a vital element of successful management.

E Conflict and inefficiency are likely outcomes in teams formed entirely of members with similar roles.

Exercise B

Set for individual work. Feed back with the whole class. Point out how this comparison essay is organized by discussing all the advantages first and then all the disadvantages. (See *Skills bank* for an alternative approach to comparison.)

If you wish, you could take this exercise further, asking students to build on the topic sentences by suggesting what ideas could follow the topic sentence in each paragraph. For this, they will need to refer to ideas in the text. Note that disadvantages of diversity in a team are not discussed in the text, so ideas for this paragraph would need to be researched further. A web search is a good place to start for this.

Answers

Model answers:

Topic sentences	Paragraph topic
D The efficiency of teams operating in a business context is a vital element of successful management.	introduction
A In business teams, roles can be seen as a function of the personality of the individual.	roles; advantages of good quality team diversity
E Conflict and inefficiency are likely outcomes in teams formed entirely of members with similar roles.	disadvantages of poor diversity in teams
C However, there is another kind of diversity that can affect team performance.	effects of language, cultural and other diversity in groups
B In conclusion, it is evident that a diversity of roles in a team is a major contributor to the successful operation of teams.	conclusion

Exercise C

Discuss question 1 with the whole class. Set the research and planning (question 2) for group work, and the writing for individual work (this could be done at home). Students can do web searches to find more information on groups and teams in business, or even on fair-trade projects.

Answers

1 Model answer:

This essay is largely analytical since it requires (possible) causes for the group's failure. It also asks students to think critically about possible problems with a system that is thought to be very good.

2 Possible essay plan:

- **Introduction:** importance of group composition to team success; reference to case study; aims of essay.

- **Definition of key roles necessary to a successful team:**
  - adaptor, administrator, team member, finisher – practical, goal-oriented workers
  - plant, innovator, shaper, leader – creative problem solvers
  - necessity for strengths to complement each other
  - necessity for shortcomings inherent in each role to be compensated by strengths of other team members.
  - examples
- **Causes of dysfunction in groups (*not necessary to include all*):**
  - imbalance between practical and creative team members
  - over-dominance of group by strong team members
  - lack of sufficient technical expertise
  - poor leadership
  - poor material support from the company
  - poor planning – lack of clear critical path analysis
- **Conclusion:** team for Collins's project; general comments about group formation and success.

Closure

Ask students if they can remember a word from the unit …

	Example(s)
beginning with *c*	comprise
beginning with *i*	impress
ending with *y*	diversity
ending with *s*	impress, analysis, stress
with two syllables	value, shaper, starter, stable
with three syllables	introvert, extrovert, interview
with four syllables	minority, motivating, intelligence
which is a verb	impress, forecast
which is an uncountable noun	interdependence, induction, discrimination, cooperation
which is an adjective	reliable, sympathetic, personal
which goes together with another word	emotional intelligence, personal specification, job analysis, job evaluation
which is difficult to pronounce	physically disabled (students' answers will vary)

Accept all reasonable answers.

1 Work through the *Vocabulary bank* and *Skills bank* if you have not already done so, or as a revision of previous study.

2 Use the *Activity bank* (Teacher's Book additional resources section, Resource 8A).

A Set the wordsearch for individual work (including homework) or pairwork. Establish that the words are uncountable in the context in which they are used in the unit, although some can be countable in other contexts.

Answers

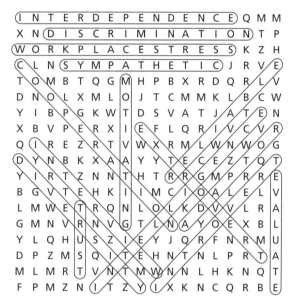

B Set the spelling exercise for individual work and pairwork checking. If students are having difficulty, give them the first two letters of the word.

Answers

Jumbled word	Correct spelling
hreifnis	finisher
noniuditc	induction
ytnimori	minority
sledrhu	hurdles
stiatr	traits
frwookecr	workforce
aetm	team
pahsre	shaper
tineer	entire
gmtoavinit	motivating

3 Check word stress by writing the following words on the board *without* stress markings. Students have to mark the stress and pronounce the words correctly.

ana'lytical

in'duction

'finisher

'extrovert

min'ority

sympa'thetic

e'conomy

re'liable

4 Remind students of how to give definitions (see Lesson 8.2). Then select five or six familiar items (e.g., iPod, laptop, sunglasses, pen, mobile phone) and ask students to think of definitions (e.g., *it's something that you use to listen to music; you need these when it is sunny*).

This can also be done the other way round by giving the definitions and asking students to guess the word; once they get the idea, students can come up with items, questions and definitions themselves. Other forms for definitions can include:

This is a place where …

This is a company which …

If you want to buy an (X), you need to go to …

Other categories which can be used to practise both the language of definition and general business and cultural knowledge include:

- brand or company names, e.g., Marks & Spencer (well known in the UK for quality food and other necessities); also use global multinationals

- familiar places in the town or college where the students are studying

- famous people

- movies and TV programmes

An alternative is the Weakest Link TV quiz show format, e.g., *What 'A' is a well-known brand of computer?* (Apple)

9 DEVELOPING PEOPLE

This is the second of two units on human resource management, which moves beyond simply understanding workforces and looks more closely at how people are managed. Unit 9 uses lecture excerpts to focus on the notions of worker motivation and rewards, and workplace learning and development. Other HRM-related topics are touched on in the extension exercises.

Skills focus

🎧 Listening
- using the Cornell note-taking system
- recognizing digressions in lectures

Speaking
- making effective contributions to a seminar
- referring to other people's ideas in a seminar

Vocabulary focus
- fixed phrases from Human Resources
- fixed phrases from academic English

Key vocabulary

absenteeism	incentive	performance-related pay
appraisal	induction	personnel
apprenticeship	industrial relations	praise (v and n)
be promoted	job enlargement	profit share
bonus	job rotation	punishment
coaching	job-sharing	quality circles
commission	keep a confidence	quantitative
conditions	labour productivity	recession
cut back	labour turnover	recruit
distance learning	mentoring	relocation
esteem	merit (n)	reward (v and n)
expert	motivation	satisfaction
financial/non-financial rewards	motivator	soft HRM
flexibility	multi-skilled	stakeholders
graduate	needs analysis	stimulating
hard HRM	outsourcing	theory X and theory Y
hierarchy	part-time	training
hygiene factors	payment	vocational
	peer	work-life balance

9.1 Vocabulary

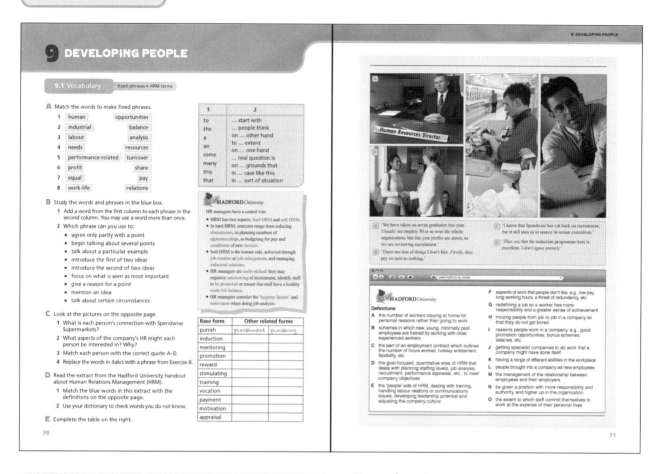

General note

Read the *Vocabulary bank* at the end of the Course Book unit. Decide when, if at all, to refer students to it. The best time is probably at the very end of the lesson or the beginning of the next lesson, as a summary/revision.

Lesson aims

- understand and use some fixed phrases/compound nouns from business studies
- understand and use some fixed phrases from academic English

Introduction

Introduce the topic for this unit. Ask students to say what Human Resource Management (HRM) is and arrive at a definition on the board, such as:

HRM is the integrated, strategic management of an organization's people in order that they help the company achieve its objectives.

Exercise A

This gives revision of some compound noun phrases (noun + noun, adjective + noun) from previous units.

Set for individual work or pairwork. Check that students remember the meanings and that they can pronounce the compounds with the main stress on the correct word. Accept any reasonable alternatives which apply in HRM. Ask students to make sentences with the compounds.

Answers

Model answers:

human	re'sources	n + n
industrial	re'lations	adj + n
labour	'turnover	n + n
'needs	analysis	n + n
per'formance-related	pay	adj + n
'profit	share	n + n
equal	oppor'tunities	adj + n
work-life	'balance	adj + n

Exercise B

Set for individual work and pairwork checking. Point out that some of the words on the left must be used more than once. Feed back with the whole class.

Answers

Model answers:

to start with	begin talking about several points
many/some people think	mention an idea
on the other hand	introduce the second of two ideas
to an/some extent	agree only partly with a point
on the one hand	introduce the first of two ideas
the real question is	focus on what is seen as most important
on the grounds that	give a reason for a point
in a case like this	talk about a particular example
in this/that sort of situation	talk about certain circumstances

Exercise C

1/2 Set for pairwork discussion.

3 Set for individual work and pairwork checking.

4 Set for individual work. Check with the whole class, asking students to read out the quotation with the alternative phrase inserted in place of the original words in italics.

Answers

Model answers:

Accept any reasonable answers. The following answers are prompts for eliciting discussion and vocabulary only.

1/2 A is the HR Director of Spendwise Supermarkets – likely to be interested in the company staffing situation, human resource development, identifying training needs.

B is a part-time employee of Spendwise (a cashier) – likely to be interested in wage rates and working conditions.

C is a headhunter – likely to be interested in maintaining his contract with Spendwise by providing good, high-level candidates for selection as executives.

D is a management inductee – likely to be interested in how Spendwise's systems work and understanding her area of responsibility as quickly as possible.

3 A (**HR Director**) 'We have taken on seven graduates this year. *Usually* we employ 30 or so over the whole organization, but this year profits are down, so we are reviewing recruitment.'

B (**part-time employee**) 'There are lots of things I don't like. *Firstly*, they pay us next to nothing.'

C (**headhunter**) 'I know that Spendwise have cut back on recruitment, *but* it still uses us to source its senior executives.'

D (**management inductee**) '*They say* that the induction programme here is excellent. I *don't agree entirely*.'

4

A *Usually*	*In this sort of situation*, we employ 30 or so over the whole organization.
B *Firstly, ...*	*To start with*, they pay us next to nothing.
C *..., but*	*... on the other hand*, they still use us to source their senior executives.
D *They say*	*Many/Some people think* that the induction programme is excellent.
D *don't ... entirely*	I agree *to an/some extent*.

Exercise D

This exercise gives some key HRM terms.

Set students to read the handout extract first and ask them to discuss in pairs which of the blue words they know and which are new for them. Feed back with the whole class to establish how much is known. Where students give correct explanations, tell them they are right, and where they are wrong also tell them, but do not give the right answer at this point.

Set the exercise for individual work and pairwork checking. Feed back with the whole class, checking the meaning of other possibly unknown words.

For extra practice at this point if you wish, set students to work in pairs. One student should shut his/her book. The other student should say one of the words for Student B to explain. Students then swap roles.

Answers

Model answers:

hard HRM	the goal-focused, quantitative area of HRM that deals with planning staffing levels, job analysis, recruitment, performance appraisal, etc., to meet company objectives
soft HRM	the 'people' side of HRM, dealing with training, handling labour relations or communications issues, developing leadership potential, and adjusting the company culture
absenteeism	the number of workers staying at home for personal reasons rather than going to work
apprenticeships	schemes in which new, young, minimally paid employees are trained by working with older, experienced workers
conditions	the part of an employment contract which outlines the number of hours worked, holiday entitlement, flexibility, etc.
recruits (n)	people brought into a company as new employees
job rotation	moving people from job to job in a company so that they do not get bored
job enlargement	redefining a job so a worker has more responsibility and a greater sense of achievement
industrial relations	the management of the relationship between employees and their employers
multi-skilled	having a range of different abilities in the workplace
outsourcing	getting specialist companies to do work that a company might have done itself
be promoted	be given a position with more responsibility and authority, and higher up in the organization
work-life balance	the extent to which staff commit themselves to work at the expense of their personal lives
hygiene factors	aspects of work that people don't like, e.g., low pay, long working hours, a threat of redundancy
motivators	reasons people work in a company, e.g., good promotion opportunities, bonus schemes, salaries

Exercise E

Set for individual work. Tell students to use their dictionaries to check the meanings and grammatical categories of the words if they are not sure. Explain that many of the base words may only have one other related form.

Feed back with the whole class, pointing out that most of the words have a particular use in the area of HRM (those that can have more general use are shaded in the table in the Answers section). Check students can pronounce all the words correctly, particularly those where the word stress shifts.

Answers

Model answers:

Base form	Other related forms	
in'duction (n, U/C)	induct'ee/or (n, C)	(n used as adj)
'mentoring (n, U)	'mentor/ee (n, C)	mentor (v)
pro'motion (n U/C)	pro'mote (v)	(n used as adj)
re'ward (v)	re'ward (n, C)	rewarding (adj)
'stimulating (adj)	'stimulate (v)	
'training (n, U)	'trainer/'trainee	(n used as adj)
vo'cation (n, U/C)		vocational (adj)
'payment (n, C)	'payer/pay'ee(n, C)	payable (adj)
moti'vation (n, U)	'motivator (n, C)	motivating (adj)
ap'praisal (n, C)	ap'praise (v)	(n used as adj)

Language note

With a good class, you can spend plenty of time on the issue of whether each noun is used as countable or uncountable or both, i.e., can the word be made plural, and if so, does that change the meaning? For example, *finance* = funding for a company/project; *finances* = general issues relating to income and expenditure.

Closure

On the board, write some terms from the lesson and ask students to give a definition; choose items from Exercises A and D. Or read out a definition and ask students to tell you the appropriate word or phrase. Check the pronunciation. This exercise can also be done as a dictation.

Alternatively, write the words and definitions on different cards and give a card to each student. The student then reads out the word or the definition and the rest of the class must produce the correct answer.

If any of the students have worked in a company, ask them if the word has had any relevance to their work experience.

2 Revise note-taking symbols and abbreviations by using Extra Activity 3 at the end of this unit.

3 Introduce the elements of the Cornell note-taking system. Try to elicit some of the R words. Ask students to try to think of five words beginning with *re-* with six or seven letters that are good strategies to use when studying and taking notes. Write the words as follows on the board:

RE _ _ _ _ (= *record*)

RE _ _ _ _ (= *reduce*)

RE _ _ _ _ (= *recite*)

RE _ _ _ _ _ (= *reflect*)

RE _ _ _ _ (= *review*)

Discuss with the class what each word might mean when taking notes. Try to elicit the following, helping where needed.

record Take notes during the lecture.

reduce After the lecture, turn the notes into one- or two-word questions or 'cues' which help you remember the key information.

recite Say the questions and answers aloud.

reflect Decide on the best way to summarize the key information in the lecture.

review Look again at the key words and the summary (and do this regularly).

Tell students that in this lesson they will be introduced to this system of note-taking – which can be used both for lectures and also for reading, and for revision for exams later. Do not say much more at this point; they will see how the system works as the lesson progresses.

General note

Read the *Skills bank – Using the Cornell note-taking system* at the end of the Course Book unit. Decide when, if at all, to refer students to it. The best time is probably at the very end of the lesson or the beginning of the next lesson, as a summary/revision.

Lesson aims

- use the Cornell note-taking system

Further practice in:

- listening for an established purpose
- understanding fractured text
- recognition of fixed phrases and what type of information comes next
- using abbreviations and symbols in note-taking

Introduction

1 Review key vocabulary from this unit by writing a selection of words from Lesson 9.1 on the board and asking students to put the words in groups, giving reasons for their decisions.

Subject note

The Cornell system was developed by Walter Pauk at Cornell University, USA. (Pauk, W. and Owens, R. (2007). *How to Study in College* (9th edition). Boston: Houghton Mifflin). Pauk advised students to use a large, loose-leaf notebook, with holes punched for filing. This is better than a bound notebook, because you can organize the notes in a file binder. You can also take out notes and rewrite them. Pauk's method, which is now called the Cornell system, is based on a specific page layout.

Pauk told students to divide up the page into three areas. The first area is a column 5 cm wide on the left side of the page. This is the cue area. The main part of the page is the note-taking area. At the bottom of the page, there is a row 8 cm high, which is the summary area. The basic grid with information on what each section should contain is reproduced in the additional resources section (Resource 9B).

The note-taking and learning process involves the *Five Rs* in the order listed in the introduction to this lesson. There are many references on the Internet for this system. A useful one at the time of writing is:

www.clt.cornell.edu/campus/learn/LSC_Resources/cornellsystem.pdf

Exercise A

Set for pairwork discussion. Refer students to the lecture slide. Tell them to look at the title and bullet points, and for each bullet point to make questions which they expect the lecturer to answer. Do not explain any words from the slide or allow students to check in their dictionaries at this point, as the meanings of these words will be dealt with in the lecture.

Feed back with the whole class, asking several students to read out their questions. Write some of the questions on the board if you wish.

🎧 Exercise B

1–3 Refer the students to the notes at the bottom of the page. Tell them that this student has used the Cornell system to take notes but has not managed to complete everything and so has left some gaps.

(Note that this is quite a normal occurrence in note-taking – details may need to be filled in later, for example, by checking with other people.)

Allow the students time to read the gapped notes. Also make sure they read question 2 and are ready to listen out for a story.

Play Part 1, pausing after each major point if you feel the students are struggling and need more time.

Tell students to work in pairs to compare their answers to questions 1 and 2, and to complete the summary in 3. Feed back with the whole class, using an OHT or projection of the answers if you wish. (The completed notes are reproduced in Resource 9C, in the additional resources section, to facilitate this.)

4 Now focus on the *recite* element of the Cornell system. Point out that here the student has completed the *Review* section. Cover up the *Notes* section of the answer and ask students if they can say anything about the first and second questions in the review. Then put the students in pairs to test each other on the remaining notes.

Answers

Model answers:

1/3/4   See table below and Resource 9C.

Review	Notes	Motivation:

4 theories of motivation are ...?	1. <u>4 key theories</u>
	    a. <u>Maslow</u>
	    b. <u>Mayo</u>
		– Hierarchy of *needs*
		– scientific ➔ human *relations/relationships*

Theory X people are ...?
Theory Y people are ...?
	c. <u>McGregor</u>
	
	    d. *Herzberg*
		– Theory X and Theory Y
		    Theory X = people who are *lazy*
		    Theory Y= people who like *responsibility*
		– Motivators = job satisfaction, etc.
		– Hygiene Factors = negative things, e.g., *low pay or threats*

3 forms of motivation are ...?	2. <u>3 methods of motivation:</u>
	    a. <u>payment</u>
	
	    b. *incentives*
		– wage/salary/commission/fees/benefits
		– management – pay rates competitive?
		– employees – pay fair?
		PRP – links pay to targets or work *performance*
		– bonuses – for good performance or reaching *targets*
		– commissions – more business = more commission

3 types of non-financial rewards are ...?	c. <u>non-financial rewards</u> Basically non-fin. rewards	– job design ➔ job satisfaction – opportunity for more *responsibility* – social life, holidays, etc. – Mgmt can give job *enlargement/enrichment* or job *rotation* = making staff *feel good*

Summary
There are four key theories relating to motivation – from Maslow to Herzberg, and three ways of motivating workers: payment, incentives and non-financial rewards.

2 The lecturer talks about his/her own experience of bad human resources management. It is not in the notes because it is a digression – because as a personal experience it is not essential information for the subject.

Transcript 🎧 1.39

Part 1

Quiet, please! As future managers of people, this morning you're going to learn about motivating and developing employees – and making the best of people. I'll outline some of the most important thinking about motivation and rewards, and I'll go on and talk about learning and development later on.

But before we begin, I have a little story to tell you … I once worked for an importing and distribution company with a very dynamic boss with fantastic ideas. There was a gap in the market, and his business was ready to fill it and make a lot of money. However, he failed because he never invested anything in his staff. There were never any bonuses, never nice words said or respect given, nor were there any courses. The workers and their conditions were miserable. After our international customers had telephone contact with deeply unhappy workers, they quickly gave up on us because of the unfriendly response they got. I lost my job after a year because the company went bust.

Of course, the point of the story is that people are the most important resource in your company, so pay attention to them! So, OK … to get back to the main part of my lecture.

Now, in terms of motivation, let's start with some basic concepts managers need to know. Motivation is all about satisfying people's needs. And research has shown that there are a lot of aspects to consider in understanding how people are motivated and satisfied or dissatisfied. It's complex. So there are a number of experts that must be mentioned first.

Firstly, look at this pyramid: Maslow (that's M-A-S-L-O-W) … in 1954 … categorized needs into groups by writing a 'hierarchy of needs' shaped like a pyramid … with physical needs at the bottom, security and safety next up, love and belonging third, esteem or respect fourth, and self-actualization (being able to use your creativity to let things happen) at the top.

Another area of thinking, by Elton Mayo (that's M-A-Y-O) in the 1930s, was a move away from management being scientific and only focused on time, efficiency and waste. It was towards 'human relations' theory, which claimed people work better when they feel they belong and are happy in their team relationships.

Douglas McGregor, in 1960, divided workers into 'Theory X' and 'Theory Y'. Theory X people tend to be lazier and are motivated by pay or punishment only – they need controlling by management. Theory Y people are self-motivated and appreciate being independent in their work – management can give them projects to take charge of.

Another great mind, Herzberg, that's H-E-R-Z-B-E-R-G … examined satisfaction … in 1960 … he found two factors that affect satisfaction. 'Motivators' are things that give you job satisfaction, like being praised or promoted. 'Hygiene factors' (that's hygiene, H-Y-G-I-E-N-E, like the word meaning cleanliness) are factors that make a worker unsatisfied – negative things like low pay, punishment, dangerous situations, etc., to be avoided.

All of these thinkers, and many others, have helped us to understand what makes people feel motivated to work well or more effectively.

OK, so to start with, let's take a few moments to consider practical ways to motivate workers. Basically, it's all about rewards. You have financial rewards and non-financial rewards. Financial rewards are about giving people money. Non-financial are other ways to make them happy. There are three important aspects of rewarding people.

The first one is the most common: payments. You can pay staff a wage by the hour or day, or a salary by the month. Sometimes there are set fees for jobs. Then there are commissions (like paying people 10% of the turnover of a job or a transaction). And there are also benefits, like giving healthcare or insurance or the use of a car. It could be argued that payments are the only way to reward. But as we shall see, there are useful ways other than financial rewards.

From the point of view of management, payments work well because the main reason people work is for money. However, there are many considerations, like how your pay compares with your competitors. Who is going to recruit the best and brightest people, do you think? That's right – the highest paying companies do … usually.

For employees, issues to think about are whether the pay is fair, whether it lets them have a good standard of living and how it compares with other professions and other people's incomes. For Theory X workers, it keeps them going. It pays the bills for the needs at the lower end of Maslow's hierarchy: home costs, food, safety and such things.

The second area for discussion is called incentives. Increasingly, we find that businesses and other organizations give bonuses or profit share, or even company shares, to their staff for reaching a target or for working well during the year. This is performance-related pay (or PRP). Many companies do this: try to measure what you produce or achieve and link your level of pay to it. Or they measure merits, like your flexibility or punctuality. There are 'piece rates', for example, where you get paid for each item you make or task you carry out. It's really payment for results, which seems like a good incentive to employees. And commissions are often an incentive, because the bigger the business, the bigger the commission paid. Like recruitment agents: the higher the salary of the successful applicant they find, the higher their reward will be (the commission).

However, incentives can be hard to make completely fair. How can you truly measure a merit like cooperation? Will these schemes distort how people work? What I mean is, will they find ways to cheat? It's true to say that PRP has a good effect on productivity. But some people come to expect their bonus and see it as a normal part of their salary rather than a reward for doing well. So its purpose is lost.

The third area to look at is non-financial rewards. What I mean by that is that most companies now realize that it takes more than money to satisfy workers and make them do a good job. And so you 'design' a job to give a sense of achievement, or recognition for doing well, or stimulating things to do in a safe environment. Theory Y type people might welcome taking on more responsibility. Others may appreciate a social life, breaks, events and holidays. When we look at non-financial rewards from a management point of view, we talk about job enlargement and enrichment (which mean increasing a worker's range of work, responsibility or challenge, and perhaps their power to make decisions). And there's job rotation (which means letting workers change jobs regularly to avoid getting bored). This allows them to become multi-skilled or able to do a greater range of tasks. Also, letting people become part of advisory teams, like quality circles that advise on products, gives them the respect of being an expert.

OK, so non-financial rewards are about making staff feel good. So it should be clear that money is not everything and workers do want a healthy work-life balance, that is, a life that includes stimulation, community, social activity, support in times of stress or ill health, and so on. ... (fade)

🎧 Exercise C

1 Tell the students to divide up a page of their notebooks into the three sections of the Cornell system. They should try to take notes in the *Notes* section as they listen. Warn them that they may not be able to complete their notes while writing, so they should leave spaces which they can fill in later. Play Part 2 straight through. Then put the students in pairs to complete any gaps in their notes. Feed back with the whole class. Build up a set of notes on the board.

2/3 Set the students to work in pairs to complete the review questions and the summary. Feed back with the whole class.

4 Discuss with the class the extent to which their pre-questions in Exercise A have been answered.

Answers

Model answers:

Review	Notes
	Learning and development
Role of induction training?	Induction training places new employee within the system and company culture
Training for who ...?	Training: @ 3 levels → combat skills shortages a. Org. level, e.g., to train staff in a new system b. Dept. level c. Individual level → meet needs of individuals [Recession = training cutbacks – training costly]
Training types ...?	Types of training: a. graduate – trains new grads. 4 mgmt roles b. vocational – gives qualification c. in-house training – within company d. e-learning/distance learning in employees' own time e. job rotation and/or working alongside others – e.g., apprenticeship, coaching, mentoring Training process: = needs analysis → course → post-course evaluation Training decisions: made @ appraisal
Appraisal ... ? Its function is to ...?	Appraisal = meeting manager ←→ employee → a. identify employee goals & fit → company goals b. confirm employee feels extended/challenged/growing c. identify learning & development needs
What types ...?	Types of appraisal: a. *self-appraisal* – employee appraises own performance vs company-given guidelines b. *peer appraisal* – colleagues ←→ self c. 360° appraisal – colleagues/self/people ↑ & ↓

Management responsibilities are ...?	Ownership of appraisal: by management – essential.
	Managers must be trained
	                       keep confidences
	Process must be open and clear
	                       involve everyone
	                       be efficient
	                       set achievable actions

Summary
Learning and development is an HRM function that identifies training needs at appraisal and supplies appropriate training and monitors training outcomes.

Transcript 🎧 1.40

Part 2

Of course, you will probably be thinking that one of the best ways to motivate through non-financial rewards is to give the worker the promise of self-improvement and promotion, and yes, you are right – this can be achieved through supporting them in learning and development. So let's now turn to learning and development.

In fact, the first piece of learning an employee does, i.e., the first training a company tends to offer an employee, is their induction programme. A good induction helps a worker understand the company and their position in it and is important as newly employed individuals are the most likely to resign and leave a company.

Apart from inductions, there is simply a need for training because, with the fast-moving nature of industry, there is often a shortage of skills. Governments usually help companies address this problem. They often provide training schemes or incentives for companies to train.

Training may be necessary at the organizational level if there are completely new operational systems for everyone to implement, for example. Or it may be smaller-scale: at the departmental level. Or it may be individual, according to the needs of a single person.

In times of recession, training in companies may need to be cut back, and it does tend to be provided *less* when times are hard. Training is costly. There are not only the costs of the training, but also the lost productivity of a trainee not working on the days of the training.

Training can take place in many forms. There is graduate training which prepares newly employed graduates for management positions. There are formal vocational courses that can earn the trainee a recognized qualification. Then there are in-house courses (these are put on by the employer, either with internal or external trainers, and either in the premises or away). Then there are various e-learning or online courses and distance-learning courses that employees can attempt in their own time and at their own speed. Of course, there are all sorts of apprenticeship schemes where a worker learns the job alongside another worker. A similar approach is job rotation, where a worker learns about the company by trying a variety of jobs. These are sometimes called on-the-job training, while an away-day would be off-the-job training. Finally, there are mentoring and coaching schemes, where an individual mentor or coach works with a person one-to-one to allow them to grow and develop.

Of course, all training, whether it is learning a new computer software system, a health and safety procedure or communication skills such as making presentations, must be planned. There must be a needs analysis beforehand – research into what people need. And afterwards, the people who took part normally give an evaluation of the training's success. Usually this is done by passing around a questionnaire.

So the question remains, who decides on training and when? And, of course, how? Well, perhaps the most obvious time to discuss and agree on training needs is at appraisal. What is appraisal? Appraisal is a meeting that employees have, usually with their line manager or another superior. In it, they identify what their goals are, how they fit with the company's goals and are thus contributing, and whether they feel they are extended, challenged and growing. Appraisal is a time when learning and development needs are often identified. It's collaborative – between the senior and junior members. But there's also self-appraisal, where the worker appraises him or herself according to guidelines given, and reports it. Or there is peer appraisal, whereby your colleagues appraise you and vice versa. There is also what is known as 360-degree appraisal. 360-degree appraisal asks for the opinions of all these people and also people *below* you in the hierarchy.

Um. Now, where was I? Oh yes, I was about to talk about the importance of appraisal systems … to be successful, they must be 'owned' and controlled by all the managers who administer the process. And these managers must be trained properly and able to keep confidences (I mean be anonymous) when appropriate. The process must be clear and open with a chance for everyone involved to participate fully. They must be efficient. And 'actions' that come from the appraisals must be easy for people to implement.

So what exactly have we looked at this morning? Well, to sum up, we need to first emphasize that the development of people is profoundly important in … (fade)

🎧 Exercise D

Allow students time to read the phrases and the types of information, making sure that they understand any difficult words. Note that they are being asked not for the words that the speaker uses but what *type* of information the words represent. Note also that the information types may be needed more than once.

Play the sentences one at a time, allowing time for students to identify the type of information which follows. Check answers after each sentence, making sure that students understand what the information actually is that follows.

Answer

Model answers:

Fixed phrase	Type of information which follows	Actual words/information
1 In terms of …	an aspect of a topic the speaker wants to focus on	motivation, …
2 Research has shown that …	a statement the speaker agrees with	there are a lot of aspects to consider in understanding how people are motivated and satisfied or dissatisfied.
3 It could be argued that …	an idea the speaker may not agree with	payments are the only way to reward.
4 As we shall see, …	information about a point the speaker will make later	there are useful ways other than through financial rewards.
5 From the point of view of …	an aspect of a topic the speaker wants to focus on	management, payments work well because the main reason people work is for money.
6 Increasingly, we find that …	a developing trend	businesses … give bonuses or profit share, or even company shares, to their staff for reaching a target or for working well during the year.
7 It's true to say that …	a statement the speaker agrees with	PRP has a good effect on productivity.
8 So it should be clear that …	a conclusion	money is not everything and workers do want a healthy work life-balance …

Transcript 🎧 1.41

1 Now, in terms of motivation, let's start with some basic concepts managers need to know.

2 And research has shown that there are a lot of aspects to consider in understanding how people are motivated and satisfied or dissatisfied.

3 It could be argued that payments are the only way to reward.

4 But as we shall see, there are useful ways other than through financial rewards.

5 From the point of view of management, payments work well because the main reason people work is for money.

6 Increasingly, we find that businesses and other organizations give bonuses or profit share, or even company shares, to their staff for reaching a target or for working well during the year.

7 It's true to say that PRP has a good effect on productivity.

8 So it should be clear that money is not everything and workers do want a healthy work-life balance, that is, a life that includes stimulation, community, social activity, support in times of stress of ill health, and so on.

Closure

Predicting information: play short sections from Part 2 of the lecture again. Stop the recording just before a word or phrase you want the students to produce and ask them what comes next in the lecture. For example:

… the first training a company tends to offer an employee, is their induction programme. A good induction helps [STOP] *a worker understand the company and their position in it.*

… Training can take place in many forms. There is graduate training which [STOP] … *prepares newly employed graduates for management positions.*

Alternatively, do this exercise by reading out parts of the transcript.

9.3 Extending skills

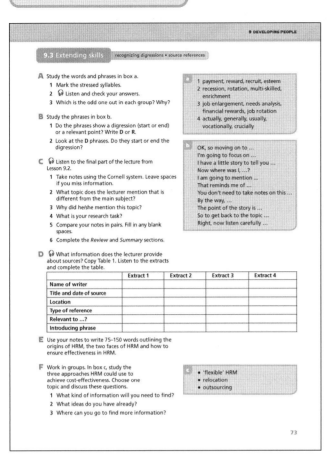

Lesson aims

- recognize digressions: start and end
- understand reference to other people's ideas: source, quotes, relevance

Further practice in:

- stress within words and phrases
- leaving space in notes for missing information – especially digressions

Introduction

Revise the lecture in Lesson 9.2 by asking students to use their Cornell notes. They should cover up the *Notes* section and use the *Review* and *Summary* sections to help recall the contents of the lecture. They could work in pairs to do this.

🎧 Exercise A

1 Set for individual work and pairwork checking. Students can underline the stressed syllables.

2 Play the recording for students to check their answers.

3 Set for individual work and pairwork checking. Tell students they need to identify the odd one out in terms of stress (not the meanings of the words).

Feed back with the whole class, checking students' pronunciation, especially of the compound words, and eliciting the odd ones out.

Answers

Model answers:

1/3 (odd one out in italics)

1 'payment, re'ward, re'cruit, es'teem
2 re'cession, ro'tation, *'multi-'skilled*, en'richment
3 'job en'largement, *'needs a'nalysis*, fin'ancial re'wards, 'job ro'tation
4 'actually, 'generally, 'usually, *vo'cationally*, 'crucially

Transcript 🎧 1.42

1 'payment, re'ward, re'cruit, es'teem
2 re'cession, ro'tation, 'multi-'skilled, en'richment
3 'job en'largement, 'needs a'nalysis, fin'ancial re'wards, 'job ro'tation
4 'actually, 'generally, 'usually, vo'cationally, 'crucially

Exercise B

Set for individual work and pairwork checking. Feed back with the whole class. Note that some of these phrases are from this final part of the lecture but some of these phrases are recycled from earlier parts, in Lesson 9.2. Note also that the end of a digression is actually a transition back to the main point.

Answers

Model answers:

1/2 OK, so moving on to ... R

I'm going to focus on ... R

I have a little story to tell you ... D (start)

Now where was I, ...? D (end)

I am going to mention ... R

That reminds me of ... D (start)

You don't need to take notes on this ... D (start)

By the way, ... D (start)

The point of the story is ... D (end)

So to get back to the topic ... D (end)

Right, now listen carefully ... R

🎧 Exercise C

Refer the students to the lecture slide in Lesson 9.2. Ask them what they know already about HRM. What would they like to know?

159

Tell them to prepare a page to take notes using the Cornell system. Remind them that they may not get all the information. If they miss something, they should leave a space. They can fill it in after the lecture.

Let them read the questions through and tell them to listen out for the answers to questions 2, 3 and 4.

1 Play Part 3 straight through.

2–4 Set for pairwork. Feed back with the whole class. Ask for suggestions for phrases to use to find out about the importance of digressions, e.g., *Why did he/she start talking about …? I didn't understand the bit about … Is it important?* and so on (see *Skills Bank*).

5/6 Set for pairwork. Students compare their notes, complete any blank spaces and then write the *Review* and *Summary* sections.

Feed back with the whole class, building a set of notes on the board.

Answers

Possible answers:

1 See notes below.

2 The Cornell note-taking system.

3 It's important to know how to take good notes.

4 To prepare a case study of a company that has done one of these three options:

- exploited flexibility to cut costs
- relocated to cut staffing costs
- outsourced to cut staffing costs

5/6 See notes.

Review	Notes
What's hard/soft HRM?	Quantitative analysis and planning v. the 'people' side Drucker 1954 coined HRM (prev. Pers. Mgmt) McGregor 1957 soft HRM
What is the best measure of effectiveness for HR?	Keeping HRM cost-effective: Number of ways: labour turnover/absenteeism, relations, profitability/productivity Measure of success of good HRM is cost-effectiveness
What does 'flexibility' in HRM mean?	Atkinson 1985 – Inst. of Manpower Studies: Flexibility – % of staff flexible in way they work • workers who work only when required
Methods?	• e.g., P-T/occasional/self-empl/job-share Relocation: – moving whole/part of business ➔ country with lower labour costs

	Outsourcing: – getting another co. to run part of your operation, e.g., Indian call centres

Summary:

Hard and soft HRM are two faces: one analytic for planning, the other for supporting and developing people. Several factors measure success of HRM. Atkinson's flexibility principle suggests ways of keeping HRM cost-effective, including different worker terms of employment, relocation and outsourcing.

Transcript 🎧 1.43

Part 3

OK, so moving on to look at other important concepts in human resource management. I'm going to focus on what people mean by 'hard' and 'soft' HRM and what makes HRM 'successful'; I'm going to explain what is meant by a 'flexible' workforce, and I am going to mention 'relocation' and 'outsourcing', two other key ideas for managers of people.

The concept of human resource management took the place of the earlier concept, 'personnel management'. Personnel management was simply managing people, as organizations have always had to manage people. Then American academics began to see human resources as a bigger area of study and called it HRM. The term originated in the 1950s with academics like Peter Drucker (who wrote a book called *The Practice of Management* in 1954). But it didn't really make it to Europe and Britain until the 1980s.

With the greater focus on the growing profession, it then split into two areas: 'hard' HRM and 'soft' HRM. Hard HRM is about predicting and planning employment levels – that is, a quantitative approach. Such forecasting and planning means you have to understand changes in the market and the business, technology, the population, the competition and government legislation, among other things. So a lot of analysis! And, of course, hiring and firing. Soft HRM, on the other hand, is about supporting, motivating and satisfying workers, training and developing them and managing the culture (and perhaps industrial relations) within an organization.

Oh yes, that reminds me of the other important thinker in the field. It was a few years after Drucker's work. His name was D. McGregor, whose book in 1957 was called *The Human Side of Enterprise*. It's in the library. So you can see where the origins of HRM lie, and how it divided into 'hard' and 'soft'. Make sure you note the difference.

By the way, speaking of note-taking, I see that some of you are using the Cornell note-taking system. That's great. Do you all know about this? No? Right, well, if you want to know more about it, I suggest you look at *How to Study in College* by Walter Pauk (that's P-A-U-K), the 9th edition I think, published in 2007. It's very good, and it should be in the university library, too. I'm sure that you all know how important this is.

So to get back to the topic ... how do you tell if HRM is effective? Well, there are a number of ways. If labour turnover is low (in other words, if people tend to stay a long time in the company) and absenteeism is low (i.e., people are not always away sick), then these are good signs. Relations with stakeholders outside the company and industrial relations within the company are also important. But perhaps most important is simply profitability and labour productivity. The key questions you can ask yourself are: Are the staff committed? Are they cost-effective (i.e., cheap to employ compared with what they achieve)? Are they competent? And do they have the same goals as management?

Now, when being lean through cutting costs became popular back in the 80s, the idea of (and I quote) 'the flexible firm' was coined by John Atkinson of the Institute of Manpower Studies ... in 1985. Since then, 'flexibility' has become a popular term and is also considered a sign of successful HRM. The idea is to have a proportion of your company flexible in the way they work: part-time, occasional (or temporary), self-employed, job-sharing or hourly paid, for example. These kinds of workers only work when they are required to. It can suit people such as young mothers, though many people would disagree and claim that it exploits them. It certainly saves a company money.

Another way to save money is outsourcing and relocation. These days, with globalization it is very easy to reduce costs by moving your business or part of your business to a lower-cost country ... or perhaps enter a contract to get another company to manage or run some of your work for you, e.g., an operation – usually less expensively than you can do it. In India, the average salary is lower than in Europe, so many companies have taken advantage of the country's excellently educated and English-speaking population and have moved their telephone call centres to India.

Now, I think that's all I'm going to say for the moment on HRM. Are there any questions so far? (*Pause*) No? Good. Now when I see you in tutorials, we'll look at this in more detail. In the meantime, I'm going to set you a research task. Right, now listen carefully ... your task is to find a case study on how a company has managed to have its staff become more flexible ... OR how a company has relocated operations or outsourced to save money. I'd like you to work in groups of three. Each group should research one company case study and report back on your findings.

🎧 Exercise D

Tell students that lecturers will often give references while they talk, and it is important to note down any references. The kinds of information may differ – they may just be names of books or articles, they may be an exact quotation (a 'direct quote') or they may be a paraphrase (sometimes called an 'indirect quotation'). Refer students to the table and check that they know what each row represents.

Play each extract and allow students time to complete the sections of the table. Check with the whole class.

Answers

Model answers:

	Extract 1	Extract 2	Extract 3	Extract 4
Name of writer	Peter Drucker	D. McGregor	Walter Pauk	John Atkinson
Title and date of source	*The Practice of Management* 1954	*The Human Side of Enterprise* 1957	*How to Study in College* 9th edition 2007	1985
Location	not mentioned	library	university library	not mentioned
Type of reference	indirect (concept only): name of book	indirect (concept only): name of book	indirect (concept only): name of book	direct quotation: possibly from a journal article (not stated)
Relevant to ...?	Origins of HRM	Origins of hard/soft HRM	Cornell note-taking	the idea of flexible HRM
Introducing phrase	The term originated ... with academics like ...	Oh yes, that reminds me of the other important thinker in the field. ... His name was ...	I suggest you look at ...	... the idea of (and I quote) 'the flexible firm' was used for the first time by ...

Transcript 🎧 1.44

Extract 1

Personnel management was simply managing people, as organizations have always had to manage people. Then American academics began to see human resources as a bigger area of study and called it HRM. The term originated in the 1950s with academics like Peter Drucker (who wrote a book called *The Practice of Management* in 1954). But it didn't really make it to Europe and Britain until the 1980s.

Extract 2

Soft HRM, on the other hand, is about supporting, motivating and satisfying workers, training and developing them and managing the culture (and perhaps industrial relations) within an organization. Oh yes, that reminds me of the other important thinker in the field. It was a few years after Drucker's work. His name was D. McGregor, whose book in 1957 was called *The Human Side of Enterprise*. It's in the library.

Extract 3

By the way, speaking of note-taking, I see that some of you are using the Cornell note-taking system. That's great. Do you all know about this? No? Right, well, if you want to know more about it, I suggest you look at *How to Study in College* by Walter Pauk (that's P-A-U-K), the 9th edition I think, published in 2007. It's very good, and it should be in the university library, too.

Extract 4

Now, when being lean through cutting costs became popular back in the 80s, the idea of (and I quote) 'the flexible firm' was coined by John Atkinson of the Institute of Manpower Studies … in 1985. Since then, 'flexibility' has become a popular term and is also considered a sign of successful HRM.

Exercise E

Set for individual work – possibly homework – or else a pair/small-group writing task. If the latter, tell students to put their writing on an OHT or other visual medium so that the whole class can see and comment on what has been written. You can correct language errors on the OHT. Attempt to elicit the corrections from the students before correcting them yourself.

For prompts, see the transcript. For weaker groups, one student can be taken aside and shown the transcript for a few minutes before returning to their group to share the content assimilated during the diversion.

Exercise F

Tell students to work in groups of three or four. Either give each group a topic or allow them to choose. Make sure that each topic is covered by at least one, or preferably two groups.

Feed back on questions 1–3 with the whole class. Tell students that each student should now carry out research into the group's topic. They should each look at a different source and so will need to decide who is going to look at which one. You will also need to arrange the date for the feedback and discussion of the information – this is the focus of Exercise D in Lesson 9.4. Tell students that in Lesson 9.4 they will take part in a seminar on this topic.

Answers

Possible answers:

1 Information to find: What are the concepts involved in each idea? How do companies apply them in real life? What are the advantages and disadvantages of each one? What strategies could a company adopt to manage the disadvantages? What criteria could HRM use to choose the best strategy for cost-cutting?

2 a Flexibility is arranging for a proportion of staff to work in ways that suit them, e.g., self-employment, part-time, job sharing, etc.

   b Relocation, for this purpose, is moving the whole or part of a company to a country with cheaper labour costs, e.g., call centres being located in India.

   c Outsourcing is contracting out part of a company's operations to another company which can do it more cheaply.

3 Use subject textbooks, books found in the library catalogues, articles found using online e-resources (academic directories) and the Internet (e.g., search engines like Google or Google Scholar and various news media like the BBC) to find out the necessary information.

Alternatively (or in addition) – depending on your teaching situation and access to the sources of information – you can refer the students to the information on page 105 of the Course Book. Some additional sites are given in Resource 9D in the additional resources section.

Closure

Resource 9E is a description by a young graduate trainee of her new job in HRM at Spendwise Supermarkets.

1 Ask students to go to Resource 9E and complete the gaps in the text with key terms.

Answers

1 hard
2 staffing
3 competitor/rival
4 technological
5 recruits
6 assessment
7 conditions
8 verbal
9 soft
10 coaching

2 Ask students to work in pairs to discuss what other skills training she could be offered and what the follow-up procedures should be once she has completed the course.

Answer

Accept any reasonable suggestion. In softer HR, she may need to have good training skills, and eventually, perhaps coaching or mentoring skills. In harder HR, she may also need some of the above and also good interviewing techniques. She would need substantial IT training in the company's particular information system applications for forecasting and modelling labour requirements. She is bound to have to use advanced spreadsheets. She might also benefit from presentation skills training as HR professionals often have to present, and communication skills are paramount. During her first year she may be mentored. Her appraisals will be a suitable time to follow up and talk about all these needs.

9.4 Extending skills

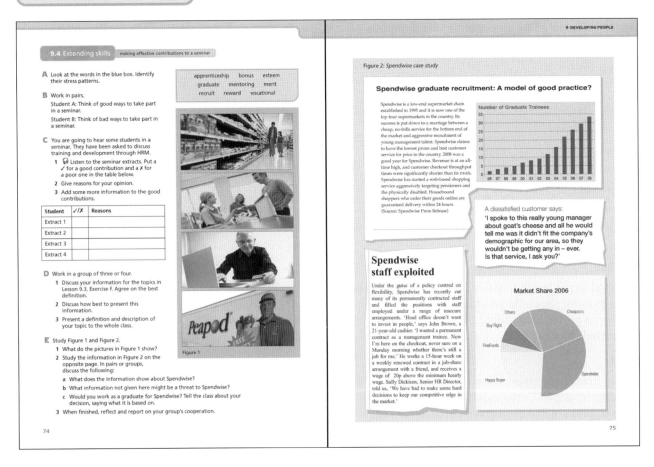

Lesson aims

- make effective contributions to a seminar

Further practice in:

- stress within words

Introduction

Use a few of the review cues from the Cornell notes in Lesson 9.3 for students to try to recall the ideas on HRM in the lecture. If the students appear to be having difficulty remembering, ask them to look again at their own notes from Exercise C in Lesson 9.3. Check that students are clear about the difference between hard HRM and soft HRM. Ask them to give the main differences:

- Hard HRM involves making strategic staffing level decisions, job analysis, recruitment and performance appraisal
- Soft HRM involves development and maximization of employee potential, training schemes, nurturing of corporate culture, handling labour problems

Exercise A

Set for individual work and pairwork checking.

Answers

Model answer:

Oo	bonus, merit
oO	esteem, recruit, reward
Ooo	graduate, mentoring
oOoo	apprenticeship, vocational

Exercise B

This is revision from Unit 5. Draw on the whiteboard two columns for *Do's* and *Don'ts*. Set for individual work and pairwork checking. Feed back with the whole class. Give a time limit and see which pair can think of the most *Do's* and *Don'ts* in the time. Refer to Unit 5 Lesson 5.4 for suggestions if you need to.

Answers

Possible answers:

Do's	Don'ts
prepare the topic beforehand	
ask politely for information	demand information from other students

use as correct language as possible	
speak clearly	mumble, whisper or shout
say when you agree with someone	get angry if someone disagrees with you
link correctly with previous speakers	
build on points made by other speakers	
make a contribution, even if you are not sure if it is new or relevant	stay silent, waiting for 'the perfect moment'
be constructive	be negative
explain your point clearly	
give specific examples to help explain a point	be vague
listen carefully to what others say	start a side conversation
allow others to speak	dominate the discussion
paraphrase to check understanding	
use clear visuals, if appropriate	

🎧 **Exercise C**

Check that students understand the topic for the seminar discussion. Ask them what they might expect to hear. Work through these extracts one at a time. Complete questions 1–3 for each extract before moving on to the next.

1 Set for individual work.

2 First check that students have understood the extract as well as possible. Then ask for opinions from the whole class on the contribution.

3 Once everyone has a clear notion of whether the contribution is a good one, ask for suggestions for additional points. Alternatively, set this part for pairwork after you have completed questions 1 and 2.

Answers

Model answers:

	✓ or ✗	Reasons	Possible additional information
Extract 1	✓	Speaks clearly, explains the point clearly, answers correctly, uses good fixed phrases, the answer is short though.	Training may result in/from job design being adjusted to provide a sense of achievement; using job rotation, enlargement or enrichment; Theory Y people will react to more responsibility; workers becoming multi-skilled.
Extract 2	✗	Does not speak clearly, does not answer the question, doesn't define soft HRM, poor use of visuals.	
Extract 3	✓	Speaks clearly, is extending the question, answers precisely, uses good fixed phrases, has prepared well. Information could be better organized.	Perhaps: on-the-job training through job rotation to teach a variety of skills.
Extract 4	✓	Speaks clearly, explains the point clearly, answers correctly, uses good fixed phrases, has prepared well, has a good visual.	Perhaps: 1 appraisal is collaborative – how? 2 explaining the need for employees to feel extended, challenged and that they are growing.

Transcript 🎧 **1.45**

Extract 1

It seems quite clear that training and development is one of the best non-financial incentives to develop a workforce that is proud of its capabilities, satisfied in its work, and is more ready to stay in a company long-term.

Extract 2

Erm, I think one big thing about soft HRM is the development of people. This is very important. It is possible, we can see, how this is very important. So let's look at the diagram and ... oh, sorry, that's the wrong one, just a minute ... right, so here is the overlap between 'hard' and 'soft' HRM ... er, you can see I think, this bit here ... do you have any questions about this bit? ...

Extract 3

We could ask the question: how can training be delivered in an organization? Well, the answer is clear. You can enrol workers on a course that gives them a qualification. It could be external or by distance learning or online learning at their own pace. Or you could have in-house training where you provide or bring in trainers. There are other ways to train on the job as well: you can create apprenticeships, mentoring or coaching schemes, where people pair up and may train each other. And most graduates need some induction training.

Extract 4

What is appraisal? Well, appraisal is when employees meet with their line manager to identify their goals and how they fit with the company's goals. They might discuss how they can be extended through training. There is also self-appraisal, where the employee appraises him or herself and reports it. You can see the types on this chart. There is also peer appraisal, from your colleagues, and 360-degree appraisal, from everyone you work with.

Exercise D

Students should work in the same groups as their research groups from Lesson 9.3, Exercise F. They will need to have with them the research they have done individually on the group's chosen topic.

Decide how you want students to present their information, e.g.,

- short talk with/without projection, an OHT, or other visual medium
- to the whole class or to another group

Make sure that students understand the options for the presentation types.

1 Tell each group to discuss the information that they have found and agree on the best definition and description of the type of strategy they have researched.

2 In discussing this question, students will need to decide who is going to speak when and say what. Encourage them to practise presenting to each other before talking to the whole class.

3 Allow each group a maximum of five minutes for the presentation. Then allow some time for questions. If more than one group have done the same topic, encourage disagreement and critical analysis.

Exercise E

1 This is a case study of a fictitious 'no-frills' supermarket which will give more practice in discussion. To set the context, first refer students to the pictures of a supermarket interior in Figure 1. With the whole class, elicit the words needed to discuss the different stages of supermarket operations (e.g., ordering, supply chain, distribution networks, online shopping, cashier, checkout, delivery van). Discuss supermarket shopping with the class. Ask them where they shop for food and what they like in a supermarket and its staff. What aspects of the supermarket operation do they think a 'cheap' supermarket would need to focus on in order to cut costs and keep food cheap for its customers?

2 Put the students in pairs (or threes). At stage c, each pair can join another pair and agree a decision.

a In their pairs, students can divide the information between them and then summarize the information for their partner. If there are words that they do not understand, they will need to check meanings in dictionaries or online.

b Students will briefly need to think here about social, political or environmental factors which might have a negative effect on Spendwise's business. For example, as air travel is used to fly fresh vegetables into the country, supermarkets can be considered to be a big polluter, and countries may decide to impose more tax on air travel in the future which will force food costs up. Equally, competition from other supermarkets, and economic conditions dictating consumer spending power, will need to be mentioned.

c In reaching some level of consensus on this (or agreeing to differ) and coming to a conclusion, students should use the graphs as well as the factual information given in the short texts, or any other factors they feel are relevant, to justify their answer.

3 Ask a representative from each group to reflect and report on the discussion. Emphasize the features of a good seminar from Exercise B. What phrases were used to include everyone? Who tried to include and elicit ideas from others? Who listened the most? Compare the reflections of each representative to allow the whole class to understand what being constructive and collaborative means, and the part they played – and will play next time – in achieving this.

Closure

Use the *Vocabulary bank* at the end of the Course Book unit to check that the group can remember the meaning, spelling and pronunciation of HRM vocabulary.

Extra activities

This unit contains technical and semi-technical vocabulary. Students will need practice with the vocabulary.

1 Work through the *Vocabulary bank* and *Skills bank* if you have not already done so, or as revision of previous study.

2 Use the Activity bank (Teacher's Book additional resources section, Resource 9A).

A Set the crossword for individual work (including homework) or pairwork.

Answers

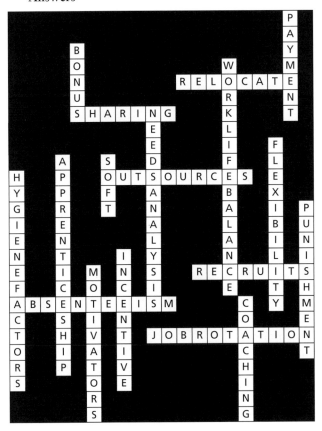

B Ask students to think about each of the nouns in the box: are plural forms of the nouns possible? Tell students to use an English–English dictionary or online definitions to help them find out the answers to the following questions.

1 Which forms are countable and which uncountable?

2 Do the countable and uncountable forms have different meanings?

Answers

Noun	Normally countable or uncountable?	Notes
flexibility	U	in HRM terms this refers to aspects of employment conditions offered to workers
induction	U	a training period for a new employee
conditions	C	the non-monetary aspects of your working arrangements
mentoring	U	when an experienced worker guides a less experienced worker
coaching	U	one-to-one work on development
payments	C/U	providing money in exchange for work done
stakeholder	C	a person who is affected by the company in some way, e.g., shareholders, neighbours, suppliers
training	U	the process of teaching and learning
relocation	U	moving a company or part of its operations to a country with low labour costs
reward	C	a positive motivator
incentive	C	a concrete reason to do something

3 Revise note-taking symbols – see the list at the back of the Course Book. Check back to Unit 5 if necessary. Give the meanings and ask students to write down the symbol (or do it the other way round). Then ask students to think about and discuss which ones they actually use. Are there any other ones that they have come across that they think are useful?

Alternatively, write the meanings on a set of cards. Put students in groups of about six, with two teams in each group. Give each group a pile of cards. A student from each team picks a card and, without showing the members of his/her team, draws the appropriate symbol. The members of his/her team must say what the symbol stands for. If the student writes the correct symbol and the team gets the meaning right, the team gets a point. If the student writes the wrong symbol and/or the team gets it wrong, the team loses a point. The teams take it in turns to pick a card.

10 INDUSTRIAL RELATIONS

Unit 10 builds on the previous unit themes in managing human resources and extends into the related and important area of industrial relations. While this topic is fundamental to the historical development of how Western managers have come to manage people, it may be alien or unusual to some students from more recently developed economies without traditions of unionism. By means of a well-referenced academic text, the evolution and procedures in industrial relations are explained.

Skills focus

Reading

- recognizing the writer's stance and level of confidence or tentativeness
- inferring implicit ideas

Writing

- writing situation – problem – solution – evaluation essays
- using direct quotations
- compiling a bibliography/reference list

Vocabulary focus

- 'neutral' and 'marked' words
- fixed phrases from industrial relations
- fixed phrases from academic English

Key vocabulary

accept	flexible worker	reject
arbitration	independent	relationship
collective bargaining	industrial action	reputation
commit	industrial dispute	scheme
competitiveness	industrial relations	sidestep (v)
compromise (v and n)	job redundancies	strike (v)
consultation	legislation	trade union
controversial	lock out	tribunal
cross a picket line	mediation	undermine someone's livelihood
dialogue	migrant labour	union membership
dismissal	negotiate	wage rise
employment contract	picket (v)	working conditions
enterprise bargaining	popular myth	
'fixed' demands	redundancy	

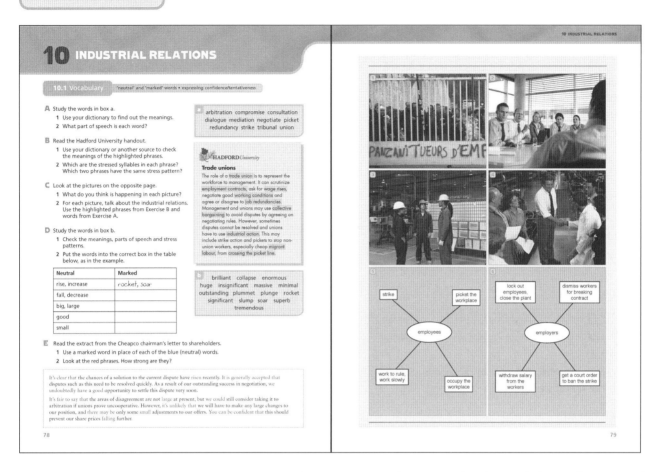

General note

Read the *Vocabulary bank* at the end of the Course Book unit. Decide when, if at all, to refer students to it. The best time is probably at the very end of the lesson or the beginning of the next lesson, as a summary/revision.

Lesson aims

- understand when words are 'neutral' and when they are 'marked' (see *Vocabulary bank*)
- understand and use phrases expressing confidence/tentativeness (see *Vocabulary bank*)

Further practice in:

- fixed phrases/compound nouns from the discipline
- fixed phrases from academic English
- synonyms

Introduction

1 Revise HRM words and phrases from the previous unit, such as:

flexibility – using a wide range of employee-employer relationships, including part-time, self-employed and job sharing

performance-related pay – linking salary to worker objectives

multi-skilled – workers having a range of skills transferable from one operation to another

team – group working together to complete a specific project or area of work

job description – company's articulated view of a job, including the duties and areas of responsibilities and the range of skills or qualifications a worker needs to have

equal opportunities – a policy in a company to offer work/promotion to everyone regardless of race, gender, sexual orientation, age or disability level

workplace stress – pressure generated by a working situation, e.g., production line issues where workers find it is too fast for them to easily complete tasks

incentive – a bonus or other arrangement offered to a worker to increase productivity

conditions – the working arrangements agreed between a company and its staff, including holidays, convenience of workspace, penalties for lateness

downsizing – a strategy in a company to increase efficiency by reducing the number of work roles

outsourcing – subcontracting part of a company's operation to an external company who may be able to do it more cheaply

Give definitions and ask students for the words/phrases.

2 Revise the following phrases used in academic writing. Ask students to recall what sort of information will follow these phrases.

On the other hand …

In conclusion …

To put it another way …

As Patel (2002) points out …

Research has shown that …

Part of the difficulty is …

To start with, …

This can be defined as …

As a result, …

Finally, …

Given what has been demonstrated above …

Exercise A

Set for individual work and pairwork checking. Feed back with the whole class.

Answers

Model answers:

Word	Part of speech	Meaning/synonym
arbitration	n (U)	a legal process in which a neutral person helps management and unions settle a dispute after both sides have given evidence
compromise	v (I/T) n (C)	giving up something important that you want as part of reaching agreement
consultation	n (U)	a process in which management asks workers for their input over decisions to be made
dialogue	n (C)	a process of discussion or negotiation
mediation	n (U)	a process in which a neutral organization like ACAS tries to solve disputes between different parties
negotiate	v (T)	a process of communication that aims for parties with different goals to achieve a solution

picket	v (I/T)	an organized protest against management, usually by striking members of a union outside a place of work
redundancy	n (C)	a worker losing his/her job because the company no longer needs his/her role
strike	n (C) v (I)	an action by workers when they refuse to work in protest against something management has done
tribunal	n (C)	a legal body that meets to consider and settle disputes, for example where an employee thinks he/she was unfairly fired
union	n (C)	a recognized group of workers who represent workforce interests against those of management

Exercise B

1 Set for individual work and pairwork checking. Other sources besides dictionaries could be business textbooks, other reference books or the Internet.

2 Show students how they can draw the stress pattern for the whole word as well as just locating the stressed syllable. If they use the system of big and small circles shown below, they can see the pattern for the whole phrase quite easily.

Answers

Model answers:

1

trade union	an organization of workers who act collectively to protect workers' rights
employment contract	a legal agreement between a worker and a company setting down the work arrangements
wage rise	an increase in money earned, usually done once a year
working conditions	the terms of employment between an employer and employee, and the quality of the facilities and work environment
job redundancies	when workers are required to stop working because their job no longer exists – they may be paid compensation
collective bargaining	shared protocols agreed between management and labour on handling potential areas of conflict

industrial action	collective employee actions to try to force management to change its tactics in a dispute
migrant labour	workers from outside the country who will sometimes work for lower than market rates of pay
cross the picket line	the action of going to work when there is a strike in your workplace and union members are protesting in front of it

2

trade union	O Oo
arbitration	OoOo
employment contract	oOo Oo
wage rise	O O
working conditions	Oo oOo
job redundancies	O oOoo
collective bargaining	oOo Ooo
industrial action	oOoo Oo
migrant labour	Oo Oo
cross the picket line	O o Oo o

Note: *migrant labour/arbitration* share the same stress patterns

Exercise C

Set for pairwork or class discussion. Encourage students to speculate about what might be happening. Students should use the highlighted phrases and other words that are useful from the text in Exercise B; they can also use words from Exercise A.

Feed back with the whole class. Accept anything reasonable.

Answers

Possible answers:

1 Some union members are preventing workers going to work. They are **striking** and **picketing** the factory.

2 Two teams are engaged in an **arbitration** process using the facilities at ACAS or some other **mediation** service.

3 A busload of non-union labour, possibly **migrant labour**, is aiming to **cross a picket line**.

4 A member of a trade union is talking to a group of workers, probably about **wage rises** or **working conditions**.

5 A range of tactics **trade unions** can use to take **industrial action**.

6 A range of tactics management can use to combat **industrial action**.

Exercise D

Introduce the idea of 'neutral' and 'marked' vocabulary (see *Language note* below and *Vocabulary bank*). Set for individual work and pairwork checking.

Feed back, discussing any differences of opinion about whether the words are marked, and in what sense they are marked. (Some students may argue that *minimal, significant* and *insignificant* are not marked, for example. Others may argue that they are marked, because they suggest not just that something is big/small, but that it is important/unimportant. Compare *There is a small problem with the program* and *There is an insignificant problem with the program*.)

Answers

Model answers:

Neutral	Marked
rise, increase	'rocket, 'soar (v)
fall, decrease	co'llapse (v and n), 'plummet (v), 'plunge (v and n), 'slump (v and n)
big, large	e'normous, huge, 'massive, sig'nificant, tre'mendous* (adj)
good	'brilliant, out'standing, su'perb, tre'mendous*
small	insig'nificant, 'minimal (adj)

* *tremendous* can mean both very large and very good, so students may place this word in either category

Language note

One way of looking at vocabulary is to think about 'neutral' and 'marked' items. Many words in English are neutral, i.e., they are very common and they do not imply any particular view on the part of the writer or speaker. However, there are often apparent synonyms which are 'marked' for stance or opinion. Neutral words typically might be verbs or adjectives, but other parts of speech are possible (e.g., nouns). The words are usually thought of as basic vocabulary (the adjectives often have opposites, e.g., *big/small; light/dark*). Marked words tend to be less frequent and are therefore learnt later.

The marked words in Exercise D are not totally synonymous. Their appropriate use and interpretation will be dependent on the context and also on collocation constraints. For example, one can say that a building is 'massive' but not (in the same sense) 'significant'.

Exercise E

1 Set for individual work and pairwork checking. Make sure that students understand any words they are not sure of. Feed back with the whole class by asking individual students to read out a sentence. Make sure that the pronunciation and stress patterns of the marked words are correct.

2 Put the table from the Answers section on the board or project it. Make sure that students understand *confident* and *tentative*. Elicit answers from the whole class and complete the table. Point out that these phrases are usually found in conversation or in informal writing such as this. Academic writing also requires writers to show degrees of confidence and tentativeness. The mechanisms for this will be covered in the next lesson.

Answers

Model answers:

1 It's clear that the chances of a solution to the current dispute have (*risen*) soared/rocketed recently. It is generally accepted that disputes such as this need to be resolved quickly. As a result of our outstanding success in negotiation, we undoubtedly have a (*good*) tremendous/superb opportunity to settle this dispute very soon.

It's fair to say that the areas of disagreement are not (*large*) enormous/huge/massive at present, but we could still consider taking it to arbitration if unions prove uncooperative. However, it's unlikely that we will have to make any (*large*) enormous/huge/massive changes to our position, and there may be only some (*small*) minimal/insignificant adjustments to our offers. You can be confident that this should prevent our share prices (*falling*) plummeting/plunging/slumping/collapsing further.

2

	Very confident	Fairly confident	Tentative (= not confident)
It's clear that	✓		
It's generally accepted that		✓	
we undoubtedly have	✓		
It's fair to say that		✓	
we could			✓
it's unlikely that		✓	
there may be			✓
you can be confident that	✓		

Closure

1 For further practice of neutral and marked vocabulary, ask students to write down some basic words, e.g., four verbs, four nouns and four adjectives. Put a list of these on the board and ask students if they are neutral or marked. See if you can find any opposites. Ask the students to find some synonyms for neutral words – they can use a dictionary. A synonyms dictionary or the Microsoft Word thesaurus can be useful here as well.

2 Ask pairs or groups to define – as accurately as they can – three of the fixed business phrases from the *Vocabulary bank*. Give them a few minutes to think of their definitions, then feed back and discuss as a class.

10.2 Reading

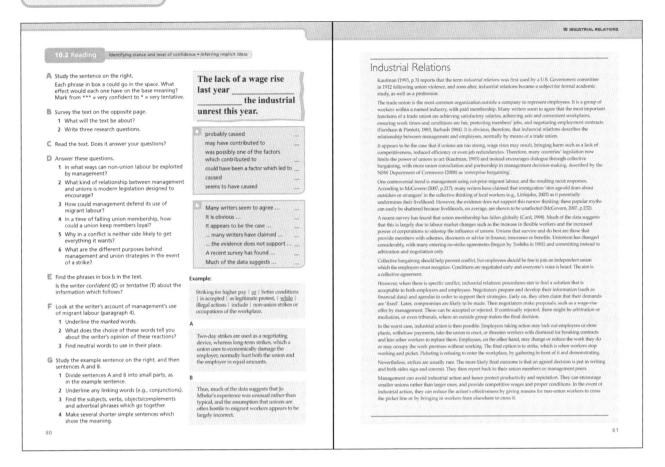

General note

Read the *Skills bank* at the end of the Course Book unit. Decide when, if at all, to refer students to it. The best time is probably at the very end of the lesson or the beginning of the next lesson, as a summary/revision.

Lesson aims

- identify writer's stance on information from use of marked words
- identify writer's level of confidence in research or information
- infer implicit ideas

Further practice in:

- finding main information in a sentence

Introduction

Introduce the idea of degree of confidence in information, which is usually shown in academic writing. More often that not, writers will avoid very categorical statements such as 'X was the cause of Y' and will demonstrate the extent to which they are sure about something through various different linguistic devices such as modals and hedging words and phrases. Use this table to help explain the idea:

100% *** definitely true. The writer is very confident	X caused Y
75% ** probably true. The writer is a little tentative	X probably/is likely to have caused Y
50% * possibly true. The writer is very tentative	X may/might/could have/possibly caused Y

Exercise A

Make sure students understand the idea of a wage rise. Ask students what they think the effects of not getting a rise might be on worker morale.

Set the exercise for pairwork. Feed back with the whole class, pointing out the aspects of the language that contribute to the degree of confidence.

Answers

Model answers:

Word/phrase	Rating	Words which show less than 100% confidence
probably caused	**	probably
may have contributed to	*	may contributed (i.e., there were other reasons)
was possibly one of the factors which contributed to	*	possibly one of the factors (i.e., there were several factors) contributed
could have been a factor which led to	*	could a factor (i.e., there were other factors)
caused	***	–
seems to have caused	**	seems

Exercise B

Explain to the students that surveying the text means scanning and skim-reading to get an approximate idea of the text contents. They should:

- look at the title
- look at the first few lines and the final few lines of the text
- look at the first sentence of each paragraph

Note that this is in order to get a very approximate idea of the contents of the text. This will enable students to formulate questions about the text for which they might try to find answers. Students should be discouraged from reading deeply at this point, as they will be able to do this later.

Set for pairwork discussion. Each pair should agree three questions. Feed back with the whole class. Write a few research questions on the board.

Exercise C

Set for individual work followed by pairwork discussion. Feed back with the whole class. Ask whether the questions you have put on the board have been answered in the text.

Exercise D

These questions require students to 'infer' information – that is, understand what is not directly stated.

Set for individual work and pairwork checking. Feed back with the whole class, making sure that students understand the answers.

Answers

Model answers:

1 Non-union labour is unprotected and vulnerable to exploitation by management, e.g., unfair pay rates, hours and working conditions, unsafe physical conditions, management-determined employment contracts and no defence against management excesses.

2 Governments want to discourage unions from becoming too powerful and they support 'collective bargaining' whereby the two sides work cooperatively to resolve demands by either side, for instance by entering no-strike agreements.

3 Management might explain firstly that migrant workers are cost-effective, and secondly that research shows that migrant works do not noticeably affect union members' jobs or standard of living.

4 A union can increase loyalty by offering reasons to stay with it, such as advice on finance, discounts, cheap insurance deals or other member benefits outside of its traditional role of representing the workforce to management.

5 Industrial relations is about achieving a practical solution to conflicts, which can usually only happen if both sides are willing to compromise, i.e., sacrifice something in order to reach agreement.

6 In a strike situation, management may need to keep the operation running to avoid serious losses in earnings. However, the union needs to put management under economic pressure by depriving the company of income, to encourage it to meet its demands.

Exercise E

Set for individual work and pairwork checking. Feed back with the whole class. Point out that these phrases are very important in academic writing and will help to determine whether something is a fact or an opinion – an important aspect of reading comprehension. They are also used by writers in developing their arguments for or against a particular point of view.

Answers

Model answers:

Many writers seem to agree that the most important functions of the trade union are …	T
It is obvious, therefore, that industrial relations describes the relationship between management and employees …	C
It appears to be the case that if unions are too strong, wage rises may result …	T
… many writers have claimed that immigration 'stirs age-old fears about outsiders or strangers' in the collective thinking of local workers …	T

... the evidence does not support this narrow thinking ...	C
A recent survey has found that union membership has fallen globally.	C
Much of the data suggests that this is largely due to labour market changes ...	T

Exercise F

Set for pairwork. Feed back with whole class. Discuss any differences in students' answers, and whether neutral equivalents are hard to find for some of the words.

Answers

Possible answers:

1 One controversial trend is management using <u>cut-price</u> migrant labour, and the resulting <u>racist</u> responses. According to McGovern (2007, p.217), many writers have <u>claimed</u> that immigration 'stirs <u>age-old fears</u> about outsiders or strangers' in the collective thinking of local workers (e.g., Littlejohn 2003) as it potentially undermines their livelihood. However, the evidence does not support this <u>narrow</u> thinking: these <u>popular myths</u> can easily be <u>shattered</u> because livelihoods, on average, are shown to be unaffected (McGovern 2007, p.232).

2 The choice of words emphasizes the writer's dislike for the union response to the use of migrant labour, which he/she feels is bigoted.

3

Marked word	Neutral alternatives
cut-price	cheaper, less costly
racist	discriminatory
claimed	stated
age-old fears	long-standing prejudices
narrow	limited
popular myths	widespread misunderstandings
shattered	clarified, dispelled

Exercise G

Draw the table from the Answers section on the board. Ask students to look at the example sentence and say which box each part of the sentence should go in. Complete the table for the example sentence as shown. Point out how each of the noun phrases is made up of several words. In each case, elicit which words are the core of the noun phrases (shown in bold in the table below). Do the same with the verb phrases. Ask students to suggest how the sentence can be rewritten in several short, very simple sentences in which noun phrases and verb phrases are reduced to the core meaning as far as possible. Demonstrate with these examples if necessary:

Striking for higher pay is a protest.

Striking for better conditions is a protest.

Illegal actions include non-union strikes.

Illegal actions include workplace occupations.

Point out how in the actual sentences the noun phrases have been expanded so that there is:

striking + for higher pay + or + better conditions

non-union strikes + or + occupations + of the workplace

Set questions 1–4 (relating to sentences A and B) for individual work and pairwork checking. Feed back with the whole class.

Answers

Model answers:

1/2 A Two-day strikes | are used | as a negotiating device, | <u>whereas</u> | long-term strikes, | which a union | uses | to economically damage | the employer, | normally hurt | both the union | and | the employer | in equal amounts.

   B <u>Thus</u>, much of the data | suggests| <u>that</u> | Jo Mbeke's experience | was | unusual <u>rather than</u> typical, | <u>and</u> | the assumption | <u>that</u> | unions | are | often hostile to migrant workers | appears to be largely incorrect.

3 (see table below)

Example	Subject noun phrases	Verb phrases	Object/complement noun phrases	Adverbial phrases	Notes
	Striking for higher pay or better conditions	**is accepted**	as **legitimate protest**		*or is a linking word here but it joins two noun phrases*
	illegal actions	include	**non-union strikes** or **occupations** of the workplace		*while is a linking word between two main clauses*
A	Two-day **strikes**	are used	as a **negotiating device**		*whereas is a linking word between two main clauses*
	long-term **strikes**	normally **hurt**	both the **union** and the **employer**	in equal amounts	*long-term strikes is the object of the relative clause which follows*

	a **union**	uses	which (= **long-term strikes**)	in order to damage the employer	the phrase with *in order to* has been designated as adverbial rather than having to explain non-finite clauses
B	much of the **data**	suggests **(that)**	Jo Mbeke's **experience** was unusual rather than typical		the clause beginning *Jo …* is the object of *suggests*
	Jo Mbeke's **experience**	was	**unusual** rather than typical		*rather than* is a conjunction used here in the sense of *not*
	the **assumption**	appears to be	largely incorrect.		
	unions	are	often hostile to migrant workers		

4 Possible sentences:

Sentence A
Strikes are used as a negotiating device.
A union uses strikes to damage the employer.
Long-term strikes hurt unions and employers.

Sentence B
Jo Mbeke's experience was unusual.
Data suggests something.
Jo Mbeke's experience was not typical.
There is an assumption.
The assumption appears to be largely incorrect.
Unions are hostile to migrant workers.

Closure

Here is some campaigning language from the website of a union that is defending its position in the energy business. Project the excerpt or put it on the board and ask students to identify any marked vocabulary items in each sentence and to suggest more neutral words. Feed back, comparing answers and discussing any differences of opinion.

> *The unfair prices you pay for either oil or gas are soaring.*
> *Our gas reserves are being burnt up at a frightening rate.*
> *We have been utterly wastefully burning vast quantities of gas in power stations.*
> *We have massive coal reserves waiting inside sealed-up coal mines.*
> *We have lost the thousands of skilled mineworkers to other industries through an insane policy of making mineworkers redundant.*
> *In the future, we will grab oil and gas from weak dictatorial governments.*
> *Our energy supply will be vulnerable, relying on pipelines that can be blown up by terrorists at any time.*

Possible changes:

The (*unfair*) high prices you pay for either oil or gas are (*soaring*) increasing substantially.
The gas reserves are being (*burnt up*) consumed at a (*frightening*) substantial rate.
We have been (*utterly wastefully*) unnecessarily (*burning*) consuming (*vast*) substantial/considerable/sizeable quantities of gas in power stations.
We have (*massive*) substantial/considerable/sizeable coal reserves (*waiting*) sitting/located inside (*sealed-up*) closed coal mines.
We have lost (*thousands*) a substantial number of skilled mineworkers to other industries through an (*insane*) inadvisable policy of making mineworkers redundant.
In the future, we will (*grab*) obtain oil and gas from (*weak dictatorial*) unstable, undemocratic governments.
Our energy supply will be (*vulnerable, relying*) dependent on pipelines that (*can be blown up by terrorists at any time*) are constantly exposed to unofficial military attack.

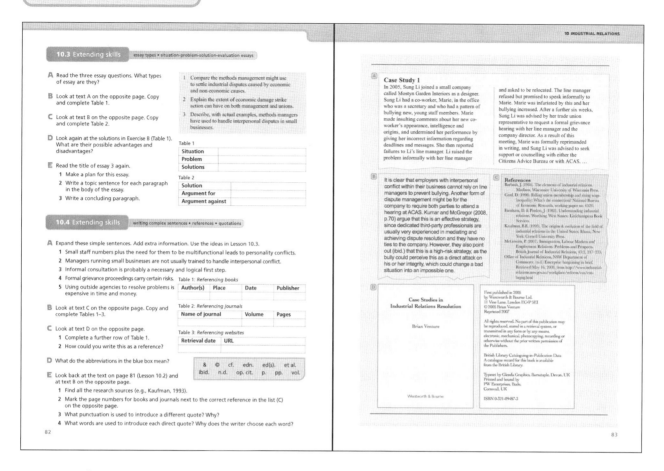

Lesson aims

- understand situation – problem – solution – evaluation structure in essays
- understand the use of information in this type of essay structure to:

describe

give cause and effect

compare

evaluate

argue for

Further practice in:

- identifying required essay types
- producing an outline
- writing key sentences – which can be expanded in the next lesson into longer sentences

Introduction

Revise the different types of essay that were examined in Unit 8. Say or write on the board some key words or phrases from essay titles such as the following:

State …

Outline …

Describe …

Compare …

Evaluate …

Discuss …

Why …?

How …?

To what extent …?

How far …?

Ask students to say:

- what type of essay is required
- what type of organizational structure should be used

If students find this difficult, refer them to the *Skills bank* for Unit 8.

Exercise A

Set for individual work and pairwork checking. Feed back with the whole class. Point out that in real life, essays given by lecturers often involve several types of writing in one essay. This is the case with essay 3. Tell students that, in fact, a possible structure for essay 3 would be the following, which is commonly found in many types of writing (including newspapers and academic writing).

177

Situation: description of a state of affairs, often giving some reasons and background information	description
Problem(s): the problems which are caused by the state of affairs; plus the effects of these problems	description (cause and effect)
Solution(s): ways of dealing with the problems (i) which may have been tried in the past or are being tried now; (ii) which will, may or could be tried in the future; suggestions for further solutions	description (+ possibly suggestion)
Evaluation of solution(s): comparison of solutions; opinion on how successful the solutions are or could be + justification; an opinion on which is the best option + justification	comparison and argument

Tell students they will plan (and possibly write) this essay.

Answers

Model answers:

1 Comparison and contrast, plus some evaluation

2 Analysis: cause and effect

3 Description, then some comparison and some evaluation/argument/opinion, plus support (see table above).

Exercise B

Set for individual work and pairwork checking. Feed back with the whole class.

Answers

Model answers:

Situation	Sung Li joined a company; she faced bullying by Marie.
Problem	The line manager would not move Sung Li, both when she complained and after the formal grievance hearing; the bullying intensified as a result.
Solutions	• Informal conversation with line manager • Grievance hearing • Written reprimand for Marie • Counselling outside the company for Sung Li

Exercise C

Set for individual work and pairwork checking. Feed back with the whole class.

Answers

Model answers:

Solution	Take the dispute to a third party like ACAS.
Argument for	The arbitrator may give good, impartial advice.
Argument against	The bully may become defensive and retaliate.

Exercise D

Set for pairwork discussion. Feed back with the whole class. Accept any reasonable suggestions. Common-sense answers are also suitable here.

Answers

Possible answers: (see below)

	Advantages	Disadvantages
Informal conversation with line manager	1. alerts line manager to the problem and context 2. gives him/her the opportunity to solve the problem informally 3. protects the manager's relations with both members of staff	1. has no official status as a complaints procedure 2. short-term measure only 3. could be misunderstood by bully as tacit approval
Grievance hearing	1. official, therefore cannot be ignored by bully 2. offers formal protection and support to victim	1. could create a sense of grievance or offence in the bully 2. could create a confrontation between bully and victim
Written reprimand to bully	1. provides evidence of company disapproval that cannot be ignored 2. evidence that could be used if dismissal proceedings are instituted	1. could damage the working relationship between bully and victim permanently 2. could undermine sympathy of other workers for victim 3. bully could use the reprimand as evidence of how 'tough' he/she is

Exercise E

1 Set for pairwork discussion. Remind students to refer back to the text in Lesson 10.2 for ideas and information, as well as the texts they have discussed in this lesson. Remind students about the basic structure of an essay (introduction – main body – conclusion).

If you wish, you can give students the first two columns of the table in the Answers section, with the third column empty for them to complete. The table is reproduced in the additional resources section (Resource 10B) for this purpose.

Feed back with the whole class. Build the plan on the board, using the ideas in the answers section to help.

2 Ask students to write some topic sentences for the four paragraphs that make up the body of the essay, using the information in the plan. Remind students that topic sentences need to be very general. Set for individual work.

Feed back with the whole class, writing some examples on the board.

3 Set for pairwork, then discussion with the whole class. Or if you prefer, set for individual homework. The ideas should be those of the students. Remind them to introduce their ideas with suitable phrases.

Note: Students will need their essay plans again in Lesson 10.4.

Answers

1 Possible essay plan:

Introduction		Examples of ideas
introduce the topic area give the outline of the essay		General: focus on issues of industrial relations in small businesses ➜ Specific: potential difficulties with staff *In this essay, I will discuss interpersonal difficulties …* *I will illustrate/describe …* (examples) *I will consider …* (solutions) *Finally, I will suggest …* (best solution)

Body	Para 1:
	situation/problems (general)
		interpersonal problems ➜ major concern for management ≠:
		1. small staff numbers + need to multifunction ➜ stress ➜
		   personality conflict (evidence: a number of surveys)
		2. minimal HRM = no mechanisms for conflict resolution –
		   problems delegated to managers, often no code of practice for
		   employees in place (not the case for large businesses)
		3. potential to escalate to union involvement

	Para 2: problems (specific examples)	examples of cases: Sung Li – victim of bullying Maria Smythe – bully who is bullied by own line manager Brian Benzoni – typical 'plant', i.e., cannot step outside area of own expertise, creates havoc with others in team
	Para 3: solutions	1. informal consultation with both sides – handled by a line manager 2. formal grievance procedure – in-company 3. consult external mediator, e.g., ACAS or other

	Para 4:
	evaluations of solutions
		1. informal consultation is probably a necessary and logical first step
		2. formal in-company grievance procedures ➜ certain risks
		   (i.e., staff not trained for this kind of procedure – may handle a
		   difficult situation inappropriately) but a necessary first step if
		   management want the later option of dismissing the bully
		3. use of outside agency for mediation ➜ expensive in time and
		   costs but useful ➜ neutral advice + experienced at handling
		   conflict – identify key issues not personalities

Conclusion		*In my view/As I see it, the best option is … because …* *Firstly …* *Secondly …* *Thirdly …*

2 Possible topic sentences:

Intro	Small businesses do not typically suffer the industrial relations issues of larger bureaucracies; however, an equivalent difficulty they do experience might be managing personal grievances that arise from interpersonal conflict.
Body Para 1	In small businesses, these kinds of disputes are potentially problematic in various ways.
Body Para 2	Such challenges can be specifically illustrated with case studies from industry.
Body Para 3	There are a number of solutions available to small enterprises.
Body Para 4	All of these approaches have a range of disadvantages as well as advantages.

3 Students' own concluding paragraphs.

Language note

Although 'situation – problem – solution – evaluation of solution' is often said to be an organizing principle in writing, in practice it is sometimes difficult to distinguish between the situation and the problem: they may sometimes seem to be the same thing. The important thing is to be clear about the main *focus* of the essay – that is, the answer to the question: *What am I writing about?* – and to structure the essay around this.

Closure

Set up a role-play situation involving negotiations between experienced managers and the workforce.

Put students in groups of four. Within each group, students work in pairs. One pair is management and one pair union representatives. Each pair works on the scenario from its point of view. The pairs work together, assembling their own argument, anticipating counter-arguments likely to be put forward by their opponents and developing refutations for those counter-arguments.

Workers prepare a short presentation: state their grievance clearly, suggest solutions and explain why the optimum solution is a good idea – i.e., how it benefits the company.

Managers state their view of the problem, the cost to the company in worker hours or money, their solution and why their solution is a good idea – i.e., how it benefits the company, including the workers.

When both pairs are ready, they should take in it turns to give their presentations, listen to the opposing presentation and formally offer their reaction. From there, they should proceed to negotiate to achieve the best result that they can for their side.

Scenario 1: Pay rise next year

Workers: have accepted an inflation-linked pay rise for the last two years. The cost of fuel has doubled, with a knock-on effect throughout the economy. They anticipate an inflation rate increase of 2% and are demanding an inflation-proof pay rise of 7%.

Managers: have borrowed heavily to finance the factory modernization programme which was instituted at worker insistence. Management cannot afford any pay increase at all. Could afford an inflation-linked pay increase for staff if staff agree to increase productivity by 10% and agree to a lay-off of 10% of the workforce.

Scenario 2: Modernization

Workers: are very worried about jobs. A new computerized production line means that 30% of jobs are likely to be lost in this plant. The remaining jobs require a skill set that workers currently do not have. Workers want assurances that there will be a minimum number of redundancies, a generous redundancy package for employees who accept redundancy and extensive retraining of the remaining workforce.

Managers: agree with the unions that 30% of the workforce need to be redistributed. They can accommodate 25% if they will relocate to another part of the country. Management is willing to accept the remaining 5% as part of natural erosion through retirement, illness, etc. The company cannot afford redundancy packages, and only offers redundancy to a worker who has been with the company for more than ten years. They will support training programmes, but training must take place outside working hours.

Scenario 3: Health and safety

Workers: have a high rate of absenteeism due to illness. Water-borne chemicals released from waste water and from leakage from storage ponds in a metal-refining processing plant are thought to be causing illness. They want toxicity tests conducted on local groundwater – they suspect arsenic and cyanide compounds (poisons) in the water. The trade union wants safer storage facilities built and a treatment plant that extracts the chemicals from waste water before it is released into the environment. They also want a danger bonus for all staff working in the production process.

Managers: view absenteeism as a result of laziness in the workforce – statistics show absenteeism occurs on Fridays, Mondays and on days when the local football team plays. They conducted tests five years ago, soon after the company start-up, on water in local rivers, and found it is within safe limits. They refuse to go to the expense of another set of tests. They demand evidence of the link between groundwater and illness of staff from the union. All storage facilities have safety certificates. They accuse environmentalists of poisoning the ground around the storage facility.

10.4 Extending skills

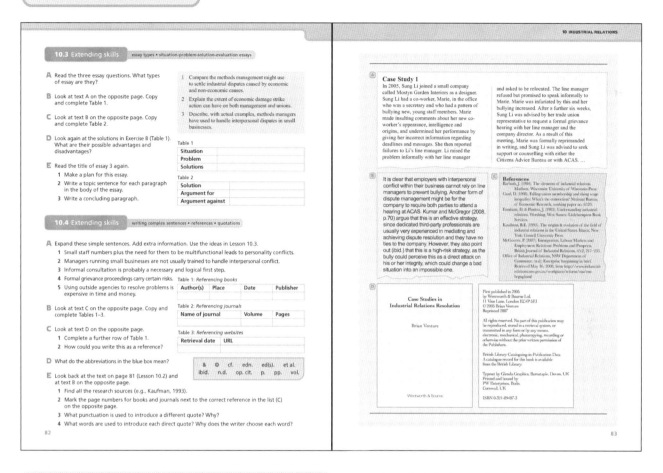

General note

This lesson focuses on writing references for a bibliography according to the APA (American Psychological Association) system. Before the lesson, it would be useful to familiarize yourself with this system. See the *Skills bank*, and for more detailed information, websites such as: http://owl.english.purdue.edu/owl/resource/560/10/ or http://www.thomsonedu.com/bcomm/guffey

Lesson aims

- use quotations with appropriate punctuation and abbreviations such as *ibid*.
- write a reference list (APA system)

Further practice in:

- the reverse activity to Lesson 10.2, i.e., putting extra information into simple sentences in an appropriate way

Introduction

Introduce the idea of using sources in writing. Look back at the text in Lesson 10.2 and ask students to find all the places where a reference to a source is

mentioned. Ask them whether first names or surnames are normally used. Where a date is given, ask weaker students the easy question of what date the author was published. Ask them to find a quotation and a paraphrase. What are the main differences?

Exercise A

Remind students of the essay plan in Lesson 10.3. If you wish, you can reproduce the following simplified table cells for them. Alternatively, choose a sample paragraph from the plan. They should try to get all the information in each numbered point into one sentence.

1 small staff numbers + need to multifunction → stress → personality conflict (evidence: surveys)
2 minimal HRM = no mechanisms for conflict resolution
1 informal consultation – probably necessary & logical 1st step. Opp solve informally + protect rel'ships
2 formal in-company grievance procedures; risks (bully defensive, intensify confrontation); a necessary first step; opp later dismiss bully
3 use of outside agency; expensive (time/cost) but useful → neutral/experienced/identify key issues not personalities

Do the first sentence with the whole class as an example on the board. Students should feel free to add words as appropriate to make a coherent sentence; they can also paraphrase (e.g., *don't often give* ➔ *are reluctant to give*).

Set the remaining sentences for individual work.

Answers

Possible answers:

1 A number of surveys have shown that small staff numbers plus the need for them to be multi-functional leads to increased personality conflicts.

2 Managers running small businesses are not usually trained to handle interpersonal conflict and, since they have minimal HRM function, they are unlikely to have mechanisms in place for proper conflict resolution.

3 Informal consultations are probably a necessary and logical first step as it gives a manager an opportunity to solve the problem informally and allows him/her to protect his/her relationship with both workers.

4 Formal in-company grievance proceedings may be a necessary first step and, although they carry certain risks and could make the bully defensive, which could intensify the confrontation between the bully and his victim, they provide the opportunity for later dismissing the bully.

5 Although involving an outside agency is expensive both in time and costs, it has the benefit of providing neutral and experienced mediation that will focus on issues rather than on the personalities.

Exercise B

Tell students that this is a list of references from the text in Lesson 10.2. Note that it is called 'References' because it lists all the references actually given (it is not a list of all the references the author might have consulted but not referred to – this is a bibliography).

Set for individual work and pairwork checking. Note that these tables are intended to help students identify some key information. For a full set of categories to include in a reference list, see the *Skills bank*. Tell students that when writing a reference list, they will need to pay close attention to the detail of the layout which is in the APA (the American Psychological Association) system. See the *Skills bank* for relevant websites which give further details. In particular, students should note and will need to practise:

- putting the names of writers and multiple writers in the correct alphabetical order according to family name, with the right spacing and punctuation

- writing all numbers correctly, including dates and page references

- using punctuation, including the role and placing of full stops, commas and colons

- laying out the references in the correct style with the correct positions (e.g., of indents and tabs)

- using standard APA style features such as italic and brackets

Language and subject note

No matter how extensive your instruction on reference lists, a few students are always likely to confuse reference list detail (as in text C) with in-text reference detail (surname, year and page number) because the area of instruction can be dry. So, you may find, for example, students inserting website addresses or book titles in essay paragraphs, or reference lists written with incomplete information. To ensure against this, constant and basic concept checking is needed. Regularly ask students to scan texts for references and elicit the reference detail, to consolidate their learning and ensure it becomes applied to their own work. Similarly, ensure reference lists and bibliographies are regularly scanned and discussed, to demonstrate their importance and relevance.

Answers

Table 1:

Author(s)	Place of publication	Date of publication	Publisher
Barbash, J.	Madison	1984	University of Wisconsin Press
Farnham, D. & Pimlott, J.	Worthing	1983	Littlehampton Book Services
Kaufman, B.E.	Ithaca, New York	1993	Cornell University Press

Table 2:

Name of journal	Volume	Pages
British Journal of Industrial Relations	45	217–235

Table 3:

Retrieval date	URL
May 16, 2008	http://www.industrialrelations.nsw.gov.au/workplace/reform/eas/entbrgng.html

Language and subject note

In the case of journals, there is an increasing tendency to refer to the volume number only in reference lists, omitting the issue number. Thus, for example, *English for Specific Purposes, 16 (1), 47–60* might become *English for Specific Purposes, 16, 47–60*.

Exercise C

Set for individual work and pairwork checking.

Answers

1

Author(s)	Place of publication	Date of publication	Publisher
Venture, B.	London	2005	Wentworth & Bourne Ltd.

2 Venture, B. (2005). *Case Studies in Industrial Relations Resolution.* London: Wentworth & Bourne.

Language and subject note

In the APA system, titles of books (but not titles of articles) are in italics, sentence case – that is, initial capital letter only, unless the title contains a proper noun. If the title contains a colon, the first word after the colon is also capitalized.

Journal titles (the names of the journals) are in italics and 'headline' style – that is, all key words are capitalized but not conjunctions and prepositions. For example: *Journal of Small Business Management*. However, journal articles are in sentence case, no italics.

Exercise D

Many of these were covered in Unit 5, so ask students to check back if they are not sure or they can refer to the list at the back of their books; they can also check online at the APA site and/or the other sites given in the *Skills bank*.

Set for individual work and pairwork checking.

Answers

Model answers:

&	and
©	copyright
cf.	compare
edn.	edition
ed(s).	editor(s)
et al.	and other authors
ibid.	same place in a work already referred to
n.d.	no date (used in a reference list if there is no date – as is often the case with web articles)
op. cit.	the work already referred to
p.	page
pp.	pages
vol.	volume

Exercise E

Remind students (if you have not done so already) of the two main ways in which students can use sources (i.e., references to other writers' work) in their writing:

- by giving the exact words used by another writer
- by paraphrasing another writer's ideas, i.e., rewriting the ideas using their own, different words but retaining the meaning

The first method is referred to as quotation or direct quotation. Short direct quotations should be in quotation marks and incorporated into the paragraph. Quotations of more than one sentence should be 'display quote' style, i.e., on a new line, and indented.

The second method is referred to as paraphrase, summary or indirect quotation. Note that over 90% of the paraphrase should be new words.

1/2 Set for individual work. Tell students to look for all the direct quotations and to identify the research sources. They should then locate the source in the reference list on page 83 of the Course Book. Writing the page numbers on the reference list may seem a mechanical exercise, but it is useful for students to get into the habit of doing this. It will enable them to find an original source book, refer to the relevant part of the book and read more about the subject.

3/4 Students should identify the punctuation and introducing phrases used.

Feed back with the whole class.

Language and subject note

If the quotation is a full sentence, it begins with a capital letter inside the opening quotation mark and ends with a full stop inside the closing quotation mark.

If there are some words missing from the original quotation that were at the start of the original sentence, the quotation does not begin with a capital letter.

Original spelling/punctuation conventions are retained in a quotation.

Answers

Model answers:

1/2 Kaufman (1993, p.3)
Farnham & Pimlott, 1983, Barbash, 1984
NSW Department of Commerce (2008)
McGovern (2007, p.217)
Littlejohn, 2003
McGovern (2007, p.232)
Card, 1998
Kumar and McGregor (2008, p.70)

Quote	Source	Punctuation/ formatting before/within each direct quote	Introducing phrase + reason for choice
'enterprise bargaining'	website reference from Office of Industrial Relations, NSW Department of Commerce. *Enterprise Bargaining in Brief.* http://www.industrialrelations.nsw.gov.au/workplace/reform/eas/entbrgng.html [16 May 2008]	'xxx'	Such as described by the NSW Department of Commerce Reason: what follows is a definition
'stirs age-old fears about outsiders or strangers'	page 217 of McGovern, P. 'Immigration, Labour Markets and Employment Relations: Problems and Prospects' *British Journal of Industrial Relations* 45:2 June 2007 0007–1080 pp.217–235	'xxx'	… many writers have claimed that immigration reason: what follows is an opinion

Language and subject note

An ampersand (&) is used with multiple authors, preceded by a comma.

The full stop at the end of the reference is omitted in the case of URLs.

Dates are (for example) April 7, not April 7th.

Closure

Refer students to the *Skills bank* for a summary of writing references. Study how the following are used:

- names (order)
- punctuation (capital letters, full stops, commas, colons)
- layout (indentation, spacing)
- style features (italics, brackets)

For further practice, use Resource 10C from the additional resources section. Ask students to check the references on a library database or on the Internet (discuss which sources are likely to be the most accurate and give them all the information they need – often the best way to check bibliographical details is to use a university library catalogue, as information found on the Internet is frequently inaccurate or incomplete). They should also make any necessary changes to ensure the references fit the APA models used in this unit. If possible, they should use the online website references (see *Skills bank*) to help them. Remind students that they will also need to put the references in the right alphabetical order. Note: do not allow students to refer back to the course book where Lesson 10.4 exhibits the correct list.

Correct versions are:

Barbash, J. (1984). *The elements of industrial relations.* Madison, Wisconsin: University of Wisconsin Press.

Card, D. (1998). Falling Union Membership and Rising Wage Inequality: What's the Connection? *National Bureau of Economic Research*, working paper no. 6520.

Farnham, D. & Pimlott, J. (1983). *Understanding industrial relations.* Worthing, West Sussex: Littlehampton Book Services.

Kaufman, B.E. (1993) *The origins & evolution of the field of industrial relations in the United States.* Ithaca, New York: Cornell University Press.

Littlejohn, R. (2003) Will Labour prove Enoch right? *The Sun*, p.33.

McGovern, P. (2007). Immigration, labour markets and employment relations: problems and prospects. *British Journal of Industrial Relations*, 45:2, 217–235.

Office of Industrial Relations, NSW Department of Commerce. (n.d.) *Enterprise bargaining in brief.* Retrieved May 16, 2008, from http://www.industrialrelations.nsw.gov.au/workplace/reform/eas/entbrgng.html

Extra activities

1 Work through the *Vocabulary bank* and *Skills bank* if you have not already done so, or as a revision of previous study.

2 Use the *Activity bank* (Teacher's Book additional resources section, Resource 10A).

   A Set the wordsearch for individual work (including homework) or pairwork.

Answers

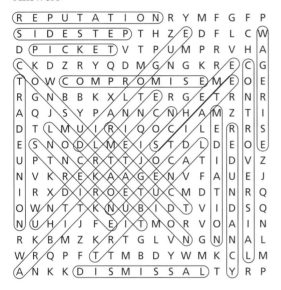

   B Set for individual work (including homework) or pairwork. Accept all reasonable answers. Students should be able to explain the meaning.

Answers

Possible answers:

collective	bargaining
employment	contract
enterprise	bargaining
industrial	action/dispute
industrial	relations
job	redundancies
migrant	labour/worker
trade	union
union	membership
working	conditions

3 Ask students to choose one of the other essays in Lesson 10.3 and make a plan. They can also write topic sentences for each paragraph in the essay.

11 MARKETING MANAGEMENT

Unit 11 looks at marketing management, initially focusing on defining market-orientation, markets and market share, and then exploring marketing objectives, strategies and branding, which are usually all top-down concerns of senior management involved in corporate strategy. This is delivered through two parts of a lecture. Then, as a foundation to the subject area, the basics of the marketing process, from market analysis to marketing mix formulation, are touched on through seminar discussions.

Skills focus

🎧 Listening

- recognizing the speaker's stance
- writing up notes in full

Speaking

- building an argument in a seminar
- agreeing/disagreeing

Vocabulary focus

- words/phrases used to link ideas (*moreover, as a result*, etc.)
- stress patterns in noun phrases and compounds
- fixed phrases from academic English
- words/phrases related to environmental issues

Key vocabulary

See also the list of fixed phrases from academic English in the *Vocabulary bank* (Course Book page 92).

a weak brand	fashion	niche marketing
advertising	focus	objectives
anticipate	formulate	perception
attitude	fulfil (objectives)	personality
behaviour	growth	position (a product) (v)
brand	have an edge over someone	product development
brand blindness	image-conscious	product orientation
brand equity	innovation	promotion
brand loyalty	launch (v)	psyche
brand preference	logo	psychology
business philosophy	maintain (v)	recognition
competition	market challenger	respond
competitive strategies	market development	segment (v and n)
competitor analysis	market entry	slogan
consumer	market expansion	specialization
cost leader	market followers	strategy
demand	market leader	supply
dialogue	market orientation	target (n and v)
(un)differentiated/ differentiation	market penetration	tastes
disposable income	market share	top-down
distinguish	marketing mix	trademark
diversify	mass marketing	trust
emotional	mass-produced	unique selling point (USP)

11.1 Vocabulary

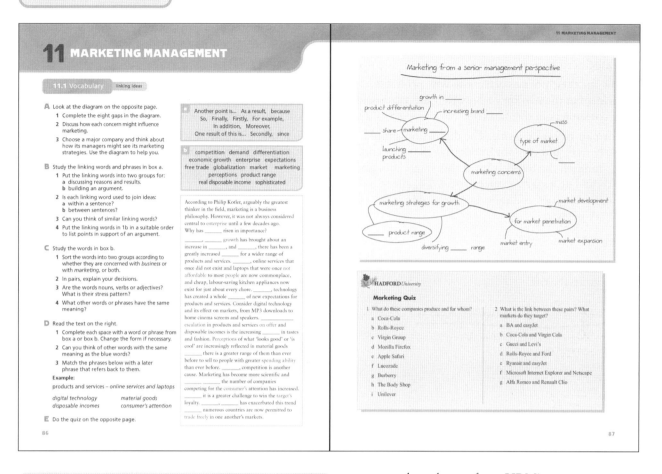

General note

Read the *Vocabulary bank* at the end of the Course Book unit. Decide when, if at all, to refer students to it. The best time is probably at the very end of the lesson or the beginning of the next lesson, as a summary/revision.

Lesson aims

- use rhetorical markers: to add points in an argument; to signal cause and effect (between- and within-sentence linking)
- further understand lexical cohesion: the use of superordinates/synonyms to refer back to something already mentioned; building lexical chains

Further practice in:

- synonyms, antonyms and word sets from the discipline
- abbreviations and acronyms

Introduction

1   Revise some vocabulary from previous units. Give students some key words from the previous two units (in italics below) and ask them to think of terms connected with these words (for example,

some key phrases from HRM).

enterprise bargaining, *'fixed'* demands, *flexible* worker, industrial *relations*, industrial *action*, industrial *relations tribunal*, job *enlargement*, job *enrichment*, job *redundancies*, job *rotation*, *labour* turnover, migrant *labour*, trade *union*, *union* membership, working *conditions*

2   Introduce the topic. Write the word *marketing* on the board. Before asking students to open their books, ask them what are the main areas of concern that senior managers need to plan well if they wish to market their products/services successfully. Accept any reasonable suggestions.

Exercise A

1   Ask students to open their books and look at the diagram on page 87. Check the meaning of the words in the diagram. If necessary, give some examples of marketing concerns, e.g., *the marketing mix* and the four Ps (product, price, promotion, place). Provide prompts for them to fill the gaps. It is more important that they say them, spell them and think about them than fully understand them at this stage.

2   Set for pairwork. Encourage students to think in terms of overall managers' objectives, for example with regard to:

- market share
- consumer appeal of products and how they should react as managers
- what role the company plans to play in the market – how to enter, and once in, what strategies to pursue
- how far their policies affect the way products perform in the market or how they are perceived by consumers in the market

3 Set for pair or group work. The discussion should be fairly free, and it is not imperative that students understand all the terms fully at this stage, though they should at least hear them vocalized, check a few in dictionaries and raise questions about how they may be used.

Answers

Possible answers:

1 See diagram (below).

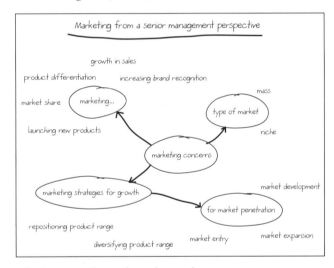

2 Answers depend on the students.

3 Answers depend on the students.

Exercise B

1 Set for individual work and pairwork checking. Feed back with the whole class, building the table in the Answers section.

2 Explain what is meant by 'within' and 'between' sentences: 'within-sentence' linking words or phrases join clauses in a sentence; 'between-sentence' linking words or phrases connect two sentences. Demonstrate with the following:

Within-sentence linking words:

Globalization has <u>exacerbated this trend because</u> many more countries now trade freely …

Tell students that within-sentence linking words precede subordinate clauses.

Between-sentence linker:

Marketing has become more scientific and sophisticated. <u>As a result</u>, it is a greater challenge to win the target's loyalty.

Point out that between-sentence linking words often have a comma to divide them from the rest of the sentence.

Ask students to say which of the other linkers in box a are 'between' and which are 'within'.

3 Ask for suggestions for synonyms and add to the table.

4 First make sure that students understand the basic principle of an argument, which is:

Statement

+

one or more support(s) for statement (= more facts, reasons, results, examples, evidence, etc.)

Constructing a complex argument will usually entail a statement plus several supports.

With the whole class, elicit suggestions for how to use the linkers when constructing an argument. Build the table in the Answers section on the board.

Answers

Possible answers:

1/2/3

Linking words	Use for	Within or between sentence linker	Other similar words/ phrases
Another point is …	building an argument	between	And another thing,
As a result,	reasons and results	between	Consequently,
because	reasons and results	within	as
So,	reasons and results	between	Therefore,/ Thus,/Hence,
Finally,	building an argument	between	Lastly,
Firstly,	building an argument	between	To begin with,/ To start with,
For example,	building an argument	between	For instance,
In addition,	building an argument	between	Also,
Moreover	building an argument	between	Furthermore,
One result of this is …	reasons and results	between	One consequence of this is/ because of this
Secondly,	building an argument	between	Next/Then,
since	reasons and results	within	as

4 A typical argument is constructed like this:

Firstly,	making the first major support point
For example,	supporting the point with a specific example
In addition,	adding another related point in support
Secondly,	making the second major support point
Another point is …	adding another related point in support
Moreover,	adding more information to the point above
Finally,	making the last point

Language note

1 Note that within-sentence linking words may be placed at the beginning of the sentence with a comma after the first clause, as in:
Because executives thought that demand was created by supply, they felt that there was no need to market their products.

2 Although the between-sentence linking words are described above as joining two sentences, they can, of course, take on an adverbial role and link two independent clauses joined by coordinating linking words _and_ or _but_, as in:
Economic growth has created an increase in real disposable income and, as a result, there has been greatly increased demand for a wider range of products.

Exercise C

1 Set for individual work. Note that students should try to put each word into one of the two categories, even if it is not immediately clear how it could be relevant. If they are not sure which category to use, they should try to think of a phrase containing the word and imagine how it could be relevant to one of the categories.

2 Ask students to compare their answers and to justify their choices. Feed back with the whole class, discussing the words for which students feel the category is not obvious. If no decision can be reached, say you will come back to the words a little later.

3/4 Set for pairwork. Feed back with the whole class if you wish.

Answers

Model answers:

Word	Suggested categories	Part of speech	Other words/ phrases
compe'tition	business/ marketing	n (U)	business competitors/ rivals
de'mand	business/ marketing	n (U)	consumer need (for a product/ service)

differenti'ation	marketing	n (U)	becoming more diverse; developing a unique selling point, or USP
eco'nomic growth	business	n (U)	expansion of the economy
'enterprise	business	n (U/C)	(U) business activity (C) company/ firm/business (as an organization)
expec'tation(s)	marketing	n (C)	customer tastes/ opinions/ hopes
free 'trade	business	n (U), adj	unregulated trade
globali'zation	business	n (U)	interconnection of worldwide commerce
'market	marketing	n (C) adj v	who you sell to related to notion of market to sell in a targeted way
'marketing	marketing	n (U) adj	the process of understanding buyers and selling to them related to this process
per'ceptions	marketing	n (C)	opinions, feelings, understanding
'product range	business/ marketing	n (C)	different types of related products
'real disposable 'income	marketing	n (U)	spending money
so'phisticated	marketing	adj	well-developed, mature, good-quality, complex

Exercise D

Note: Students may need to use dictionaries in question 2.

Students should first read through the text to get an idea of the topic.

1/2 Set for individual work and pairwork checking. Feed back with the whole class.

Point out that having done these questions, it should now be possible to say whether the words in box b can be put into a 'business' or a 'marketing' group. (In the cases of _competition_, _demand_ and _product range_, a case can be made for both groups.) The point here is that the context will make clear what the meaning of a word should be. Point out that this is important when it comes to making a guess at the meaning of a word you are not sure of initially.

189

3 Since the text is about marketing, ask students to identify all the words first about *business*, and then about *marketing*. Set for individual work and pairwork checking. Feed back with the whole class, if you wish using an OHT and two coloured pens, or other visual medium. Point out that these ideas are to be mentioned in the text.

Tell students that a particular topic will have groups of words which are connected to or associated with it – known as 'lexical chains'. These lexical chains show us the themes that run through the text and which help 'glue' the ideas together to make a cohesive piece of text. It is a good idea, therefore, to learn vocabulary according to topic areas. It is common, then, to use synonymous words and phrases to refer back to something already mentioned. Ideally, use an OHT, or other visual medium, of the text (see Resource 11B in the additional resources section), and with a coloured pen draw a line to show how *products and services* is referred to later in the text by *these things … online services and laptops*. Set for individual work and pairwork checking. Feed back with the class, (linking the phrases with coloured pens if using Resource 11B).

Answers

Model answers:

1

According to Philip Kotler, arguably the greatest thinker in the field, marketing is a business philosophy. However, it was not always considered central to enterprise until a few decades ago. Why has <u>marketing</u> risen in importance?

<u>Firstly</u>, <u>economic</u> growth has brought about an increase in <u>real disposable income</u>, and <u>so/as a result</u>, there has been a greatly increased <u>demand</u> for a wider range of products and services. <u>For example</u>, online services that once did not exist and laptops that were once not affordable to most people are now commonplace, and cheap, labour-saving kitchen appliances now exist for just about every chore. <u>Moreover/Furthermore</u>, technology has created a whole <u>range</u> of new expectations for products and services. Consider digital technology and its effect on markets, from MP3 downloads to home cinema screens and speakers. <u>One result of this</u> escalation in products and services on offer and disposable incomes is the increasing <u>differentiation</u> in tastes and fashion. Perceptions of what 'looks good' or 'is cool' are increasingly reflected in material goods <u>since/because</u> there is a greater range of them than ever before to sell to people with greater spending ability than ever before.

<u>Secondly</u>, competition is another cause. Marketing has become more scientific and <u>sophisticated</u> <u>because/since</u> the number of companies competing for the consumer's attention has increased. <u>As a result/So</u> it is a greater

challenge to win the target's loyalty. <u>Moreover/Furthermore</u>, <u>globalization</u> has exacerbated this trend because numerous countries are now permitted to trade freely in one another's markets.

2

Word	Synonym
enterprise	business
growth	expansion
not affordable	too expensive
people	consumers
escalation	growth
on offer	available
perceptions	attitudes towards
spending ability	disposable income
consumer's	customer's
target's	consumer's
trade freely	deal/sell without restriction

3

First phrase	Second phrase
digital technology	from MP3 downloads to home cinema screens and speakers
disposable incomes	spending ability
material goods	greater range of them
consumer's attention	target's loyalty

Exercise E

Time this marketing quiz if you wish. Alternatively, set it for homework for students to research the answers. Make sure that students understand they need to say what the company sells and what kind of market it targets.

In order to be able to follow the lecture in Lesson 11.2, students will need to be at least superficially familiar with these organizations and bodies.

Answers

Model answers:

1 What do these companies produce and what kind of market do they target?

Coca-Cola – soft drinks, sports drinks, health drinks, worldwide market with mass appeal

Rolls-Royce – Luxury cars for the wealthy (also aero-engines)

Virgin Group – over 200 companies, including music for many markets, media – cable TV, phone, mobile and TV channels, finance and money services, airlines and train services

Mozilla Firefox – Internet browser, for the mass market – challenger to Microsoft Internet Explorer

Apple Safari – Internet browser from Apple, aiming to challenge other browsers

Lucozade – sports energy drink, aimed at the health/mass market

Burberry – clothing, originally for the practical-minded but has moved upmarket

The Body Shop – cosmetics produced ethically, targeting ethical consumers

Unilever – produces a huge range of household products (under different brand names), a huge range of target markets

2   What is the market relationship between these pairs of companies?

BA and easyJet – both are airlines; BA is primarily a scheduled route carrier offering quality service particularly to business clients; easyJet is a budget airline specializing in cheap tickets catering for the price-conscious.

Coca-Cola and **Virgin Cola** – Coca-Cola is a market leader in soft drinks; Virgin Cola is a market follower that is unlikely to achieve a huge market share.

Gucci and **Levi's** – Gucci is a niche market high-end fashion provider; Levi's is a mass-market supplier of jeans.

Rolls-Royce and **Ford** – Rolls-Royce produces luxury cars for a niche market, while Ford produces a wide range of products aimed at different segments of larger markets.

Ryanair and **easyJet** are competitors for the budget airline market, offering cheap flights mostly within Europe.

Microsoft Internet Explorer and **Netscape** were rival Internet browser providers, but Netscape has fallen from prominence.

Alpha Romeo and **Renault Clio** – They are both cars; the Alpha Romeo is a high-performance car for a niche market, while the Clio is a small family car.

Closure

Ask students to review the lesson by listing any factors associated with marketing objectives and marketing strategies, including marketing penetration strategies. Ask student groups to rank them in order of importance for:

a managing the launch of a new product into existing markets

b managing an American company with a portfolio of products wanting to break into East Asian markets

11.2 Listening

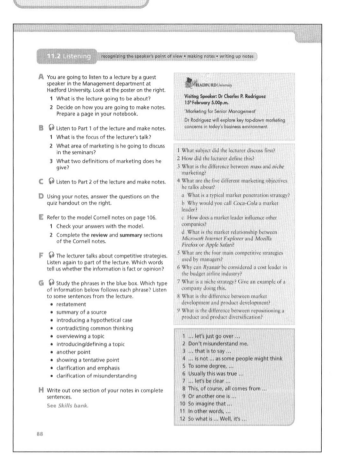

General note

Read the *Skills bank – Writing out notes in full* at the end of the Course Book unit. Decide when, if at all, to refer students to it. The best time, as before, is probably at the very end of the lesson or the beginning of the next lesson, as a summary/ revision.

Lesson aims

- recognize and understand phrases that identify the speaker's point of view
- use background knowledge in listening comprehension
- convert notes into full sentences and paragraphs

Further practice in:

- making notes (use of heading systems and abbreviations)
- referring to sources
- general academic words and phrases

Introduction

1 Review phrases indicating a speaker's view of the truth value of a statement. Write a sentence such as the following on the board (i.e., a 'fact' about which there may be differences of opinion): *A product can only be sold successfully with an effective promotional campaign.*

Ask students to say whether they think this is true or not. Elicit phrases they can use before the sentence to show how certain they are about their opinion.

Dictate or write on the board the following phrases. Ask students to say what the effect of each phrase is when put before the sentence on the board. In each case, does it make the writer sound confident or tentative?

> *The research shows that …*
>
> *A survey found that …*
>
> *The evidence does not support the idea that …*
>
> *It appears to be the case that …*
>
> *The evidence suggests that …*
>
> *The evidence shows that …*
>
> *It is clear that …*
>
> *It is possible that …*

2 Revise the Cornell note-taking system. Elicit the R words. Ask students to describe how to divide up the page (refer to Unit 9). Revise the other ways to take notes (see Units 1 and 3).

3 Revise note-taking symbols and abbreviations (see Units 5 and 9, and Unit 9 extra activity 3).

Exercise A

Refer students to the Hadford University lecture announcement. Tell them to look at the title and the summary of the talk.

Set the exercises for pairwork discussion. Feed back with the whole class.

Answers

1 Accept any reasonable suggestions.

2 The lecturer is clearly going to focus on aspects of marketing and the reasons/features of them. This suggests that possibly a spidergram or the more conventional numbered points system might be a suitable form of notes (as in Unit 1), as well as the Cornell system (which is used here).

🎧 Exercise B

Play Part 1 once through *without* allowing students time to focus on the questions.

Put students in pairs to answer the questions by referring to their notes. Feed back with the whole class, building a set of notes on the board if you wish.

Ask students which method they are going to use to make notes, now that they have listened to the introduction. They should make any adjustments necessary to the page they have prepared in their notebooks.

Answers

Model answers:

1 typical marketing concerns and objectives from a senior management perspective

2 the marketing process

3 he gives two definitions:
   a activity that helps buyers and sellers exchange things
   b process used by managers to identify and profitably satisfy consumer needs/wants

Transcript 🎧 1.46

Part 1

Good morning. I'm Charles P. Rodriguez, and it's a pleasure to be here today. My aim is to clarify what it means for a company to have a marketing orientation. I'm also going to talk about what typical marketing objectives and strategies are, from a management perspective. We'll talk about what market share is, and touch on branding; that is to say, I shall introduce you to all the aspects of marketing that concern corporate *senior* management.

The marketing process itself we'll leave for your seminars, as we're taking a strictly top-down approach today. Don't misunderstand me, I don't want to imply that this is all there is to marketing. Of course, a marketing manager has to analyze the market, segment it, target her customers, position the product and formulate a marketing mix. But our scope today is just a senior management view.

Now, before we get going, let's be clear that marketing is not the same as selling … as some people might think. What is marketing? To some degree, every organization – no matter what it does – is involved in marketing activity. So firstly, let's just go over the definition of marketing that you see here on the screen: it's any activity that helps buyers and sellers exchange things – goods and services. Or you can use this one: the process by which managers can identify and then anticipate consumer needs, and maybe wants, too, and then satisfy them profitably. So you can see – there's a lot to it.

🎧 Exercise C

Play the whole of the rest of lecture through *once* without stopping. Students should make notes as they listen.

Answer

See *Notes* section of the table in the Answers section for Exercise E.

Transcript 🎧 1.47

Part 2

So what is *market orientation*? Well, it's a move on from *product orientation*. It is said that, in the past, companies used to be more product-orientated, that is to say, they were centred on the product and the production process. 'A good product will sell itself,' they thought. And so, according to this view, advertising is hardly needed. In other words, demand is simply created by supply! Usually this was true for unique, new products with little or no competition … often products that were mass produced. You can imagine the very first toasters or vacuum cleaners or other inventions for the home. Just the *usefulness* of the product was enough to move it – to sell it.

Then, as competition grew, people began to realize that branding was needed to distinguish your products from others. And so market orientation was born. A market-orientated company identifies and keeps reviewing the needs of consumers, to try to meet them. Sony is famously market-orientated. So is Apple, with its fresh ideas for laptops, cutting-edge designs, varied and smaller mobile music players and so on. These companies anticipate and respond fast as the market changes … to changes in what people want, where they want it, how they want it and the price they expect to pay. They are in constant dialogue with customers to fully understand their wishes.

A similar concept to think about is *mass marketing* as opposed to *niche marketing*. Mass marketing is where products are undifferentiated … they're all the same. Mass-marketed products like the original Coca-Cola are the same the world over (and they're therefore also an example of 'global' marketing). The opposite of mass marketing is differentiation through customization (that's designing products specifically for individuals), or niche marketing. A niche is a small segment of a market. Rolls-Royce cars are marketed to the rich who want to appear rich. A presentation skills trainer only markets to professionals who are nervous about talking to audiences. These are examples of where businesses focus, or 'niche', to a specific segment.

Now, there are several reasons why a company may engage in marketing. These are called marketing objectives.

First of all, they may simply want to grow by increasing their sales and their revenue. Growth is usually a central concern of companies.

Secondly, they may want to get market share. *Market share* means the *portion* of the market that your company has. So imagine that the Virgin Group, a strong brand with a fairly global reach, wants to launch Virgin jeans – yes, blue jeans like Diesel and Levi's – it might want just one per cent of the market. The global jeans market is worth perhaps over $40 billion. You can imagine that one per cent of $40 billion is a lot of money. So it'd be worth it. They might even develop a *market penetration strategy* … market penetration is doing whatever it takes to get into a market and get some market share. You could sell your jeans for less than they cost you, for example – in other words, you could even lose money, simply to win market share. 3 Mobile did exactly this a few years ago in Britain to capture mobile phone market share from the big players at the time: Orange, T-Mobile, Vodafone and O2. Yes, increasing market share is a popular marketing strategy. And maintaining it is, too.

The company with the biggest share of the market is called the *market leader*. Microsoft is the market leader in the software industry. Smaller companies will often follow the pricing of the market leader. And sometimes, they will follow their quality and standards and other things, too. The companies with the next biggest share are called market challengers. In the business of Internet browsers, the market challengers to Microsoft's Internet Explorer software are Mozilla Firefox and Apple Safari. Netscape was a challenger and now no longer is. Smaller companies that don't want to be market leaders or challengers are called market followers. Virgin Cola, for instance, or a supermarket's own-brand cola, *copy* the market leaders, Pepsi and Coke, but don't try to challenge them for first and second place.

Then there are less obvious marketing objectives, like launching new innovations – new products. Then there is *differentiating* your products from your competitors.

Or another one is to become well-known – to get your brand into the minds of the public – to increase their *recognition* of your brand.

Now, to achieve your goals – that is to say, to fulfil the marketing objectives – you need *marketing strategies*. A strategy is 'how' something is done. For corporations, marketing strategies are linked to objectives.

They could be competitive strategies, for example. For these sorts of strategies, you would need to do what's called *competitor analysis*. You need to do detailed research into your competitors' behaviour: who are they? (They might not just be those that produce the same product; they might be those that satisfy the same need in a different way) … what are their strengths and weaknesses? … and what are their strategies? Lots of research to do. This, of course, all comes from Michael Porter's excellent

book *Competitive Strategy*, published in 1980 … and others he has written since then.

One particularly effective competitive strategy he discusses is to become the *cost leader*. The purpose here is to be known as the cheapest. Ryanair, for example, became Europe's first cost leader in the airline industry, and the evidence indicates that easyJet was close behind.

Another strategy is *differentiation* – to be different. This is linked to the objective I mentioned before: differentiating your product. This is to try to give your company an 'edge' over others. British Airways, for example, actually used to try to indulge its high-price-paying customers in little luxuries that you wouldn't expect.

Another strategy is *focus*. Or *niche*. Gucci, for example, only focuses on people with high disposable incomes who are image-conscious – that is to say, it likes its image to signify a higher status in society. Other examples include specialist organic supermarkets as opposed to normal supermarkets.

Or they could be strategies for *growth*. Most large companies want this.

Or they could be other strategies … strategies for *market penetration* (like I mentioned a few moments ago – an idea first written about in the *Harvard Business Review* in 1957 by a fellow called Igor Ansoff – he's responsible for a few of these!), *market entry* (which is entering a new country, for instance) or *market expansion*, *product development* (that's introducing new products, like chocolate manufacturers do all the time with new types of chocolate bar), *market development* (that's pushing existing products in new markets, like banks that open up overseas … or retail chains moving into new countries).

Or strategies could be about changing the feeling that people have about a product in relation to other products (that's called '*positioning*'). Lucozade used to be a drink for the sick – to recover. Now it's seen as a sports drink. That's an example of *repositioning*. Burberry used to be a practical weatherproof clothing brand associated with a particular segment of the market, mostly elderly ladies. In 1998, it actively repositioned its products as luxury items. Now, it's commonly believed that it always was a luxury brand!

Or a strategy could be in *diversifying*. Mercedes was always known for having large cars … until one day it woke up and decided to capture the lower-priced but higher-volume small-car market as well. Now it covers both types and more – vans and things, too! In my view, it's risky business. But that's called diversification.

OK. Now, I'm going to stop at this point and …

Exercise D

Put students in pairs to answer the questions by referring to their notes. Feed back with the class to see how much they have been able to get from the lecture. If they cannot answer something, do not supply the answer at this stage.

Answers

Model answers:

1 Market orientation

2 A market-orientated company identifies and reviews consumer needs and reacts to market change to determine what products/services it offers.

3 Mass marketing is marketing the same products over a large market, e.g., Coca-Cola. Niche marketing is marketing products that are customized to individual or small, specialized target groups, e.g., Rolls-Royce produces luxury cars for people who want to appear wealthy.

4 market growth – most companies want to expand their sales and revenues
market share – market leader, challenger or follower launching new products
product differentiation – increasing awareness of what makes your product unique
increasing brand recognition

   a selling a product at below cost price to gain market share for a new product

   b Coca-Cola has the largest share of the market

   c a market leader often sets prices, quality of products, production standards

d *Explorer* is the market leader, and *Mozilla Firefox* and *Apple Safari* are market challengers

5 To become a *cost leader*, differentiate products/services from those of the competition, establish products/services in a focus or niche market, adopt market penetration strategies.

6 *Ryanair* has the lowest prices, so it is a cost leader.

7 Niche strategy is selling products to a select and specialized market, e.g., Gucci targeting fashion-conscious consumers with high disposable incomes.

8 *market development* = taking existing products into a new market
product development = increasing your product range, e.g., new kinds of chocolate bars

9 *repositioning a product* = adjusting the feeling a target consumer has towards a product, e.g., Burberry from the sensible granny market to a luxury upmarket market.
product diversification = producing a wider range of products, e.g., Mercedes Benz produced large executive cars and now also target the small-car, truck and van markets.

Exercise E

1 Set for individual work.

2 Set for individual work and pairwork checking. Feed back with the whole class.

Answers

Possible answers: (see table below)

Review	Notes
Product orientat'n is … ?	<u>Market Orientation</u> 1. ≠ product orientation: product supply ➔ demand true for single products, e.g., 1st toaster/vacuum cleaner 2. ↗ competition ➔ idea that branding is important to differentiate own products ⬅ others.
Mkt-orient'd is … ?	3. <u>market-orientated co.</u> identifies and reviews consumer needs & supplies products & services to suit. a Sony and Apple – fresh ideas for laptops, etc., & respond rapidly to mkt changes
Mass mktg is … ?	b *mass vs niche marketing: mass mkting* = undifferentiated products to the whole mkt., e.g., Coca-Cola
Niche mktg is … ? e.g.s of each … ?	*Niche mkting* = customized products for individuals or specialized groups, e.g., Rolls-Royce = luxury cars for high-end users or presentation skills tutor for smll grps of unconfident speakers

What are the 6 main mkting objectives?	4. <u>Marketing objectives:</u> (reasons why co.s engage in marketing)
	a growth of co. sales/revenue
	b mkt share – e.g., Virgin jeans target 1% of $40bn
	c mkt penetration strategies are:
	  i. sell new product below cost price to gain entry and profile, e.g., 3 Mobile in UK mkt.
	  ii. choose what role co. wants to have in mkt.
	    • *mkt leader*, i.e., co. with largest section of mkt, e.g., Coca-Cola of soft drinks mkt.

Mkt leader is … ? e.g., …	• mkt leader often benchmarks prices and stds and quality criteria

Mkt challenger is ...? e.g., ...	• <u>mkt challenger</u>, i.e., co.s that are close to mkt leader, e.g., Mozilla Firefox & Apple Safari mkt challengers ➔ Microsoft Internet Explorer
Mkt follower is ... ? e.g., ...	• <u>mkt follower</u>: – co.s that can't compete and accept and smaller slice of the mkt, e.g., Virgin Cola looking for small part of mkt.
	d launching new products e product differentiation f increasing brand recognition
Name 5 mkting strategies.	5. Marketing strategies:
Competitive analysis is ... ?	a <u>competitive strategies:</u> – need to do competitor analysis – research their behaviour, e.g., strengths/weaknesses/strategies (ref: Michael Porter Competitive Strategy, 1980)
e.g., of cost leader – why?	• cost leader – i.e., to be known as cheapest – e.g., Ryanair
How do companies differentiate?	• differentiation – i.e., to known to be different – e.g., BA luxury for business users cf Ryanair
Why is Gucci niche mkt?	• focus/niche – e.g., Gucci products ➔ consumers with high disposable income or organic supermarkets vs ordinary supermarkets
	b <u>strategies for growth</u> – aim of most co.s
	c <u>strategies for mkt penetration:</u> (ref: Ansoff 1957) – key concepts – mkt entry = entering a new country – mkt expansion = increasing product range – mkt development = bringing existing products into new mkts
What's the difference between mkt entry/ expansion/development ?	
Repositioning is ...?	d <u>repositioning product range</u> – changing product appeal, e.g., Lucozade ◀ health drink ➔ sports drink/Burberry ◀ Practical weatherproof clothing ➔ young luxury brand
Diversifying is ...?	e <u>diversifying product range</u> – e.g., Mercedes known for large executive cars ➔ small family cars & vans

Summary

Market orientation is responding to the needs and wants of the consumer and reacting quickly/flexibly to meet these. Companies choose to target niche or mass markets. They set clear marketing objectives concerning market share and market penetration strategies. They need to decide on strategies that might include: competitive, growth, differentiation, niche, product positioning and range diversification, or market penetration for market entry, expansion or development strategies.

Note

Source references for lecture:

Ansoff, I. (1957). Strategies for diversification. *Harvard Business Review*, 35(5), 113–124.

Porter, M.E. (1980). *Competitive strategy*. Free Press, New York.

🎧 Exercise F

Discuss the question with the whole class. Ask them if they can remember any phrases which signal whether comments are true or just opinion.

Play the extract. Ask students to tell you to stop the recording when they hear key phrases. Write the phrases on the board.

Remind students that it is important to recognize when someone is giving only their opinion, which others might well disagree with.

Answer

Model answers:

Michael Porter's *excellent* book (*Competitive Strategy*, published in 1980.)	Whether something is 'good', 'excellent', etc., is always a matter of opinion.
One *particularly effective* (competitive strategy he discusses ...)	This is a continuation of 'excellent.' His opinion is favourable.
The evidence indicates that ... easyJet was close behind. (This suggests the speaker has previously seen factual survey data on comparative pricing.)	Without the actual source, information cannot be truly verified as fact, although sometimes people put forward their case so strongly to present opinions as facts. In this case, it is most probably fact.

British Airways … *actually* (used to try to *indulge* their high-price paying customers in *little luxuries* that you wouldn't expect.)	*Actually* here shows surprise or reaction, indicating something contrary to what might be seen as correct, especially as it is linked to words like *indulge* and *little* luxuries. In other contexts, *actually* can be used to show stronger disbelief or suspicion. This is subjective and thus opinion.
It's *commonly believed that* (most large companies want this.)	This phrase can be used to give both a speaker's own as well as others' opinions. The passive distances the claim slightly from the speaker, allowing space for it to be the opinion of others rather than fact.
In my view (it's risky business.)	This is clearly the lecturer's opinion.

Transcript 🎧 1.48

This, of course, all comes from Michael Porter's excellent book *Competitive Strategy*, published in 1980 … and others he has written since then.

One particularly effective competitive strategy he discusses is to become the *cost leader*. The purpose here is to be known as the cheapest. Ryanair, for example, became Europe's first cost leader in the airline industry, and the evidence indicates that easyJet was close behind.

Another strategy is *differentiation* – to be different. This is linked to the objective I mentioned before: differentiating your product. This is to try to give your company an 'edge' over others. British Airways, for example, actually used to try to indulge their high-price-paying customers in little luxuries that you wouldn't expect. [fade out]

[fade back] In 1998, it actively repositioned its products as luxury items. Now, it's commonly believed that it always was a luxury brand!

Or a strategy could be in *diversifying*. Mercedes was always known for having large cars … until one day it woke up and decided to capture the lower-priced but higher-volume small-car market … as well. Now it covers both types and more – vans and things, too! In my view, it's risky business. But that's called diversification.

🎧 Exercise G

Allow students time to read the phrases and the types of information, making sure that they understand any difficult words. Remind students that 'type' of information tells you what the speaker *intends to do* with the words. The words themselves are something different.

Ask students to try to match the phrases and types of information as far as they can. Note that it is not always possible to say what the function of a phrase is outside its context, so they may not be able to match all the phrases and information types before hearing the extracts. Note that some types of information are needed more than once.

When they have done as much as they can, play the extracts one at a time, allowing time for students to identify the type of information which follows. Check answers after each extract, making sure that students understand the information that actually follows the phrase. If possible, students should also give the actual words.

Answer

Model answers:

Fixed phrase	Type of information which follows the phrase
1 Let's just go over …	overviewing a topic
2 Don't misunderstand me.	clarification of misunderstanding
3 … that is to say …	restatement
4 … is not … as some people might think	contradicting common thinking
5 To some degree, …	showing a tentative point
6 Usually this was true …	showing a tentative point
7 … let's be clear …	clarification and emphasis
8 This, of course, all comes from …	summary of a source
9 Or another one is …	another point
10 So imagine that …	introducing a hypothetical case
11 In other words,	restatement
12 So what is … Well, it's …	introducing/defining a topic

Transcript 🎧 1.49

Extract 1
So firstly, let's just go over the definition of marketing that you see here on the screen … .

Extract 2
Don't misunderstand me, I don't want to imply that this is all there is to marketing.

Extract 3
We'll talk about what market share is, and touch on branding; that is to say, I shall introduce you to all the aspects of marketing that concern corporate *senior* management.

Extract 4
… marketing is not the same as selling … as some people might think.

Extract 5

To some degree, every organization – no matter what it does – is involved in marketing activity …

Extract 6

Usually this was true for unique, new products with little or no competition … often products that were mass produced.

Extract 7

Now, before we get going, let's be clear that marketing is not the same as selling … as some people might think.

Extract 8

This, of course, all comes from Michael Porter's excellent book *Competitive Strategy*, published in 1980 …

Extract 9

Or another one is to become well-known – to get your brand into the minds of the public …

Extract 10

So imagine that the Virgin Group, a strong brand with a fairly global reach, wants to launch Virgin jeans – yes, blue jeans like Diesel and Levi's …

Extract 11

In other words, demand is simply created by supply!

Extract 12

So what is market orientation? Well, it's a move on from product orientation.

Exercise H

Use this section from the Cornell notes to demonstrate what to do:

Market Orientation:

1. ≠ product orientation ➔ product = supply ➔ demand true for single products, e.g., 1st toaster/vacuum cleaner

2. ↗ competition ➔ idea that branding is important to differentiate own products ⬅ others

---

Elicit from students suggestions on how to write up the notes in complete sentences. Write the suggestions on the board.

Ask students to say what they need to add into the notes to make a good piece of writing, e.g.,

Grammar: relative pronouns, articles and determiners, prepositions, auxiliary verbs, linking words, 'there was/were' clauses

Vocabulary: some vocabulary may need to be added, particularly where symbols are used in the notes, or where extra words are needed to make sense of the information or give a good sense of flow in the writing

Note that this, of course, works the other way: when making notes, these elements can be excluded from the notes.

Possible rewrite of the notes:

> Market orientation **is not the same as** product orientation, in which product supply is enough to **create** demand. **This was often true in** the case of unique products **such as** toasters **or** vacuum cleaners **entering the market for the first time.**
>
> **Increasing** competition **led to** companies needing branding to differentiate their products **from** other products **in the market.**

Set another section for individual writing in class or for homework. Either ask students to refer to their own notes, or to the Cornell notes on page 106 of the Course Book.

Closure

1 Tell students to review and make a list of the main topics and arguments presented in this lesson. Then ask them to try and summarize the viewpoints, using some of the language they have practised.

2 They could also give a two- or three-sentence summary of anything that they themselves have read, e.g., *I read a useful article on X by Y. It said that …*

3 Ask students to do some research and to make a list of useful or interesting books/articles/websites on the topics in this lesson. They should draw up a list, correctly referenced, and share their sources with other students.

11.3 Extending skills

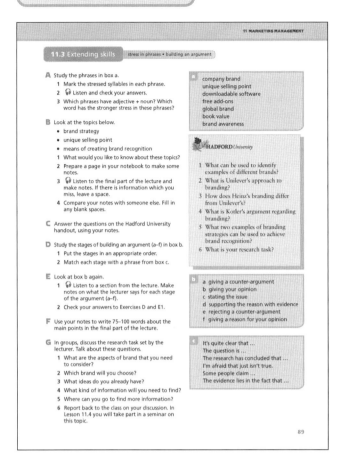

89

Lesson aims

- recognize stress patterns in noun phrases
- understand how to develop an argument:

  stating the issue

  giving a counter-argument

  rejecting a counter-argument

  giving opinions

  supporting opinions
- understand more general academic words and phrases mainly used in speaking

Further practice in:

- expressing degrees of confidence/tentativeness
- reporting back

Introduction

1 Revise the lecture in Lesson 11.2. Ask students to use the model Cornell notes on page 106. They should cover up the notes section and use the review and summary sections (which they completed in Lesson 11.2) to help recall the contents of the lecture. They could work in pairs to do this.

2 Revisit the expressions students highlighted in Lesson 11.1 as difficult. Check that students are clear on their meaning now and provide meaning if they are still unsure.

3 Revise phrases which express degrees of confidence in 'facts'. Dictate these phrases. Do they show that the speaker is certain or tentative?

There is no question that (= certain)

We have to accept the evidence that (= certain)

Some people claim that (= tentative)

What is obvious to us is that (= certain)

As everyone is aware (= certain)

To some degree (= tentative)

This means ultimately that (= certain)

It's quite clear that (= certain)

We could argue that (= tentative)

🎧 Exercise A

1/2 Set for individual work and pairwork checking. This is an exercise in perceiving rhythm. At this point, there is no need to distinguish between different levels of stress. Students can underline all the stressed syllables. They will also need to count all the syllables.

Feed back with the whole class, checking pronunciation of the phrases and meanings.

3 Discuss this with the class first. Demonstrate with ˌcompany ˈbrand, showing how if you say ˈcompany ˌbrand, it appears that a contrast is being made with another type of brand. Tell students that the usual pattern for the adjective + noun phrase is for a heavier stress to go on the noun. Set students to pick out the other adjective + noun patterns, writing each one on the board. Elicit the stress patterns and give students time to practise the phrases. Note that there is plenty of natural variation in native speech, so it is not necessary to impose these patterns as 'rules' in the students' minds; this is simply an awareness-raising exercise.

Answers

Model answers:

1/2 company ˈbrand

uˈnique ˌselling point

downˌloadable ˈsoftware

ˈfree ˌadd-ons

ˌglobal ˈbrand

ˈbook value

ˌbrand aˈwareness

3 Adjective + noun (second word often – but not always – has stronger stress): unique selling point, downloadable software, free add-ons, global brand.

199

Transcript 🎧 1.50

company 'brand

u'nique ,selling point

down,loadable 'software

'free ,add-ons

,global 'brand

'book value

,brand a'wareness

🎧 Exercise B

1 Look at the three topics. Discuss with the class what they know already about these topics and find out what opinions they may have. Put students in pairs and ask each pair to write down one question to which they would like an answer in the lecture.

2 Set for individual work.

3 Play Part 3 straight through; students make notes.

4 Put students in pairs to compare their notes and fill in any gaps they may have.

Transcript 🎧 1.51

Part 3

OK, let's move on to brand. Yes, I can see a few … and a few brands worn here in the front row [faint laughter]. So. The question is, what is brand exactly? Well, on the *most basic level*, brand is anything that lets a consumer identify a company's goods or services: it could be their name; a slogan (a few words or phrases); a colour (think of Shell, think yellow; think BP, think green); a logo, sign, symbol or design (think of the apple on Apple computers); or a tune. In fact, it could be all of these together … trademarked, of course (legally protected so others can't copy it).

Now with the likes of Shell, it's a company brand. But sometimes the brand is just a product. BMW is a good illustration. Mini Cooper is a brand that is owned by BMW but quite different from the traditional BMW brand. Giant companies like Unilever will brand all their soap powders differently for different market segments, making them look like they are competing with each other. Others, like Heinz, will put the name on all its products. Others combine: think of Nestlé's product Nescafé. Others extend their brand: think of Pepsi and then Diet Pepsi or Wild Cherry Pepsi. And then others stretch their brand: think of Camel cigarettes; now think of Camel shirts and baseball caps.

Now, some people claim that brand represents a product's USP. What's USP? It's the 'unique selling point'. It's what makes a product different from others. The unique selling point for a certain Hong Kong hotel might be its perfect mountain peak views that no other hotels in Hong Kong have; the USP for a business school might be its amazing marketing department with world-famous lecturers; the USP for certain downloadable software might be that it includes free add-ons that everyone wants, unlike all its competitors. It's claimed that brand simply reflects the USP of a product or service.

Well, I'm afraid that just isn't true. Yes, brand does sometimes reflect a product's USP, but it's much much more than that. Let's take a look and see.

Experts often try to place a value on brand; these experts work out what this 'thing' called brand is worth and call this *brand equity*. This can sometimes run into the multimillions. Now this wouldn't happen if brand were simply a name, logo and USP. Let's think about this.

Philip Kotler is one of the all-time gurus of management, especially the marketing side. He claimed that many of the great global brands are worth much more than even the book value of the assets that together were used to make the brand … in other words, the value of the brand as it grows often becomes worth more than the physical value of companies. Of course, this is important as it increases the price a business can be sold for. If you buy a company, your accounting statements can reflect this amount. So, what is this extra 'thing' that can create incredible brand equity? Well, it's quite clear that it's more than just a name, a logo and USP.

The research has concluded that having a strong brand means you have high brand awareness. This is because people recognize it. Such research, according to Kotler, is the work of countless branding and marketing agencies who work with companies on brand and then test the responses of the public. Yes, exposure and hopefully *recognition* is very important. Then people are more likely to choose the brand (this is called *brand preference* and then *brand loyalty* if they stick with it). A strong brand also means you can be more flexible with price. Consumers loyal to their Apple computers, for instance, will not be tempted by a drop in Dell's computer pricing, nor be too worried by a rise in Apple's. If the brand was weaker, they'd easily switch.

Now, some people today talk about *brand blindness*, which means not noticing brands as there are so many competing for our attention. So it is harder and harder to achieve brand recognition and awareness, let alone preference or loyalty. Thus, the marketer has to dig into our psychology.

Basically, there are two ways to do that. The first is called *attitude* branding. This is about representing feelings. The Body Shop brand was originally about making people feel *trust*. Nike makes many people feel *rebelli* ... yes, like your attitude, you in the front row with the Nike logo on your shirt and cap! Just kidding! OK, and the second just takes it further ... it's *personality*. Essentially, a brand has 'personality' so that an individual's psyche can enter a relationship with it based on their experience with it ... you know: adventurous, bold, slick, playful, or whatever mix of these it might be. The consumer in the street needs to respond *emotionally* with the brand for it to be successful. It's like they're responding to another human.

On first glance, you may question whether it's really possible to build a brand that people can respond to in this way. The evidence lies in the fact that many companies have done it and done it perfectly ... just take a few minutes to think about the psychology of how you respond to the Body Shop, or – you there – Puma ... or Audi or Alpha Romeo cars, or the Renault Clio, for that matter. [fades]

Now I'm going to set you a task which will involve investigating some of these aspects I've discussed. I want you to do some research. Choose a brand and identify for us all the components of brand, like logo and so on, also its USP, its brand equity if it's possible to find out, any studies or data into recognition, awareness and preference or loyalty. And then, most importantly, a brief analysis into what you think and what others think about attitude or personality in the brand. See what you can do. I hope you can come up with some great stuff for the workshops next week.

Exercise C

Set for individual work and pairwork checking. Feed back with the class on question 6 to make sure that it is clear.

Answers

Model answers:

1 names, slogans, colour (Shell and BP), logos, signs, symbols, designs, tunes.

2 Unilever uses multi-branding. Soap powder brands are marketed separately to create the impression of competing products; who owns the product is not clear to the consumer.

3 Heinz, in contrast, exhibits its brand on all its products.

4 Kotler argues that branding is more than logos, tunes, etc., because brand equity is a greater worth than the assets and resources that built it – this includes brand recognition and value derived from brand loyalty.

5 Companies can use attitude branding or developing brand personality to create strong brand recognition.

6 Firstly, students must choose a brand to analyze and identify:

- brand components
- USP
- brand equity (if possible)
- studies revealing amount of brand recognition, awareness preference or loyalty.

Then students need to analyze their own reaction to the brand, and find out what others think about the attitude or personality of the brand.

Exercise D

1 Set for pairwork discussion. Point out that there is no one 'correct' order; students should try to identify the most logical sequence for the argument. Explain that a 'counter-argument' means an opinion which you do not agree with or think is wrong. 'Issue' means a question about which there is some debate.

2 Set for individual work and pairwork checking. Do not feed back with the class at this point, but move on to E, where the answers will be given.

Exercise E

1 Play the extract. Tell students to stop you when they hear each item. Make sure students can say exactly what the words are in each case. Ask them also to paraphrase the words so that it is clear that they understand the meanings.

2 If necessary, play the extract again for students to check that they have the phrases and types of statement correct. Ask how many students had the stages of an argument (Exercise D question 1) in the same order as the recording/model answers below. Discuss any alternative possibilities (see *Language note* below).

Answers

Model answers for Exercises D and E: see table on next page.

Language note

A common way in which an argument can be built is to give a counter-argument, then reject the counter-argument with reasons and evidence. There are, of course, other ways to build an argument. For example, the counter-arguments may be given after the writer's/speaker's own opinion. Or all the arguments against may be given, followed by all the arguments for an issue (or vice versa), concluding with the speaker's/writer's own opinion.

Type of statement	Phrase	Lecturer's words
c stating the issue	The question is ...	*The question is:* what is brand exactly?
a giving a counter-argument	Some people claim ...	*Some people claim* that brand represents a product's USP.
e rejecting a counter-argument	I'm afraid that just isn't true.	*I'm afraid that just isn't true.*
b giving your opinion	It's quite clear that ...	*It's quite clear that* it's more than just a name, a logo and USP.
f giving a reason for your opinion	The research has concluded that ...	*The research has concluded that* having a strong brand means you have high brand awareness.
d supporting the reason with evidence	The evidence lies in the fact that ...	*The evidence lies in the fact that* many companies have done it and done it perfectly.

Transcript 🎧 1.52

OK, let's move on to brand. ... [fades out, fades in] ... So. The question is, what is brand exactly? Well, on the most basic level, brand is anything that ... [fades out, fades in] ... Now, some people claim that brand just represents a product's USP. What's USP? It's the 'unique selling point'. It's what makes a product different from others ... [fades out, fades in] ... Well, I'm afraid that just isn't true. Yes, brand does sometimes reflect a product's USP, but it's much much more than that. Let's take a look and see. ... [fades out, fades in] ... So, what is this extra 'thing' that can create incredible brand equity? Well, it's quite clear that it's more than just a name, a logo and USP ... [fades out, fades in] ... The research has concluded that having a strong brand means you have high brand awareness. This is because people recognize it. Yes, exposure and hopefully *recognition* is very important. Then people are more likely to choose the brand (this is called *brand preference* and then *brand loyalty* if they stick with it). A strong brand also means you can be more flexible with price ... [fades out, fades in] ... It's like they're responding to another human. On first glance, you may question whether it's really possible to build a brand that people can respond to in this way. The evidence lies in the fact that many companies have done it and done it perfectly ... just take a few minutes to think about the ... [fades out]

Exercise F

Set for individual work – possibly homework – or else a pair/small group writing task. If the latter, tell students to put their writing on an OHT or other visual medium, so that the whole class can look and comment on what has been written. You can elicit from them corrections to language errors.

Exercise G

Play the last section of Part 3 again ('Now I'm going to set ...') and ask students to listen and take notes. In pairs, students compare their notes with what they already have. Feed back and explain on the whiteboard all elements that may be discussed.

Set students to work in groups of three or four. Allow each group to choose their brand. Guide a few of them to think outside the box and consider brands like Madonna or Beckham, or organizations like Greenpeace or the Olympics Committee, rather than the usual Starbucks and Nokia that many students immediately choose. Ask one person from each group to present the results of the group's discussion.

1 Set for group discussion. Encourage them to identify some particular brand strategy or focus before choosing their brand. This will make it easier later. For example, multi-branding leads to such examples as Unilever or Proctor & Gamble, while brand extension or 'stretching' leads to Apple's i-series (iPod, iTunes, iPhone, etc.).

2 The group should decide for themselves, but will need to check with the teacher that their choice is likely to be interesting and doable, and relates to brand strategies or aspects of brand discussed.

3 Groups need to brainstorm at this point and come up with a mind map.

4 Get groups to focus on the different areas of the task; they will need to compare notes. (Note that if they choose to research brand equity (the value of the brand), they might find it useful to consider the following. Brand equity is sometimes known in accounting terminology as the main component of 'goodwill', which is part of the value of the sale of a company which represents intangible value. Therefore, it is difficult to ascertain brand equity unless an enterprise has been sold (and in most accounting systems it is improper to include it as an asset unless it has been bought). Nevertheless, there are professionals in the real world with dedicated vocations in brand equity valuation. Knowing all of this may help in searching and choosing search terms.)

5 Elicit from the class the likely sources of information on the brand itself: company websites, professional journals in marketing, academic journals specializing in marketing. Try to encourage them to seek a balance and not rely on Google alone.

Elicit from the class how they will find information regarding brand personality and attitude. Steer them towards both secondary research and primary – by conducting questionnaires of classmates or others. Ask them to question people and organize and analyze the responses.

6 They could prepare a brief report summarizing what they have discovered in terms of brand attitude and personality. You can set a realistic word limit according to how much time is available. Alternatively, you could keep it spoken. You will also need to arrange the date for the feedback and discussion of the information – this is the focus of Exercise G in Lesson 11.4.

Closure

Arguments, counter-arguments and giving opinions

Before you ask students to look at the statements below, tell them they should think about the methods seen in this unit to build an argument. Then ask them to think about whether they agree with the statements below. They should prepare a brief summary of their viewpoints on the topics; they should also try to use some of the phrases used in this lesson. They should try to state a counter-argument and then reject it.

1 A brand is only a mixture of USP and features like colour, logo design and strapline ... nothing more.

2 The multi-branding strategy that companies like Unilever use to present their brands is basically dishonest.

3 Branding and marketing have created too much choice for consumers, which has resulted in the wasteful use of resources.

4 Letting market orientation (i.e., consumer needs and wants) determine what companies produce is an irresponsible use of resources.

5 Companies spend far too much on packaging which just gets thrown away as rubbish.

6 The fact that consumers can develop brand blindness is proof that we live in a world with too much choice, which creates unnecessary stress on the population.

7 Managers should plan their marketing on good principles of sustainability, not simply on what sells best.

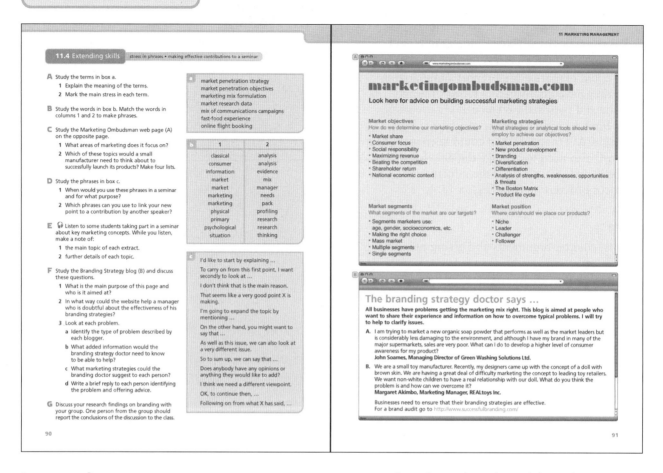

Lesson aims

- recognize stress in compound phrases
- link a contribution to previous contributions when speaking in a seminar
- understand vocabulary in the area of marketing issues

Further practice in:

- taking part in seminars:

  introducing, maintaining and concluding a contribution

  agreeing/disagreeing with other speakers

Introduction

1 Remind students that they are going to be presenting their research findings later in this lesson. Check that they can remember the main points from Lesson 11.3 lecture extracts; key phrases from the lecture could be used as prompts, e.g.,

> *The question is* (what is branding?)
>
> *What are typical components of brand?* (colour, logo, tunes, slogans, name)
>
> *In what way is the assumption that brand is simply a product's USP wrong?* (Brand recognition is an important element of what a brand is and is achieved through a range of strategies involving a brand's core values, its essence, its attitude and even its 'personality'.)
>
> *Other elements of branding* (brand recognition leads to brand loyalty)
>
> *The big question is ...* (how do we achieve brand recognition?)
>
> *Two methods ...* (attitude branding or creating brand personality)

2 The following activity is a good way to check that students are familiar with the terminology and vocabulary from Lesson 11.3. Ask students to write down 5–10 words or expressions from the previous lesson relating to branding and branding strategy. Then use two or three students as 'secretaries'. Ask the class to dictate the words so that the secretaries can write the vocabulary on the board. Use this as a brainstorming session.

Exercise A

These are more complex noun phrases than in Lesson 11.3, since they are made up of three words. In some cases, the pattern is noun + noun + noun. In this case, there may be a compound made from the first two nouns, or the last two nouns. In other cases, the pattern is adjective + noun + noun, in which the second and third words make a compound. These patterns should become clear once the meaning is understood.

1 Discuss *market penetration strategy* with the class as an example. Elicit that it is a strategy developed to help the company penetrate new markets. Set the remaining phrases for individual work and pairwork discussion. Feed back with the whole class, writing each phrase on the board and underlining the words which make a compound noun.

2 Tell students to try to identify where the main stress should come in each phrase. The key to this is finding the two- or three-word compound which is at the base of the three-word phrase. The stress will normally fall in the same place as if this two-word compound was said without the third word. Demonstrate this with *market penetration strategy*. The two-word compound here is not *penetration strategy* but *market penetration*. This is a noun + noun compound, so the rules say this will normally be stressed on the first noun: *'market penetration*. The main stress remains in its original place when the third word is added.

Tell students only to identify the syllable on which the heaviest stress in the phrase falls. (See also *Language note*.)

Answers

Model answers:

The basic compound is underlined in each case.

'market penetration strategy	strategy a company chooses in order to enter a market or increase its market share
'market penetration objectives	what a company wishes to achieve when it penetrates a market
'marketing mix formulation	creation of a mixture of the four Ps to develop a successful marketing strategy
'market research data	information gathered by either primary or secondary research for use in developing a marketing mix
mix of 'communication campaigns	the tactically staged use of combinations of media, e.g., TV advertising, online pop-ups, sports sponsorships, etc., to communicate with target consumers
'fast food experience	the process a customer goes through when he/she buys fast food
online 'flight booking	the process we use to book flights using the Internet

Language note

Stress placement, especially in complex compound noun phrases, is notoriously unstable. There will be apparent exceptions to the rules explained in Exercise A. Stress may often move, depending on the context: for example, *bad 'tempered* – but *'bad-tempered 'teacher*. It's also possible that some native speakers may not agree about some of the phrases above. The main point is to try to notice where the main stress is, and to focus on and rehearse the three words together as a chunk of unified meaning.

Exercise B

Set for individual work and pairwork checking. Tell students that although in some cases it will be possible to make a phrase with more than one option, they must use each word once, and they must use all the words.

Feed back with the whole class. Check that the meaning of all other phrases is understood. Check pronunciation.

Answers

Model answers:

classical	thinking
consumer	needs
information	pack
market	analysis
market	research
marketing	manager
marketing	mix
physical	evidence
primary	research
psychological	profiling
situation	analysis

Language note

Although in most noun–noun compounds the main stress comes on the first element, there are some compounds where this is not true. Definitive pronunciation of compounds can be found in a good pronunciation dictionary.

Exercise C

Refer students to the web page on the opposite page. Set for pair or small group discussion. In question 2, students should identify which points can help companies reduce costs or may involve them in more costs.

Answers

1 market objectives, marketing strategies, market segments and market position

2 Possible answers:

Market objectives

- Market share – has to decide how much market share he/she wants to or is able to penetrate and gain.
- Consumer focus – he/she needs to have a very clear idea of who is the ideal customer.
- Beating the competition – he/she needs to have pricing and brand-positioning strategies to compete successfully against others. This might have risky turnover implications.

Marketing strategies and analytical tools

- Market penetration strategy – this will affect product placement, pricing, etc. Decisions that managers make will be concerned with market entry.
- New product development – both for the new products he/she has developed and ideas for follow-up product development – tooling up and design can be very costly, and it can take a long time to recoup investment capital.
- Branding – brand recognition will be nil, so he/she needs to have a clear brand-building strategy; this is expensive but necessary.
- SWOT analysis of competitors, i.e., their strengths, weaknesses, opportunities and threats. This is only expensive if he/she hires consultants to do this.

Market segments

- He/she will need to decide which segments of the market are likely customers and to target these segments in advertising. This will assist in cost effectiveness in promotions.

Market position

- He/she needs to decide on the subtle relationship between the product and its competitors, and whether he/she can in time become a market challenger. He/she might be content to simply be a market follower. If he/she wishes to become a market challenger or leader this will entail a long-term strategy and a lot of capital investment – unless the products are something completely new, like certain cutting-edge technologies – in which case the product, if it captures consumer interest, could easily become the market leader.

Exercise D

This is mainly revision. Set for individual work or pairwork discussion. Feed back with the whole class.

Answers

Model answers:

Phrase	Use in a seminar
I'd like to start by explaining …	= beginning
To carry on from this first point, I want secondly to look at …	= maintaining/continuing a point
I don't think that is the main reason.	= disagreeing
That seems like a very good point X is making.	= confirming
I'm going to expand the topic by mentioning …	= adding a new point to someone else's previous contribution
On the other hand, you might want to say that …	= disagreeing
As well as this issue, we can also look at a very different issue.	= adding a new point to someone else's previous contribution
So to sum up, we can say that …	= summarizing/concluding
Does anybody have any opinions or anything they would like to add?	= concluding/inviting closure
I think we need a different viewpoint.	= disagreeing
OK, to continue then, …	= maintaining/continuing a point
Following on from what X has said, …	= adding a new point to someone else's previous contribution

🎧 Exercise E

Before students listen, tell them to look at the exercise and questions. Check that students understand the topic for the seminar discussion. Ask them what they might expect to hear.

Play each extract one at a time and ask students to identify the main topic and some further details. Feed back with the whole class.

Answers

Model answers:

	Main topic	Further details
Extract 1	market analysis	situation analysis, demand, market research, primary and secondary research
Extract 2	market segmentation	reasons for segmentation, psychological profiling of consumers, product positioning

| Extract 3 | marketing mix formulation | product, price, promotion, place |
| Extract 4 | 7 Ps | the 4 Ps plus people, physical evidence, process |

Transcript 🎧 1.53

Extract 1

DINA: The lecturer last week asked us to each report on steps in the marketing process, and I was given the first one: market analysis. So, in my part of the seminar, I'd like to start by explaining that market analysis is basically understanding a market and its potential. They talk about measuring 'market size' by volume or by value. They might first carry out a situation analysis to understand the environment, and then look at demand for the product, or changes in demand, such as changes in fashion, existing supply of the product and its price, or rising incomes. And so then there's market research. Market research collects data about how people consume goods and services and how they react to marketing ideas, and then collates and analyzes it. OK? It could be secondary research (that's looking up information already there) and primary research (that's asking the questions yourself).

Extract 2

ELENA: OK, following on from what Dina has said, I'm going to expand the topic by mentioning segmentation. Markets need to be segmented, which means being divided into groups of people with similar needs. So you could divide them up by age, gender, education, social class or income. Or it could be more subtle things like their politics, religion, ethnicity, lifestyle or family characteristics. In fact, today marketers talk about psychological profiling, so they're really digging deep. It seems like a very good point Dina is making about market research, because this can help the marketer in segmenting, too. OK. Now I'd like to mention some important points about why we segment. It's to get the information we need to sell products. With the increase in knowledge, we can increase how we satisfy the needs and wants of the consumer. Therefore, we can 'target' them more effectively without wasting time and money marketing to the wrong people. Now, on the other hand, you might want to say that *any or all* companies operating in a market do this. Well it's true. And this is why we need the next stage: 'positioning'. Positioning is how you 'position' your product against the competition, in terms of how the customer perceives it, in terms of price, that sort of thing … it's being a little different from the others in the eye of the buyer.

Extract 3

BRUCE: Right. Thank you, Elena. I'm going to expand the topic by mentioning the last stage in the process. It's called the marketing mix formulation. Marketing managers have to control the balance between all the elements of the mix. The mix is these things: product, price, promotion and place. Let me try and make this clearer with examples. In thinking about a product, they might consider design and packaging. And for price, they have a very complex job, because price relates to strategy and competitors – market penetration objectives might mean one company undercuts the others and becomes a cost leader, for example. Promotion includes a whole mix of communications campaigns that might cover advertising on TV with coordinating banner ads online, in the press and on the radio and billboards. Or publicity and visibility through sponsorships and charitable work and so on. And place is how the products or services are distributed. For instance, they could reach the consumer through shops and supermarkets, online downloads or in the post. So to sum up, we can say that the four Ps have to be integrated in just the right way … they are a delicate balance and interdependent. Does anybody have any opinions or anything they would like to add?

Extract 4

LEILA: As well as the four Ps model, we can also look at a slightly different sort of approach. I think we need a different viewpoint, and although Bruce has researched the classic thinking on the marketing mix, there's now a bit more to it than that. So here, I'm going to explain the seven Ps. OK, the seven Ps include the four Ps, but there are three more that apply especially to services (you know, like education, insurance, things like that) where there is not always a tangible product. Right, these extra Ps are: People, Physical Evidence and Process. *People* means the face (or the voice) that a customer experiences when he or she have contact with the company or uses the service. It's very important. Think how often a rude person has put you right off a company … for good! Secondly is *physical evidence*. Some services have nothing tangible, so they need to ensure there's something to see or touch as evidence. Business cards, flyers and information packs do this. Or the famous shape of the building. Or membership cards … that sort of thing. OK, to continue then to the last one: *process*. Process is where the service is done a special way which the consumer is involved in, and is thus part of marketing. Think of the fast-food experience and its quick-n-ready convenience. Or think of the process of online flight bookings. These are good examples.

Exercise F

1/2 Set for pairwork. Tell students to study the branding strategy doctor's blog. Feed back with the whole class.

3 Divide the class into small groups. Each group is to discuss either problem a or problem b. Groups feed back to other groups discussing their problem. Then feedback to the whole class.

   a–c Ask students to brainstorm questions – they can use the website for suggestions. Make a list of information needed and of suggestions.

   d Ask students to form two groups, one group dealing with problem A and the other with problem B. The whole group makes suggestions and prepares written advice on an OHT or a file for projection.
   Use the projection as an opportunity for eliciting peer correction of written errors. Feedback with the whole class.

Answers

Possible answers:

1 The main purpose of the page is to give managers an opportunity to share problems in discussion with others. It is probably aimed at small businesses where managers are multi-tasking.

2 He/she could have an 'audit' done, i.e., an evaluation of the way the company brands its products and the nature of the brand as it stands, and he/she can get advice on how to improve the branding strategy.

3 a problem A – lack of brand awareness among consumers, resulting in poor sales

   problem B – product differentiation; similar products already exist

b

Problem A	Problem B
● target market position – niche, leader, challenger, follower? Is this realistic? ● which market segments is product aimed at? Do age, gender, social responsibility matter for your consumer? ● market penetration strategy – pricing? ● branding – what strategies has he used? What media? ● product focus? Do you think you have the focus right, and how could you improve it?	● new product development ● differentiation – plans to achieve this? How is your doll different? ● branding – what strategies used so far? ● market position – is it realistic? ● market penetration – what is your pricing compared with others; your quality; what reasons are there to choose yours? What outlets have you targeted; are there other outlets that

● consumer focus? Is it right – what kind of consumer are you targeting?	might be more effective? Do you think you are in a market entry, development or expansion phase?

c

Problem A	Problem B
● **target market position** – product is niche – establish a strong presence in the niche market then move it up to supermarket level. ● **market segment** – target different outlets, e.g., organic supermarkets, small health food shops, etc. Aim to reach people with green awareness – probably mid-30s, good income, middle class – target the places they shop and the media they read and view. ● **market penetration strategy** – could try cutting price to undercut market leaders, but can you afford to risk a price war? ● **branding** – high-profile TV advertising will create consumer awareness but is expensive. Can you afford this? What alternatives are there? ● **product focus** is on environmentally aware consumers; get endorsement from green groups, e.g., Friends of the Earth, Greenpeace. ● **consumer focus** is too mainstream, better to focus on consumers who will feel guilty if they don't buy product.	● **new product development** – is there anything you can add to make the product more appealing to parents of children: a cuteness factor? ● **differentiation** – major problem – nothing different from existing dolls that already cater to these markets. You need to focus on and develop your product's uniqueness. Develop a clear identity of its USP – if it has none, should you cut your losses and get out? ● **branding** – high-profile advertising campaign, celebrity endorsement, etc. ● **market position** – essentially you are a follower – is this product going to challenge your competitors – need to increase brand awareness in costly promotion campaign to achieve brand recognition. ● **market penetration** – what outlets have you targeted? You could try e-commerce.

d

Problem A:

John, your problem appears to be a lack of consumer recognition for your product, but in fact the problem is primarily one of market position. Your product is strongest as a niche market product. Place it in green supermarkets or other outlets and get green endorsements for it from Friends of the Earth, etc. Once you have established a strong presence there, you can move it up into the bigger supermarkets.

Alternatively, you could try an expensive advertising campaign or a campaign mix to raise general consumer awareness, but then you are challenging sophisticated market leader brands powerfully supported by Unilever or Proctor & Gamble and you could find yourself unable to beat the competition.

Problem B:

Margaret, you have a really serious problem with product differentiation, and in short I feel there is not much you can do to combat this. What do you think is your product's USP? You say you think non-white children will develop a real relationship with the toy. This may be true, but you need to find a way to distinguish yourself from your competitors who produce the same types of doll.

You could review your market penetration strategy and release your doll more cheaply on eBay or other e-outlets and see how well it sells there. You could advertise it with clear celebrity endorsement – this might make it more acceptable to retail outlets. You don't have a niche market you can aim at, and your product is very much a market follower, so you might need to look at market penetration strategies, like pricing.

Exercise G

In their groups, students should now present their research findings on the brand they have chosen to the rest of the group. Remind them that the task was to:

- identify all the components of the brand, its USP, brand equity (if possible) and research any studies into such aspects as brand recognition, awareness, preference or loyalty (they might have come across brand core values, brand essence and other similar aspects as well).
- decide what you and others think about the brand's attitude and 'personality'.

Encourage students to use the seminar language practised in this unit and earlier. When they use predictable or unadventurous phrases for discussions, provided they are not too shy, interrupt and prompt them with phrases learnt in this unit. In addition, students can, of course, make use of the information in Lesson 11.4.

They should be looking at, or at least mentioning, some or all of the following (depending on their ability):

- brand components or features – colour, jingles, tunes, logos, names, straplines, images, design, etc., whether the brand is presented by product or by company/organization/person
- brand USP – comment on how it differentiates itself from rival brands – state what these brands are and how it has established its identity
- present information on brand equity if they can find it – either from the commercial press, e.g., *Financial Times, Economist*, etc., or from academic articles on the subject. Note that brand equity is sometimes referred to as the main component of 'goodwill', which is part of the value of the sale of a company which represents intangible value.
- present information on brand preference, awareness and loyalty – from academic or professional press sources if possible
- present their findings on brand attitude and personality from their questionnaires to classmates

As a group, students should try to come to an overall conclusion regarding brand personality and attitude. This conclusion should be presented to the rest of the class, together with supporting evidence from students' own research.

Closure

The aim of this task is to integrate all the concepts students have come across in the unit.

Put the students in small groups. Ask them to imagine that they are senior managers in a new company selling revolutionary desalination systems that are nuclear powered but 'cleaner', yet very expensive, and perfectly suited to irrigating the drying agricultural land belts of the Middle East, the Mediterranean and Mexico. The systems are technologically amazing compared with previous systems. They are much smaller and neater. They are very futuristic. Ask them to brainstorm the major decisions they need to make with regard to branding. Each group should write its decisions on an interactive whiteboard and then compare.

Useful prompts could be:

- market share
- consumer focus
- brand appeal
- market penetration strategies
- market segments to be targeted
- market position
- social responsibility and communication campaigns

Extra activities

1 Work through the *Vocabulary bank* and *Skills bank* if you have not already done so, or as a revision of previous study.

2 Use the *Activity bank* (Teacher's Book additional resources section, Resource 11A).

   A Set the crossword for individual work (including homework) or pairwork.

Answers

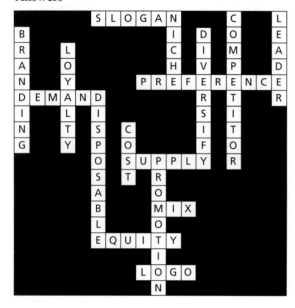

   B Set for individual work (including homework) or pairwork. Check students understand the meanings.

Possible answers

brand	personality
business	philosophy
market	orientation
marketing	mix
mass	produced
niche	marketing
product	development
product	placement
unique	selling point
weak	brand

3 Tell students to add other words to each of the words below to make as many two-word phrases as possible. Elicit one or two examples, then set for individual work or pairwork.

   ● market
   ● brand
   ● marketing

Possible phrases:

market leader, market challenger, market follower, market orientation, market penetration, market share

brand awareness, brand equity, brand loyalty, brand strength, brand personality, brand recognition, brand blindness

marketing mix, niche marketing, mass marketing, marketing strategy, marketing objectives

4 Use an extended activity to allow students to practise some of the concepts they have studied in this unit. Tell students to work in groups. They are going to design a marketing campaign for a 'widget'. This could be something small and useful in people's everyday lives, for example, a unique can opener or a piece of hardware like a new satellite dish. They need to decide:

a what a widget is and what it does

b who their target consumers would be

c which segments of the population would most welcome it

d what the product's strengths are; what its USP is

e how they are positioning the product against similar products

f what personality or attitude (if any) they might wish for their brand

g what their pricing policy will be in order to penetrate the market

h what potential for diversification the widget may have in the future

i what media they will use to raise brand awareness

j what policies they may use to build brand loyalty, e.g., after-sales service

When they have made these decisions, they present their strategy and recommendations to the rest of the class as if they were members of the Board of Directors. The class can question them about their choices and their reasons for them. Groups vote on which presentation is the best statement of their case.

Ask students to vote using these criteria:

1 clarity of their choices

2 effectiveness of their justifications for their choices

3 creativity or inventiveness

4 the way they handled the questions asked

Each group awards five points for each category, making a possible total of 20.

Remind groups that voting other groups down only attracts revenge voting, so is self-defeating.

You need to take notes of language and factual errors in each presentation and after each presentation briefly feed back on the positives of the presentations and on common language or pronunciation errors made during the presentations. Staged and immediate feedback like this is useful to students still waiting to speak. It increases the relevance of the feedback.

12 MANAGEMENT INFORMATION SYSTEMS

This final unit, on the topic of applied technology, is concerned with particular information systems designed for management needs, with the key ideas presented via a case study which is slightly journalistic in style. The focus is on the technology being led by specific need (in this case, management need) rather than general technology for its own sake. The unit also provides an opportunity for revision of many of the concepts and vocabulary items used throughout the book.

Skills focus

Reading

- understanding how ideas in a text are linked

Writing

- deciding whether to use direct quotation or paraphrase
- incorporating quotations
- writing research reports
- writing effective introductions/conclusions

Vocabulary focus

- verbs used to introduce ideas from other sources (*X contends/suggests/asserts that …*)
- linking words/phrases conveying contrast (*whereas*), result (*consequently*), reasons (*due to*), etc.
- words for quantities (*a significant minority*)

Key vocabulary

application (software)
assert (v)
audit
B2B
bankrupt
budgeting
business relationship
coherent
coincidence
contractor
crisis
data
database
deadline
dotcom crash
e-commerce
extranet
gross turnover

grow organically
implement (v)
in its infancy
information communication technology (ICT)
integrated
interconnected
interface
intranet
key performance indicators
made redundant
management information systems (MIS)
manufacturer
navigate
networks (people)

order (n)
ordering (gerund)
plan
player (in the market)
programming (software)
project
retain clients
revolutionize
scheduling
subsystem
sue (v)
supply chain
SWOT analysis
synchronize
task
update
up-to-date

12.1 Vocabulary

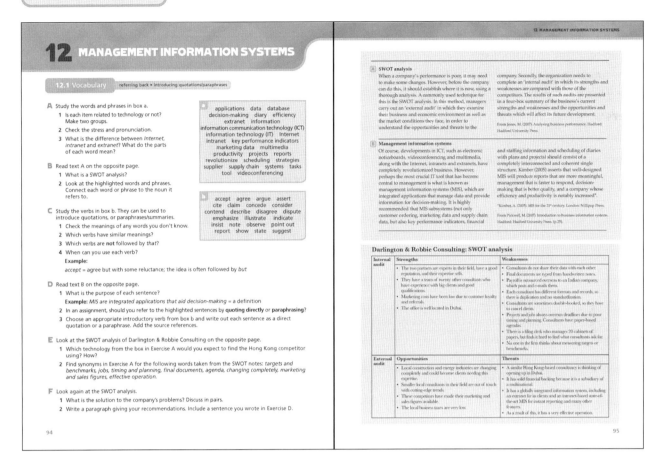

General note

Read the *Vocabulary bank* at the end of the Course Book unit. Decide when, if at all, to refer students to it. The best time is probably at the very end of the lesson or the beginning of the next lesson, as a summary/revision.

Lesson aims

- understand deictic reference – pronouns and determiners
- refer to sources: the choice of introductory verb and stance of writer towards reference
- choose whether to quote or paraphrase

Further practice in:

- words and phrases from the discipline

Introduction

1 Revise the following words and phrases from the two previous units. Ask students to say which grammar class the words belong to and to provide definitions of them.

dismissal (n, U)

mediation (n, U)

controversial (adj)

distinguish (v, T)

penetration (n, U)

formulate (v, T)

diversify (v, T/I)

2 Introduce the topic of the unit: write the phrase *information systems* on the board. Ask students what this refers to. Is it simply the existence of computers in the workplace or does it refer to something beyond that? Brainstorm examples of types of data and information in business that *information systems* might need to be created to handle. Accept any reasonable suggestions. Do not elaborate, but tell students that a particular type of information system (management information systems) will be the topic of this unit.

Exercise A

1/2 Set for pairwork. Ask students to mark the most strongly stressed syllable in the compounds.

Feed back with the whole class, checking meanings. Note that the word *applications* when countable means software programs for computers, and when uncountable it has a non-IT meaning; *systems* in business usually means computer-based information systems; also *revolutionize, data, information* and some others are categorized as general/non-technology, though they are very often used in referring to technology.

3 Draw attention to the prefixes. Set for pairwork. Feed back with the whole class.

Answers

1/2 Model answers:

Technology terms	video 'conferencing
	'database
	infor'mation tech'nology (IT)
	'Internet
	'intranet
	'extranet
	infor'mation communi'cation tech'nology (ICT)
	multi'media
	appli'cations (as a countable noun)
General terms	de'cision-making
	sup'ply chain
	produc'tivity
	key per'formance indi'cators
	'diary
	'scheduling
	'tasks
	su'pplier
	'projects
	'strategies
	e'fficiency
	'marketing 'data
General, but sometimes technology-specific or used in technology contexts	'systems
	infor'mation
	'data
	revo'lutionize
	re'ports
	'tool

3 Model answer:

Internet (You may wish to mention that the word is sometimes capitalized as the name of a unique 'item', though the convention is changing and internet is becoming equally as commonly used)	a network which is open to the public and via which any computer can interconnect, to share and receive data or information	*inter* = between *net* = network

intranet	a smaller 'Internet' with internal access only, inside an organization	*intra* = within *net* = network
extranet	a smaller 'Internet' which has controlled external access, for example, only to suppliers or customers outside the business	*extra* = outside *net* = network

Exercise B

1 Set for small group discussion. Feed back with the whole class.

2 Introduce the idea of textual cohesion, created by referring back to words or ideas already mentioned with pronouns such as *it* and *this* (pronouns and determiners). Say that this an important way in which the sentences in a text are 'held together'. In reading and understanding, it is important to know what is being referred to by such words.

You can build up the answers to question 2 by copying Resource 12B in the additional resources section onto an OHT or other visual medium. Set for individual work and pairwork checking. Feed back with the whole class, building the table below. Establish why a writer might use a particular referring word (see table on next page).

Answers

Model answers:

1 A technique which enables a company to evaluate itself and the situation it finds itself in, by analyzing strengths, weaknesses, opportunities and threats.

2 SWOT analysis

When a company's performance is poor, it may need to make some changes. However, before the company can do this, it should establish where it is now, using a thorough analysis. A commonly used technique for this is the SWOT analysis. In this method, managers carry out an 'external audit' in which they examine their business and economic environment as well as the market conditions they face in order to understand the opportunities and threats to the company. Secondly, the organization needs to complete an 'internal audit' in which its strengths and weaknesses are compared with those of the competitors. The results of such audits are presented in a four-box summary of the business's current strengths and weaknesses and the opportunities and threats which will affect its future development.

Word	Refers to	Comments
the + noun	a previously mentioned noun	one of several ways in which choice of article is governed
it, they	a noun	generally refers to the nearest suitable noun previously mentioned or the subject of the previous sentence
its, their	a previously mentioned noun, indicating possession	other possessive pronouns used in text for reference: *his, her, hers, theirs*, etc.
this	an idea in a phrase or a sentence	often found at the beginning of a sentence or a paragraph; a common mistake is to use 'it' for this purpose also used with prepositions (e.g., *for this*)
this/these + noun	a previously mentioned noun/ noun phrase	also used with prepositions (e.g., *in this method*).
those	a previously mentioned noun/ noun phrase	also used with prepositions In this text, 'those of the competitors' means 'the strengths and weaknesses of the competitors'; there is no need to repeat 'strengths and weaknesses'. *Those of* + noun is a useful construction to learn. *Those* – not *these* – is used to show distance between the writer/ speaker and the objects/concepts themselves.
such + plural noun	a previously mentioned noun	Meaning is: 'Xs like this'. Note that when referring to a singular noun, *such a X* is used (e.g., *in such a situation*).

Language note

Clearly, in this text, there are also relative pronouns which refer back to previously mentioned nouns in relative clauses. However, the grammar of relative pronouns is not covered here.

This is a complex area of written language. The reference words here are commonly found, and arguably, students should be able to use them in their writing. There are, of course, various other ways to refer back to a word or idea, such as when comparing: *the former … the latter …; some … others …* For more information, see a good grammar reference book.

Exercise C

1–3 Set for individual work or pairwork. Feed back.

4 Discuss this with the whole class, building the table in the Answers section. Point out to students that the choice of introductory verb for a direct or indirect quote or a paraphrase or summary will reveal what they think about the sources. This is an important way in which, when writing essays, students can show a degree of criticality about their sources. Critically evaluating other writers' work is an important part of academic assignments, dissertations and theses.

Answers

Possible answers:

2 accept, agree, concede

argue, assert, claim, contend, insist

consider, note, observe, point out, state

disagree, dispute

illustrate, indicate, show

3/4 Possible answers:

		Used when the writer ...
accept	*that*	reluctantly thinks this idea from someone else is true
agree	*that*	thinks this idea from someone else is true
argue	*that*	is giving an opinion that others may not agree with
assert	*that*	is giving an opinion that others may not agree with
cite	+ noun	is referring to someone else's ideas
claim	*that*	is giving an opinion that others may not agree with
concede	*that*	reluctantly thinks this idea from someone else is true
consider	*that*	is giving his/her opinion
contend	*that*	is giving an opinion that others may not agree with
describe	*how;* + noun	is giving a description or a definition
disagree	*that; with* + noun	thinks an idea is wrong
dispute	+ noun	thinks an idea is wrong
emphasize	*that*	is giving his/her opinion strongly
illustrate	*how;* + noun	is explaining, possibly with an example
indicate	*that*	is explaining, possibly with an example
insist	*that*	is giving an opinion that others may not agree with

note	*that*	is giving his/her opinion
observe	*that*	is giving his/her opinion
point out	*that*	is giving his/her opinion
report	*that*	is giving research findings
show	*that*	is explaining, possibly with an example
state	*that*	is giving his/her opinion
suggest	*that;* + gerund	is giving his/her opinion tentatively; *or* is giving his/her recommendation

Language note

Note that these are all verbs of saying and thinking. As such, they can be followed by a noun. Where *that* can be used, it indicates that the verbs are followed by a noun clause. The verbs may also be used with other kinds of construction. For more information on possible uses, see a good dictionary.

Exercise D

Discuss with the students when it is better to paraphrase and when to quote directly. Refer to the *Skills bank* if necessary.

1/2 Set for individual work and pairwork checking. Feed back with the whole class.

3 Set for individual work. Remind students that if they want to quote another source but omit some words, they can use three dots (…) to show words are missing.

Language note

When deciding between quoting directly and paraphrasing, students need to decide whether the writer's original words are special in any way. If they are, then a direct quote is better – for example, with a definition, or if the writer has chosen some slightly unusual words to express an idea. If the writer is giving factual information or description, a paraphrase is better. Opinions also tend to be paraphrased.

Answers

Possible answers: (see table below)

1–3

Original sentence	The writer is ...	Direct quote or paraphrase?	Suggested sentence
a Of course, developments in ICT, such as electronic noticeboards, videoconferencing and multimedia, along with the Internet, intranets and extranets, have completely revolutionized business.	setting context	paraphrase	Pickwell (2007) observes that the world of commerce has changed entirely due to ICT.
b However, perhaps the most crucial IT tool that has become central to management is what is known as management information systems (MIS), which are integrated applications that manage data and provide information for decision-making.	giving an opinion and giving a definition	quote	Pickwell (2007) describes management information systems as important 'integrated applications that manage data and provide information for decision-making'.
c It is highly recommended that MIS subsystems (not only customer ordering, marketing data and supply chain data, but also key performance indicators, financial and staffing information and scheduling of diaries with plans and projects) should consist of a completely interconnected and coherent single structure.	giving a strong opinion	paraphrase with a direct quotation of the last few words, which make a 'special' phrase	Pickwell (2007) emphasizes the need for the many components of MIS to be an 'interconnected and coherent single structure' (p.25).

d Kimber (2005) asserts that well-designed MIS will produce reports that are more meaningful, management that is faster to respond, decision-making that is better quality, and a company whose efficiency and productivity is notably increased.	quoting from another writer; the other writer is stating consequences	mostly paraphrase but quote a 'special' from the other writer directly	Pickwell (2007) cites Kimber (2005, p. 11), who insists that properly planned MIS will result in 'meaningful' reports, good decisions and more effective operations.

Exercise E

1/2 This exercise relates the vocabulary discussed in Exercise A to this case study. It will help prepare students for work later in the unit. Refer students to the picture and the SWOT analysis. Make sure they understand that a consultancy is a company or partnership that *provides* advice to businesses on particular aspects of business. This usually involves dealing with a lot of information and producing reports for clients at the end of projects.

Set for pairwork discussion. Feed back with the whole class if necessary.

Answers

1 Information technology (IT), information communication technology (ICT), videoconferencing, Internet, intranet, extranet, multimedia, applications, systems, database

2

Term from SWOT	Term from Box A
targets and benchmarks	key performance indicators
jobs	tasks
timing and planning	scheduling
final documents	reports
agenda	diary
changing completely	revolutionize
marketing and sales figures	marketing data
effective operation	productivity/efficiency

Exercise F

1 Set for pairwork discussion, followed by class discussion.

2 Before setting the students to write, tell them they should refer to text B in their answer.

Answers

1 It needs a coherent management information system (MIS).

2 It is clear that, despite its tremendous reputation and professional expertise, Darlington & Robbie Consulting is at a crisis point. This is because the company, having grown organically, has never planned a coordinated approach to managing its information. As a result, it is now failing to be efficient. A management information system could integrate strategy, project planning, individual tasks and the consultants' electronic diaries, so there would be no more overruns or double bookings. It would standardize the way work is done and how client information and reports are produced. It could tie in performance indicators with financial information. Pickwell (2007) emphasizes the need for the many components of MIS to be an 'interconnected and coherent single structure' (p.25) and (2007) cites Kimber (2005, p. 11), who insists that properly planned MIS will result in 'meaningful' reports, good decisions and more effective operations. Therefore, it is possible that Darlington & Robbie Consulting would turn their business around and avoid losing business to their Hong Kong-based competitor.

Closure

Ask two or three students to take turns reading their paragraph to the class. Elicit peer correction of intonation errors of phrases or sentence fragments. Drill the corrected versions. If you have a paper document projector, project randomly chosen students' work onto a screen and elicit whether the referencing is correctly done. Offer corrected versions if necessary. Comment on how to improve any other features of the writing that might require it. If you have no such technology, allow students to present their work in small groups to others and elicit the same improvements.

Using these observations and discussions on the students' texts, encourage them to create a SWOT framework for their own writing ability. This can be done in small groups. The object of the exercise is to see how SWOT can be a practical motivator and also to reflect on their own competence and progress.

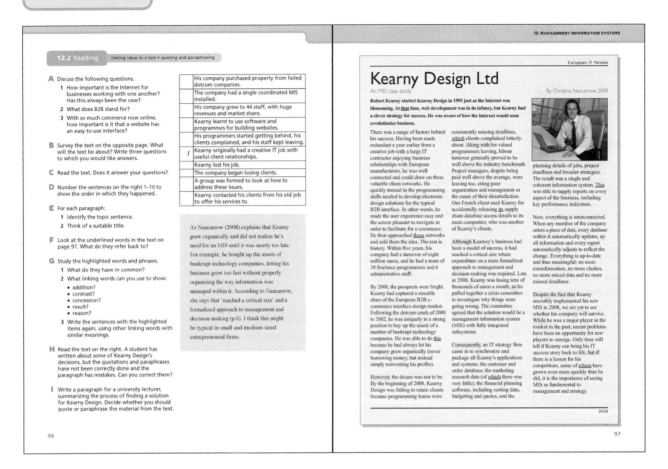

General note

Read the *Vocabulary bank* and *Skills bank* at the end of the Course Book unit. Decide when, if at all, to refer students to them. The best time is probably at the very end of the lesson or the beginning of the next lesson, as a summary/revision.

Lesson aims

- understand rhetorical markers in writing (*but* and *so* categories)
- use direct quotations from other writers:
  common mistakes
  missing words
  fitting to the grammar of the sentence
  adding emphasis to a quote
  continuing to quote from the same source

Further practice in:

- indirect quotations/paraphrases/summaries
- summarizing with a series of topic sentences
- rhetorical markers (adding points)
- deictic reference and relative pronouns

Introduction

Review the previous lesson. What does MIS stand for? What benefits does an MIS bring?

Exercise A

Set for pairwork or class discussion. Questions 2 and 3 are mainly to ensure students are exposed to vocabulary items *B2B*, *commerce* (in order to recognize e-commerce), and *interface*.

Answers

Possible answers:

1 These days, it is often extremely important. Sometimes it is the basis of the business relationship. Companies often have an extranet that suppliers, customers or clients can access. They even often synchronize applications. However, this has not always been true. The Internet only became widely available in 1995. Before that, companies did not tend to use online facilities.

2 B2B stands for business-to-business e-commerce. Compare it with B2C (business-to-consumer, such as Amazon), and C2C (consumer-to-consumer, such as eBay).

3 It is very important.

Exercise B

Remind students about surveying a text (skim-reading to get an approximate idea of the contents by looking at the title, the first and last few lines, and by looking at the first sentence of each paragraph).

Set for individual work and small group discussion. Each group should agree three questions. Feed back with the whole class. Choose a few clear and relevant questions to write on the board.

Exercise C

Set for individual work followed by small group discussion. Feed back with the whole class. Ask whether the questions you have put on the board have been answered in the text.

Exercise D

Set for individual work and pairwork checking. This activity could also be done using Resource 12C in the additional resources section. Photocopy and cut up the sentences and hand them out jumbled up. Tell students to put them in the correct order.

Answer

Model answers:

6	His company purchased property from failed dotcom companies.
10	The company had a single coordinated MIS installed.
5	His company grew to 44 staff, with huge revenues and market share.
3	Kearny learnt to use software and programs for building websites.
7	His programmers started getting behind, his clients complained, and his staff kept leaving.
1	Kearny originally had a creative IT job with useful client relationships.
2	Kearny lost his job.
8	The company began losing clients.
9	A group was formed to look at how to address these issues.
4	Kearny contacted his clients from his old job to offer his services to.

Exercise E

1/2 Set for individual work and pairwork discussion. The topic sentences should suggest a suitable title.

Answer

Possible answers:

	Topic sentence	Para title
Para 1	Robert Kearny started Kearny Design in ...	The man behind Kearny Design
Para 2	There was a range of factors behind his success.	The origins of the company
Para 3	By 2000 the prospects were bright.	The company's highest point
Para 4	However, the dream was not to be.	Problems at Kearny Design
Para 5	[his business] ... had reached a critical size where expenditure on a more formalized approach to management and decision-making was required.	Time to seek a solution
Para 6	Consequently, an IT strategy firm came in to synchronize and package all Kearny's applications and systems ...	Gathering systems into one MIS
Para 7	Now, everything is interconnected.	MIS benefits
Para 8	... Kearny smoothly implemented [his MIS, but] we are yet to see whether his company will survive.	Looking to the future

Exercise F

Set for individual work and pairwork checking.

Answer

Model answers:

Word	Refers to
that	1995
these	client networks (his business relationships)
this	buy up assets of bankrupt technology companies
which	missed deadlines
its	the French client
which	marketing research data
this	coherent information system
whom	his competitors

Exercise G

1 Refer students to the highlighted words. Elicit that they are all linking words and phrases. They act as signposts in the text.

2 With the whole class, elicit from the students some linking words that can be used for:

- contrast and concession (i.e., words which have a *but* meaning)

- results or giving reasons (i.e., words which have a *so* or *because* meaning)

Build the table in the Answers section on the board, reminding students of the difference between between- and within-sentence linking words (refer to Unit 11 *Vocabulary bank*).

3 Set for individual work. Encourage students to rewrite the sentences using a different type of linking word from the original (i.e., swapping between– and within– sentence linkers). Monitor and elicit corrections to errors in their sentences.

Answers

Possible answers:

	Between-sentence linkers	Within-sentence linkers
Addition (*and*)	Furthermore, … In addition, … Additionally, …	… and … … too … also … … along with … … together with
Contrast (*but*) used when comparing	However, … In/By contrast, … On the other hand, …	… but … … whereas … … while …
Concession (*but*) used to concede/accept a point which simultaneously contrasts with the main point of a sentence or paragraph	However, … At the same time, … Nevertheless, … Despite/In spite of (*this/noun*), … Yet, …	… although … … despite/in spite of the fact that …
Result (*so*)	So, … As a result, … Consequently, … Therefore, …	…, so … … so that … … with the result that …
Reason (*because*)	Because of (*this/ noun*), … Owing to (*this/ noun*), … Due to (*this/ noun*), …	… because … … since … … as … … due to/owing to the fact that …

Yet/In spite of this, the dream was not to be.

Together with his valued programmers leaving, labour turnover generally proved to be well above the industry benchmark.

Programmers were leaving, *and* labour turnover generally proved to be well above the industry benchmark.

Programmers were leaving; *also*, general labour turnover proved to be well above the industry benchmark.

Despite his business hav*ing been* a model of success, it had reached a critical size …

His business had been a model of success; *yet* it had reached a critical size …

Kearny was losing tens of thousands of euros a month. *Therefore*, he pulled together a crisis committee …

Due to the fact that Kearny was losing tens of thousands of euros a month, he pulled together a crisis committee …

Kearny pulled together a crisis committee *since* he was losing tens of thousands of euros a month.

Kearny pulled together a crisis committee *as* he was losing tens of thousands of euros a month.

As a result, an IT strategy firm came in to synchronize and package all Kearny's applications and systems …

Therefore, an IT strategy firm came in to synchronize and package all Kearny's applications and systems …

… every database within it automatically updates, *with the result that* all information and every report automatically adjusts to reflect the change.

… every database within it automatically updates. *Consequently*, all information and every report automatically adjusts to reflect the change.

In spite of the fact that Kearny smoothly implemented his new MIS in 2008, we are yet to see whether his company will survive.

Kearny smoothly implemented his new MIS in 2008. *However*, we are yet to see whether his company will survive.

Kearny smoothly implemented his new MIS in 2008. *At the same time*, we are yet to see whether his company will survive.

Although he was a major player in the market in the past, recent problems have been an opportunity for new players to emerge.

He was a major player in the market in the past. *Yet* recent problems have been an opportunity for new players to emerge.

Only time will tell if Kearny can bring his IT success story back to life. *On the other hand*, if there is a lesson for his competitors …

Only time will tell if Kearny can bring his IT success story back to life. *However*, if there is a lesson for his competitors …

Exercise H

Set for individual work and pairwork checking. Feed back with the whole class.

Answers

Model answers:

Corrected version	Comments
As Nancarrow (2008) explains,	Note the grammar here: either *As Nancarrow explains*, or *Nancarrow explains that*, but not both together. This is a common mistake that should be highlighted.
… did not realize his need for …	Students sometimes misplace *his* and *he's* due to the similar sound.
For example, he bought up 'the assets of … bankrupt technology companies', letting his … (p.6).	1. The words which are the same as the original need quotation marks around them. 2. Some words have been left out. Where this happens three dots are used to signify an omission. It is important that a quote is exactly the same as the original. Any changes (such as omitting words) need to be clearly shown. 3. The page number should be given in brackets at the end of the quote.
Nancarrow further points out that the company had 'reached a critical size' where a 'formalized approach to management and decision-making' becomes necessary (ibid.).	1. When continuing to refer to a source, you can use *further* or *also* or other similar words; *says* is not a good choice of introductory verb since it is too informal. You do not need *according to* as well as a verb of saying. This is another common error that should be highlighted. 2. When referring to the same place in the same source, use *ibid.* instead of the full source reference. If it is the same publication (but not the same place in the text), use *op. cit.* 3. It is important to make a quotation fit the grammar of a sentence. Here the grammar is fixed by inserting a subject (*the company*) and constructing a *where* clause. Failing to integrate quotes properly is a common mistake for students. 4. The quotation marks must be placed around the words which are the same as the source.
This might be typical in small and medium-sized entrepreneurial firms.	1. While not incorrect to personalize (*I think*), it can often be avoided as it is usually clear that a sentence following a cited claim is the response (opinion) of the writer. 2. The word *think* is not very academic and can often be avoided.

Exercise I

Set for individual work, possibly for homework. Alternatively, set for pair or small group work. Students can write the paragraph on an OHT or other file for projection on a screen, which you can display and give feedback on with the whole class.

Answer

Possible answers:

Nancarrow (2007) explains that Kearny Design Ltd was the result of an entrepreneur being well placed to exploit corporate contacts and build a business in designing the B2B interface for e-commerce. The enterprise grew organically; for example, initial financial success allowed it to purchase assets of failing dotcom companies and grow quickly, without properly managing its growing information needs. Nancarrow refers to the 'critical size' it had reached, where a 'formalized approach to management and decision-making' had become necessary (p.6). Poor service to clients and resigning staff led to the formation of a crisis group to seek a solution. They soon had an MIS implemented as it appeared that all the problems stemmed from the lack of a centrally controlled information system (ibid.).

Closure

Ask students to discuss these questions.

1 At what point do you think a growing company would need a centralized MIS? Is there a particular employee number? Is the industry or the operation important?

2 Brainstorm a list of the kinds of people that work for and have contact with Robert Kearny. What specific information needs would each of them have? What access might they have to the system? What access would Robert Kearny and his senior management team have? Why?

Accept any reasonable suggestions.

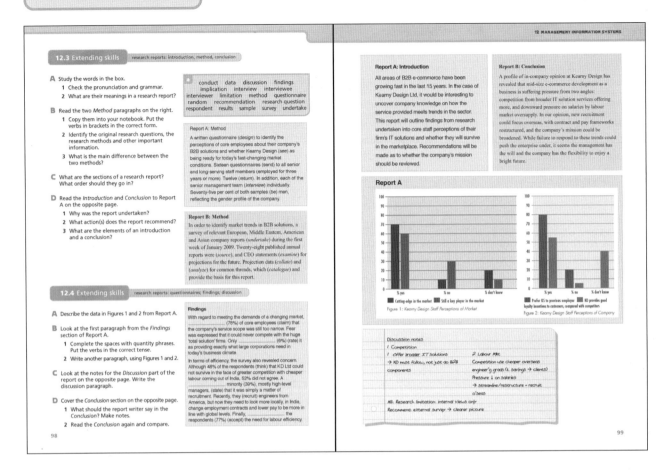

Lesson aims

- Structuring a research report:

  introduction

  method

  conclusion

Further practice in:

- essay structure
- research methods

Introduction

In preparation for looking at the structure of a research report, revise the sections for an essay: introduction, body, conclusion.

Ask students what should go in each section. Elicit ideas for introductions and conclusions. Do not correct at this point.

Raise the idea of methods for doing research. Ask students what kinds of research would be appropriate if you wanted to find out what users of an information system think of it, or what potential users of an MIS might expect from it. (Primary sources are best: survey, questionnaire, interview; both quantitative and qualitative methods.)

Ask students what kinds of research would be appropriate if you wanted to find out what business activities companies in a particular sector are involved in. (Secondary sources are the easiest, e.g., Internet research, company reports, trade magazines.)

Tell students that the next two lessons will focus on writing up research in reports. Ask for suggestions for suitable sections of a research report. Do not correct at this point.

Language note

In the model presented here, the report is executed at a very simple level. For instance, in a real academic research report, there will usually be a literature review section before the methods section, and the research questions will be linked with this review; there will also generally be a findings and a discussion section that leads to the conclusion. There are different models for reports. For example, a business report (as opposed to an academic research report) may put conclusions and recommendations near the beginning and the findings as the final section. For the complete text of the report, see Resource 12D in the additional resources section.

Exercise A

Set for individual work and pairwork checking. Feed back with the whole class.

Answers

Model answers (see table):

Word	Notes on pronunciation and grammar	Meaning in a research report
con'duct	v (noun is pronounced: 'conduct)	do (some research, a survey, an experiment)
'data	pl n	information; can be numerical and aiming to be objective (quantitative) or verbal and more subjective (qualitative)
dis'cussion	n (U/C)	the title of the section in a research report which discusses the findings. Sometimes the discussion is included in the *findings/results* section.
'findings	pl n	the title of the section in a research report which details what has been found out; each finding should be linked with a research question. The title *Results* can also be used for this section.
impli'cation	n (C)	a possible effect or result of the findings
'interview	n (C), v	noun: when someone is asked questions in a survey; verb: to ask someone questions in a survey
interview'ee	n (C)	the person being questioned
'interviewer	n (C)	the person asking the questions
limi'tation	n (C)	a problem with the research methods; an aspect which the research could not address
'method	n (C)	the title of the section in a research report which clearly explains how the research was carried out.
question'naire	n (C)	a written set of questions to collect data
'random	adj	a way of selecting a sample: in no fixed order or with no organizing principle
recommen'dation	n (C)	a suggestion for action as a result of the findings of the research
re'search question	n (C)	what the researcher wants to find out
re'spondent	n (C)	a person taking part in a questionnaire survey
re'sults	pl n	the same as *findings*
'sample	n (C), v	noun: the group of people taking part in the research; verb: to select people for research
'survey	n (C), v	a type of research in which the researcher sets out to describe a situation or set of ideas or behaviours by reading a variety of documents or asking people questions
under'take	v	do (research, a survey)

Exercise B

Explain to the students that these are examples of a typical *Method* section of a research report.

1 Set for individual work. Ask students to copy the text into their notebooks and put the verbs into the correct form. Feed back with the whole class, drawing students' attention to the use of the past tense when reporting methods of research, as well as the use of the passive.

2 Set for individual work and pairwork checking. Tell students that they should transform the research questions into real, direct questions. Feed back with the whole group, pointing out that the information

given in the *Method* sections should include these types of details.

3 Set for brief pairwork discussion. Then compare different pairs' views.

Answers

Possible answers (see table):

	Research questions	Research method	Other important information
Report A: Method A written questionnaire (*was designed*) to identify the perceptions of core employees about their company's B2B solutions and whether Kearny Design (*is/was seen*) as being ready for today's fast-changing market conditions. Sixteen questionnaires (*were sent*) to all senior and long-serving staff members (employed for three years or more). Twelve (*were returned*). In addition, each of the senior management team (*was interviewed*) individually. Seventy-five per cent of both samples (*were*) men, reflecting the gender profile of the company.	1. What are your perceptions of KD's B2B solutions? 2. Is KD seen as ready for the current market?	written questionnaire	16 questionnaires, sample of senior and long-serving KD staff, 12 returned
		interview	management team interviewed
			75% of both samples: male
Report B: Method In order to identify market trends in B2B solutions, a survey of relevant European, Middle Eastern, American and Asian company reports (*was undertaken*) during the first week of January 2009. Twenty-eight published annual reports were (*sourced*) and CEO statements (*were examined*) for projections for the future. Projection data (*was collated*) and (*analyzed*) for common threads, which (*were catalogued*) and provide the basis for this report.	What are the likely future trends in the B2B systems sector?	survey: text analysis; data collection, analysis and cataloguing	global sample of 28 companies

Report A is 'primary' research: methods include questionnaires and interviews that find out new information. Report B is 'secondary' research: methods involve searches for information that already exists.

Language note

The impersonal use of the passive for research reports is not absolutely required. It is often possible to find students' work (assignments, dissertations) which contains the use of the first person singular. This tends to be where the writer's perspective is important. However, in very formal writing, such as in many journal articles, the passive is widely used to depersonalize the text. Also, it is commonplace in *Methods* sections, which normally prioritize the process over the participants.

Exercise C

Use this to confirm that students understand the organization of a research report. Elicit answers from the whole class.

Answers

Model answers:

Section	Order in a research report
introduction	1
methods	2
findings/results	3
discussion	4
conclusion	5

Language note

Different disciplines and reports for varying purposes may have different section names or organization. The model suggested here is a basic and general one, and is a pattern commonly adopted in an academic context, though there are variations depending on the level of the writing (whether, for example, it is a Master's or PhD dissertation). If students are going to write about 500 words only, you may wish to include *discussion* with *findings/results* or with the *conclusion*.

Exercise D

Explain to the students that these are examples of a typical introduction and conclusion for a short research report. Set for pairwork discussion. Feed back with the whole class. Bring the class's attention to the tenses that are used here (present perfect, present simple, future) as well as the use of the passive.

Answers

Model answers:

1 It was undertaken to measure whether the company's services are meeting trends in the sector.

2 The recommendations are to recruit overseas and restructure contracts and pay, and broaden its solutions provided/broaden its mission.

3 The typical functions of introductions and conclusions are given in the table below.

Good introduction	Example sentences
Introduce the topic: give some background information to bring the reader into the topic.	All areas of B2B e-commerce have been growing fast in the last 15 years.
Say why the topic is important, relevant or of interest.	In the case of Kearny Design Ltd, it would be interesting to uncover company knowledge on how the service provided meets trends in the sector.
Say what you will do in the report. Give a statement of the purpose of the research.	This report will outline findings from research undertaken into core staff perceptions of their firm's IT solutions and whether they will survive in the marketplace. Recommendations will be made as to whether the company's mission should be reviewed.

Good conclusion	Example sentences
Give a general summary; restate the findings; conclude.	A profile of in-company opinion at Kearny Design has revealed that mid-size e-commerce development as a business is suffering pressure from two angles: competition from broader IT solution services offering more, and downward pressure on salaries by labour market oversupply.
Say what your recommendations are.	In our opinion, new recruitment could focus overseas, with contract and pay frameworks restructured, and the company's mission could be broadened.
Set out the implications of not taking action.	While failure to respond to these trends could push the enterprise under, ...
Comment on future possibilities if action *is* taken.	... it seems the management has the will and the company has the flexibility to enjoy a bright future.

Closure

1 Refer students to the *Skills bank* to consolidate students' understanding of the sections of a research report and their contents.

2 Ask students to choose a company into which they would like to carry out some customer research. They should think about aspects such as quality, service, reliability, customer perceptions, etc. What topics would they ask customers about in a questionnaire?

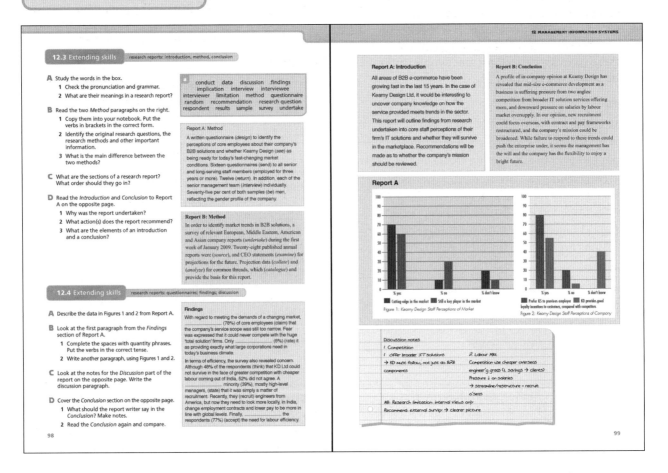

Lesson aims

- write part of a research report: findings and discussion
- analyze and use research data and information

Further practice in:

- talking about numbers and quantities

Introduction

Write up the table below, or project it, on the board. Give some example phrases and ask students to say approximately what percentage they represent, e.g., a large majority = perhaps 80%?

A/An	overwhelming large significant slight small insignificant tiny	majority	
		minority	
		number	(of + noun)
Over		half	
More	than	a quarter	
Less		a third	
		x%	

Note that *of* is needed if the category for the numbers is given: *A slight minority of respondents said that …* but *A slight minority said that …*

Ask students: what is the difference between *many* and *most*?

Exercise A

Set students to work in pairs to talk about the key elements of the numbers shown in the charts. If you wish, ask students to give examples of use. Feed back with the whole class, writing some example sentences on the board. Ask the class what these results show about Kearny Design (some of its strengths).

Answers

Possible answers:

Figure 1

A majority (60%) of respondents said that Kearny Design was still a key player in the market.

A significant majority (70%) of respondents said the service was cutting-edge.

A significant minority (30%) said the service was no longer a key player.

A very small minority (20%) replied that they did not know if the services were cutting-edge or not.

226

Figure 2

An overwhelming majority of respondents (80%) said they preferred working at KD compared with their previous employers.

Over half (55%) of respondents said they thought Kearny Design provided good loyalty incentives to customers, compared with other companies.

A tiny minority (5%) disagreed that Kearny Design provided good loyalty incentives to customers, compared with other companies.

Exercise B

1 Set for individual work and pairwork checking. Tell students that each space may be for more than one word. They will also need to practise the expressions they used for quantity in Exercise A. Feed back with the whole class, pointing out the use of past tenses when reporting findings.

2 Set for individual work. Remind students to use linking words and to begin with a topic sentence. This paragraph continues the *Findings* section of the report.

Answers

Possible answers:

1 With regard to meeting the demands of a changing market, a large majority (78%) of core employees (*claim*) claimed that the company's service scope was still too narrow. Fear was expressed that it could never compete with the huge 'total solution' firms. Only a small minority (6 %) (*rate*) rated it as providing exactly what large corporations need in today's business climate.

In terms of efficiency, the survey also revealed concern. Although 48% of the respondents (*think*) thought that KD Ltd could not survive in the face of greater competition with cheaper labour coming out of India, 52% did not agree. A significant minority (39%), mostly high-level managers, (*state*) stated that it was simply a matter of recruitment. Recently, they (*recruit*) had/have recruited engineers from America, but now they need to look more locally, in India, change employment contracts, and lower pay to be more in line with global levels. Finally, most of the respondents (77%) (*accept*) accepted the need for labour efficiency.

2 The survey also revealed some positive aspects. Firstly, considering the market and competition, a majority (60%) of respondents said that Kearny Design was still a key player in the market, and most (70%) considered it was 'cutting-edge' in its service. In comparison with other companies, although only about half (55%) of respondents thought Kearny Design provided good loyalty incentives to customers, a little less than half (40%) were not sure and only a tiny minority (5%) thought it did not. Secondly, considering staff satisfaction, an overwhelming majority of respondents (80%) said they preferred working at KD compared with their previous employers, while a minority (20%) did not.

Exercise C

Tell students to look at the notes on the right-hand page. Ask checking questions about the information in the notes, e.g.,

> *What are the two issues?*
> *How does 'broader' solutions compare with what Kearny Design already delivers?*
> *What does 'grads' stand for?*
> *How do salaries need to change?*
> *What can the company do to compete?*
> *What does 'limitations' mean?*
> *What was wrong with the research? Why is an external survey likely to be better?*

Tell students that the discussion section of a report is where they interpret findings by speculating and giving their opinions on the findings. They should write a paragraph using the ideas in the notes. Set for individual work.

Answers

Possible answers:

Discussion

Clearly, the findings indicate that Kearny Design needs to confront a number of issues quickly. It is probable that corporate clients increasingly prefer companies that can provide the whole IT solution, not just the B2B components and usability design. Moreover, it seems that competitors are benefiting from cheaper engineering graduates from overseas, and savings are probably being passed on to clients. To compete, perhaps streamlining or restructuring is needed, along with possible recruitment from overseas.

A limitation of this research, however, was that it was internal only; administering the same survey externally, across a number of companies including key clients, too, might provide a clearer picture.

Exercise D

1 Get students to cover the *Conclusion*. They may well remember what it said but, even if they don't, they can work out what it *should* say based on the *Findings* and the *Discussion* and, of course, the *Introduction*. Set for individual work and pairwork checking. Do not confirm or correct.

2 Refer students to the *Conclusion* to check their ideas.

Closure

1 Ask students to work out the original questions used in the Kearny Design employee survey.

First, suggest some question types for questionnaires. Elicit the following:

- yes/no
- multiple-choice
- open-ended

Tell students to concentrate on the *yes/no* or *multiple-choice* types (open-ended questions will elicit qualitative information which is often hard to analyze) and to look at the data in Figures 1 and 2 and the sample *Findings* paragraph. They should try to formulate the actual questions given in the employee survey questionnaire.

Set for pairwork. Feed back with the whole class, writing examples of good questions up on the board. Refer to the model questionnaire in the additional resources section (Resource 12E).

2 Set a research report based on a questionnaire survey for homework. Students can use the ideas they have already discussed in this unit. They should write questionnaires, carry out the research amongst a suitable group of employees (20–40 respondents is fine) and then write up the report. See extra activity 4 for suggestions for topics. Alternatively, students could choose to find out about the business activities of several global companies in the same sector.

Extra activities

1 Work through the *Vocabulary bank* and *Skills bank* if you have not already done so, or as a revision of previous study.

2 Use the *Activity bank* (Teacher's Book additional resources section, Resource 12A).

   A Set the wordsearch for individual work (including homework) or pairwork.

   Answers

```
A P P L I C A T I O N S O F T W A R E
P N D J N A V I G A T E S T R P Z Y Q
S I M P L E M E N T N I V D N B Y 2 R
H U Q C T K C I K Y M X E Q N R R Z G
D D P C O M B L N N K T W Z H E L S T
T B T P Z N R Y D T C L 2 T R K I N E
T 2 W T L F T L X E R D C U W S T Z P
R B E H B Y K R N R W A T T Y G I K T
E K T Q H R C N A L P C N L H N T P K
C C M I C T O H H C A H A E O P U E I
Y H O N J C N K A F T N B I T R G X N
P C D M R J T Q U I A O T F K M T T T
X V A E M Z M N L T N U R N T Z T R E
T K T M Z E A B O G L D A T L C M A R
C N A R D M R W Z O T B P Z E M G N F
I G B R D V S C V M T P C J C G F E A
K K A P 2 K R E E L P B O R H X H T C
D W S F C N R D K Q L R Y R N N X R E
K L E B F Z Z H Z R P D E A D L I N E
```

   B Set for individual work and pairwork checking.

   Answers

95%	the great majority
70%	a significant majority
53%	just over half
50%	half
48%	slightly less than half
10%	a small proportion
2%	a tiny minority

3 Set Resource 12F for individual work and pairwork checking.

Answers

Monty & Boot Ltd was losing money. It was under pressure from bankers and other lenders. <u>In addition</u>, shareholders were not happy when the share price dropped to an all-time low of 11p.

<u>Consequently</u>, a decision was made to undertake a strategic review of the company. <u>First</u>, the management team set out to establish the views of all staff. <u>Next</u>, management was persuaded to agree to more ambitious efficiency targets. Finally, plans for implementation were set up.

<u>As a result of</u> the actions in the plan, the company had a management information system installed, which <u>led</u> to improved communication and real-time information availability. Better MIS <u>also</u> meant staff could understand their key performance indicators and reach their targets more easily.

These steps soon <u>resulted</u> in increased customer and supplier confidence, and sales quickly returned to previous highs.

4 Ask students to practise making questionnaires for surveys. They could choose from the following topics (or other appropriate topics):

- Which of the two do customers prefer, e.g.,

  two popular websites?

  two brands of mobile phone?

  two brands of computer?

  two online information services?

- What do customers think of:

  online shopping?

  a mobile phone brand?

  a TV channel?

  a new piece of personal entertainment equipment?

  cosmetics for men?

Activity bank

A Solve the crossword.

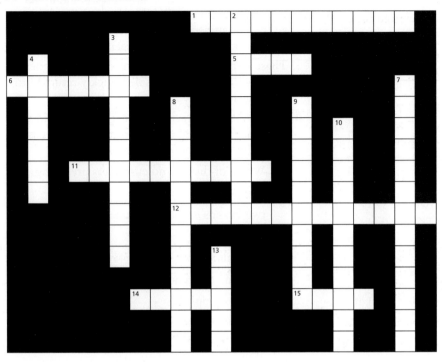

Across

1 The more trust and freedom we give Andrew's team, the more we will see a sense of ... within them as people, and the better their results will be.

5 Her particular ... within the management team is to advise the other managers on financial projections.

6 We raised our start-up ... by borrowing from friends and family.

11 Bill is so ... . He allows his staff to make many day-to-day decisions.

12 I would call Henry a ... leader, because he has complete authority but he really does look after his staff.

14 We are a market leader in the ... of electronic innovation.

15 Our ... for this coming year is to double our turnover.

Down

2 Somehow his ... manner convinced his staff to accept a pay freeze for two years.

3 He is so ... . It's like he lights up the office the moment he enters it.

4 A leader who ... his/her team properly should have no real problem getting a project done on time.

7 He has really good ... skills. He can tell you exactly what he wants, simply, clearly and very effectively.

8 I could never be an ... because I hate risk. I just want a steady salary and quiet life without all that stress and worry.

9 ... tasks to the right team members is one of John's great strengths.

10 I really don't like autocratic managers. I think we should all ... in the decision-making process.

13 If you follow the business ... we've developed for you, I am sure you will find your company will be very successful.

B Play noughts and crosses. Use the words in context or explain what they mean.

flexibility	cross-border	expertise	transformational	leadership	land
indecisive	characteristic	consultative	capital	easyJet	team
incompetent	charismatic	entrepreneurship	objective	Gandhi	stamina

Activity bank

A Find 20 words from this unit in the wordsearch.

- Copy the words into your notebook.
- Check the definition of any words you can't remember.

V	A	L	U	E	S	I	N	E	V	I	T	A	B	L	E
V	I	S	I	B	L	E	C	Y	K	T	Q	F	B	Y	X
T	X	E	T	Z	C	E	Y	O	C	D	Q	Y	N	N	C
H	H	W	N	I	G	T	G	A	U	F	V	O	C	I	Q
G	F	H	N	T	C	R	F	I	E	R	I	C	G	L	T
K	U	H	Y	Q	R	E	E	I	S	T	T	E	K	N	G
B	T	R	Y	A	T	E	L	S	A	L	T	E	A	B	P
E	X	L	U	R	S	E	P	V	I	A	A	D	S	K	N
G	P	L	A	T	B	S	O	R	R	S	N	T	D	Y	E
K	Y	J	M	Q	R	N	U	T	E	U	T	J	I	R	B
V	F	N	H	J	N	W	S	M	D	N	N	A	U	O	N
T	A	L	L	I	A	N	C	E	P	K	E	T	N	G	N
P	M	Y	J	V	K	Z	R	B	K	T	L	U	Y	C	Y
L	E	V	I	D	E	N	C	E	B	U	I	J	R	G	E
P	R	X	Y	E	M	B	R	A	C	E	V	O	Y	X	T
R	C	O	M	P	E	T	I	T	I	O	N	T	N	K	T

B Do the quiz.

1 What are the different types of culture that can affect management?

2 Culture can be seen in behaviours that result from which three things?

3 Who is Geert Hofstede?

4 Who is Edgar Schein?

5 What were Schein's three levels of measuring culture?

6 How important is it to understand company culture if you are in change management?

7 The opening up of new markets among China's middle classes, consumer tastes for carbon-neutral products, and new techniques and new legislation are all examples of what?

8 Who is ultimately responsible for change management?

9 How is it possible to overcome resistance to change?

10 What is the popular term for a company which continually invests in training and development, communication and empowerment?

Before senior management can develop a strategy for change, it needs to understand organizations, organizational culture and how this affects internal communication. Every organization has its unique company culture, which will affect how change management strategies should be developed and communicated to staff. Change management often fails because managers misunderstand the pre-existing culture they are dealing with.

Defining organizational culture is fairly straightforward. According to Edgar Schein, an organization's culture is like general culture, which is identified by national or ethnic boundaries. General culture is said to be a set of beliefs, values and attitudes that are learnt. It results in behaviours in common across countries, regions and languages. These characterize a particular group. In the same way, the common behaviours of people in a particular organization characterize the organizational culture of that company.

It is possible to categorize the differences between people in different cultures. For example, world-renowned cross-culture guru Geert Hofstede, in his research spanning decades, has measured differences in the way people around the world see things. These include how they view authority, how they identify either collectively or individually, how they accept or reject traditional views on masculinity and femininity and whether they accept or avoid uncertainty.

However, to be useful to corporate management, we need a more specific definition that relates to organizations. Schein (2004) suggests that organizational culture includes basic assumptions that arise from a group trying to survive and integrate. He adds that they are shared by people throughout an organization. They are mostly unconscious and taken for granted, and include such things as a company's view of itself. Culture is a naturally occurring phenomenon that arises where social situations exist over time.

Organizational culture can therefore be identified by listening to what people say is peculiar to their workplace. Discussions may reveal that certain values and norms are common across one company and quite different across another. For example, an employee from a young and exciting Internet service company, which celebrates their award-winning customer experience, leaves her job. She begins a new job for an uncompromising, ruthless and conservative law firm. She will quickly find that these new values, communicated to her and repeatedly affirmed by the people around her, displace her old ones.

How can organizational culture be measured? Schein maintains that it includes aspects on different levels (ibid.). The first level is visible. At this level, we see people's behaviours and 'artefacts', such as the way they dress (or do not dress) and the way they arrange their desks. On the second level are the employees' values – what they are ready to say is true or precious to them, such as courtesy, entrepreneurialism or creativity. On the deepest level, we find their assumptions and beliefs. They are often unaware of these feelings and take them for granted.

Managers need to be familiar with organizational culture because it affects the way they manage the process of communicating change. Most managers have to implement training, which involves personal change, and sometimes major restructuring, which involves corporate change. Schein asserts that we cannot see how organizational learning and planned change can work unless we realize first that culture is the main basis for resisting change (ibid.). Therefore, managers must become conscious of the cultures they operate in, otherwise the cultures will manage them, rather than vice versa. Communicating and effecting change is a basic part of leadership. Therefore, getting to the bottom of organizational culture is fundamental for any leader to be able to lead effectively.

Many factors bring about the need for change management in a business. Market changes, population changes and evolving consumer tastes are major factors. Obvious examples are the opening up of new markets among China's middle classes or the trend towards carbon-neutral products. Also, new technology can force change. New production techniques can make workers redundant or increase the need for specific IT training. Finally, legislation may demand it. New laws could, for example, require higher safety standards or impose biting taxes on polluters.

The effects of change are substantial, and successful companies recognize the need to be adaptable. Product life cycles are getting shorter, and company research and development departments are increasingly under pressure to respond to the needs of fast-moving markets. Both product innovation and quality assurance need to be cutting-edge to keep one step ahead of the competition. Human resource management (HRM) needs to plan for a changing workforce. However, perhaps the most expensive effect is the constant need for newer production methods and IT, and associated training.

Ultimately, HRM is responsible for managers disseminating new requirements and procedures throughout the company. New procedures could include applying performance-related pay, or empowering individuals or teams to take on more responsibility and become self-motivated. Such moves could be applied as a whole package – a complete restructuring, for instance – or they could be introduced as gradual piecemeal initiatives, consisting of meetings about quality, better communication, new work practices, outsourcing or pay incentives.

Businesses are always likely to face widespread resistance to change, but this can be overcome. The reason for this is that many people are afraid of the unknown. They fear becoming unemployed, not performing satisfactorily or simply not working with their friends. Blake et al suggest that resistance to change is part of existing company culture and behaviour dynamic (1989). To minimize such resistance, managers need to take certain measures. They should keep employees informed through discussions, both face-to-face and online. If these are consultative, the workers will feel involved in the change process and are more likely to accept them. Managers can convince their teams to cooperate by preventing rumours and misinformation spreading, and by advising of requirements such as unavoidable legislation. Training can be offered if necessary.

If an organization moves towards a culture that accepts and embraces change, it is more likely to reduce resistance. Although it is claimed that culture is difficult to shift because people's beliefs and values are established over time, there is real-world evidence to show that it is possible. Sony, for example, is a company well known on the one hand for its strong and distinctive company culture, and on the other hand for its culture of innovation and accepting change as inevitable.

A term used to describe a company that embraces change constructively is 'the learning organization'. According to Senge et al, a learning organization is one which absorbs knowledge and skills actively and quickly, resulting in the company's 'memory' growing. This type of business has HRM as key to its overall company strategy. It accepts employee training and manager coaching as a constant process to address changes in markets and the business environment. It is ready to put its trust in teams to find their own solutions to problems. Most of all, it expects to communicate and is ready to communicate. Such companies are said to grow and develop naturally and become stronger as a result.

Grammar review: Linkers and relative pronouns

Clauses in a sentence are often linked together using linkers. Place the words *so*, *because*, *because of* and *since* in the gaps where they fit.

Some clauses are conditional. Place *if* in a gap where it fits.

Some clauses are, in fact, infinitives. Place *to* in a gap where it fits.

Some clauses are relative, and relate to a noun or noun group. Place *which*, *who*, *when* and *where* in the gaps where they fit.

1 The CEO should stick to his original plans _____ he doesn't want people to think of his leadership as unpredictable.

2 Our entrepreneurial CEO asked for information about the changes to be distributed to all front-of-house staff _____ customers needed to know as well.

3 The CEO asked for information about the changes to be distributed to all front-of-house staff _____ the need for customers to know as well.

4 The straightforward restructuring plan was quickly communicated to all employees _____ it would inform them of the possibility of job losses.

5 The conference hall, _____ the restructuring plans were announced, was filled with many angry employees.

6 The restructuring plans had been carefully considered _____ ensure the company would survive and succeed in a difficult commercial environment.

7 The CEO, _____ wanted to displace the marketing department in the restructure, was conscious of the problems it would cause.

8 The communication style, _____ was peculiar to the CEO and his directors, was not popular with the marketing department.

9 Most of the staff in the marketing department lost their jobs _____ the restructure took place.

10 Our entrepreneurial CEO requested the changes to be implemented immediately _____ the new directors could begin their new jobs without any uncertainty.

Activity bank

A Solve the crossword.

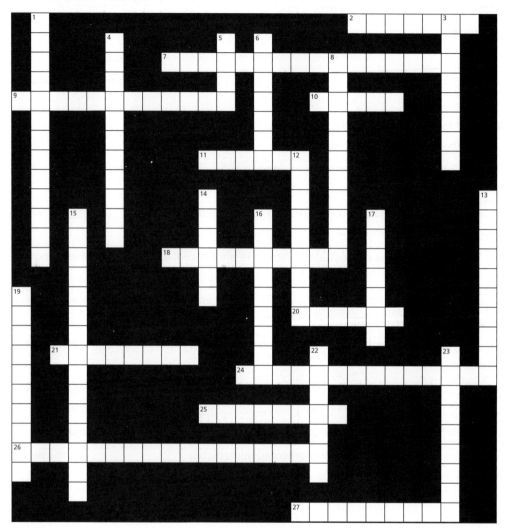

Across

2 An order of this size was a ... for the team.
7 The project was ... but worth the effort.
9 The employees valued their ... .
10 ... production is where a number of products are made at once.
11 The ... of the company was very important to the managers.
18 A hierarchical tree with ... arms is an example of a matrix structure.

20 He was considered to be an ... in his field.
21 A ... hierarchy exists within the team.
24 A ... from each area of the company will provide feedback to the team.
25 The two men had an ... discussion before they went into the meeting.
26 Flow production is more ... than labour-intensive.
27 Bob made sure the group were aware of his ...

Down

1 The staff didn't have to ask Head Office because power was completely ... .
3 The employees were lucky to have ... working hours.
4 A ... is the traditional type of hierarchical structure.
5 The company was advertising a management ... in the newspaper.
6 The company were very pleased with the results of the ... .
8 The manager had ... values.
12 Large international companies often have a centralized ... .
13 The new acquisition had ... to the company.

14 The ... is an example of an organizational model.
15 The man was successful because he had an ... spirit.
16 The manager explained the correct ... to his employee.
17 People in an informal ... share trust, information and advice.
19 The employee was a model of ... .
22 The idea of economies of scale is ... to job, batch and flow methods.
23 A matrix is an example of a structure which has a vertical ... .

B Play bingo.

- Think of words for each of the categories and write them on card 1. Think of a word from another category for the last square ('another word').
- Each student says one of their words. Cross the squares on card 2 when you hear a word from that category.

1

type of organization	characteristic	type of production
phrase	adjective	another word/s

2

type of organization	characteristic	type of production
phrase	adjective	another word/s

Activity bank

A Find 20 verbs from the first four units in the wordsearch.
  - Copy the verbs into your notebook.
  - Write the noun for each verb.

```
J  E  J  V  M  W  X  E  V  A  L  U  A  T  E  B  H
M  C  D  E  T  A  P  I  C  I  T  R  A  P  Z  M  L  L
E  A  J  T  R  E  S  C  H  E  D  U  L  E  N  H  D
Z  R  T  N  T  Y  B  R  L  T  L  M  Y  R  M  Y  E
I  B  C  O  N  C  E  P  T  U  A  L  I  Z  E  X  B
L  M  X  K  X  W  R  D  Z  K  R  N  B  X  M  M  A
A  E  L  C  O  I  E  T  A  G  E  L  E  D  E  V  T
R  T  Z  P  C  L  M  G  T  M  G  Z  P  T  Z  E  E
T  H  M  I  A  O  B  P  A  J  I  L  A  T  B  Z  T
N  E  Y  Y  S  V  O  N  R  L  L  C  T  B  Q  I  P
E  P  E  F  N  N  A  R  A  O  I  N  M  I  T  N  T
C  R  C  V  I  G  W  I  D  N  V  L  Y  N  F  A  Y
N  B  M  T  E  L  C  O  U  I  W  E  N  S  Z  G  V
X  D  L  N  L  E  A  M  D  D  N  T  R  P  X  R  C
W  N  H  C  P  M  M  U  R  W  N  A  Q  I  B  O  T
K  J  W  S  M  O  M  B  Q  D  L  Q  T  R  P  M  W
R  L  R  K  C  E  T  A  V  I  T  O  M  E  K  G  C
```

B Play noughts and crosses. You must say the abbreviation or acronym and give the original words to place your symbol in a square.

BPR	SMART	JIT
COQ	CM	ANOVA
USP	TQM	BM

ISO	MBO	BM
QA	COQ	BPR
JIT	USP	SMART

To be successful, management must plan and control a company's production.

Process engineering (or re-engineering) is a concept crucial to the management perspective.

There is one approach to organizing business processes which is particularly oriented towards results. It is called *management by objectives* (MBO).

Of course, not all managers are at a senior level, and another important area is the study of managing smaller units in business.

Whatever the size of a company, or the management level involved, the key element to control in the production process is quality.

ANOVA	ANSI
BPR	BM
CM	COQ
ISO	JIT
MBO	QA
SMART	TQM
USP	

Activity bank

A Solve the definitions crossword. Find words and phrases with the same meaning as the clues.

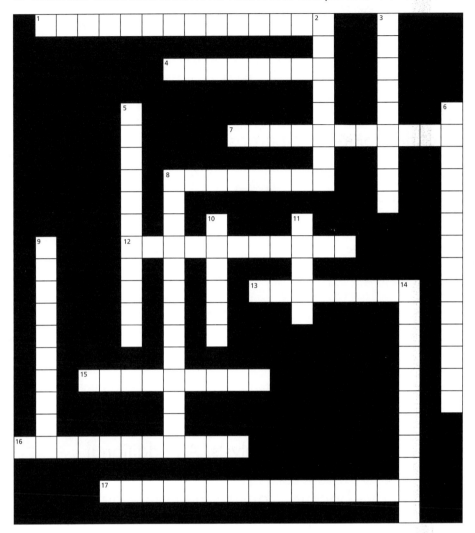

Across
1 A situation analysis tool.
4 Company providing resources or equipment.
7 Rival companies.
8 One company's complete control of market supply.
12 Substitute.
13 Doable, achievable.
15 Contracting of external companies to perform operations.
16 People with a strong interest in a company's success, e.g., shareholders, government, union members.
17 A backup plan.

Down
2 Long-term plan and approach.
3 Motivation, motivating factor.
5 Relating to population.
6 Support systems.
8 A very large company operating in many countries, e.g., Microsoft.
9 A company breaking into the market.
10 Emergency situation.
11 Competitor.
14 Context, surroundings.

B Play opposites bingo.

- Choose six words from the box and write one word in each square of your bingo card.
- Your teacher will call out some words. If you have the **opposite** word on your card, cross it out.
- The first person to cross out all the words on their card is the winner.

competition	decrease	diversify
expansion	feasible	inflation
monopoly	rigid	rise	rival
sharply	slightly	slow

Faculty: Management Studies

Lecture: Strategy development

Key _____ of developing an overall plan for managers are:

- having a clear idea of the company's purpose.

- protecting those with vested interests in the company.

- understanding what is possible.

Good information is _____ in developing a plan. One

_____ of data collection is _____ _____ rival business

analysis. This is _____ to understanding the business environment.

Another _____ is _____ a PESTEL analysis. An additional

_____ of planning is to have backup plans so the company can

react to a serious problem if it arises.

One measure of the success of business strategies is that they offer a

powerful inducement for the growth of the company.

Describing trends

Verbs	Nouns	Adverbs	Adjectives
rise		gradually	
increase		sharply	
grow		slightly	
improve		markedly	
fall		significantly	
decrease		rapidly	
drop		steeply	
decline		steadily	

Poor contributions	Student A	Student B	Student C
disagrees rudely			
doesn't explain how the point is relevant			
doesn't understand an idiom			
dominates the discussion			
gets angry when someone disagrees with him/her			
interrupts			
is negative			
mumbles or whispers			
says something irrelevant			
shouts			
sits quietly and says nothing			
starts a side conversation			
other:			

- -

Good contributions	Student A	Student B	Student C
allows others to speak			
asks for clarification			
asks politely for information			
brings in another speaker			
builds on points made by other speakers			
contributes to the discussion			
explains the point clearly			
gives specific examples to help explain			
is constructive			
links correctly with previous speakers			
listens carefully to what others say			
makes clear how the point is relevant			
paraphrases to check understanding			
says when he/she agrees with someone			
speaks clearly			
tries to use correct language			
other:			

Activity bank

A Find 20 nouns from this unit in the wordsearch.

- Copy the nouns into your notebook.

L	R	A	N	G	E	R	C	L	T	Y	R	Y	E
Q	R	S	T	V	A	L	U	E	T	Z	G	C	B
D	A	C	C	O	U	N	T	I	P	X	I	A	L
K	K	F	S	O	Q	P	L	N	A	R	P	S	H
T	P	Z	U	L	R	I	N	T	P	R	O	S	O
A	Z	L	M	X	B	E	G	L	S	D	R	E	L
S	P	G	A	A	F	M	C	I	M	K	T	T	D
T	M	P	I	N	T	Y	S	A	T	Y	F	T	I
R	E	L	R	S	N	Y	C	T	R	J	O	C	N
A	R	M	O	O	L	I	T	M	M	D	L	L	G
T	G	C	N	A	A	V	N	L	F	R	I	W	S
E	E	R	N	R	X	C	G	G	L	L	O	D	K
G	R	A	E	D	G	E	H	Z	N	N	O	N	X
Y	P	W	M	A	R	K	E	T	Y	Q	T	W	C

B Think of a word or words that can go in front of each of the words below to make a phrase from management studies. Explain the meaning.

Example: *asset = fixed asset*

_____ analysis	_____ holdings	_____ scorecard
_____ account	_____ liability	_____ sum
_____ approach	_____ market	_____ strategy
_____ asset	_____ planning	_____ tax
_____ cost	_____ portfolio	_____ value
_____ edge	_____ price	
_____ flow	_____ range	

1   Fixed assets have been adjusted for their _____ in value.

2   There was _____ in the value of capital reserves between the two years.

3   The value of goodwill has _____ over the year, with a small company takeover.

4   Share values _____ sharply when the company was faced with a takeover in the summer.

5   Intangibles like goodwill are a/an _____ part of this company's valuation.

6   Funds raised from shares are included in the _____ section of the balance sheet.

1   Fixed assets have been adjusted for their depreciation in value.

2   There was an increase in the value of capital reserves between the two years.

3   The value of goodwill has risen over the year, with a small company takeover.

4   Share values rose sharply when the company was faced with a takeover in the summer.

5   Intangibles like goodwill are an essential/important part of this company's valuation.

6   Funds raised from shares are included in the capital section of the balance sheet.

a   *In 2008, capital reserves were valued higher than they were in 2007.*

b   *An organization trying to buy the company mid year caused a jump in share price.*

c   *Goodwill is a non-physical asset, but in the case of the company, its worth needs to be recorded.*

d   *One of the capital entries in the balance sheet is the money raised from share sales.*

e   *The value of fixed-asset values includes an adjustment for loss in value due to age.*

f   *The company's reputation, brand and customer loyalty has increased in value during the previous year, due to the purchase of a minor enterprise.*

Original sentence	Student A	Student B
Regardless of the level of management, valuation and appraisal are two key financial skills a manager must have.	Management must use valuation and appraisal at any level as these are key financial skills.	Appraising investments and valuation are vital managerial skills used in financial decisions.
	not satisfactory: not enough changes: this is patch-writing	*acceptable paraphrase: reordering the information/words are changed, e.g., key > vital*
Therefore, a fixed amount paid in the future will be worth less than a fixed amount today.	So, a fixed quantity in the future will be less in value than a set quantity today.	Consequently, when a sum of money is paid back ten years from now, the currency is likely to have a lower value than the same sum paid this year.
	not acceptable: although the words have been changed, the vocabulary used is inappropriate for the context of money *(e.g., quantity; also sentences should not start with a conjunction (linker).)*	*acceptable paraphrase: note that most of the vocabulary has been changed, that although the times are more specific they are still general enough to retain the meaning of the original.*

Original sentence	Student A	Student B
'Net book value' is what appears on the balance sheet to show what assets minus depreciation are worth.	'Net book value' is seen on the balance sheet and shows the worth of assets less depreciation.	'Net Book Value' is a balance sheet entry for asset value after depreciation is deducted.
	not satisfactory: not enough changes: this is patch-writing	*acceptable paraphrase: use of passive voice, e.g., what appears on* ➜ *entry; key vocab changes, 'minus'* ➜ *'deducted'*
In recent years, following a number of large-scale scandals, regulation of accounts has become tighter in order to reduce the manipulation of accounts by managers.	In the past few years, following some big scandals, the official control of accounts has become stricter, so that they reduce the manipulation of accounts by management.	Recently, as a result of infamous financial scandals, there has been stronger application of regulations governing accounts, so that account manipulation is diminished.
	not satisfactory: not enough changes; this is patch-writing	*acceptable paraphrase: replacement with subject 'there' ('regulation of accounts has become tighter'* ➜ *there has been.); vocab and change of adjective phrase to noun phrase ('tighter'* ➜ *'stronger application of'). Note 'manipulation' and 'accounts' are the same as the original but this is acceptable as they are key terms.*

Regardless of the level of management, valuation and appraisal are two key financial skills a manager must have.

The value today of a sum of money available in the future is called the net present value (NPV).

Valuation is a difficult area for managers.

There are a great number of financial ratios that can be used to understand a company's accounts, which help management decide, for example, whether to purchase a company.

Apart from DCF, managers may use other several other techniques in valuing.

There are, however, serious problems with valuation methods.

In fact, some managers are even guilty of manipulating accounts to show incorrect valuations.

	Main subject	Main verb	Main object/ complement	Other verbs + their subjects + objects/ complements	Adverbial phrases
A	the name (of the steel company)	has changed	to (HSH Haka Steel Holdings)	which* was known as LBS	in the UK, previously
B	three of the many ways	will be described		in which financial ratios can be calculated	here
C	managers	can also use	the DCF	which is useful, which requires some prediction, which is uncertain	obviously
D	a manager	must under-stand	the new tighter financial accounts regulations	as well as not manipulating accounts	fully deliberately
E	some managers	have caused	a number of serious scandals	having manipulated accounts in the process of valuation	

A		B	
A	added	B	value
A	asset	B	management
A	cash	B	flow
A	competitor	B	analysis
A	current	B	asset
A	current	B	liabilities
A	customer	B	services
A	fixed	B	asset
A	fixed	B	liabilities
A	float	B	a company
A	historical	B	cost
A	human	B	judgement
A	investment	B	capital
A	labour	B	intensive
A	loan	B	money
A	market	B	capitalization
A	share	B	holding
A	share	B	portfolio
A	share	B	price
A	share	B	value
A	situation	B	analysis
A	unit	B	cost

Activity bank

A Solve the crossword.

Across

3 We will reach ... point when our income covers our costs.

4 This week there have been wild ... in the FTSE.

7 In ... accounting, information is collected for managers to use in-company.

9 When there is a high level of risk, managers need to have a contingency ... in place.

11 Before investing in a new venture, managers need to do a careful ... analysis.

12 Risk can be reliably calculated using a mathematical ... .

13 ... decision-making uses mathematical tools to help plan a budget.

15 ... is the total money a company turns over in a year.

17 I ... that we will overspend on the projects by about 1.3 million euros, though I could, of course, be wrong.

18 I'm afraid we don't have the financial or human ... to undertake this project.

Down

1 In planning our budget, we need to take our ... into consideration, which is what it costs us just to keep the business in operation.

2 Every budget has to include both fixed and ... costs for a project.

5 The Balanced Scorecard uses ... indicators to measure how well a strategy is working.

6 A company can ... risk by outsourcing high-risk activities to other companies.

8 I have ... £30,000 to cover the cost of stationery for the year.

10 ... is how easy or difficult it is for a company to gather funds to pay its debts as they fall due.

14 It is difficult for managers to forecast market ... , i.e., the way in which share prices move.

16 A ... is an agreed plan for expenditure, usually calculated over a year.

	Fixed phrase	Followed by ...	Actual information (suggested answers)
1	Yes, there are ...	a comment about a diagram, picture or slide	
2	What do I mean by ...?	introducing a new aspect of the topic	
3	As you can see on this slide, ...	an explanation of a word or phrase	
4	However, ...	offering an alternative view	
5	But of course, ...	redefining a concept	
6	In other words, ...	a contrasting way of looking at something	
7	In fact, ...	linking to a result or implication	
8	The point is ...	extending an idea by giving examples	
9	In this way, ...	a key statement or idea	

7.4 Student A

Business risk 2
Political risks

- How stable is the government? Does it have a strong party system? What is the average life of a parliament/government? How does the country manage political change?

- Political protest: how does the government handle dissent? How does it deal with political insurgents, and is there any such threat to the proposed location of the production unit? What is the cost of security?

- Is there a prospect of government grants for establishing a business, for example in a poor area?

- How well does the government police environmental issues in the area?

7.4 Student B

Business risk 2
Natural disasters

- What kinds of natural disasters is the area prone to? How frequent are they? What facilities does the government have for dealing with disasters? What studies have there been to calculate the likelihood of a natural disaster?

- What impact would a natural disaster have on the business? Is the production unit going to be at risk in its proposed location? How would distribution networks and access to raw materials be affected? Would the export capability be seriously affected, and for how long?

- What skills/training does the labour force have for dealing with natural disasters, and what would it cost to train them adequately?

7.4 Student C

Business risk 3
Economic risks

- How competitive in the market is our product against its nearest rivals? What percentage of the market do our competitors control and with what products?

- What is the size of the market available and what is its potential for development? Is there real investment potential? If so, can the market carry high or low fixed costs such as rent, or land purchase finance? What is the cost of energy?

- How strong is the economy, what is the rate of inflation and how stable is the local currency? Are labour costs static or escalating, and if escalating, by how much?

- How regulated is the economy, and what is the potential skills level and labour cost of the staff?

7.4 Student D

Business risk 4
Social conditions

- What level of crime is there in the area, and what kind of crime is most common?

- What are the most serious social problems in the area and how are they likely to impact on our operation? For example, high unemployment figures probably mean a low skills base. Poverty and malnutrition mean low levels of concentration and productivity.

- Environmental effects: does the environment offer the clean air and water we need?

- What support will managers need if they go there? Language support? Cost of living quarters: how expensive will it be to settle people there? What level of education is available for managers' children?

Activity bank

A Find 15 words from this unit in the wordsearch. All the words are uncountable nouns in the texts in this unit.

- Copy the words into your notebook.
- Check the definition of any words you cannot remember.

I	N	T	E	R	D	E	P	E	N	D	E	N	C	E	Q	M	M
X	N	D	I	S	C	R	I	M	I	N	A	T	I	O	N	T	P
W	O	R	K	P	L	A	C	E	S	T	R	E	S	S	K	Z	H
C	L	N	S	Y	M	P	A	T	H	E	T	I	C	J	R	V	E
T	O	M	B	T	Q	G	M	H	P	B	X	R	D	Q	R	L	V
M	N	O	L	X	M	L	O	J	T	C	M	M	K	L	B	C	W
Y	H	B	P	G	K	W	T	D	S	V	A	T	J	A	T	E	N
X	B	M	P	E	R	X	I	E	F	L	Q	R	I	V	C	V	R
Q	I	R	T	Z	R	T	V	W	X	R	M	L	W	N	W	O	G
D	Y	N	B	K	X	A	A	Y	Y	T	E	C	E	Z	T	Q	T
Y	I	R	T	Z	N	N	T	H	T	R	R	G	M	P	R	R	E
B	G	V	T	E	H	K	I	I	M	C	I	O	A	L	E	L	V
L	M	W	E	T	R	Q	N	L	O	L	K	D	V	V	L	R	A
G	M	N	V	R	N	V	G	T	L	N	A	Y	O	E	X	B	L
Y	L	Q	H	U	S	Z	I	E	Y	J	Q	R	F	N	R	M	U
D	P	Z	M	S	Q	I	T	E	H	N	T	N	L	P	R	T	A
M	L	M	R	T	V	N	T	M	W	N	N	L	H	K	N	Q	T
F	P	M	Z	N	I	T	Z	Y	I	X	K	N	C	Q	R	B	E

B Rearrange the letters in the words to form a correctly spelt word from this unit.

Jumbled word	Correct spelling
hreifnis	
noniuditc	
ytnimori	
sledrhu	
stiatr	
frwookecr	
aetm	
pahsre	
tineer	
gmtoavinit	

Activity bank

A Solve the crossword.

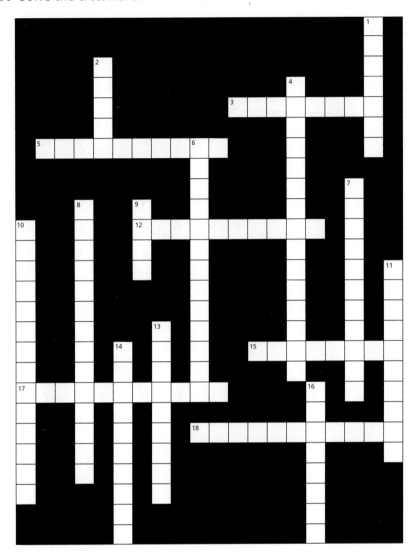

Across

3 Our company will ... to Indonesia because labour costs there are so much cheaper.

5 Ross works in the morning, and Sally in the afternoon, doing the same work. They do this because they are ... .

12 When a company ..., it contracts part of its operations to another company.

15 New ... should undergo a period of induction training to familiarize them with the ways of the company.

17 Not being at work when you should be.

18 Moving people from one type of work to another within a company to make the work less boring.

Down

1 Most workers think that the level of ... is the most important aspect of choosing a job.

2 Extra money paid for good work performance.

4 Some executives work too hard and spend almost no time at home. Their ... is very poor.

6 A process that works out what areas of a staff member's skills need further development.

7 ... allows people to work according to the hours and kind of contract that suits them best. Some might job-share, others work part-time, and still others want to be self-employed.

8 Ella has a/an ... with the company which means that she works with an older, more experienced worker who offers her on-the-job training.

9 ... HR managers have to be able to support and develop staff, train in leadership, solve labour disputes, and identify and provide other training needs.

10 Things like inconvenient conditions, poor pay, bossy line managers and a blame culture make a company unpleasant to work for; we call these things ... .

11 Theory X type workers respond best to pay or ... to stop them being lazy.

13 An ... encourages a staff member to work harder for a company.

14 Factors that make employment attractive to a staff member, e.g., bonus schemes, good promotion prospects.

16 Working on a one-to-one basis with a colleague at work to guide him/her in developing his/her potential.

B Are the nouns countable or uncountable? Use a dictionary to check.

HRM terms	Countable or uncountable?	Notes
flexibility		
induction		
conditions		
mentoring		
coaching		
payments		
stakeholder		
training		
relocation		
reward		
incentive		

Review reduce + recite + review	Notes record
Here you write only important words and questions; this column is completed *after* the lecture. Later, this column becomes your study or revision notes. You can use it by covering the right-hand column and using the cue words and questions here to remember the contents on the right.	This column contains your notes. You should underline headings and indent main ideas. After the lecture or reading, you need to identify the key points and write them in the **review** column as questions or cue words.

Summary

reflect + recite + review

After the class, you can use this space to summarize the main points of the notes on the page.

Review	Notes

4 theories of motivation are …?	1. <u>4 key theories</u>
	
	  a. <u>Maslow</u> – Hierarchy of *needs*
	
	  b. <u>Mayo</u> – scientific ➔ human *relations/relationships*

Theory X people are …?
Theory Y types are …?
	c. <u>McGregor</u> – Theory X and Theory Y
	       Theory X = people who are *lazy*
	       Theory Y= people who like *responsibility*
	
	  d. <u>Herzberg</u> – Motivators = job satisfaction, etc.
	       – Hygiene factors = negative things, e.g., *low pay or threats*

3 forms of motivation are …?	2. <u>3 methods of motivation:</u>
	
	  a. <u>payment</u> – wage/salary/commission/fees/benefits
	       – management – pay rates competitive?
	       – employees – pay fair?
	
	  b. <u>incentives</u> PRP – links pay to targets or work *performance*
	       – bonuses – for good performance or reaching *targets*
	       – commissions – more business = more commission

3 types of non-financial rewards are …?	c. <u>non-financial rewards</u>
	       – job design ➔ job satisfaction
	       – opportunity for more *responsibility*
	       – social life, holidays, etc.
	       – Mgmt can give = job *enlargement/enrichment* or job *rotation*
	       Basically non-fin. rewards = make staff *feel good*

Summary (suggested)

There are four key theories relating to motivation – Maslow to Herzberg, and three ways of motivating workers: payment, incentives and non-financial rewards.

Further definitions may be found at the following web pages. Where links are no longer working, placing the search terms in a good search engine may help to find useful definitions and introductions to the concepts.

1 Soft and hard HRM

http://www.hrmguide.co.uk/introduction_to_hrm/hard-hrm.htm

http://wiki.answers.com/Q/What_is_the_difference_between_hard_and_soft_Human_Resource_Management

http://www.revisionworld.co.uk/a2-level/business-studies/people-operations-management/human-resource-management/hard-soft-hrm

2 Theory X and Y

http://en.wikipedia.org/wiki/Theory_X_and_theory_Y

http://www.envisionsoftware.com/articles/Theory_X.html

http://www.nwlink.com/~donclark/hrd/history/xy.html

http://www.valuebasedmanagement.net/methods_mcgregor_theory_X_Y.html

3 Hygiene factors

http://en.wikipedia.org/wiki/Hygiene_factors

http://www.netmba.com/mgmt/ob/motivation/herzberg

http://www.uwex.edu/disted/conference/Resource_library/proceedings/02_13.pdf

4 Motivators

http://www.businessballs.com/herzberg.htm

http://www.mindtools.com/pages/article/newTMM_74.htm

http://www.accel-team.com/human_relations/hrels_05_herzberg.html

http://en.wikipedia.org/wiki/Frederick_Herzberg

Name: Fatima Hameed
Job Title: HR Analyst
Joined: September last year
Degree   BSc (Hons) Business Studies, Lancaster University

I applied to join Spendwise while I was on holiday in Spain after taking a gap year. I was attracted to Spendwise because it aggressively promotes the opportunities it offers young graduates and because, as a company, it is a market leader in its field.

I was amazed at the level of responsibility given to me. I work in 1 _____ HRM, not soft HRM, so my analytical skills are really important. My current project is to predict 2 _____ levels for next year, and to do that I have to find out and factor in first, what our 3 _____ supermarkets might be doing, next, what our own projected turnover is likely to be, how 4 _____ change like our main supplier's new information system will affect our efficiency and thus our required staff levels, and so on. The really exciting thing is that my next assignment is likely to be taking part in the interview process for new graduate 5 _____. I will meet them the day before they come to our 6 _____ centre in Leeds so they can chat to me about the company and working 7 _____ at Spendwise. I think this is really useful. The next day, I will be scoring them on their mathematical, 8 _____ reasoning and talent-screening tests.

After that, I am due to spend six months working in 9 _____ HRM. I will be working with an experienced trainer who will be 10 _____ me so that I can develop my own soft skills and identify my own development goals. That is the thing about Spendwise: the whole focus is on helping me maximize my potential to fit the company's own objectives.

Activity bank

A Find 20 words from this unit in the wordsearch.
- Copy the words into your notebook.
- Check the definition of any words you can't remember.

R	E	P	U	T	A	T	I	O	N	R	Y	M	F	G	F	P
S	I	D	E	S	T	E	P	T	H	Z	E	D	F	L	C	W
D	P	I	C	K	E	T	V	T	P	U	M	P	R	V	H	A
C	K	D	Z	R	Y	Q	D	M	G	N	G	K	R	E	C	G
T	O	W	C	O	M	P	R	O	M	I	S	E	M	E	O	E
R	G	N	B	B	K	X	L	T	E	R	G	E	T	R	N	R
A	Q	J	S	Y	P	A	N	N	C	N	H	A	M	Z	T	I
D	T	L	M	U	I	R	I	Q	O	C	I	L	E	R	R	S
E	S	N	O	D	L	M	E	I	S	T	D	L	D	E	O	E
U	P	T	N	C	R	T	T	J	O	C	A	T	I	D	V	Z
N	V	K	R	E	K	A	A	G	E	N	V	F	A	U	E	J
I	R	X	D	I	R	O	E	T	U	C	M	D	T	N	R	Q
O	W	N	T	T	K	N	U	B	I	D	T	V	I	D	S	Q
N	U	H	I	J	F	E	I	T	M	O	R	V	O	A	I	N
R	K	B	M	Z	K	R	T	G	L	V	N	G	N	N	A	L
W	R	Q	P	F	T	T	M	B	D	Y	W	M	K	C	L	M
A	N	K	K	D	I	S	M	I	S	S	A	L	T	Y	R	P

B Think of a word or words that can go after each of the words or phrases below to make a phrase from management studies. Explain the meaning.
Example: *bank = bank loan, bank account*

collective	
employment	
enterprise	
industrial	
industrial	
job	
migrant	
trade	
union	
working	

Introduction		Examples of ideas
introduce the topic area give the outline of the essay		
Body	**Para 1:** situation/problems (general)	
	Para 2: problems (specific examples)	
	Para 3: solutions	
	Para 4: evaluations of solutions	
Conclusion		

J. Barbash The Elements of Industrial Relations. 1984.

David Card 'Falling Union Membership and Rising Wage Inequality: What's the Connection?' **National Bureau of Economic Research**. Working Paper No. 6520 April 1998

Farnham, D. & Pimlott, J,, 1983: Understanding Industrial Relations. Littlehampton Book Services,

Kaufman, B.E. *The Origins & Evolution of the Field of Industrial Relations in the United States*. Ithaca, New York: Cornell University Press, 1993.

9 May 2003, p.33 Littlejohn, R. 'Will Labour prove Enoch right?' *The Sun*.

McGovern P 'Immigration, Labour Markets and Employment Relations: Problems and Prospects' British Journal of Industrial Relations 45:2 June 2007 0007–1080 pp.217–235

[16 May 2008] Office of Industrial Relations, NSW Department of Commerce. Enterprise Bargaining in Brief.
http://www.industrialrelations.nsw.gov.au/workplace/reform/eas/entbrgng.html

J. Barbash The Elements of Industrial Relations.1984.

David Card 'Falling Union Membership and Rising Wage Inequality: What's the Connection?' **National Bureau of Economic Research**. Working Paper No. 6520 April 1998

Farnham, D. & Pimlott, J,, 1983: Understanding Industrial Relations. Littlehampton Book Services,

Kaufman, B.E. *The Origins & Evolution of the Field of Industrial Relations in the United States*. Ithaca, New York: Cornell University Press, 1993.

9 May 2003, p.33 Littlejohn, R. 'Will Labour prove Enoch right?' *The Sun*.

McGovern P 'Immigration, Labour Markets and Employment Relations: Problems and Prospects' British Journal of Industrial Relations 45:2 June 2007 0007–1080 pp.217–235

[16 May 2008] Office of Industrial Relations, NSW Department of Commerce. Enterprise Bargaining in Brief.
http://www.industrialrelations.nsw.gov.au/workplace/reform/eas/entbrgng.html

Activity bank

A Solve the crossword.

Across

1 In the 1980s, Coca-Cola successfully used 'It's the real thing' as its ... .

8 When a shopper chooses to buy a Zen MP3 player over an Apple iPod, she is showing brand ... .

9 The number of customers who want to buy a product is called ... .

12 The amount or quantity of a product that is available for sale is called ... .

14 The four Ps of product, price, promotion and place together are what we call a marketing ... .

15 The value of a brand when a company is sold is sometimes called brand ... .

16 This little image like a tick is Nike's ... .

Down

2 Gucci has chosen to market its products to a small, highly select group of consumers. This is called ... marketing.

3 One of the things managers have to do when they are thinking of launching a new product is a ... analysis, i.e., an investigation of the strengths and weaknesses of other products in the market at that time, and of the companies producing them.

4 I think we have to admit that Coca-Cola is the market ... for the soft drinks market because it is known all over the world and it sets standards for this kind of product.

5 The process of creating consumer awareness of a brand is, naturally, called ... .

6 Sales of our main product are down. I think we need to ..., in other words, we need to develop a range of products so we hit a wider spread of the market.

7 When a consumer always chooses the same brand, this is an example of brand ... .

10 The amount of money a consumer has to spend freely is his ... income.

11 A company like easyJet has the lowest air fares, so it is the ... leader for the budget airline market.

13 The way a company advertises its products is part of ... . This is one of the four Ps.

B Match a word in the first column with a word in the second column to make a two-word phrase. Make sure you know what they mean.

brand	produced
business	brand
market	mix
marketing	development
mass	orientation
niche	selling point
product	philosophy
product	personality
unique	marketing
weak	placement

English for Management Studies – Copyright © 2009 Garnet Publishing Ltd.

According to Philip Kotler, arguably the greatest thinker in the field, marketing is a business philosophy. However, it was not always considered central to enterprise until a few decades ago. Why has marketing risen in importance?

Firstly, economic growth has brought about an increase in real disposable income, and so/as a result, there has been a greatly increased demand for a wider range of products and services. For example, online services that once did not exist and laptops that were once not affordable to most people are now commonplace, and cheap, labour-saving kitchen appliances now exist for just about every chore. Moreover/Furthermore, technology has created a whole range of new expectations for products and services. Consider digital technology and its effect on markets, from MP3 downloads to home cinema screens and speakers. One result of this escalation in products and services on offer and disposable incomes is the increasing differentiation in tastes and fashion. Perceptions of what 'looks good' or 'is cool' are increasingly reflected in material goods since/because there is a greater range of them than ever before to sell to people with greater spending ability than ever before.

Secondly, competition is another cause. Marketing has become more scientific and sophisticated because/since the number of companies competing for the consumer's attention has increased. As a result/So it is a greater challenge to win the target's loyalty. Moreover/Furthermore, globalization has exacerbated this trend because numerous countries are now permitted to trade freely in one another's markets.

Activity bank

A Find 20 words from this unit in the wordsearch.
- Copy the words into your notebook.
- Check the definition of any words you can't remember.

A	P	P	L	I	C	A	T	I	O	N	S	O	F	T	W	A	R	E
P	N	D	J	N	A	V	I	G	A	T	E	S	T	R	P	Z	Y	Q
S	I	M	P	L	E	M	E	N	T	N	I	V	D	N	B	Y	G	R
H	U	Q	C	T	K	C	I	K	Y	M	X	E	Q	N	R	R	Z	G
D	D	P	C	O	M	B	L	N	N	K	T	W	Z	H	E	L	S	T
T	B	T	P	Z	N	R	Y	D	T	C	L	Y	T	R	K	I	N	E
T	2	W	T	L	F	T	L	X	E	R	D	C	U	W	S	T	Z	P
R	B	E	H	B	Y	K	R	N	R	W	A	T	T	Y	G	I	K	T
E	K	T	Q	H	R	C	N	A	L	P	C	N	L	H	N	T	P	K
C	C	M	I	C	T	O	H	H	C	A	H	A	E	O	P	U	E	I
Y	H	O	N	J	C	N	K	A	F	T	N	B	I	T	R	G	X	N
P	C	D	M	R	J	T	Q	U	I	A	O	T	F	K	M	T	T	T
X	V	A	E	M	Z	M	N	L	T	N	U	R	N	T	Z	T	R	E
T	K	T	M	Z	E	A	B	O	G	L	D	A	T	L	C	M	A	R
C	N	A	R	D	M	R	W	Z	O	T	B	P	Z	E	M	G	N	F
I	G	B	R	D	V	S	C	V	M	T	P	C	J	C	G	F	E	A
K	K	A	P	N	K	R	E	E	L	P	B	O	R	H	X	H	T	C
D	W	S	F	C	N	R	D	K	Q	L	R	Y	R	N	N	X	R	E
K	L	E	B	F	Z	Z	H	Z	R	P	D	E	A	D	L	I	N	E

B Match the percentages with a suitable phrase to describe numbers of respondents.

95%	a significant majority
70%	a small proportion
53%	a tiny minority
50%	half
48%	just over half
10%	slightly less than half
2%	the great majority

SWOT analysis

When a company's performance is poor, it may need to make some changes. However, before the company can do this, it should establish exactly where it is now, using a thorough analysis. A commonly used technique for this is the SWOT analysis. In this method, managers carry out an 'external audit' in which they examine their business and economic environment as well as the market conditions they face in order to understand the opportunities and threats to the company. Secondly, the organization needs to complete an 'internal audit' in which its strengths and weaknesses are compared with those of the competitors. The results of such audits are presented in a four-box summary of the business's current strengths and weaknesses and the opportunities and threats which will affect its future development.

	His company purchased property from failed dotcom companies.
	The company had a single coordinated MIS installed.
	His company grew to 44 staff, with huge revenues and market share.
	Kearny learnt to use software and programs for building websites.
	His programmers started getting behind, his clients complained, and his staff kept leaving.
1	Kearny originally had a creative IT job with useful client relationships.
	Kearny lost his job.
	The company began losing clients.
	A group was formed to look at how to address these issues.
	Kearny contacted his clients from his old job to offer his services to.

Report A: Survey at Kearny Design Ltd

Introduction

All areas of B2B e-commerce have been growing fast in the last 15 years. In the case of Kearny Design Ltd, it would be interesting to uncover company knowledge on how the service provided meets trends in the sector. This report will outline findings from research undertaken into core staff perceptions of their firm's IT solutions and whether they will survive in the marketplace. Recommendations will be made as to whether the company's mission should be reviewed.

Method

A written questionnaire was designed to identify the perceptions of core employees about their company's B2B solutions and whether Kearny Design was seen as being ready for today's fast-changing market conditions. Sixteen questionnaires were sent to all senior and long-serving staff members (employed for three years or more). Twelve were returned. In addition, each of the senior management team was interviewed individually. Seventy-five per cent of both samples were men, reflecting the gender profile of the company.

Findings

With regard to meeting the demands of a changing market, a large majority (78%) of core employees claimed that the company's service scope was still too narrow. Fear was expressed that it could never compete with the huge 'total solution' firms. Only a small minority (6%) rated it as providing exactly what large corporations need in today's business climate.

In terms of efficiency, the survey also revealed concern. Although 48% of the respondents thought that KD Ltd could not survive in the face of greater competition with cheaper labour coming out of India, 52% did not agree. A significant minority (39%), mostly high-level managers, stated that it was simply a matter of recruitment. Recently, they recruited engineers from America, but now they need to look more locally, in India, change employment contracts, and lower pay to be more in line with global levels. Finally, most of the respondents (77%) accepted the need for labour efficiency.

Discussion

Clearly, the findings indicate that Kearny Design needs to confront a number of issues quickly. It is probable that corporate clients increasingly prefer companies that can provide the whole IT solution, not just the B2B components and usability design. Moreover, it seems that competitors are benefiting from cheaper engineering graduates from overseas, and savings are probably being passed on to clients. To compete, perhaps streamlining or restructuring is needed, along with possible recruitment from overseas.

A limitation of this research, however, was that it was internal only; administering the same survey externally, across a number of companies including key clients, too, might provide a clearer picture.

Conclusion

A profile of in-company opinion at Kearny Design has revealed that mid-size e-commerce development as a business is suffering pressure from two angles: competition from broader IT solution services offering more, and downward pressure on salaries by labour market oversupply. In our opinion, new recruitment could focus overseas, with contract and pay frameworks restructured, and the company's mission could be broadened. While failure to respond to these trends could push the enterprise under, it seems the management has the will and the company has the flexibility to enjoy a bright future.

Model questionnaire

Kearny Design Internal Survey

To all our staff: Please help us to improve our strategic vision to ensure a more prosperous position in the marketplace in the medium and long term, by completing this questionnaire. Please indicate your answer by circling your choice.

1 Do you consider that Kearny Design is still cutting-edge in the marketplace?

    yes   no   don't know

2 Do you consider that Kearny Design remains a key player in the marketplace?

    yes   no   don't know

3 As the market changes, in particular the competition, do you feel we provide the scope of service that our customers require? Is our scope of service:

    A wide enough?   B satisfactory?   C too narrow?   D don't know

4 Can we compete with the multinational 'total solution' firms?

    A definitely   B sometimes   C never   D don't know

5 Do you consider that we address the needs of our large corporate customers?

    A yes, exactly   B sometimes   C no, rarely or never   D don't know

6 Do you consider that we provide suitable loyalty incentives to customers, compared with what our competitors provide?

    yes   no   don't know

7 The increase in efficient Indian competitors or competitors who recruit mainly from India has been mentioned as a threat. Do you agree that this threatens our survival?

    yes   no   don't know

8 What is the solution to this threat?

    A raise labour efficiency   B stop USA recruitment   C recruit from India   D don't know

9 Do you like working at Kearny Design more than your previous employer?

    yes   no   don't know

10 Do you have any other comments? Please elaborate on any of the above answers you have made. There is space on the back of this questionnaire for further comments.

Thank you for your help!

Use the words and phrases in the box to complete the text below.

> also   as a result of   consequently   first   in addition   next   led   resulted

Monty & Boot Ltd was losing money. It was under pressure from bankers and other lenders. _____, shareholders were not happy when the share price dropped to an all-time low of 11p.

_____, a decision was made to undertake a strategic review of the company. _____, the management team set out to establish the views of all staff. _____, management was persuaded to agree to more ambitious efficiency targets. Finally, plans for implementation were set up.

_____ the actions in the plan, the company had a management information system installed, which _____ to improved communication and real-time information availability. Better MIS _____ meant staff could understand their key performance indicators and reach their targets more easily.

These steps soon _____ in increased customer and supplier confidence, and sales quickly returned to previous highs.

Use the words and phrases in the box to complete the text below.

> also   as a result of   consequently   first   in addition   next   led   resulted

Monty & Boot Ltd was losing money. It was under pressure from bankers and other lenders. _____, shareholders were not happy when the share price dropped to an all-time low of 11p.

_____, a decision was made to undertake a strategic review of the company. _____, the management team set out to establish the views of all staff. _____, management was persuaded to agree to more ambitious efficiency targets. Finally, plans for implementation were set up.

_____ the actions in the plan, the company had a management information system installed, which _____ to improved communication and real-time information availability. Better MIS _____ meant staff could understand their key performance indicators and reach their targets more easily.

These steps soon _____ in increased customer and supplier confidence, and sales quickly returned to previous highs.